vel vey
&&

A NORMAL
LIFE

A story of abuse, survival
and finding a new life

AURA ANGEL

A NORMAL

LIFE

A story of abuse, survival and finding a new life

MEMOIRS
Cirencester

Published by Memoirs

MEMOIRS
PUBLISHING

25 Market Place, Cirencester, Gloucestershire, GL7 2NX
info@memoirsbooks.co.uk www.memoirspublishing.com

A NORMAL LIFE

ISBN: 978-1-909544-67-3

Contents

Unknown Warrior

Introduction

1. First memories   Page 1

2. On the move   Page 22

3. The worst place ever   Page 34

4. My new life   Page 47

5. Boys – nothing but trouble   Page 59

6. The best time ever   Page 68

7. A second chance?   Page 76

Unknown Warrior

I am an unknown warrior
Like many who lose their way
I'm fighting for the freedom
I hope to find one day

I share the warriors' unknown gift
And give what I have to share
For many warriors are unknown
And no one can see us there

18.04.12

Introduction

Rain was pounding on the windows the day I came into the world, or so I was told. The labour was fraught with difficulties and lasted 36 hours, unusual for a third child. My mother had an ulcer and at the age of 32, this increased the risks. I was the biggest of her second family of three children, weighing a mighty 6lbs. The month was November, making me a Scorpio. At times I like to think that the determination of this sign has helped me through the tough times, and believe me there were many of those.

Back then when we used to talk, my mother said I was a difficult child. Now I fill with anger and irritation and I can't stay long in a room with her; I never know when she's going to kick off. This happens every time I see her, which is not very often; to my relief I'm not ready to tackle those demons yet. Don't get me wrong, I visit my mother birthdays, Easter and Christmas. Ironic really, considering I don't believe in God. I suppose there is some guilt there now, seeing her living on her own with no support except from the warden who visits three times a week, but then where was she when I was growing up? I have selfish thoughts too, just like everyone else. Maybe the tranquillizers prescribed by the doctor for depression had something to do with it, or maybe it was and is because she has a mental illness - who knows?

Tell it to someone who cares, I hear you say; ah, but I don't. Not today, not yesterday, but there's always tomorrow. Quite cynical for a thirty-something, maybe I'll mature with age.

When I was born in the late sixties, I had a father too. He didn't hang around long; I was supposed to be a boy. When the boy did come along, he left with him. Then he brought him back, I'm not sure if it was because he had to or he found out how hard it was to balance his care for him with the women he wanted. Back then in the late sixties, early seventies, I suppose men (in general) were the ones who left the baggage, and if they were lucky (fortunately for us we were) they would get a visit now and then. He and mother tried to reconcile when I was about eight, but I wasn't having a bar of it. Children can be so selfish, can't they? I didn't understand the concept of love; even now I find it hard. My mother loved him for her own reasons. She never married again and never had a regular boyfriend; most people were scared of her, they didn't know when she was going to kick off.

My mother was thirteen years older than my dad - I say was, because he died on December 31st 2002 age 54 (I think). I know some of her childhood she told us in bits, maybe they're the only bits she remembers. She was born to a single mum and moved south with her. Her mother (whose name I don't know) became house staff to a man she eventually married and they had another two children, boys. She only told me some of her childhood, and said her father was a musician. The man her mother married became her father, and no doubt she had her trials and tribulations living with the damage of the war. She mentioned once that they had ration books but didn't elaborate on it. Most of her past she keeps private, or maybe she doesn't remember. She trained as a nurse but didn't continue into employment. She married young and had a boy from that marriage. It didn't last; they separated and the son stayed with his father's mother.

My dad I know even less. He met my mother when he was stationed with the army in the south. I don't know if they married because my mum got pregnant or if he actually did love her. When he finished his time in the army they moved to the West Midlands. In fact, I think my dad moved up first because my mum was doing time for stabbing him; then when she was released she came too. We kids stayed with his parents. When mum came we took residence in a council house just up the road from them. My granddad (Ted) used to sit me on his knee and show me his finger. He kept it in a baccy tin on the shelf next to where he spent most of his time in an armchair; he said he had lost it in the war. It took me a few minutes to realise that when he put the tin back he always had five fingers, but I always told him to show me every time I visited (nearly every day). Inside the tin there was cotton wool lining the bottom, with a hole just big enough for his finger to fit in. The blood was food colouring I think, to make it look authentic.

I have a few photos of the time they took me and my sister to the seaside, but I have no recollection of the event. It must have been when we were living with them. My brother wasn't born then, he was doing time with my mum in Tonevale (Bristol) then Powick (Worcestershire). My granddad died in 1975 when I was about six; he had cancer. One day he was there, then he was gone. No explanation, no excuses, just gone. I don't think of him much now but when I do I always remember his tin. I'm smiling now just thinking about it.

My grandmother lived a while longer, having settled down with a taxman called John. She moved to the next town, where she lived until I was 19 and she was 66. John died shortly afterwards of leukaemia. I didn't feel much moved by her death as she was bedridden and spent most of the day sitting in a chair. Her bed was in the same room because she couldn't get up the stairs. There was a commode next to it, and I always sat on it next to my Nan. There was always a smell in the house of decay.

John was kind to me, although he always seemed to be sad. After she died I didn't keep in touch with any of the cousins or aunts, though I do see them around; we ask how each other are and how the kids are but that's it. I like it that way because I can't fall out with any of them if I don't know them, we have no regular contact. I see them any time, usually in town.

I hope you enjoy reading my journey. I'm writing it as a counselling tool for me. I need to grieve for the past, live in the present and look forward to a future.

CHAPTER ONE

First Memories

The council house in York Road was cold, always cold. There were no carpets on the floor. There was one chair in the living room and a table in the kitchen with two chairs. The fire was an open hearth and when it was lit (which was not very often) it gave the room a light orangey glow. At those times I used to sit as close as I could and hated to leave it to go to bed. I shared a mattress on the floor with my sister at the back of the house. If I started to whinge my dad would get out a newspaper, roll it up and whack me round the side of the face several times. Even though I would be crying after the first blow he carried on; I couldn't go anywhere because he used to corner me.

The front door was at the back of the house, so the kitchen door, at the side of the house, was used all the time. The kitchen was at the front of the house and the living room was at the back. The stairs were in the living room along with the front door. We had a lot of garden and played in it often, as Mum didn't like us playing in the streets. It felt like prison most of the time, but it was better than being in the house.

The arguments between Mum and Dad got worse. She would end up crying and he would storm out. As the time went on he started to hit her, every time they argued (daily). We kids would sit behind the garden shed huddled together, and most times we would cry. I used to think, why does he stay? He causes nothing but misery.

I only have two happy recollections of family events:

One day my dad bought me and my sister matching skirts, brown coloured nylon with big red flowers. I wore mine from the shop; we went to the pub and as children do, played outside in the garden while Mum and Dad sat inside drinking. We stayed all day and returned late, and my dad, in a drunken state, lit the fire; he was feeling generous with the coal. Mum and Dad were in the kitchen talking (for a change). I was so happy with my new skirt that I took it off and started dancing with it in the front room, waving it in the air then hugging it close. I twirled one too many times and the skirt flew out of my hands and into the fire. I tried to get it out, but nylon melts quickly. I was more upset watching it burn than I was of the beating I had for losing it. I never had anything else new from him again; just like he promised.

Another was when we went to the brook, a little bubbling stream between trees. We picnicked on the grassy side and paddled in the stream, and the sun was warm and the air was fresh. We were there not even an hour when my brother cut his foot. My dad panicked and ran off to the car with him to take him to the hospital. Mum, my sister and I had to pack up the picnic (hardly touched) and carry it all home. Two happy memories at least.

My dad would come home from wherever he had been. I don't know where that was, but he didn't work. Sometimes he would just come in and sit in the only chair in the living room. More often than not, he would be in a bad mood. He would start ordering us around to get us from under his feet. Eventually when he came home we would run upstairs and stay huddled on the mattress in the dark. I hate the dark, and even now I have to sleep with a light on.

Sometimes I think maybe I was thick because I used to get hit the most. He would always hit the left side of my head, around the ear; eventually I went deaf in that ear and then I would get another whack, because he thought I was ignoring him. I didn't know I was deaf, as I didn't have any checkups and I didn't think I had a problem because most of the time I was in my own world. It wasn't until I went to school it was discovered, when I wouldn't answer the teacher.

Another day another argument, but this day was different. They were arguing over my brother. My dad came out, took him from behind the shed and left. I tried to stop him but he was too strong, and I ended up in the kitchen with my right hand crushed between the frame and the door as he slammed it on the way out. I was there screaming a long time before mum came downstairs, and then she only came down to smack me and tell me to shut up. When she opened the door to release my hand, it hurt more.

We spent several days locked in the house without my brother; she didn't answer the door to callers, usually the milkman, and only went out on her own to get supplies. My dad brought my brother back and left again. Then we all moved into Mum's room, sharing the double bed.

It was winter, there was shouting outside the bedroom window, it woke us all up. It was my dad, shouting to be let in. My mother told him to fuck off and he went mad. We ended up throwing his clothes out of the window.

"Fuck off you wanker!" I said to him. "And don't come back, we all hate you." Pretty impressive, I thought then; I was only five.

"Where did you hear that kind of language? You're not talking to me like that!" he shouted.

"I learned it from you, you old bastard. You don't live here any more so go back to your slapper!" I was screaming then.

He freaked out and started throwing stones at the windows. Then he started kicking the door and jumping up and down, swearing. Someone must have called the police, because then they showed up. Eventually he left in the police car. I felt really good but also scared. I didn't feel safe in the house and sleep evaded me. One thing my mother didn't like was fidgeting, so I got plenty of whacks from her. I fidgeted a lot. Soon I started to hate going to bed, even though it was the only warm place in the house. The television was brought upstairs and we spent the whole winter there. We even ate what meagre food we had for meals there.

The council decided to modernise the houses in our street, a good job too as we were running out of floorboards to burn. The winters were colder and we only spent one in the bedroom, much to my joy. We were sent to the other side of the town to live in a caravan. We had a taxi to school and back every day. I liked it there, it was near fields and lanes; I used to walk them alone when I could escape for an hour or so, daydreaming of a day without being scared.

One time when we were in the van our cat, Bonzo, killed a bird and brought it into the van. Within a few minutes there were birds everywhere. They started throwing themselves at the windows and screeching their anger. It carried on until Mum threw the bird outside. That frightened me and my brother, but I didn't believe my sister when she said she wasn't scared. I have since gained admiration for birds' loyalty to their own.

When we moved back the council gave us a different house, number 13 in the same road. Mum didn't like the neighbours, but this was something that always happened when we moved. To date I have moved 27 times and I have been to eight different schools, one of them twice. At this address mum got addicted to bingo. She used to leave us for long periods and spend all the government benefits.

Our then neighbour was kind to us; she would pop in to see if we were all right and bring us something to eat. My sister started to hit me when my brother and I were left with her. So when Mum was at the bingo I used to lock myself in the airing cupboard. At least when Mum used to beat me she knew when to stop, but my sister used to have rages and used things like pokers and spades. I have since found out why she did this, but you can't explain it to a seven-year-old. I thought everyone hated me. The people I was supposed to trust used to beat me; maybe that's why I found the smallest act of kindness hard to accept. I was always wary of the neighbour, but grateful for her kindness. Most of the beatings I got from my mum were forgotten almost before they had begun. I became detached from everything, and even the physical pain didn't hurt any more. She never hit my head or face; it was always body and limbs. Maybe she knew what she was doing hiding the bruises under clothes, explaining the limb bruises as "well, children will play." I never had any friends to play with after school. For the first year I was there, Mum didn't allow it, and the ones I had at school didn't last long.

We didn't have new clothes; Mum would go to jumble sales. The stick I used to get from the other kids when they saw me wearing one of their old dresses or jumpers! My brother used to get new clothes and was growing fast. Sometimes I would be fortunate enough to get a pair of jeans that still had the ass left in them. I always got the hand-me-downs from my sister, who would have her clothes from a jumble too. I got these when they were too small for her.

All three of us used to go scrumping on the main road. We crept into the owner's garden and stuffed our faces and our pockets (I always felt hungry). A few times the owner came out and the rush of excitement used to fuel our escape. Although, I think he didn't want to catch us. We used to take only the ones off the floor and most of the time they were rotten.

Once I knocked on the door and asked if he needed them all. He laughed and said, "Help yourself, I end up throwing most of them away because I can't use them quick enough. You can come at any time and help yourself, but don't tread on the flowers." He was old and had kind eyes, but his smile was sad.

My family were poor, and kids can be cruel. Although whatever they said and even when eventually they started to hit me, it wasn't a patch on what my mum did. I can remember thinking 'You're my mother, you should be here to protect me and love me and make me feel safe'. What a load of garbage, eh? In the twelve years I lived with her, she never once made me feel any of those. I endured self-hate, self-loathing and physical abuse. Not a day went by without me thinking I deserved it; even now I struggle with the concept.

The first time she hit me I didn't understand why.

She slapped me on the arms and legs, then pulled my hair. I ended up on my knees on the kitchen floor. Confused, I picked myself up went back outside to play; I don't remember if I cried then. This happened maybe once a week, and I was 5.

When I started school just after my dad left they became more frequent. The slaps turned into punches and the hair pulling became more savage, sometimes banging me into furniture and walls. My brother and sister used to huddle in corners and cry as they watched, helpless. I saw my sister get a few good hidings too; I knew what that felt like. I never saw my brother get any though.

The beatings became more regular and they hurt more. As I got older she started using things like brooms and metal kitchen utensils, anything she could lay her hands on. She used to say, "I can't use my hands any more because I can't hit you hard enough without hurting my hands." How selfish. I quickly learnt that if I cried harder she would hit me for longer, and if I cried too soon she would hit harder. Afterwards she would stand there and just stare, there would be a sense of calm, I would be lying on the floor feeling pathetic and angry but I would know not to move until she left the room; my anger I had to contain. I didn't know why this was happening. All I could do was wish I was somewhere else as I let my anger consume me and destroy my sense of feelings.

The first day back at school after my first summer holidays, my English teacher asked the class what they did, and then she told us to write a story about it. My story filled the whole book; I considered the holidays to be boring. Apart from staying in with mother and listening to her rantings and ravings, I didn't do anything. I couldn't really write about all the good hidings I felt I deserved, could I? So I invented my own stories. I went to the Safari Park and went on all the rides, even though I didn't know what they were called. I said I had been on holiday to Spain and stayed out of the sun; that's why my tan was not very brown. I went canoeing down a white-water river, and got wet. I don't know where these stories came from. I guess they were what I wanted to do, but I impressed the teacher; she gave me a gold star for effort.

The journey to school was one to be feared. A group of girls a few years older took a dislike to me and my sister. They used to walk in front facing us and say nasty things which I used to ignore, stick and stones and all that. Then one day they started hitting my sister round the mouth with a buckle belt; she just had four teeth out. I went ballistic. I jumped on the one who had the belt and clawed her back with my nails. I felt really wild. Then I repeatedly head-butted her in the back of the head until she fell to the floor. Then I started on another one, kicking her in the legs and punching her in the chest (I could only reach her chest) and I didn't stop until she too was on the ground.

Standing there, I was shaking with anger. "Come on then, you want some?" I shouted to the other two. They backed off. I helped my sister to school and took her to a teacher, and her face was a mess. She had blood pouring out of her mouth, scratches down her face and some hair missing. I told the teacher what happened and what had been happening every day we came to school. Then I thought, oh shit, my mother's gonna kill me for fighting, but surely she won't be too angry? I was protecting my sister. But I knew mum. "She can look after herself," she would say. "Why did you get involved?" How little she knew how much my sister was a coward. She only picked on me because I never fought back. I was three years younger than her and a lot smaller. My mother surprised me, because she didn't say a thing. Although, the next beating I had, I thought I was gonna die.

I don't remember ever having a birthday party,

although I can remember going to one. I stuffed my face with everything. I didn't know what a lot of it was but it all tasted really good. Afterwards we all played chase outside, mainly kiss chase. I hated kiss chase. I never got caught and tried really heard not to catch anyone either. I did catch the birthday boy though, and he punched me in the stomach when I refused to kiss him, which made me throw up everywhere. I was more upset about losing my food than him punching me.

One Christmas we had some rag dolls made for us by an old woman down the street. They were really good and I took mine everywhere until my mum used it to start the fire with.

The second year at school my mother let us play in the streets with the other children. They already had their friends and joining a group was hard. My first real friends were a brother and sister, twins, her name was Alison. They lived in a cul-de-sac on the same estate and we played in the park between my house and hers.

The park was a safe place for me. There was a small forest at the bottom where we used to play 'tracking'. I was always the tracker because I was good at it, and it was something that was done alone. The other children used to hide together in small groups because the forest was dark under the trees. I loved tracking in the dark on my own and even developed skills to help me move silently.

The tracking game became popular with other kids who would normally not play with the younger ones. But they too found enjoyment in the chase. Very rarely would I be the hunted. No one argued and we always had fun; we even used to wait until it was darker to get the eerie effect.

When I wasn't playing in the forest I was playing in the road. I developed a liking for chewing gum, not just any old gum; it had to be already used and thrown on the floor. My addiction lasted about a year. I would hunt the streets for it, scrape it up off the floor and chew it, tarmac too. Some would still have the taste in it, and the tarmac would make my teeth go black.

"Sssh!" I said to my brother. "If we get found out we'll never be allowed here again." We crept into our grandmother's garden at the end of the road and went into the greenhouse; it had been Granddad's when he was alive. The smell was musty to my nose, the air was moist and warm and the plants stood lined up in row on the table. I started to giggle; I was so scared of being found out.

My brother found a blade and started to slash at

the plastic window panes, and I began to pull the plants out of their pots and throw them on the floor. We totally trashed everything. We didn't get caught, but we were found out. Nan was in tears when she knew I had been involved. "I expected your brother to do something like this, but not, not you" she said. Then she started to cry, I felt nothing. I felt that she had cheated on granddad and she deserved it. What did I know about how the heart works when it comes to love and forgiveness?

Although, after it happened she never spoke of it again. The greenhouse was dismantled and she didn't grow anything in the garden of that house any more. I still went round for her kind words, tea and sympathy. She used to blame herself for what my dad did to us. I never blamed her for that, it was my dad who did the deeds, not her, but not once did I tell her that.

Mum did try to take us on holiday, down the river, camping. The excitement was electric. We put up the tent and went straight to sleep, but when I awoke the next morning my sister and mother were gone. I panicked, woke my brother and started to pack up the tent. When we had finished we started to walk home. I didn't know what else to do, I was so scared. Mum used to threaten us with, "I'll have you all put into care if you don't start behaving yourself". I didn't know then that the staff who looked after you couldn't by law hit you, otherwise I'd have gone sooner.

So my brother and I were walking through town to get back when we bumped into my sister and mum. My mother's face! Her explanation was that she had to get some milk. Instead of buying some from the shop they had walked all the way home to get it off the doorstep! Madness.

We all begged her to go back to the river and camp, but she said, "What's the point? We're all packed up now." She turned and stalked off home. I endured the dirty looks from both siblings all the way and carried most of the stuff myself. Oh joy, I thought, another kicking from my sister.

I would like to tell you a story about when we all went to the river for a swim. I am telling it from a third person point of view, so maybe you would have some idea of what other people might see. I wrote this for an assignment in a writing workshop, and it was received with much success. The names have been changed.

A mother and three children were walking on the town side of the river Severn. The eldest, a girl of maybe eight years old, walked confidently beside her mother. Her mousy brown hair, cut short in the fashionable pageboy style, bounced in unison with the spring in her step. She babbled on incoherently, excited that they were out on a trip.

"Oh shut up Tina!" snapped her mother. "You're giving me a headache." Worry lines creased her brow. Tina's head snapped up and she gave her mother such a glare, but she stayed quiet.

The other two lingered behind, occasionally hitting one another. The shorter girl had a longer hairstyle in the same colour. She wore identical clothes to Tina, a dark blue barrel-shaped nylon dress to the knees with a white collar dotted with blue spots, white ankle socks and scruffy black shoes. She was obviously a few years younger, maybe five or six. She looked small for her age and thin. She lingered behind as if in hope of not getting noticed.

The boy had blond hair cut short and features as pretty as a girl's. His smile could have melted the heart of angel. He gleefully slapped the smaller girl across the head. She slapped him back, only harder.

"Mum, mum!" he wailed. "Julie's just hit me again, wah, wah!"

The mother turned sharply on her heel. "Stop hitting your brother or I'll hit you!"

Julie shuffled to a stop. "But he hit me first!"

"So?" she yelled, "He's younger than you, you bully!" Her voice rose to a shriek. She turned abruptly and *stalked off. The boy instantly stopped crying, turned and smiled.*

"See," he said. "Mum always believes me." Then he poked out his tongue and ran off to catch the other two.

Julie stood and watched her brother run off. Then she started to shuffle in the same direction. When she had caught up with the others they had already settled in a spot on the grass, shaded in trees. Both had started to strip down to their underclothes whilst their mother stared into the distance, smoking a No. 6. That's if you can call a fag just hanging out the side of her face smoking.

Julie approached and started to copy the ritual of undressing. By the time she was ready to paddle, the other two were already splashing and shouting in the river. The river had wide banks and looked as if it could flood. It was low now, being in the middle of summer, and the bottom was muddy.

The mother stood up and dropped her fag on the floor, treading on it. She started to undress. Underneath she wore a costume. She trotted over to the water's edge. Putting her hands on her hips, she said, "Now you lot stay by the edge, I'm going to swim over to the other side. I mean it, you stay close to the bank, because I won't be able to help you if you get into trouble, and I will be very pissed off with you, do you hear me?"

"Yes mum" they mumbled in unison.

She waded out to her waist and began to swim across. Her pace was relaxed and a slow left arm lazily entered the water, followed by the right. Her feet kicked in co-ordination with the swing of her body.

Tina splashed water into the air and stood as it cascaded down over her head. Julie stood at the edge stomping in the shallows, causing the water to splash up to her knees. The boy looked quite gaunt without his overclothes, but he ran and jumped merrily, dragging both arms through the water, scooping it up in his hands and throwing it behind him.

The mother had reached the middle of the river. The current looked strong there; her slow, lazy strokes were becoming more rapid. The leg kicks were more frantic as she struggled with the force of the water. Her breath became more laboured, but she wasn't going anywhere. Her hazel brown eyes grew large, her thin lips opening and shutting, gulping for air.

Her head disappeared under the water and was lost to the eye for a few seconds. It reappeared further down as she resurfaced, her arms flailing for control. After a few seconds it appeared she was moving again, this time at a hysterical pace. She reached the other side and grabbed for the edge. Then she scrambled for the grass and pulled herself up. She lay on the grass breathing heavily and slowly rolled over on to her side and sat up. She raised her hand and waved to the children on the other side, but they didn't notice.

Julie was squatting in the shallows scooping mud and letting it slip through her fingers and plop back into the river. Tina shrieked, "Robert, stop splashing me!" then she shoved him hard. Robert fell backwards and landed on his bottom, chest high in the river. He stood up as quick as he could and splashed Tina again in the face. She chased him up the bank, back to where they had left their clothes. Julie stood and started to walk the water's edge.

Tina caught Robert and wrestled him to the ground, then sat on his chest and put her knees over each of his arms, pinning him to the ground. She was bigger than him and was using her weight to hold him there. Then she proceeded to do the typewriter, tapping him hard on his chest with her fingers.

"I told you to stop splashing me!" she said, then she slapped him hard across the face. Tapping again, she said, "but you didn't listen did you?" and slapped him again on the other side. Robert started to shout and scream.

"Get off me, bitch!" he yelled. "You wait till mum gets back, she's gonna kill you!"

Tina tapped out the words again in syllables and shouted over his noise, "Yeah, so? I don't care, you spoilt little brat!" She slapped him again.

Julie ignored them, as if this happened a lot. She carried on slowly kicking the water as she lifted her foot and put it back in; she seemed to be in her own little world. Suddenly she slipped and fell into the water. She gasped out. She reached for her right foot and tried to sit upright, but fell sideways several times. After gulping a few mouthfuls of water and coughing hard enough to retch, she gained control and sat in the shallows, holding her foot. She felt a sharp pain and looked to see that a rusty corned beef tin was stuck in her heel. She sat there crying.

Through eyes filled with tears and cheeks red and wet, she pulled the tin out. Blood started to come, slowly at first and then in a stream. She held her leg and cried harder. Robert managed to throw Tina off with his wriggling and screamed words of insult. He walked over to her shoes, picked them up and ran over to the river. Before Tina could catch him, he had thrown them into the river.

Tina punched him in the back and he fell forward, the wind knocked out of him. She ran over to the clothes and picked up his trousers. Dragging the trousers behind her, she ran to the river and threw them in.

The slender body of their mother emerged from the river. She was breathing hard as she stopped to get her breath. Tina and Robert stood quietly, waiting for the explosion. She walked over to Julie, lifted her out of the water and carried her to the grass. Julie just sobbed.

"Tina, fetch me your brother's T-shirt, now!" she snapped.

Tina ran over and passed the white T-shirt to her mother. She snatched it from her and wrapped it around Julie's foot.

"*Hold it there and press. You two get dressed.*"

"*I haven't got any trousers*" *Robert whimpered.* "*Tina threw them in the river.*"

"*What! What's been going on here? For god's sake I've only been gone five minutes, and you wonder why I don't take you anywhere!*" *she shrieked. Stiffly she walked over to her clothes and got dressed over her costume.*

"*Tina, give Robert your dress.*"

"*But then I won't have anything to wear*" *Tina replied.*

"*Well you should have thought of that before you threw his trousers in the river, you stupid bitch!*"

"*He threw my shoes in first and they're my school ones.*"

The mother turned and slapped Tina hard on the mouth.

"*Don't backchat me, you wait until I get you home, I'll beat you black and blue. Now give him your dress!*"

It would appear that this was the way it always was between them. Tina gave Robert her dress. The mother turned to Julie sitting on the floor.

"*Well I'm not carrying you, you can bloody walk. Come on Robert, give me your hand, we're going home.*"

This may appear strange and in no way relevant, but I was Julie.

CHAPTER TWO

On the move

A few years after moving into number 13, we moved. The next town was only three miles away, but to an eight-year-old it was the ends of the Earth. I wouldn't be able to visit my Nan, I wouldn't be able to go for tea and home-made biscuits, and I wouldn't have anywhere to go and feel safe. I was devastated. I felt alone and isolated. Maybe this was my punishment for destroying the greenhouse.

The new house was in the middle of a street with houses in front and behind. My mother, true to form, fell out with the neighbours within two months of our arrival. At least the beatings were fewer and not as severe, and we used to play outside with other children. That was until she fell out with their parents; we weren't allowed to play with them after that. Although what she didn't know wouldn't hurt her, or us.

The neighbourhood was rough and there were places you didn't go. I never played on the park; it was full of big kids. Here my sister and brother and I used to go round at Christmas and sing carols, and we were so excited at all the money we earned, £25. Mum let us spend £5 it on sweets and fizzy pop and chocolate; she kept the rest, her addiction for the bingo still going strong.

She still left my sister, now 11, in charge. I used to lock myself in the bedroom with a slide lock I fitted, which I'd found down the garden. The garden wasn't very good to play in, as it was full of junk. My mother had taken to burning things she didn't want any more. Although at least I had a bed and my own room. It was the smallest room, only big enough for a bed. I didn't have many clothes, so wardrobe space wasn't a problem. My sister had the bedroom at the front of the house, big enough for a double bed, and my brother still slept with my mother.

My brother found an old pushchair on the side of the road. It had hard wheels of plastic and a metal frame with hood. I was sitting in it with my hands underneath the wheels when my brother began to push it, unaware that my hands were still there. Trapped under the weight of the pushchair, I could not get them out. The drag of my hands made the chair slow, so he pushed harder, not heeding my cries to stop.

When the chair reached the bottom of the hill he stopped. I fell out of the chair in agony. There was blood all over my fingers and when I lifted them up it started to run down my hands and arms. I rolled around on the floor for a while, and then an adult came out of one of the houses and carried me home. The only good thing that came of that was that the warts I had on two of my fingers were completely ripped off. I never had any after that, and still don't.

On Mondays mum used to get paid by the Social. We went to the shops and bought chocolate and fizzy pop and crisps, and ate it all in one day. That was our lot though, as the only other meal we had was from school. They were free, although I think Mum tried to keep us healthy; but we didn't have a chance with her addiction. She used to say, "The Social don't give me that much, how am I expected to feed us all and clothe us on what they give me?"

Moving into this area was a mistake; I started to skive off the local school. Eventually Mum fell out with everyone in the street. Maybe this was a good thing, as they wouldn't tell her when they saw me coming back into the house after she left for work. She didn't last long in a job; there were many. She kept saying the bosses only wanted to get into her knickers and she was sick of them. I used to hide in the coalhouse, which was inside the house in a separate room attached to the kitchen.

One day she came home before I had left to pretend to be at school. The door of the coalhouse opened and I was sitting there on top of a blanket with the cat-shit smell and the darkness. She dragged me out by my hair, pinned me up against the wall by my throat and punched me in the face. I was so scared. Then she squeezed. This is it I thought, I'm going to die.

But that didn't happen; instead she dragged me by my hair all the way to school. When I got away from her on a few occasions she chased me, tripped me over on to the floor and grabbed my hair again. After what seemed like hours I lay outside the school gates. I was sobbing and hysterical; I just wanted to kill her. My hair had had big clumps taken out of it; I had lost my shoes and had made my heels bleed trying to stop myself from being dragged.

The caretaker came out and my mum shouted hysterically, "I don't know what to do with her any more!"

He tried to pick me up, but I wouldn't let him grab me. I kept trying to punch him or scratch him.

The tears ran down the sides of my face to my ears so I couldn't see properly. Eventually I became tired, and the fight was over, but the hysterical sobbing was still there.

The caretaker carried me into the sick room and sat me on a chair, telling me to stay there while he went to get the headmistress. To make sure I didn't go anywhere (not that I had anywhere to go), he locked the door. My mother was nowhere in sight.

The headmistress came and tried to talk to me, but I said nothing. Maybe I should have then, but all I asked for was an apple. She kept me there for the rest of the day. I just slept on the bed that was there.

I skived more. I ate little and became heedless of rules. When I was at school it was for the dinner, then I used to sneak out and go to a small brook I had found at the back of the school. I just used to sit there and daydream. I was nine years old, with no hope for a decent future. The question was - did I have one?

I didn't learn anything at school that I can remember. I had no interests or hobbies, joined no clubs and had no friends. My family were what? I had no answers. I used to envy the children who had both parents and a home life. I started smoking at the age of eight and used to walk around looking for dog ends, or scavenge in the ashtray for my mum's leftovers. She never noticed because I used to empty them at the same time.

I knew a girl called Vicky then. We used to go to a boy's home (Dr Barnardo's) just off the estate and sit there smoking her dinner money. When we got found out her dad made her smoke 20 cigars one after the other, and she was sick. We didn't hang around after that. In fact she and her elder sister, Kim, became very bitchy towards me. They used to taunt me on the way home from school, on the days I went.

Mum had the truant officer call. She went absolutely mental; I didn't have a side that didn't hurt after that one for at least a week. I started to go to school though, for a while. On one of the good days I would be left alone from the bullies, but that wasn't often. One day after school I hurried on home so I wouldn't be caught by them. But they were already there. The girl who smoked 20 cigars and another (from a one-parent family) stopped me on the path. Each grabbed a side of my hair and I grabbed their hair. They pulled this way and that way until I felt like a yo-yo. I managed to pull them down with me, and the strength that I had experienced before came back. Then I was mad. As I fell to the floor they fell with me and I held one pinned to the floor with my strongest hand, my left, and started head-butting the other with the side of my head. When she fell silent I started on the other.

They didn't bully me after that, though the single parent one's mother came round to our house to have a go at my mum. Mum soon told her where to go; after all I had ended up with a nose bleed from that fight. My mother got so stressed out about it she kept me off school for a week.

Then the truant officer came back and I had to start going again. I got into a routine of attending two days and skiving one. It worked too, until my mum fell out with the headmistress over something my brother had done, so she took us all out of that school and sent us to another, a Catholic school; oh joy, new bullies to meet. My sister, being 12, went to the high school, which wasn't local so she had to catch a bus. The uniforms were paid for from a government grant then.

This school was run by two nuns; they were both already old when I got there. Although, give the headmistress her due, she did pay for me to go on a school trip to Alton Towers, and paid for the coach too. We lived on the same estate but it was worth the extra travel time (late every day I was). I didn't get bullied here, so I went every day. The food was good too.

It was here that I found out I had a talent for sports. I was the fastest in the school. At lunchtime I was always the first in the dinner queue, because no one else could beat me, or maybe it was because I was hungrier.

When we used to have games I was usually the captain of the team and I had the chance to pick from all the other girls. Most wanted to be on my team because they were sure to win. I excelled at most of the games, especially track events. Rounders was a favourite of mine, and the opposite team didn't like me batting; being left handed gave me the edge, and no one was quick enough to catch the ball. Every time I hit the ball it went deep, and even their fastest couldn't get there quick enough. Usually I got the whole way round; only if there was a slow person in front did I stop (I couldn't run out one of my team).

I used sport as a release from frustration. I played for all I was worth and used my pent-up anger as the energy. My sporting prowess meant the bullies left me alone a lot of the time.

My mum started to go to a social club, I can't remember where. We used to sit outside with a glass of pop and a packet of crisps. We would send my brother in to ask Mum for more, but he only ever came out with one, for him.

He used to tell tales too. If he thought my sister and I were leaving him out, he used to go into Mum and whine. She would come out and say, "If you don't play with your brother, we'll go home now". I didn't want to go home, so we would play with him. She stopped going to that club, I don't know why. She started hitting me more often after that and I would cry myself to sleep at night.

One day mum decided that I couldn't have my bedroom any more and made me move in with my sister. It was fine by me, because I used to get so cold at night and mum never put the radiators on - it took me a while to figure out what they were. At night we used to take it in turns as to which one of us would cuddle up to the back of the other. When she cuddled me, she used to really squeeze sometimes and I found it hard to breathe, so I used to kick her in the shins. She would get her own back though; she would kick me in the shins the next night. This went on for a few months, until I decided that I didn't want to cuddle her any more.

Some time after we had stopped going to the social club, Mum took us to another. Here we were allowed to go inside, and there was music there. I used to dance on the floor on my own mostly, if you could call it dancing. I used to close my eyes and get lost in the rhythm, I would get really upset when it was time to go home. Mum used to virtually drag me all the way. She started to hit me more too; it would start with "What do think you're playing at? If you don't start doing as you're told I won't bring you any more." I knew that would mean she would leave me on my own at home.

One jumble sale we went to I found a skirt, a sixties-style full circle, white with big black dots. I begged Mum to buy it me as it was only 2p. She did, and I felt so happy that I put it on to walk home in. I wore it to the club and just spun around all night, watching the skirt fly out and wave up and down. One girl came up to me and said "I like your skirt," and all I could do was smile. I felt like I was somewhere else. The music took me away from my life and the skirt made me feel special.

The next time we went to the club I looked frantically for my skirt, but I couldn't find it anywhere. I was so upset; I had to wear a scruffy pair of my brother's old jeans. When we got to the club I saw the girl who said she had liked my skirt wearing it. I was crushed. I walked up to my mum and said, "Why is she wearing my skirt?" My mum laughed and said "I gave it her".

I threw myself on to the floor and started punching it with all my worth. My mum had to leave the club because I was making so much noise. She didn't even wait until we got home. She pushed me in front of her, shouting at me about how useless I was and that I had ruined everything and that we couldn't go back there again. By the time we got home my back felt like it had been crushed. It was numb from the pushing, which turned into punches every single step.

When we got into the house she bounced me off the stairs, then dragged me by the hair into the living room. She told my brother and sister to go upstairs. Their screaming faded in my ears as I lay on the floor curled up into a ball.

I woke up on the bed with the door shut and the light off. I was too scared to move, so I just lay there for the rest of the night. Mum made me sleep in the double bed on my own for a month, not for comfort; she used to visit me regularly after the other two were in their beds. I never cried though, it used to make her worse. What had I got to lose? My life? I used to pray to a god I didn't believe in to let me die.

My mum let my sister start sleeping with me again and her bingo addiction came back with a vengeance. We spent a lot of the time on our own and amused ourselves. Sometimes we just used to beat each other. My brother used to come off worse though; I used to really lay into him. It was worth it just to see my mum's face when she came home. I knew I'd get a beating from her, but it didn't matter, whatever she did and whatever she used I couldn't feel it; she couldn't hurt me any more. I was emotionally dead. At the ripe old age of nine, I didn't care any more.

We only stayed at this house for two years. When I was 10 we moved again.

CHAPTER THREE

The worst place ever

The new house was bigger than the other one and had two downstairs living rooms; the kitchen was small but it led to a large garden which backed on to an apple orchard and allotment (I couldn't believe it, food on tap). I say food on tap because I don't remember Mum ever cooking anything. There was rarely food in the house and when there was, my brother got it all. Mum used to say, "He's a growing lad and he needs it more than you". There wasn't a day went by without hunger pains.

At this place the furnishings were few. I slept with my sister and Mum slept with my brother. I didn't think this was unusual, because he had always slept with her. All I wanted was my own room.

In this house there was a pantry under the stairs. Many a night I spent in there. It had a lock built into the door handle, and this was my safe place.

We had moved to the other side of town and Mum made us go to the local school for the area. The Catholic school was just a distant memory now, and the kids there lived even further away.

Mum went really weird here. Her ranting was more frequent and sometimes she would talk to herself. Soon she was doing it all the time. Whichever room she was in, I tried to be in the other. Most times she would find me and when she couldn't she would batter the pantry door.

I used to get myself up in the mornings when I heard the milkman; he was the alarm clock. Anything Mum used to buy she would sell within the week for fags.

Then men started to come to the house, and Mum would take them upstairs, while I went to the allotment. They used to pay her with fags or money. I didn't see faces, just legs walking up the stairs. Mother was never houseproud and most of the furniture was old. The floors were usually bare, but sometimes someone would give her a rug to sit in front of the open fire.

We used to have coal at this house, delivered in sacks. Every two weeks they brought three sacks. I used to watch the man carry them on his back round the side of the house and tip them into the bunker. It was made of concrete and had a sliding slab on top to cover the coal from the rain. When the coal got low I used to sit in it and look through the hole up at the sky, wishing I was up there with the stars.

The neighbours who lived next door, on the end, were an old couple; I used to watch the old man in the garden sometimes when he did the gardening. He used to smile at me but never spoke. One day when I was coming home from school the old woman stopped me and asked if everything was all right. I smiled and said everything was fine. She told me she could hear Mum beat us and that if we ever needed any help to shout really loud.

The next day was Saturday; Mum always got up late and was always in a mood. She would enter the room I shared with my sister and start shouting at us. My sister stood against the wall and crept around to the door. I stayed in bed, hoping the covers would protect me from her vicious words. This was a regular ritual for Mum, and it always led to a beating. I never used to reply to her if she asked me anything, it just seemed to fuel her anger. If I answered her back she'd hit me anyway.

This day I thought I would give it a go at screaming really loud. I screamed even before she started hitting me. It didn't make any difference though, I still felt lonely and angry afterwards.

Fortunately, there were no toys so she had to use her hands.

A few weeks later we had a visit from Social Services and a social worker was assigned to our family. I don't know why she bothered to come to our house as all she used to do was sit there, listen to what Mum said and reply with "um" or "yes." I tried to tell her what Mum was really like, but Mum never left us alone to talk to her.

After we'd been there for 12 months or so the physical abuse started to get more violent. My sister went to live with Dad; she never visited us after that and stayed out the picture. I silently congratulated her, but I would never live with him - he had left us with HER!

I never went into the kitchen when she was in there, as I was so scared she would try to stab me, as she had Dad. I started to run away and stay out all night sleeping in gardens and sheds. When I was found, they used to take me straight back.

Sometimes Mum took in lodgers. Some were OK, but others used to talk nasty to me. One of them used to watch me, and once he said, "I can't wait until you're sixteen". Then he would smile (ironically, my mum thought he was her long-lost son, from her first marriage). He was hanging around the door once when

I was in the kitchen; the knife in my hand put him off coming in to the room. I was so prepared to use it on him. I even invited him in, waving the knife around. I felt so angry that he even implied that he could beat me or whatever, and I said, "Don't think for one minute I won't use this." My knuckles were white, I held it so tight. *I might let my mum beat me, but you've got no chance,* I thought. I realize now how fortunate I had been. I watched him rape my sister in the bathroom, only I didn't understand what he was doing.

One lodger (a friend of the one who raped my sister) I saw on *Crimewatch*. It turned out he had raped an eight-year-old in the city. It was his cowboy hat that gave it away, the one he had in a suitcase under the bed - kids can be so nosey. I didn't realise how much Lady Luck had shined on me I was 12.

I started to be angry a lot of the time; I used to provoke my mum to beat me, even though afterwards I regretted it. I thought I deserved it, thinking bad and horrible thoughts of her death. I used to wish she would die, and then I would be free. I hated her walking behind me.

The broom head came down again, this time hitting my legs. By now I couldn't run away even if I tried to, my legs wouldn't let me. She kept raising it up and crashing it down until I couldn't feel the hits any more. I was huddled in a corner trying to use the wall to protect me. She hit at my sides and back and arms and legs. Then I felt something snap, my leg I think, but I didn't care - I just wanted it to end. Bruises had formed even before she stopped, and they were covered with more bruises.

The frenzy ended as quickly as it had started. She stopped hitting me with the broom, dropped it on the floor and hovered over me; I just waited for the encore. She turned around and left the room, shutting the door behind her. The room was dark with the curtains drawn and I just lay on the floor holding my legs to my chest and rocked. I was too scared to cry in case my whimpering brought her back. If I could have died then, I would have. For hours I lay there rocking back and forth, eyes dry and body cold. I hated this place and I always thought I would die here.

Time ticked on and nothing changed. Sometimes I looked forward to the beatings; they used to help me contain the thoughts I used to have, violent thoughts of dying in the middle of a beating used to make me laugh. I would say to myself, "Explain that then, Mum". At night I used to sit in my room and bang my head against the wall just to annoy her and make her know I wasn't a nothing, I was still here.

The social worker still visited, but she made everything worse. I was guaranteed a good beating when she left. My brother and I got in with the wrong crowd and started to become a nuisance on the estate. I had developed an attitude, I didn't care what I said or what I did; nothing anyone could do was as spectacular as what Mum could do. Running away became more frequent and it took them longer to find me. Sometimes my brother would come just for the crack. Mum used to come to the police station and just take him back. I could hear her saying, "You can bloody keep her, she's nothing but trouble."

I didn't mind, the police were kind to me and I felt safe in the cell. I knew I would have to go eventually; I just had to wait for Social Services to get their shit together. While I waited I used to promise myself I would never have kids, but if I ever did I wouldn't treat them the way I was being treated. You wouldn't treat a dog like that.

At this age I was totally out of control. All I had wanted was for my mother to love me, but I think I had gone beyond that now.

I started to smash things up. I would have explosions of anger I couldn't control. What little I had in my bedroom was broken, and what I didn't break she used to sell. I only did my own stuff, because it wouldn't be right doing anyone else's.

I lived in a world devoid of anything that could possibly make me happy. I think maybe that's why material possessions don't mean anything to me now. Don't get me wrong, I know certain things make life easier, but I live with the minimum and I don't have things I don't need. I make do with what I've got and replace it when it breaks, but only if I think I still need it.

I started to do wild things and play with danger. I knew drugs were around, but didn't touch them, I'd seen what the drugs the doctor had given my mum did to her when they started to wear off. They didn't interest me at all, but I knew my brother was taking them, and he was eighteen months younger than me. I don't know why he started to take them, but they changed him. I took each day as it came; if I went a day without a beating it was a bonus.

Then one day I lost it big time. This bully bullied everyone, so I found comfort in not being singled out. She smashed my face into the radiator and dragged me over to the desk and smashed my face off that too, several times. Then she pushed me to the floor and started to stamp on my hands and face. I didn't cry, I never cried for the bullies or for my mum now.

When she had finished she turned and walked away. This happened every time; she would kick the shit out of me and walk away. But not this time. I slowly got up off the floor as the crowd started to disperse.

I stood there and shouted, "You think that's a kicking? I've got the best teacher in the world and I ain't taking your shit any more."

I flew the distance between us and kicked her mate in the face as I passed. "This is how you do a real kicking!" I shouted. I was on her in a flash, headbutting her, kicking her and punching her. I couldn't stop myself. I frightened myself that day, because what I saw was me getting a beating from my mother. But it did feel good. I felt that I had done something for me; I left her crying on the floor. I got into a lot of trouble, but I didn't care. She never bullied me again.

It didn't last long, because Mum moved schools again. Back to the Catholic school. We still lived in the same house. This house was nearly three miles from the school, but still not far enough for a bus pass. I used to get up with the milkman's round. I used to hear the bottles rattling in the crates and I was always late for school, but I didn't care as long as I made it for dinner.

To get there I had to walk through town, and in the autumn I used to play in the puddles. I sat in them and splashed around, while people walked past shaking their heads, I used to smile at them and carry on playing. I was always kept behind after school to finish work; they didn't have to tell your parents then. But I always got it when I got home for being late. I started to run away again, just to get the kicking when I got back.

The Catholic school was still OK. The kids there were just as well off as me. The kids I had played with before had changed. The few who did speak to me stopped. I started to get to school at 10 am, stay for my dinner, then walk into town, spend the rest of the day in the multi-storey car park and then go home. I was a walking zombie. I didn't care about anyone or anything. All talk was hollow, I felt alone, stupid, no reason to live and no future.

I discovered an area of wild, the Range, a mile or so from the house. I started to go there a lot. Sometimes there were other kids there, and we used to play tracker. I found it boring and just used to lie in the grass or sit in a tree and wait to be found. These kids were different from the ones I used to play tracker with in the other town - they were harder. I had found sanctuary in this place and preferred to be on my own here. If I had known how to live there I would have. I loved the green fields, the dusty road track, the sun shining on my face as the white cotton clouds lazily floated by. I had no awareness of time and never left until the sun disappeared.

Then one day I woke up and told myself I had had enough. I went to Social Services and sat in reception. The lady behind the window was kind and brought me a drink. I told her I wanted to see Rose, my social worker, and I wasn't going to move until I did.

Time went past, and some time after dinner she arrived. I told her I wouldn't go home and I wouldn't go to school until she put me into care. Mum used to threaten me with care homes and say they used to beat you in them. I had decided that I would rather get beaten by someone who didn't know me than by my mum, who was supposed to love me.

By 9 pm I was in Rose's car. She went to a judge's house to get a care order and then took me to a residential care home called Daylesford. I watched the stars in the sky from the window of the car. I didn't know where I was going or what kind of future I was going to have, but I was going to have a future. I smiled to myself as I looked forward to being able to live instead of wishing I was dead.

My brother had come with me, but he was going somewhere else - I didn't care where.

Rose pulled on to a large drive. The house was big

and stood in a corner of a cul-de-sac. There were lights on everywhere; I had never seen so many lights in one place before. I trembled as I got out the car, but Rose told me not to worry. We walked up the steps to the door and rang the bell. Inside the reception was big and I stood there and took it all in while Rose talked to a staff member. I couldn't stop smiling. It felt warm and safe; I was starting a new life.

The staff introduced me to some of the other children; some just smiled, some said hello. I was shown to a room I was to share with two other girls. I couldn't sleep that night, as I was waiting for my mum to come storming in and take me back to that house. I did this every night for a month, until I realised she wasn't coming. I was upset that she didn't come for me, but relieved as well.

The next day the other children went to school, but I stayed. I walked round the garden; it was big and full of hiding places. Then I went back inside and cut all my hair off. I was four foot eight, weighed four and a half stone and had more bone than skin. I hadn't really thought about it then, but I must have looked a sight.

Today I was starting my new life; I had cut all my hair off so no one could pull it again. My journey had ended with my mother and I had begun another. At the ripe old age of twelve I had taken control of my life. A lot of the time I struggled with anger and control, but now I had the chance to start to heal.

CHAPTER FOUR

My new life

The first couple of days I spent just walking around the garden, which was big. Then I went back to school - not the same one as the other kids, who went to the local school. I was at the high school which continued on from my old school, still Catholic. I had to get up at 7 am to catch a coach at 7.30 which went all the way around the other estates to pick up the other kids. I was the first pick-up and the last drop-off at 5.45 pm - it was a long day.

I hated being the only one to go to a different school but the other kids at Daylesford didn't seem to mind. Everyone there was in the same boat as me. They had all had family breakdowns – that was why they were there. Some of the kids were older, some younger, but most were my age.

Three months after I arrived at the home, I had

my 13th birthday. I had some cards from a few of the kids and some money from the staff. I smiled all day like the Cheshire Cat. We had cakes and stuff for tea and I blew the candles out on my cake. I slid into my bed that night and fell asleep for the first time, happy.

I made a few friends there. Some kids didn't stay long, while others stayed as long as me. Some went to other homes and others were fostered, something they tried for me, but I was too angry to appreciate what a family had to offer. I went for a weekend stay, but felt I didn't belong there.

The first family I tried lived in Hay-on-Wye. It didn't work out; I wasn't used to having a man around. They were nice to me, but the village was too quiet. I went back to the home, and felt I belonged there. I tried another family in Cheltenham, but they were too posh for me. I remember the mother saying she would not tolerate me smoking in the street – yeah, whatever. And she didn't like tattoos. I had my first ones at the ripe old age of 13, home-made, and I think I enjoyed the pain I felt as I did them.

There were many arguments between the kids. I didn't participate, as I'd had enough at home. I was of the attitude that no one here would be bullying me, and no one did. I avoided the ones that tried and kept my own counsel.

I had a lot of problems with my cursed periods, as they were heavy, painful and made me feel like shit. I went on the pill at 13 to try and sort them out, and stayed on it until I was 30.

The years at Daylesford were good. I found my centre and was pretty much left to my own devices. I did get into trouble. such is life, but I only ran away once. Here I had all the friends I wanted. I moved into every bedroom and shared it with almost all the girls at one time or another.

The staff were great; they never took sides, they just tried to sort things out without any violence. The home manager was a man called Dave, who was nice, and his wife Liz was his right-hand man. They made a good team, and moved on to try other things.

Then there was Brian. Brian was a big man, huge to a four-foot-eight girl. He had a hardness about him, but he never shouted - he didn't have to. When Brian talked, you listened. We developed an understanding. By the time Brian had come, most of the older kids had left. At 14 I was one of the older ones now and had a way with the other kids that helped with the balance of the home. If anything needed to be sorted out, Brian would talk to me and we would negotiate a peaceful outcome. It was a give and take relationship and both of us usually got what we wanted. I got what the kids wanted and Brian had an easier time.

I have seen him since I left and he laughs "I used you for as long as was needed", and I laugh back "I let you use me for as long as was needed." Then we both laugh.

We had a holiday once with Daylesford, camping. One of the staff had a caravan which he brought along. We had all our cooked meals from there. We had two big tents, one for the boys and one for the girls, and it was the best holiday I ever had as a child. In the second week we had a really bad storm which ripped the tents down, and we all had to sleep in the camp social room. That was horrible, as all the other families had to do the same. The camp field was massive, and down the bottom was a wooden bridge that led to the sea. We went there every day for a swim, and it was magic. The kids were happy. We had ice cream and fish and chips, and I don't remember anyone arguing.

One of the staff, Eric, had the mick taken out of him every shift. We used to call him a gay boy and make up songs. He runs a fresh fish shop now, but he stills asks me how I am.

I don't pretend it was all roses. We were all involved in any decisions that were made. We had new clothes to wear and we were fed. The cook, Eunice, was fab. She always asked us what we wanted to eat and tried her best to please us all, no mean feat.

As I grew in this place I developed a liking for bullying. No more was I to be the victim. It lasted about six months. The last girl I bullied I nearly drowned in the river, and I really frightened myself. The look in her eyes was the same as the one I must have had when I had just wanted to die. She flipped out after that, I think she was a bit slow too. She climbed out of a side window on to the kitchen roof and started stripping off, singing, "Hey baby do you want to dance, drop your drawers and I'll drop my pants, let's dance." She kept on repeating it over and over, and it was four in the morning.

But let me start at the beginning. This girl started to nick things from my room and take them home at the weekend and sell them. I didn't know it was her at first, but then I caught her doing it. The bedrooms were not locked but we could lock our wardrobes. I didn't feel the need because we didn't have much to pinch. I started buying records with my pocket money - I actually had money, 75p a week. I used to save it and when I had enough, I would buy my favourite songs. I was into music in a big way. It used to keep me sane, and every moment I had I used to go to my room and play them, over and over.

When I found out it was her I challenged her, and she said she was looking for something. "In my room?" I shouted. The first time I went to the staff and told them she was nicking my stuff, I was so angry. I didn't have a lot and she was taking it.

One day I was in the games room. It had a pool table in there and a sitting area, and we used to play board games and stuff. She started shouting at me and threatening me. I was walking away because I was scared of what I would do to her. I reached the door and she was on me like a rash. Her arms were around my throat and she was squeezing. I took a step backwards and leaned forward, and she fell to the floor and I kicked the shit out of her.

I knew I had to stop because I was actually liking hurting others. I started to stay out late, sit in the garden and stare. What was I becoming? I used to cut myself every time I wanted to hurt someone. It wasn't the first time I had done it. When I was 12 and still at home and hurting, I used to cut myself because I couldn't hurt my mum. One time I went too far and cut too deep, I still carry the scar now. It's not hard to fool people. I have other scars from the tattoos I had removed when I was 15. I just tell people when they ask that it's a tattoo scar, even though it doesn't look the same. I'm embarrassed about it, a constant reminder of how close I came to the edge. I didn't want to die - I just wanted to stop myself from hurting other people. I frightened myself sometimes with the rage I felt, I didn't know what I was capable of.

So I had started again. The staff didn't know I used to wear long sleeves all the time or a sweatshirt. Sometimes I would cut my face and say someone threw a stone or something - I don't think they were aware of any of it. One girl used to do "chicken scratches" on her arms at school, or she used to pick a scab and keep on picking. Some of the other kids used to glue sniff, some used to drink. We were never out of control though, we knew when to stop.

One time some of us went down to the river and got drunk on cider and Paracetamol. We weed in a puddle and got back stinking drunk. I was the worst because it made me angry and I tried to fight them all. When we got back Brian was called, because the staff couldn't cope with it. I was in the hobbies room having a fag, although I wasn't old enough by their rules to smoke.

He tried to get me to the door to go to bed and sleep it off. I didn't want to sleep it off, I just wanted to be left alone. The only way he was getting me out of that room was to drag me out. Thinking about it now, if he didn't I was undermining his authority. But I wasn't thinking about him - I was ready to fight the world.

We struggled for a while and I just freaked out. I was hitting and punching and scratching anything; I think I did more damage to myself. Eventually he was able to get on the floor, where he sat on me. I didn't feel a thing as I was stone drunk. I wriggled and slapped and scratched and screamed him to get off me, and then I must have passed out. I woke up in the morning in my bed. I still went to school, though I couldn't face Brian.

When I got back from school I was told Brian was off sick. He had deep, long scratches down his chest that were causing him discomfort. My punishment was that I had to go to bed after tea every night for a week and I had no pocket money. That was nothing compared to how I punished myself. I never apologised, but I did realise that I had crossed the line. I slashed myself in punishment and started putting blades in my mouth, as no one could see inside. It took a few months to get our friendship back on track, but it was never the same. Kids can be so unforgiving.

At Christmas we had presents from the Round Table committee, and we had gifts from the staff and money from the Government for the staff to buy what we wanted. The dinners were excellent. I couldn't imagine what the staff went through, being there for this special day, but none of them seemed to mind. Maybe they wanted to spend it with their families, but it didn't show. We had fun. We had a social workers' party where the kids would play football against them - they were crap and we always won. Although we laughed more than we played, I used get the ball in the face. One year I got hit in the crutch, and wow that hurt.

Brian was pretty handy with the drill and saw, so we improved the hobbies room. I helped him make the seats and fix them to the walls. The kids helped to paint it and I did a snake on one of the walls as decoration. I was so proud of the fact that Brian had asked me to help.

Because I had made such a good job of the hobbies room, he asked me and one of the lads to help him paint his caravan. We had so much fun, we got more paint on ourselves than on the walls. I wore one of Brian's overalls. Even with the legs rolled up to the crutch and the arms rolled up to the pits, it was still too big and I looked a right picture. We spent the day at his house, where his wife made us some lunch and loads of squash. We forgot for a day that we were in care.

My life was pretty much well balanced and I enjoyed it to the full. Sometimes I would fall off the wagon of godliness, but my behaviour changed such that I didn't bully anyone and no-one bullied me, another choice I realized I had. I came to my senses when I saw the fear in the eyes of a victim. I knew what that felt like, and I was disgusted with myself. When I bullied, I felt the power of control wash over me, it made me feel ecstatic. I could understand the buzz it gives when you take control over someone through fear. Thankfully my bullying days were short lived.

One day at school I saw someone else getting bullied. I walked up to the bully and said, "If you want to bully someone, bully me, you'll find me harder to intimidate and I hit back." After that I became a sort of safe haven for the victims. If someone wanted help, they just hung around with me for a while, and the bullies moved on to someone else.

By this time I was at the school with the other kids. I dyed my hair blonde and had a crewcut. I started back-chatting the teachers and refusing to do any work. I used to put blakies in the heels of my shoes and clippity clop down the corridors. I never had my tie in the right place and always wore ankle socks (because they were forbidden). I was sick of the early mornings and late drop offs. My ultimatum was if they didn't change me to the regular school I would start skiving, and they couldn't make me get on the coach. I always kept my word. I had heard so many broken promises. I chose to be honest, although this was sometimes hard to achieve when I didn't want to hurt anyone.

Eventually, I stopped talking when asked my opinion just so I couldn't hurt them with my words. I know how soul-destroying words can be too.

I eventually got a balance, in the form of manipulation but always for the greater good. I would talk to my reason, even sometimes arguing with it and challenging it, but I was too young and naïve. I didn't know then how limited my vision was.

At this school was the bully I had kicked the shit out of at another school. She left me alone, but there were many others she didn't. One day I was walking up the stairs to an English lesson, late. She was walking down with four of her mates. Her gang was big and one to be feared - you didn't argue with just her if she was upset with anyone, you had the lot of them to deal with.

She just glared at me as we passed, and I couldn't resist it. "What you looking at, you ugly slag?" I said. I don't know why it just slipped out, she didn't say anything. She had four of her mates with her and she didn't say a word. I was impressed with my outburst.

It wasn't until many years later I found out that

most of her 'mates' were frightened of her and her bigger sisters. I know some of her gang still lived in the land of how big they were - quite sad really. I made it my business to check who she was bullying and was always around when she tried to get their money or something she took a fancy to.

I used to hang around the shops at dinner time; I knew she would be there and I used to get a buzz from her discomfort. I used to look at her with the look of 'come on then' she would always nervously ignore me. Eventually she stopped coming to the shops at lunchtime. Many of the others who stopped going because of her started to come back. It felt good, giving something back.

I have since become friends with one of her gang, a girl who used to hang around with her so she wouldn't bully her. I've seen her since leaving school working at a hairdresser's in the next town. I let her cut my hair with my five earrings in each ear. She kept catching them with her comb and apologising. I told her it was fine, it would take more than a few tugs to hurt me. She was so different from the way she had been at school. I suppose I couldn't imagine what it must have been like having an older sister's reputation to live up to. I was 17.

CHAPTER FIVE

Boys – nothing but trouble

I was still a virgin until the age of 15. I had no interest in boys, as I preferred to be one of the lads. I found it hard to have girlfriends, because they used to bore me to death talking about boys and who they fancied, and what would they wear for the disco or what colour eye shadow should they wear. It was so tedious. Boys had more fun and knew how to make you feel good. I didn't know if any of the ones I used to hang around with had any problems with bullies or bullying, but I wasn't stupid enough to think it didn't happen either.

We used to play chicken. We'd lie in the road and wait for cars to approach and the chicken was the first to get up and run to the path. We played chicken with knives too. Two people would face each other with their legs apart and the other would throw the knife in between - the idea was to get close to the feet. I had a few go in my shins and trainers or toes, but it was a laugh. It's amazing how many would move to avoid getting hit.

Another game we used to play was shadow hiding. We'd lie in the grass just as the sun was going down in the shadow of the fence. Some of the girls used to play too, but they always got caught first because they were too slow. We would run up to windows and doors and knock them, race back and dive for the shadow. The staff were fine with it, but whoever got caught would have to go in, I suppose it was our way of bending the rules of having to be in at nine o'clock. And the staff would give us leeway. I was one of the last few to go in, only because I couldn't knock the doors and windows at the same time.

I met Nobby when I was 15. He was 17 and so good looking. He had shoulder-length black curly hair, dark brown eyes, a lovely smile and brilliant white teeth. He was funny and he cared about me. He worked on the local trading estate as a sheet metal worker, and he worked hard. He rode a motor bike. He had five brothers and a sister, though when I knew him only two brothers and the sister lived at home. One of his brothers was in my English class when I first started the local school. I didn't know him then.

He used to come to Daylesford on his bike, and he was always polite to the staff and always left at the proper time. He was gentle and kind and we had fun. I had had other boyfriends before, but they lasted only a few weeks. The shortest lasted one day, right up to when he kissed me - it was like kissing a washing machine. Although he was upset, it was for the best.

Nobby and I started to get serious in our relationship. I met his parents and sometimes I was allowed to stay over. I was still on the pill, so I couldn't get pregnant, could I? I had my first clitoral orgasm when I was 14. Nobby and I used to go to the hobbies room, which was for the kids who were old enough to smoke (I only got caught once). We used to lie on benches we had made of chipboard and covered in cushions. We would kiss and fumble around, and I used to lie with my leg over his and we would hug. It was quite by accident the way I discovered it; I got carried away with the kissing. It made me feel all tingly and breathless. I didn't understand what had happened, but it blew me away.

Nobby was patient; he never tried to take it any further, not until I was ready. The first time we had sex was in the tree house. I didn't enjoy it, because it hurt and made me bleed. But Nobby was gentle and kept asking me if he was hurting me. I said he wasn't but couldn't wait to get back to the house. It was two weeks before my 16th birthday.

I didn't get my period and I was bricking it. What was I going to do? I waited as long as I dared (a few weeks) then I told Nobby. He said he would stick with me whatever my decision was, and he never imposed his opinion, although he looked crestfallen when I told him I was going to have an abortion. I was so scared. The staff were great – they never made me feel like dirt or anything, they just tried to comfort me when I had moments of weakness. Unknown to me, it was my hormones at work.

The doctor I saw was an asshole. He made me feel cheap and ugly and kept saying "an abortion is not to be treated lightly, there is a human being growing inside you and we don't dish them out like sweets". I didn't know that he and his wife couldn't have kids. I was only 16 – what did I know about life?

After the consultation I got an appointment at a hospital 15 miles away for four weeks' time. I was the youngest there and was kept in a side room. The doctor said I was too far gone to have a straightforward abortion, so they stuck me on a drip and induced labour. The pains came straight away and lasted the whole day. Then they gave me something to stop me from being sick, and immediately I threw up. They kept coming in to inject something into the drip which made me dozy.

At six o'clock the next morning the pains started to get worse. Most of the time I was out of it, but they hadn't topped it up so I felt everything. I called the nurse to say I wanted the toilet and she fetched a kidney bowl. I heaved myself up, feeling desperately weak, and tried to pee. I clenched my stomach and a balloon fell out. Then there was a lot of blood and a big blob of something splashed in to the bowl. The physical pain was over, but the emotional pain had just started. I named him Steven, and he would be 21 now. I knew it was a boy - I just knew.

There wasn't a day went by without me thinking - what if? I knew I wouldn't have been able to cope, as I was still trying to find out who I was. I knew I had made the right choice, and it had been my choice, but there's no replacement for the sorrow I felt. I still think of him from time to time, and even now I get emotional. Nobby was great though, he never mentioned it once. Our song was, *I Won't Run Away*, by Alvin Stardust. I used to use songs to feed my emotional needs. I liked Meatloaf and still do. His songs can overwhelm you. They make you think about what you are and what you can do to change things, if you want to.

I went back to school after the milk dried up. The first thing I saw on the toilet wall was two names - one was mine, and they said we were murderers. I never found out who wrote it, a good job really.

Time ticked on and I started to skive again. I used to go down to the canal or up over the range, which was closer than when I lived at home. Most of the time I just used to sit and stare, as thinking wasn't an option, it hurt too much. Where was I going? What was I doing? I didn't know the answers and mostly I didn't care. Now I realise just how alone I was, and how desperate to change myself.

I didn't know what to do and didn't ask for any help. I just lost myself in pity and anger and self-destruction. I kept cutting, as I hated myself down to my very soul. I was a nobody. I used to wish my mum was there so she could beat me, because I deserved it. Eventually I was just angry all the time. I used aggression towards the staff and started to punch and headbutt walls, just generally trying to hurt myself. On the outside I was calm and laughing and pretending to have fun, but on the inside I was empty.

Before I had got pregnant, I had been moved into a flat on the side of the house. Two other kids my age moved into the other bedrooms. I had my own room and we swapped regularly, doing our own shopping and housework. We argued a lot over who should do what, and I felt so isolated.

One of the kids moved to another home and another took her place. Then the flat was shut and two of the downstairs rooms were turned into bedsitters. I wouldn't sleep in the bed so I used to sleep on the floor. The room could be locked from the inside, so I used to lock it. At first it was good in there, I was closer to the other kids. They moved on and I stayed, but by this time there was only one of the original kids left and he lived in the other bedsit. I didn't have any contact with the other new kids; they were different, their problems were different. I didn't know any of them and didn't want to. I was still only 16.

I left school in the April of 1984 and started in the Youth Training Scheme. I worked in an office (because I thought that's what I wanted to do) and I hated it - I lasted six months. I was still living in the bedsit, but I was on my own. In the June of that year I moved to another town, into a council bedsit in a house which was an old Victorian building converted into four rooms. Now I was really on my own. I had one visit from a staff member and then I didn't see any of them again. Nobby worked all day and used to visit in the evening. I didn't want him to stay over. We lasted about eight months and then I called it a day.

He was devastated. I didn't see him again for three years.

I started another YTS in woodwork; I had enjoyed it at school so I thought I would give it a go. I was the only girl there, but that didn't bother me. I still had the moped Nobby had bought me and used it to get there. He was good to me and I was a bitch.

I don't remember much of this time, only that I was lonely. I used to paint pictures on my walls in black and white gloss. I painted the kitchen in bright orange gloss, because it was damp and cold and had moss growing on the inside. It smelt choky and I hardly ever used it. If I was hungry I went up the road to the chippy. I met some lads who lived up the road, Italians, and they were OK. We stayed up late and walked the town, helping ourselves to the bread left outside a shop and eating toast and jam at five in the morning.

One of the lads was in the TA, but they didn't take girls in his unit then. I did try to join the army cadets when I was 13, but got turned down because I was a girl. He told me they took girls at another unit 12 miles away, 67 Signal Squadron. He came with me on the first visit, when I was seventeen and a half. I wasn't old enough to join without parental consent, but they said I could continue with the unit and take my oath when I was eighteen. I loved it - every minute of it. I did every weekend I could and every drill night.

I got the name Lofty because I was so short. They couldn't find boots to fit me, so I wore my Doc Martens. There was no height limit - good job too. I got my name because of a situation I encountered on my first recruit weekend. We went down to Cirencester - we didn't get our uniforms until we had done the course. On the way home we stopped at a road van, and I couldn't see over the counter to get the sugar to put in my tea. The staff sergeant shouted 'Lofty' and laughed, and it stuck. I felt proud of my new name, but it was confusing later because when we had roll call no one knew who Private Angel was.

We were one of two units that made up one squadron, the other being in Stratford. There was a Lofty there too, but he was over six foot tall.

CHAPTER SIX

The best time ever

The time I spent in the TA was the best ever. I got on with everyone and I don't remember ever arguing with anybody. The weekends were hard work, but I enjoyed them. I would look forward to them. Friday night most people would be getting ready to go out and party, but I would be donning my uniform and packing a weekend bag. I used to get excited that I would be leaving civvy street and forgetting about the monotony of routine living.

I always felt pride when I wore the uniform, and I always tried my best, even if I knew I couldn't do it. The others who were in the unit were ordinary people like me. They had families of their own, and civilian jobs. I always felt welcome and was treated as part of the team. We all worked well together, and we always had a laugh. Whatever we were doing, be it lying in the rain with a rifle, waiting for an ambush or running an assault course with loads of kit to carry, we all did it as a team and everyone helped each other. They all felt like family and I fitted right in.

I learned a lot of practical stuff and how to keep going. Even if I felt I couldn't any more, there was always someone there to help, any time. I was so proud of myself when I took the oath, I had never felt so elated. I would do every weekend I could, and eventually I knuckled down for the academic subjects too. I did really well, and at one time I was the highest-paid private there. The first time I was put in for promotion it was refused because of my age (19). The opportunity doesn't come up very often. When I enrolled there were four other girls who joined at the same time, they were four or five years older and three of them got their promotion. I wasn't really bothered, because with promotion comes responsibility, and I wasn't really into that.

At field weekends we would learn everything about survival, and these were my favourites. I learned patience. During my time with the unit, I learned Morse code, how to drive, how to man a station and a radio. The experience I gained during my time with the unit was priceless.

Whilst I was still with 67 Signal Squadron, I got back together with Nobby. I'm not sure why, maybe it had something to do with my Nan's death. I was sitting in the office of the Community Programme I did as a way to get back into work. I used to go out to old people's houses and fit draught exclusion around their windows and doors. The team I was with were all male, and they were good to me. I was treated as one of them and did the same work they did, earning their respect. We were celebrating the Christmas break and at the time I was doing office duties, because I was recovering from a broken wrist (the cast had been off a few weeks and I had a support on it), but I didn't like being in the office, I wanted to be out with the crew. Such is life, I sigh, but it didn't matter - I was away the weekend with the TA doing theory. I was anticipating a good time.

As I was sitting there waiting for the crew to return to tuck into the sandwiches and cakes which had been laid on, a gust of wind passed through the door and engulfed me. I got goose bumps and shivered. It lingered, then fled through the walls. My father told me of Nan's death when he picked me up on the Sunday from the TA centre. I knew before he told me, because she had come to say goodbye.

After the funeral I got back in contact with Nobby, who was working in London at the time. We began a distant relationship and I visited him in Shepherd's

Bush, where he was a security guard. Things moved on and he moved back up here. I had moved into a two-bedroomed council flat and things couldn't be better. We decided to tie the knot on 22nd June 1988. I had my second child, Kyle, on Saturday 19th August 1989 at 9.08 am. He weighed 6lbs 7½ oz and had eyelashes to die for. He was gorgeous (though I'm biased of course). A short time after, we moved into a three-bedroomed house in the next town.

Nobby worked full time and I stayed at home with Kyle. A few weeks later, his mother started to come over. At first it was novel, but then she started to try and tell me how to run the house, feed the baby, change the baby, stop the baby crying - she was driving me up the wall. We argued a lot and it was mainly about her. Although Kyle was my second baby he was the first I had looked after as a mother. It was all new to me at the age of 21.

Eventually, it all got too much and we split up. Nobby moved out, but took Kyle with him. I don't think it was for the benefit of Kyle, it was to hurt me. Within two weeks I told him he could come back, the same day I left. It didn't feel right that he should be made to live with his family and care for a baby, and I had a bigger house. Anyway, I thought, I can't stay in this relationship - I don't love him.

I moved in with my sister. At first Nobby co-operated with weekend visits. I was still doing the TA but reduced my weekends to spend time with my son. Then he started changing the days and the times. I would have to decline weekends because he had swapped. Sometimes I didn't know whether I was coming or going. We were communicating through solicitors, and eventually there was total breakdown. If I had anything to say I would have to go to my solicitor, because he wouldn't listen. I still have all the correspondence in the hope that one day I will see my son again.

At first I found it hard. What had I done? I used to beat myself up over it. I had left my son, although I never once thought he was in any danger. Nobby loved him more than life, and I had broken his heart. I felt I had totally destroyed a family, and all because I didn't love Nobby. I found out later that he was cheating on me, but it didn't make a difference to me because I didn't love him any more (not sure I loved him in the first place or that I realised I never loved him). I have never stopped loving my son, I think about him every day. I missed his first words and his first steps, I missed his first day at school and his smile. I have seen him from a distance and I know he is doing OK.

Recently I asked the daughter of a friend, who knows him from school, to pass on my phone number in the hope he will contact me. At this time of my life I think back that if there was a god he was having a laugh, because what I got out of the TA, I lost in my personal life with my family. Eventually I left the TA, because Nobby always used it as an excuse to say that I didn't care about Kyle.

Then he moved to Newcastle-under-Lyme, though two years later through my solicitor I found him. He had by then remarried and had another child. The woman already had a child from her previous marriage (the husband had been someone I had known very well from the children's home - he was there with his brother, and we had many a good argument together).

They have since returned to this area and have made her husband's life hell. Both co-operated at first but it's turned to shit. They have done to him what Nobby did to me when we split up. As far as I know, he doesn't see his daughter.

There is no excuse for what I have done, and I can't change the past, but my son has the blood of an Angel in his veins and he is a survivor. I do know he wants to join the army, something maybe I should have done like my father and his father before him.

Maybe one day I will know who my son really is, but it's not my choice. I live in hope.

Kyle

You'll always be my shining star
As I watch you grow, stood from afar
The baby I held in my arms
A man now with so much charm

You grew so fast from the boy
My heart is filled with so much joy
I missed your first words and your walk
One day I hope to hear you talk

My heart rejoices as you show
You have room in you to grow
I'm unaware how you feel pain
Just be aware I feel the same

The pain I feel is all my own
Every day it's there, unknown
I love you son, with all my heart
These distant years tear me apart

CHAPTER SIX

What ever your choices you make in life
Make them yours and choose them right
Our lives too short to always grieve
I love you son, just believe.

I feel now that I didn't learn the lesson that was to be taught, because I started a new relationship with a man who I am in love with, still, only to have my heart broken.

CHAPTER SEVEN

A second chance?

In July 1990 I was living with my sister and her then partner. I used to spend a lot of the time in my room; I didn't go out and I had no job. I was licking my wounds, I suppose, over my failed marriage. There were a few times I found myself weak, and cried uncontrollably for days. I didn't eat, I hardly slept and I had no one to talk to.

My sister had her own problems. She used to be a DM (Dungeon Master) for a group of people who played Dungeons and Dragons. I was intrigued, so I used to sit and watch, numbly. I didn't understand the rules but got lost in their fantasy world. I started to come down regularly and make them tea and coffee all night. Although my sister wasn't there for me when I was living at home or when I went into care, she was here for me now, and that was all that mattered.

In the group there was a young man called Bertie, and he was gorgeous. He had long black shiny hair, a radiant smile and the blackest of eyes. He played the character of Delium Darius, half human and half elf, and I was fascinated. I had only been in one serious relationship before. Nobby was the one I gave my virginity to and I wasn't experienced in initiating relationships of the intimate kind. I didn't know anything about sexual relationships (I hear you laugh - but you had a child!) and that was the only time (apart from when I had the abortion) that we had sex. Unfortunate, I hear you say - you can say that again. The first time I ever had sex I got pregnant, although I didn't know then and maybe tried it a few times more. Nobby was gifted in the size department, so it hurt. We tended to just pleasure each other. When we got married, we only had intercourse once and I got pregnant again. After Kyle was born we didn't have intercourse, we just pleasured each other.

So you can understand my inexperience in the bedroom department. Here I am, 21 and only slept with one man, and only a few times. I was nervous when Bertie asked me to go for a drink with him, on my own. The previous months had been good, because when we went out it was with a crowd. I didn't want a serious relationship as I had just come out of a marriage. I had things to deal with, about me and who I was and where was I going.

It was like the Danny and Sandy scene at the beginning of *Grease* - you know, when they're fooling around on the beach. Only our place was the local park or the riverside. We used to mess about, play-fight and stuff, nothing in it, just good old-fashioned fun. I was so nervous, and thinking back now I guess he was too, as he had only just turned 18.

We went to the next town in his Mini, which was white with go-faster stickers on the side. He is about five foot nine and filled the seat with his long legs. He worked with a printing firm for meagre wages. I remember he would get a cheque at the end of the month, pay it in to the Halifax, go out for two weeks, then stay in for two weeks. Most of the time he would stay with me at my sisters.

Anyway, the first kiss lasted 20 minutes. We stood on the doorstep, me on the step and him on the path. My heart was racing, I felt sick and my hands were all sweaty. Welcome to the real world, I hear you say. It was the best kiss I had ever had. He held me gently, no groping or anything like that, and his lips were soft and warm, I should have known then that he had obviously had practice.

We continued to see each other, while I moved a

few times. The first argument we had was over his mates, as I felt he was spending too much time with them. Sometimes I wouldn't see him for a few weeks. After I had moved from my sister's house, because he wasn't there he didn't know I had moved. When I phoned him at work to meet me at her house and he turned up with some of his mates, I decided to call it a day. The beginning of the relationship was over already.

I was quite shocked at his reaction. He was saying 'I'm sorry, I will spend more time with you', as if this was the first argument we had had about how much time he spent with his mates. I was confused. We continued to see each other and he gradually started to drift back to his mates.

Having moved a few more times, I settled down as a lodger with a young widow. She had met someone else and was moving in with him, so it was just me and Bertie. We had been together for about two years when I found myself pregnant. I knew it was a girl - I didn't need any scan.

I could tell by Bertie's reaction that he wasn't happy about it, but we put our names on the council list to get a place together. When I was five months pregnant we moved in to a bedsit in the next town. He was working at an arts and crafts factory and started to do lots of overtime, but hey guess what -

he wasn't getting paid for it. We moved into a house just up the road from the bedsit, which is where I still live. We had our arguments, as in any healthy relationship. But as time went on his behaviour became more aggressive. He never hit me, but words can be just as damning.

My daughter was born on December 3rd 1992, weighing 6lbs 8ozs. Her eyes were the darkest black and she had a full head of black hair; she was gorgeous. I had a few problems with the bonding thing at first and found Bertie to be most unsupportive. I guess he was nervous - he was only 21.

As the time went by we grew apart. He wanted other things. He started going out a lot, then one day he said he was leaving. I should have let him go then, but I couldn't. We separated for about a month.

Then I met the mother of one of his mates in town one afternoon and told her we had split up. She said it was for the best, considering he was having an affair. I was devastated. I thought we had split up because we weren't getting on.

I confronted him, and he denied it of course. We both decided to give it another go. Now it was out in the open we could move on with our relationship, or so I thought. Over the years we had been together we had both changed. I had definitely changed, the way I think about friendship, love, anger, the past.

I don't remember when I decided I couldn't change any more and when I decided the relationship was over. He made it very hard to hate him; he just wanted different things. He never stopped me doing anything I wanted, but his doubts about his trust for me, by his own deeds, got in the way.

I know he has had more than one sexual encounter in our relationship, with more than one woman. One of his friends said to me once, 'it's the ones that have it done to them I feel sorry for'. I didn't understand what he meant then, and it's too late now of course - the damage has already been done. It's funny really, this person has spent most of his adult life alone and he now has a partner and he does it to her. Ironic really, that he should think that she wouldn't feel as hurt as I was. Maybe he thought that's what I wanted to hear.

We have separated now, but remain friends, I hope. I wish him well and hope he finds what he is looking for. We still have regular contact, because we have a daughter. I still love him and I think he still loves me. We have laughed together, argued together, helped each other, had a child together, lived together, but he would never marry me. I don't think I would have, because he always made me feel as if he was waiting for something better to come along.

In the 15 years (on and off, more on than off) we were together, I have been to college, worked the fields, done a factory job and had the time to share the first five years of my daughter's life. We lived on his wages; he has been a good provider for his family, and now I feel really shit, leaving him with only memories. But he probably doesn't remember half of them, he likes his smoke to much. The last few years felt like I was the only one in the relationship, so letting go was easy.

We have the financial things sorted now, and I hope we stay friends. I am sad that it's over but it's for the best, it takes two people to have a relationship. I think from the first time he cheated on me, there was only one, (in the relationship) and it was me. I still love this man and always will, he is my friend. I would have died for him, but I can't live with him any more. I didn't know then those years ago when he first cheated on me that it would end my future with him. It certainly lets you know who your friends are. But I have come to realise that with all relationships they have to be unconditional. After all, they have their shit to deal with haven't they?

I have gone from beaten to beater to saviour (for some). I was selfish, obsessive, angry, self-destructive, manipulative, ignorant, oppressive, depressed, lonely, alone, happy, sad, worried - the list goes on. As I make this list I think about all the people I know, have met, worked with, laughed with and so on. One thing I can honestly say, we are all the same in different ways, all the time.

I like watching people. I like sitting outside the local pub and listening to conversations. Most people are just going through the motions of what they think they want. Others know what they want and get it, but are we ever really truly happy? I would like to believe that happiness is there waiting for me round the corner. I just have a few things to do first.

I learned a long time ago that no one is better than me, but I'm no better than anyone else. This helps me to deal with people. I have chosen my current path, but I also know I can change it if I want to. I will not hurt others knowingly, and I will try to sort the wheat from the chaff, but I know I will make mistakes. The question is, will I learn from them? I suppose a future is what you make it, it's just how far are you prepared to go and when you call it a day.

I have recently had a priceless New Year with my friend Stella, whom I have known for 15 years. We would say hello to each other but there was no interaction, we knew each other through other people.

In August 2006, I argued with my daughter when

I found out she was smoking. She stormed off in a mood and ended up at Stella's house. From there we have become friends, and when I speak of friends I mean the kind that talk about everything, inside and out. She showed me on New Year's Eve the many possibilities of family and friends just by letting me be there. All her children hugged me and kissed me and wished me a happy New Year, I was so overwhelmed with the love they shared. I have a lot to do and a long path ahead of me, but I know I will get there. She is a true friend. I know that friends come and go and come again and I think she will be one of those friends.

Since starting my journey at the end of the relationship I have been through the process of what I want, what I need and how to get it. I would like to have a soulmate, someone who I spend time with the same interests, someone I can walk with, camp with and enjoy the feeling I used to get when I was at one with Mother Nature in the fields and lanes of the range; someone I can love and who would love me back unconditionally.

I met a man when I first moved into this town. He was young and still had to live his life, and I was already in a relationship which I wanted to work. I knew then I would meet him again, and I have. I knew back then that there was something between us, I just didn't get it.

Later when Bertie and I had the first break-up in 1997 we started to hang out as friends (he lived next door) and I didn't know then how much shit he got from his friends about it. But in my head I was still in a relationship with Bertie. Not being the type of girl to put it about, sex wasn't on the menu and that's what he wanted.

In this journey I have chosen to have as much of a future as I wish for. I have since become reacquainted with this man. It took me four months to pluck up the courage to contact him. Although I have never been a 'what if?' person I found it hard, because I used to have images in my head of what I wanted to happen between us. Some were quite scary, like the one with love in it. Currently, we have a sexual relationship, because we both have issues we need to deal with like trust and painful relationships. The moment we first kissed totally blew me away and my legs were like jelly. I had to sit in the car for a few minutes to compose myself.

We laugh a lot together, we talk about stuff we've done, stuff we want to do and stuff that we complement each other with. We talk about how many doors we've walked through and the ones that are now shut to us. We communicate, at a deeper level and feelings are always said. For now I think we can just be friends, but there's always hope.

The worst hurt of all is the breaking of trust, because no matter how much you want to change and how much you want to forgive, the doubt will always be there. I wish I could turn back the clock and be the person Bertie wanted me to be, but I can't, all I can do is be me.

Love comes in many forms, it's how hard you make it. I think forgiveness is harder - I'm still working on my mum. In a way maybe I should thank her. Has her treatment of me made me who I am? Or have I really made my own choices?

She has finally been taken into residential care as she has no cognitive behaviour and very little memory. Her social worker said she had admitted beating me and that she had beaten me the worst, I felt relieved, because she had always denied it.

I have met quite a few people in the years I have survived. I still don't trust many people (if any), but I understand that trust should be implied in any relationship, not just the personal ones. As I understand it, there are levels of trust, and only by how we perceive it can we incorporate it.

I expect in certain types of friendships that trust

doesn't exist, but that the trust is a certain kind of respect ingested to support the interaction. There are other friendships where you can't talk about your fears because of exploitation and manipulation. Last but not least, there is complete trust. My experience tells me that my broken trust at the time was not intentional, but the outcome was devastating.

There is no explanation of how it made me feel. I went through the normal grief stages of thinking it must have been my fault, then anger at "how could he?" I tried really hard to change my perception of trust and incorporate changes, but how many? I really didn't want this relationship to fail and maybe accepted more than others would have in my shoes. He is a good man and easily influenced by others who are control freaks. Don't get me wrong, I have been a jealous, selfish and manipulative little bitch, so I know the signs.

It appears that the type of people I have interacted with are those that tend to leave me alone, because their problems are more important. They don't want to know about me but already know me, or think they do. Maybe I'm too much like them, who knows? Cynically I dare say, who cares? Because I don't reveal how I feel unless I express it in anger, I'm not worth the time of day. Maybe that's a good thing. If people aren't bothered about finding out, why would I be bothered about enlightening them?

I have found that both sexes are intrigued by gossip and deal with others' less fortunate situations by saying "well they deserve it" or "it was only a matter of time before they got their just desserts", without a thought as to how their comments are so close to home. Some I find revel in others' misfortune, others try to console but many take it in their stride as if it's not their problem.

I am aware that not all friendships are like this and there are people out there who are genuine. I have even met some - I was just not ready to take that leap of faith. I think I'm getting there, but I know the journey will be a long one. I don't pretend to know it all, and I can only compare to my own experiences. I'm under no illusion that my future will be easy, but I embrace it with hope. I have glimpsed some inner peace in the decisions I have already made and look forward to a less chaotic and emotional future. I sincerely hope I have the courage to face what my future brings me, based on my decisions, rightly or wrongly.

I would like to think that I will achieve what I have set out to do, but either way I have not failed. I live with genuine respect for myself and others, and love every minute I spend with my daughter. Hopefully I will have some future with my son too.

I can't wait till I reach forty. Apparently that's when life begins.

I've already made a 'to do' list:

- Have whole body painted – front sunset, back moonlight
- Pole dance
- Learn to play the violin
- Learn to play the saxophone
- Go to an outside festival
- See Meatloaf in concert – 16.04.07 at the NEC
- Visit New Zealand and Australia
- Own a fast bike
- Get Love tattoo – 23.11.06
- Attend/have pagan wedding
- Know harmony
- Base jump
- Continue to grow spiritually and emotionally
- Form new friendships
- Maintain old friendships

- Complete my degree – working with young people
- Visit Stonehenge – summer/winter solstice 2007
- Enjoy music and keep on dancing
- Give up smoking
- Be forever friends with my daughter
- Meet my son and have mother/son relationship
- Live with the peace/love that surrounds me now
- Keep trying to be non-judgemental
- Love myself – all the time
- Stay healthy – respect my body
- Find my soulmate – dance connected
- Finish my autobiography
- Finish my fantasy novel
- Be happy
- Continue with guides for as long as I can
- Learn Tai Chi
- Be considerate of others – all the time
- Deal with anger in a positive way
- Never be alone when I'm lonely
- Treat others as I would want to be treated
- Be honest to myself

- Do the best I can in whatever I do
- Take part in a survival weekend
- Go to a murder mystery weekend
- Read lots of fantasy books
- Not be afraid of the dark any more
- Visit American Indians – learn their respect for Mother Earth
- Learn from my mistakes

There is probably some more, but I need to find them first.

As I think about how I cope now with being on my own, I realise I always have been on my own. I've just grown from hating myself to loving myself. Steady on now, I hear you say, this has been the hardest thing I've had to do - there are a lot of people out there who will never love themselves because they don't have a box to fit them.

When we remove boxes the limitations we impose on ourselves are lifted, and many of us haven't got a clue what to do with the freedom or where to start. I am a firm believer that whatever we wish to achieve, can be achieved; it's how we get there that helps us to grow. Sometimes I find that I do things that I haven't

CHAPTER SEVEN

been taught, but it feels right, then later (maybe a few years or so) I remember why, but do you think I can remember what it was I did?

The fear of living

The hurt I feel from you is like
A thousand spiders poised to bite
You never know where, when or why
Just constant jelly wobbles inside

Another day, another slap
Too scared to turn and show my back
The corners in the wall begin to shrink
It's like a journey to the brink

The darkness envelops me tight
I fight the feelings with all my might
To no avail it closes fast
I live in hope it will not last

You frighten me with your cruel words
And bully me with movements unheard
You show me no mercy or respite
I wish the ground would swallow me every night
My fantasy place seems so real

I go there every time I need to heal
This special place in which I hide
Has waterfalls and golden sunshine

Back here in reality, the world is cold
'You're useless and stupid', I'm constantly told
I don't like it here today, not ever
I know you don't love me, never

I want love, hope and someone who cares
Not you who will not share
From the outside in, you pick away
Day after day after day

June 2005

Friendship is...

Friendship is just being there
To show how much you really care
And walk the path of ups and downs
When times are tough, to be around

To help, support and share the pain
And be there when it comes again
In times of chaos within the soul
A helping hand to reach their goals

A moment shared in the feet
The feeling carried from defeat
To walk with them side by side
And show them they are still alive

To share their madness from within
And help them back from the din
A friend is there no matter what
To give them back what was forgot

October 2005

What do you want?

I don't know what you seek
In your soul so lost and deep
You wander long in your search
To find a friendship of such worth

But first you must search yourself
To open up your share of wealth
The knowledge you try to hide
Is hidden in your fear for chide

2006

Dance

Dance a little everyday
Listen to the music, you like to play
Feel the rhythm, touch the beat
Have some fun, feed the need

See yourself as you are
Warts and all and you'll go far
Accept yourself and smile away
And dance again, tomorrow, today

6th November 2004

I see you

I see you in your world of despair
Where you hide and pretend not to care
I watch you walk a path of pain
And feel the anger you contain

In you the light you have burns bright
But you choose to cover it with night
You nurture pain from within
And hold on tight to destruction

This journey you travel is yours to walk
And all you know is self taught
When chaos reins in a lonely heart
The world you knew just falls apart

From the outside I watch you destroy
The love you have without any joy
I feel your pain in my very soul
And helpless is the world foretold

Eventually you will get to where you need to be
You have the courage within to see
That here and now is where you are
And never can be lonely

I give you my heart to show you I care
Take my hand and we can step into
The unknown
The gate is open, all we have to do is
Step through

September 2005

I have met many amazing people on my journey so far, and I know I will meet many more. As I walk through this life I begin to realize they have given me many gifts, some of which they do not understand themselves.

As I mature in my wisdom (ha ha) I see them doing what they have always done, because that's all they know. Oh yes! And how do I know this? Yep, that's right, because like many I have either done it or have seen the consequences of someone else's lesson. Whether or not they have learned from it – I have.

I have the ability to learn quickly, but I still have to repeat the cycle until I can realize (sooner or later) I can let go any time I want. Many times I have embraced change, forgetting when I actually decided I was letting go and moving on. I still struggle with emotional detachments. I just recognized the damage caused by holding on.

Ever Repeat

Ever doesn't exist for it is always a gift
Never has yet to come, always is a promise for some
In my head you hurt so much make believe to keep in
touch
Busy busy is how you be, too busy wasting time on me
You play my feelings you don't understand
What I was offering was more than a hand
We will not find a place of peace
Until you stop to find what you repeat

13.09.12

You can only help people who want to be helped. You can only give what you have, but for many the best thing is to walk away....You got to where you are now. I can do nothing for anyone else but show them a way, first I need to know where I am going.

When we fall

It doesn't matter
Where we fall
As long as we
Have given all
To be just where
We are now
And find another
Piece somehow
To catch the wishes
In your hands
And learn some more
To understand
To feel another
Piece of all
And learn ourselves
Why we fall

22.08.11

I know where I want to be, I know where I am. I see my way and how I've always seen it exciting, awesome and happy. The things we need will always come, it could be a person for a day or a lifetime who walk with us for a while. It could be that resources that were not available now are. New information about a thing or just a feeling. Feelings are amazing when you realize what they mean.

As I sit here and write I am waiting for a text message from someone who I see as giving me the future I dream about – will he text me back? I hope so, because there is always hope.

I wrote 'Today I fight this fight' as a poem. The meaning behind the words I have since discovered has always been my way. Whatever the fight, it isn't about a physical fight, although determination can give you the 'rarr' to get to the other side.

Tis everyday we fight a fight: emotional, psychological, academical, intellectual... when it becomes physical to me it means I can no longer contain the fight within. I do understand the need for protection from matters that you have no control over. The biggest struggle is knowing when to stop – a consequence of choice.

We hurt ourselves more from within because it's harder to change conditioning, to be more aware and of course integrity. "Two steps forward and one step back" - the one step back is more important so we can see where we are and sometimes it's just kinder for everyone else to "GET ON".

Anyway enough of my waffle!

I hope that by reading my words it will help you discover yourself, discover that you are amazing. There are many doors, so why not enter the ones already open to us and see where they go? Not all doors are closed, it's only the eyes... but you knew it was a wrong door... right?

Every poem I have written has been about somebody, something or just a craziness that moves me emotionally. Ironic really, that some people think I don't have any emotions... Yeah, I know.

It's your shit

It's your shit so deal with it
You made it happen just like this
Not what you wanted, shame, boohoo
This is your debt, pay what's due
Not what you expected it to be
Not looking forward – obviously
Crated from inside your chaos
So stay as long as you need to be lost

Cry if you need to, long and true
Scream as loud as ears have two
Sob and wail, let it out
Find out what you are about

Hit the bottom, get back up
Catch your stars and take a look
Hold the dreams of what's to be
Let them take you where you cannot see.

02.20.09

I realise now all the poems are about me... yep, that's right, because I can only write with the experience I have of things. I can only write about my feelings and I can only write knowing how I feel. So for some my words won't make sense, for others they will smile knowing of what I speak.

Today I fight this fight
For the braves who have fought before me
For the love of my people and what I believe
I walk with my friends, my enemies and my kin
With strong heart and hope
I see my destiny
A gift should I return
A celebration should I meet the great warriors
For this day I fight
This fight

29.11.11

Forever moving forward in the knowledge we relate
Our freedom from the heart in a future we create
Every time we meet we change my shadow from within
Moving in to dance again and start how we begin
She shows me my ability, she helps me with my needs
With the knowing of humility she helps me grow the seeds
With movements unseen she dances my beat
She starts in my head and goes down to my feet
My shadow is – the part you can't see
My shadow is – the essence of me
My shadow is – me

Keysi is a street fighting application trained for protection. This method has been used in films such as *Batman Begins* and *Clash of the Titans*. I train in this application and it helps me see many things. Originally it is physical and keeps me fit, but on a closer look there is so much more to see.....

Keysi the art
Spanish born from a gypsy line
Keysi evolves with time
Consequence of real events
For instructor program development
Old traditions do not bind
Your journey of body, spirit and mind

No limits hold your learning paths
Breaking free from conditioning pasts
Always moving not standing still
Our daily learning and growing will
Be from what our hearts believe
Discovering self from the seeds

June 2010

It's right that life begins at forty, for some, but I see it now as getting to use and enjoy all I have learned on the way there. Now I get to find out who I really am. So:

Safe journey, fellow warrior
Stay on the path and you will never be lost
Should you wonder, follow your heart
Believe in hope and you will be
Where you need to be
Protect yourself with love and
Fight for what you believe
There can be only one truth
And it belongs to you

20.12.12

Paige

So out she popped so small, alone
To start her life in times unknown
Before as one but now there's two
We start our journey, me and you

As her mother I watch her grow
This time too for me unknown
Our journey not alone forever
We will share a future together
Mother, daughter start to grow
Our bond of love begins to show

A love-hate relationship both to share
Will do anything to show we care
I feel your joy and share your pain
We'll be friends forever and remain

Although we'll have our ups and downs
The love we have will know no bounds
As we walk this path in life
We'll share feelings and also strife
I hope we help each other to grow
And live with peace and love and know

June 2005

Stevan

Goodbye Stevan, I've grieved my loss
I'm letting you go from life
In 24 years I've grown much pain
So today's the day my love remains

The son I did not give birth
Lost in chaos and gone
The spirit alive and soul retained
In my head to punish me again

I decide today my anger is gone
Has turned to love for you my son
My feelings changed, and emotions new
I have always loved you, just realized
I knew
Rest in Peace – 1983

17.09.07

Without compassion we never truly live
Without integrity we never truly give
Without trust we have no friends
Without love the loneliness does not end

13.01.12

Open hands

I stand here offering you my best
My hope, my honour, my love and no less
I show you open hands because
I'm hiding nothing protected by love

Open hands of what I hide
It's nothing you can't see inside
What you see is what you get
But maybe you see nothing yet

With me you can only compare
With you, your life and moments so rare
Do you see my life full of strength?
My love, my anger, my moment's intent

I show you who I'm about to be
But will you take the time to see
Will you look beyond the wall?
And know that I reveal it all

I'm hiding nothing from your view
Your fear stops this hiding you
I stand here offering you my best
My hope, my honour, my love and no less

January 2012

Many thanks for the gifts of encouragement given to me by the people who believed in me. I apologize if it was emotional, but now you have made the first steps of many to believe in yourselves too...

Right arm raised, the fist enclosed
Touches briefly inside we knows
Getting to where we need to be
And finding more of what we see

Thank you, RJP, for keeping the door open.

Inspiration

Inspiration comes from you all
To hold out your hand or just let me fall
Whatever you choose your knowing is rite
For love and for hope your growing just mite

Show us a way that others can't see
But knowing the path we are choosing is free
To be who we are and never look back
And enjoying the moments that keep us on track

Inspiration is not about me
I get it from all in my life that I see
The friends that I have
The ones yet to meet
From a look around glance
Too intense and so deep

A word in the head
From a stranger unknown
To the words that have meaning
And say how I've grown

In music and dance
For the body to share
From a moment of chance
To one not prepared

I trust in my heart and don't question why
The hours they tick their way by
To give and be given but not question who
Inspiration is about being you

17.11.12

BOATING
ON A BUDGET

DEREK HARVEY

With original pen and ink sketches by
JULIE HAMMONDS

ADLARD COLES NAUTICAL
London

Published in 1993 by Adlard Coles Nautical
an imprint of A & C Black (Publishers) Ltd
35 Bedford Row, London WC1R 4JH

First edition 1993

ISBN 0-7136-3774-9

A CIP catalogue record for this book is available from the British
Library.

Typeset in 10 on 11pt Times by Falcon Graphic Art Ltd, Surrey
Printed and bound in Great Britain by
The Cromwell Press, Wrelksham, Wiltshire

CONTENTS

FOREWORD   v

INTRODUCTION   1

1·CHOOSING THE BOAT   5
    Money matters   7
    Essential equipment   7
    Inventory   8
    Insurance and maintenance costs   9
    Buying on credit   10
    Berthing   12
    Buying second-hand   13
    Surveyor's report   14
    Do-it-yourself projects   15
    What sort of boat?   15
    Where to buy?   18

2·SAILING CRAFT   20
    The learning process   21
    Shoal draught   21
    The question of size   24
    The matter of weight   25
    One hull or two?   26
    Small dinghies and car toppers   30
    Big dinghies and open family boats   33
    Small cruising craft   39
    Larger cruisers and catamarans   42

3·RIGS AND RIGGING   48
    How sails work   48
    Sailplans   52
    Lugsails   53
    The classic rigs   56
    One mast or two?   60
    Reefing systems   60
    Sail costs   63

4·POWERBOATS   64
    Hull forms   64
    Engine types   68
    Boats for inland waterways   71
    General purpose powerboats   73
    Sportsboats   76
    Inflatables   78
    Motor cruisers   79

5·BUILDING YOUR OWN BOAT   82
    The workshop   84
    Tools   85
    Materials for boatbuilding   86
    Frame-and-plank technique   92
    Stitch-and-tape technique   96
    Clinker or lapstrake construction   98
    Laminating and strip planking   100
    GRP kit panel construction   101
    Sailmaking   101

6·WHEELS UNDER YOUR KEEL   105
    Trailer sailing   105
    What sort of boat for trailing?   107
    The law on your trail   112
    Which type of car?   114
    The right trailer   115
    Launching tips   117

APPENDICES
    1 Helpful organisations   118
    2 Boatbuilders and importers   119

INDEX   121

FOREWORD

'Wealthy playboy yachtsman' The phrase kept running through my head, tickling my childish sense of fun, as I lay there on the muddy shingle, scraping barnacles off the bottom of my 'yacht'.

I've never called her a yacht before, though that is what she is, a thirty-foot cutter, and I suppose I *am* a yachtsman in the strict sense of the word, which a dictionary would define as a boat owned for pleasure rather than commerce.

But if we do own yachts, we never call them anything but boats, probably because we don't want to sound pretentious, and because we know we are not in the 'wealthy playboy' bracket which is such a handy cliché for some newspapers.

Most boat owners are ordinary people, with ordinary means, who have to get their own hands dirty, and tackle any jobs that they are capable of doing. Some spend more time tinkering, embellishing and repairing than they do in sailing, just as many home-owners devote endless hours of work to their gardens yet never seem to sit back and enjoy what they have created.

Some boat owners like to potter: exploring creeks and watching the wildfowl; some enjoy the keen edge of racing and the stimulus of club-room society afterwards; others are drawn to blue waters and far distant shores. The satisfaction and contentment that come from owning a boat are manifest in many forms.

There are all types of owners – but even more varieties of boat. There are so many possible choices that a newcomer to boats is in need of the sort of balanced objective guidance that this book seeks to provide. Unbalanced advice is often too readily at hand – the old codger who longed for some high performance gymnastic boat, such as an International Sailing Canoe, when he was young, may thrust his own frustrated desire into any available ear. Beware of those who are sure *they* know what will be best for *you*. Be equally wary of those who claim to know what is the 'best' kind of boat, or the 'best' rig.

A good boat may be built of steel or aluminium; of wood or glass-reinforced plastic. A good boat may have a deep keel, or two keels, or a centreboard – or even leeboards. A good boat may have a Bermudian rig, or a gaff rig, or a gunter. She may be a sloop, a cutter, a ketch or a yawl. A good boat may have one hull, or two, or even three . . .

If you were to fly in a light aeroplane over any popular boating area on a summer weekend, you would see an infinite variety of boats; power and sail, fast and slow, open or decked, large and small – every one of them giving pleasure and pride to their owners. None is 'best', yet each is best for her particular owner's circumstances, for his or her desires and means.

As Derek Harvey says somewhere in this book, the first task for prospective boat owners is to analyse themselves, and decide what they want a boat *for*. A fine, ocean-going vessel that will take you round the world is not well suited to weekend pleasure-boating. Some people see a boat as a snug and cosy variant of a weekend cottage; others see it as a declaration of competitive mettle. Some have only themselves to consider, others have families and growing children, who, one must add, stand to gain a great deal from the many lessons that boating can teach about the natural world.

It sounds complex, and indeed it can be. But for those who think well before they act, to embark on boat ownership is likely to bring a lifetime of reward.

Denny Desoutter
Wareham

INTRODUCTION

'There is nothing – absolutely nothing – half so much worth doing as simply messing about in boats', wrote Kenneth Grahame, back in 1908. In those days a yacht usually took the form of 'an open vessel, oared, engined or sailing, for cruising and for private pleasure excursions', to quote a dictionary definition of the time. And even then, it was recognised as one of the best antidotes to the stresses and frustrations of the world we live in. It was the Victorians, too, reacting to the expense, over-elegance and social tophamper of their somewhat effete style of yachting, who first recognised that the smaller and more primitive the boat, the greater the fun and sense of freedom it could provide, and the greater the achievement in making a passage in it.

Small boats have never lost their appeal, although amateur sailors occasionally aspired to move up to grander vessels as soon as they could afford to, abandoning mere boating for what some saw as the more elitist sport of 'yachting'. Not so today. In an era of escalating costs – notably those of marina berthing in countries such as Britain and the USA – there is a trend towards smaller and more characterful craft that can earn a place in our affections without burning a hole in our pockets. Boating isn't cheap, but it needn't be prohibitively expensive. It is a fact that, nowadays, anyone can afford to own some sort of boat if they are prepared to invest enough time and effort – call it sweat equity – and to make the most of what they can afford. Using one's own talents, and a sailor's ingenuity to improvise and make do with what he has, is half the happiness. The rest comes from just being out on the water, from understanding the sea and its changing moods; experiencing the periods of tranquillity, the physical excitement of rough weather and the element of danger, and above all, the escape from the boring pattern and pettiness of life. I truly believe that sailing cleanses the soul. At sea I feel more at peace with myself than in any other place; it is sometimes solitary but seldom lonely. It is a powerful therapy, at once a satisfying and hugely refreshing combination of the intellectual with the physical.

It was a very long time ago that I was irrevocably bitten by the boating bug, but I remember it as if it were yesterday. A rough wet trip in a small sailing dory is hardly the best way to convince oneself of the merits of boating, but that's the way it happened to me. It had been a damp and blustery afternoon, the wind blasting across the estuary in vicious gusts that snatched and tore at the boat covers and set the shrouds shrieking in the dinghy park. I'd been waiting for my skipper, and when word came that he'd be working late and that I was welcome to take the boat out on my own, I hesitated for as long as it took to screw up my courage and cast off. The next few hours passed in a blur of stinging rain and hissing white caps on the weather-going tide. I never got as far as the island I'd been aiming for, running instead up a sheltered creek at dusk for a breather and a flask of tea before turning back into the rough stuff and the distant lights of home. But as I trudged up the club slipway, soaked, exhausted and not a little relieved to be back on dry land, I was filled with a tremendous sense of achievement and a real affection for the little cockleshell that had served me so well. A boat may be only a plaything, but the sea is no playground.

From that moment, sailing became for me, as for thousands of others under different circumstances, a consuming passion; it is a way of life that I have since been fortunate enough to enjoy for more than half a century. There can be little else in life that gives one such a sense of achievement, or the same degree of freedom. In this book you will see that I have placed rather more emphasis on sailing craft than on their engine-driven sisters, and I freely admit to being somewhat biased in their favour. This is because, on a personal note, and without wishing to play down the attractions of any other forms of boating, I find sailing to be very fulfilling and, for me, capable of providing more scope for sheer enjoyment. I do, however, appreciate being out in powered craft, for they are usually more comfortable and much less fidgety than the average small sailboat. More importantly, for most of us who regard their leisure hours as a time for total relaxation, powerboats make fewer demands on one's personal energy and skills. Also, to a newcomer with doubts as to his seafaring ability, they appear as a much less daunting and generally more easily manageable proposition.

I hope that this book will encourage you to take up boating, of whatever kind, and that it may also dispel some of the qualms about its cost. It may perhaps help those with experience in shared or borrowed boats who long to own one if only they could afford it. It may also offer some useful suggestions to existing owners of big cruising yachts and power craft who, for reasons of finance or advancing years, would like to shed the responsibility of running a large or expensive vessel. Many are reluctant to hang up their oilskins for the last time, but are justifiably sceptical of the cheap-and-cheerful alternatives, or don't know enough about them.

With regard to cost, it would be unrealistic to impose a single ceiling figure on what I mean by the word 'budget' in the title of this book, for to do so might rule out any number of boats that would otherwise have been worth including. There is an old saying that the first thousand pounds spent on a boat produces the most fun, and each subsequent thousand shows a diminishing return. Such figures are becoming less representative as the years pass, but the principle still applies. The objective here is to limit our maximum initial outlay to a comparatively modest sum, with proportionately low running expenses. As an approximation, I have assumed that the most expensive boat that we can even consider will be priced no higher than an average-sized family car – say, around £15 000 in the UK at the time of writing. If this sounds too much for your modest budget, take heart. Boats can be found which cost far less, with some barely the price of an old 'banger'.

For convenience, and to avoid quoting hard and fast prices which can quickly become outdated, the boats are divided into four approximate new-price bands. Let us say that any boat below £2000 belongs in Group 1. There are many to be found for *less* than £1000. Most of the smaller dinghies, sail or power, and many of the second-hand Group 2 boats fall within Group 1. Group 2 runs from £2000 to £5000, Group 3 £5000 to £10 000, and Group 4 £10 000 to £15 000. The addresses of the manufacturers whose boats are mentioned in the text are given in Appendix 3, should you wish to check on current prices.

No-one can pretend that boating is the cheapest form of recreation, but by taking some sound advice on buying – or building – a suitable craft, and by judging what bits of equipment are essential, it is still possible to get afloat in safety for a surprisingly small outlay, with running costs to match. As a further perspective on prices, bear in mind that many of the mid-sized yachts – say, 30–33 ft (9–10 m) in length – cost in the region of £50 000, and there are many larger boats with price tags of anything from five to ten times that much.

Since budget boats have, necessarily, to be small ones, I have taken these to include anything from a dinghy up to, say, a much travelled and many-owned 26 footer. The fact is that the smaller the boat and the less it costs, the more it seems to get used and the more fun it can give you, compared with a larger or more luxurious yacht. Never lose sight of the fact that a small, well-found sailing craft can go anywhere that even the largest ones can – and miles beyond, even into shoal water – provided it is adequately crewed and competently handled. It becomes a ticket to freedom, rather than a status symbol.

But as in so many other fields of activity, it's a matter of picking the right horse for the course. Choosing a boat may be one of the most important decisions you will ever have to make. If what I have written helps you to make up your mind about adding this new dimension to your life, to decide what sort of boat to do it with, and to venture out on the water without worrying about what it has cost to get there, this book will have succeeded in its purpose.

'A boat is the best investment a man can make, if he values sun fresh air, freedom and contentment.' K Adlard Coles, 1945

'We look for happiness in boats.' Horace, 25 BC

1·CHOOSING THE BOAT

Despite its importance, the decision as to whether or not to take up boating is quite easily reversed. A number of people try it and don't like it for one reason or another, such as chronic seasickness, a persistent feeling of insecurity, or disappointment at the general inconvenience and discomfort. More often, it is simply because they chose the wrong sort of boat. Provided it was bought at the right price or, better still, borrowed or hired, their experience might at least have been interesting and should not have cost them very much. Others toy with the idea, often for unnecessarily long periods due to lack of sound advice, while they wait for more spare time, or cash, to come along. Many of us, however, have only to venture out once or twice in a small boat to lose our hearts to this way of life, and immediately start looking for the means to achieve it.

To start with, we should ask ourselves why do we want to go boating? Is it for the challenge and the sense of adventure, the combination of the physical and the intellectual, the 'serious kind of joy' that Arthur Ransome found in seamanship, the achievement in making a difficult passage, or perhaps for the sport and excitement of competing against other boats? Or is it for the sheer beauty of life in the open air, the peace and solitude, and the escape from everyday life?

The reality, for most of us, is the annual holiday cruise – if we're lucky – and the sailing weekends and evenings. The feeling of freedom and independence must be one of the attractions of boating, whether in an adventurous open-water passage, the thrill of a race, pottering around in creeks and rivers, or of just whiling away the day moored or at anchor, fishing or fixing this and that. In other words, messing about in boats as the fancy takes us. As well as the network of inland waterways, lakes and rivers, nowhere in Britain is more than 100 miles from the sea. There are thousands of miles of coastline to choose from, and many more within easy reach around the European continent. We are not concerned here with heroic voyages and feats of seamanship in stormy seas – our kind of boating is supposed to be fun. On the other hand, bad weather cannot always be avoided, and then it becomes a natural challenge, to be met with a certain amount of skill, nerve and judgement. Anyone who ventures out on the water and is never in some measure frightened or in awe of it must be totally lacking in imagination.

Without doubt, some of the small craft we shall be looking at are rather less sea-kindly than others in terms of the relative comfort they can provide. But all of them are seaworthy, in the sense that they are able to put to sea and to survive the worst conditions they were designed to meet without making unrealistic demands on the capabilities and stamina of their crews. Many of them, considering their modest size, also have an all-round performance that can raise the eyebrows of many a sceptic. You need to find one that suits not only your pocket but also your general outlook and temperament. Whether you choose power or sail, however, you will need some tuition in how to handle your boat. I suppose there will always be a few irresponsible people who haven't bothered to learn even the basics of navigation or how to handle their boats properly and considerately, and who take it for granted that the emergency services will always be there to get them out of trouble. The majority of small boat sailors, however, are just ordinary, reasonably intelligent folk who take pride in being self-reliant, and in behaving sensibly while at the wheel or the tiller.

It may come about that British boat owners will soon have to be tested for a Certificate of Competence and to register their boat, with a special tax to pay and an annual inspection, in the same way as for a car. Such regulations already exist in most of the Mediterranean countries and have been adopted in part by both the Belgian and Dutch authorities. So if you are planning to skipper a boat overseas – your own or a chartered one – you will need a Helmsman's Certificate and a registration document if the boat is British owned. Assuming that you have a VHF radio aboard, your ship's papers should also include a licence for it and a certificate showing that you are competent to use it. When visiting another EC country, you must also be able to show Customs officials the VAT receipts for the boat and its equipment. Unless you can prove that sales taxes have been paid, or you can pay them there and then, you may be asked to leave. So bear this in mind if you buy a second-hand boat, and insist on full VAT documentation before you close the deal. Further EEC proposals might even affect our freedom to sail the type of boat we choose by defining the areas in which each could be used (Ocean, Offshore, Coastal or Sheltered). Further information and advice on the latest legislation is available from the Royal Yachting Association.

Boating is all about freedom and the way it can temporarily transform our lifestyle. Even for an hour or two, a boat, however small, provides the environment for a total change of outlook and priorities – an entirely self-contained habitat or a 'capsule of change'. 'With your home about you, you have everything you need to feel at peace with the world which at times can seem far, far away', wrote the famous designer of small, simple boats, Maurice Griffiths.

MONEY MATTERS

Prudence is one of the essential ingredients of seamanship. A boat is for fun and relaxation, not for sailing in the shadows of financial over-commitment. Keep it simple and don't over-invest. Admittedly, we are talking here of a comparatively small scale of expenditure. Even so, it is only too easy to underestimate the genuine all-in first cost of a boat, which, in addition to its basic purchase price, should include the cost of insurance (see page 9); a survey (see page 14); and an inventory of the essential equipment without which no small craft can be considered truly fit – let alone safe – to put to sea, even for a single day. Boating is not inherently dangerous but at sea you are far more dependent on your own resources than you are on land.

ESSENTIAL EQUIPMENT

This is likely to add some 20% or more to the modest cost of a Group 1 boat, proportionately much less for the more expensive ones. Useful savings can be made by shopping around among the many suppliers who regularly advertise well-known brands of chandlery goods at well below list price, or by buying from the small ads, car boot sales or boat jumbles. Well-known brands of new outboard motors, for example, are sometimes advertised at one third below their list price. Outdated models or slow-moving stock, it doesn't really matter. But be sure that (if it's not straight out of the box) any equipment you buy is from a reputable manufacturer, or at least in sound working order.

This need not apply to boats being used on sheltered inland waterways, when no more than a few warps and fenders, plus a bilge pump and an anchor or grapnel and a stout boathook are usually all that are needed in addition to the domestic list of provisions and creature comforts, warm clothing and waterproofs. Nor is any of it needed for local dinghy sailing – except for some type of buoyancy vest, which should always be worn in windy weather or while racing, and by children and non-swimmers whenever they go afloat. The list of primary essentials, which applies to all other small craft, of whatever kind, is shown in the accompanying table as Category 1. In addition, any cruising boat, whether power or sail (other than dinghies) should include all the rest of the listed items, that is to say those in Categories 2, 3, and 4, in their inventories. Some of these pieces of equipment, however, are either inappropriate, unnecessary, or too bulky for a camp-cruising dinghy, whose inventory can therefore be confined to Categories 1 and 3, while sports powerboats on short local trips

CATEGORY 1 All small craft, including sportsboats and dinghies

- Bower (principal) anchor. Allow 1 lb/ft (1.5 kg/m) of boat length, and at least 25 m of chain, or 5 m chain and 35 m of 8 mm nylon warp. A 10 m warp without any chain is adequate for dinghies.
- Bilge pump (or for dinghies, a pair of bailers, secured to the boat on long lanyards).
- First aid kit and instructions.
- Drinking water container – allow at least 3 pints or 2 litres per person per day.
- At least one robust bucket, with a lanyard on its handle.
- Personal buoyancy aids, one for each crewmember and a spare if possible.
- If positive buoyancy is not already incorporated in the hull, enough buoyancy bags to support an open boat and crew if swamped.
- If you are liable to be out after dark, navigation lights or a powerful waterproof lamp, and a torch.
- Auxiliary propulsion: oars, or an additional engine.
- Distress flares of appropriate classification (inshore, coastal or offshore) in a watertight container, and a powerful waterproof torch.
- Horn, bell or whistle to give audible warning in mist or fog.
- Steering compass (with an up-to-date deviation card).
- Binoculars (or compass binoculars, which also enable you to take bearings).
- Radio receiver for weather forecasts (if you are going out for more than a few hours).
- Tide tables and chart(s).
- Sailor's knife, marlin spike, spare cord, rope and rigging tape.

CATEGORY 2 All cruising boats, power or sail; not dinghies

- Kedge (secondary) anchor, approx 2/3 the weight of the bower, and at least 25 m nylon cable.
- Secondary bilge pump.
- Inflatable dinghy, and/or liferaft if you are going offshore.
- Radar reflector.
- Distance-run indicator, usually mechanical (towed log), or combined distance/boatspeed electrical instrument.
- VHF two-way radio.
- Echo sounder.
- Barometer or barograph.
- Wind speed and direction indicator (sailboats only). Not absolutely essential, but if you intend cruising, it's a good idea to have one.

CATEGORY 3 All cruising boats, including camp-cruising dinghies
- Safety harnesses, one for each crewmember on sailing cruisers, and on motorcruisers for anyone working on deck in rough weather or at night.
- Hand-bearing compass (can serve as a spare, or as a steering compass on a dinghy).
- Lead-line, for taking soundings.
- Corrected charts covering your route and adjoining areas.
- Pilot books, tidal atlas and some means of plotting your course.

CATEGORY 4 All cruising boats and sportsboats; not dinghies
- Two fire extinguishers, automatic or remote-controlled on fast boats.
- At least one horseshoe lifebuoy, for throwing.
- Engine spares kit, handbook and tools.

A valuable addition to anyone's offshore inventory is an electronic position finder such as GPS, a satellite navigation receiver/computer small enough (some models) to carry in your pocket. GPS has effectively superseded Decca and Loran which, though less costly, are much less accurate and reliable; while the traditional sextant requires skill, practice, a reasonably steady deck and a clear view of the heavens to be of any use. But GPS is an expensive addition to the budget, and just how strictly essential you rate it must depend on how ambitiously the boat is used.

within sight of the shore can be covered by Categories 1 and 4 (otherwise they should be treated as cruisers).

INSURANCE AND MAINTENANCE COSTS

Insurance is an annual item, averaging somewhere around 1.5% of the value of the boat, depending on its type and where it will be used. Low value boats, oldies (especially wooden ones, I am sorry to say) and multihulls cost rather more – typically 2% or a bit over – while a powerful open sportsboat can run as high as 5%. Although not actually a legal requirement, as it is before you can license a car, comprehensive insurance is certainly advisable (it will be insisted on by any finance company) from the moment you own the boat, and before you move her. Be sure the policy includes third-party liability to indemnify you against any damage or injury you might cause to other people, or their boats, in the event of an accident.

Next, you should allow a sum for any initial repairs and refurbish-

ing that may be needed. You should also include in the budget a
'guesstimated' annual figure for upkeep, which can amount to
between 5 and 10% of the purchase price. A year's maintenance can
easily account for half of this, even if the boat is in reasonably good
condition – more if it is not. Of course, you can make some big
savings by using your own labour, but the cost of materials will still be
significant – notably such items as antifouling paint, for example. The
price of this may be around three times that of the most expensive
paint or varnish, although this is one of the savings you make if you
choose to trailer-sail. If you are buying a powerboat, you must
consider the cost of fuel, which can be a major item at current prices.
Some examples of fuel consumption are given on page 69.

BUYING ON CREDIT

If you decide to borrow the money to buy the boat, there is a
considerable range of credit facilities available to you – provided,
of course, that you are able to satisfy the lenders that you can
afford the repayments. The terms can vary widely between one
firm and another, so it always pays to shop around. To the
uninitiated, the credit market presents a veritable minefield that
warrants cautious navigation. Most finance companies are highly
reputable and they are obliged to operate within strict legal
guidelines. Nevertheless, some deals are not quite so straightforward as they might at first appear, and some are even 'negotiable',
so be prepared to haggle if you feel you are justified in doing so;
read the small print carefully, or seek professional advice.

For loans in the Groups 3 and 4 range, a marine mortgage is
generally regarded as the best alternative to extending a house
mortgage, which is the cheapest form of borrowing. The maximum
advance under a marine mortgage is usually 80% of the purchase
price or valuation, including any equipment bought for the boat at
the same time. The finance company then takes a charge over the
boat as security. At the time of writing, typical figures for this
type of credit were an interest charge of three or four percent
above Finance House Base Rate (the national average over the
previous eight weeks) and a maximum repayment period of 7–10
years, resulting in what is termed an APR (Annual Percentage
Rate) of 11–12%. APR is the commonly used basis for assessing
the true cost of the loan, taking into account the repayments and
the compound interest on the outstanding amount. It must be a
sign of the times that it is occasionally possible to obtain very
similar terms without actually pledging the vessel, but this is still
unusual.

Boats of the value that interest us do not necessarily have to be

Instant access to your boat, already afloat, with electricity and water supply points, car park, restaurant and shopping facilities. *Photo: author*

registered, unless they are being taken abroad, but they must be surveyed and insured.

Marine mortgages are not usually available for boats in Group 2, and never in Group 1, so the smaller borrowings have to be made by some other form of credit agreement. By their very nature, and because they are particularly affected by fluctuations in the market, the status of the borrower, the type of boat and its age, they tend to attract interest rates that are several percentage points higher than secured and other loans for larger amounts, allied to shorter repayment periods – typically 3–5 years. There is also a much wider variation in the ways in which they can be structured. Your bank, for example, will usually be willing to arrange a personal loan or an overdraft. But the rates – typically as high as 20% APR – are unlikely to match those of the specialist marine finance companies that form an integral part of the marine industry, and hence are much more familiar with boats and the degree of risk involved in funding them.

Hire purchase is at the top end of the credit cost range. It is quick, convenient and easy to arrange, just like buying a car or a television. HP is normally limited to new or nearly new boats, and is often the only form of finance available on high risk types such as small sportsboats and jetskis. Interest rates are mostly similar to those of credit cards or bank loans, ie 19–23% APR. However, this is the area

Free parking at home on a trailer. *Photo: David Evans, Trail Sail Association*

where some of the widest variations can be found among the various deals on offer, with APRs ranging from as low as 18% to over 25% in a few cases. The essential difference between it and other forms of credit is that the HP company actually buys the boat and simply hires it out to you, usually over a maximum period of three years, with the option to purchase. This means that until you have completed the payments, they have clear title to the boat should you default. (They are also, incidentally, liable for any damage the boat may cause while they own her, hence the need for insurance.)

I must emphasise that although the above figures were representative at the time of writing, they will always be affected by market forces and those ephemeral digits that flicker across the bankers' and brokers' video screens in accordance with the state of the world economy. They are included only as a rough guide to what you may expect.

BERTHING

One of the first things to decide is where you are going to keep your boat. With or without winter storage, it can vary from free parking at home on a trailer, to a modest fee to a sailing club for space in their boat park or on their moorings, or up to four-figure sums in a marina. The majority of boats that lie afloat during the season are found in marinas – moored in rows alongside pontoons. Here instant access is provided for the crew and for loading stores, with all the conveniences of electricity, water and fuel, chandlery and car parking;

there will also be a crane or travel-hoist for lifting-out and winter storage. It is hardly surprising that luxury facilities like these come at high prices, anything from around £700 per annum to £1700 or more for a 25 footer and pro rata. But such has been their escalation in recent years – notably around Britain's south coast areas, where for no apparent reason they are generally about double those of their counterparts on the other side of the Channel – that over a period of two or three years the cumulative cost of using a marina could easily amount to more than you paid for your boat in the first place. Even the open water moorings are nowadays mostly owned by the marina operators, who charge accordingly, often only 20% below their pontoon berth prices. In consequence, private or even club moorings are scarce and seldom available, except in a few out-of-the-way bays and rivers where you can still lay your own moorings and be charged no more than a peppercorn rent. These high costs have undoubtedly affected sales of new boats, with repercussions throughout the marine industry in general. But this has now backfired, resulting in large numbers of empty berths and discount deals becoming available. The trend towards more reasonable pricing looks set to continue.

One way of reducing expenses is to go into partnership with one or more like-minded friends. But it is essential to have a properly drawn up agreement (the RYA publishes a useful guide on the subject). The idea often works, at least for a time but unless you know your partners extremely well, and sometimes even then, it can lead to friction and resentment. There may be problems with clashing dates. For example, one needs the boat for the same weekend or holiday period that another had planned. There may be misunderstandings over the share of maintenance work that each contributes during the season, or criticisms about not leaving the boat clean and tidy when coming ashore. People's standards vary. So unless you can be reasonably sure of sufficient give-and-take in the partnership, it's probably best to forget the idea. The advantages of exclusive ownership usually outweigh those of any cost cutting.

BUYING SECOND-HAND

Buying a boat should never be considered as a potentially profitable venture, unless you are a determined and competent do-it-yourselfer. You'd get a better return on your money from Government bonds. Nevertheless, well-built and carefully maintained sailing craft are a sound investment, because depreciation is relatively slow. It would be meaningless to try to define this in real terms, in view of the various fluctuating factors such as the inflation rate and the retail price index. Let's just say that quality sailing boats can still command good market prices after ten, twenty or even thirty years of use. This is not the case, however, with the majority of powerboats, particularly the small sporty ones which are naturally liable to wear out more quickly and whose styling soon becomes outdated. The more traditional types, such as fishing cruisers, which don't usually get such a hard life, are a safer financial bet.

A new boat has, of course, all the advantages of the latest design and construction techniques, with a manufacturer's warranty, and no need for a survey. But buying second-hand is the most cost effective way of getting into boating. You gain from extra equipment that may be included in the deal, and also from the experience of the previous owner who should have sorted out any teething troubles that arose when the boat was new; he will probably have added a few improvements of his own (though not necessarily to your taste). Because you get more for your money, buying second-hand may also enable you to buy a larger boat than you first thought you could afford.

Never make the mistake of choosing an ugly old tub just because it's big or cheap. You may not claim to have a seaman's eye for such matters, but you soon learn that there are few objects more offensive to look at than an ill-proportioned vessel. You will never love her, and instead of a growing sense of attachment, there will be a gnawing resentment at her awkward, misshapen lines. She will stand out in an anchorage or boat park – an ugly duckling among the swans – and when you decide you must be rid of her, she will probably be difficult to resell.

SURVEYOR'S REPORT

Other ostensible bargains to be avoided at all costs are the hard-used, in reality worn-out, racing sailboat, however sleek and attractive she may look. Also, steer clear of any shoddily built boat or one in need of extensive repairs that are manifestly beyond your capabilities. Professional rebuilding could prove cripplingly expensive, even assuming it was practicable, and if it were not, she might be dangerous at sea. Except in the case of the smallest craft such as dinghies, always consult a surveyor or ask to see a recent report by a qualified professional. The cost varies with the size of the boat, but in the UK there is a simple guideline, which is just to multiply the length by the beam (both in feet). This gives you the fee in sterling, excluding VAT. The same formula works for multihulls, except that in their case you take only two-thirds of the resultant figure, so as to compensate for their greater overall beam.

A survey is usually mandatory if the boat forms the security on a financial credit deal, many of which are conditional on a suitable report and the rectification of any major faults it may disclose. One common example is osmosis, a form of skin blistering that can affect GRP (glass reinforced plastic) hulls, notably those built a few years ago when techniques and materials were not as good as they are today. It is not always easy to spot, but unless treated in the early stages, repairs become expensive. Partly restored, unsaleable wrecks – fit only for the bonfire, hulks that have broken someone else's heart – make a sad and all too common spectacle. A survey might have avoided this. Not only will it save you money in the long run if you decide against such a boat, it might also save your life.

DO-IT-YOURSELF PROJECTS

Without expert knowledge or advice, it is often difficult to distinguish between a seemingly well-maintained but structurally flawed hull, and one that is basically sound but looks scruffy and ill-kempt, perhaps with superficial damage which the owner hasn't the time or the inclination to put right. Provided you know exactly what you are taking on and how to go about it, with a fairly clear idea of the likely fix-up costs, this is a good way of reducing your initial outlay. You can, of course, save a great deal more by building your boat from a set of plans and the designer's list of materials (see page 82) or from a kit of parts, or by fitting out a factory built hull-and-deck assembly. You can save anything up to half the cost of a new boat by assembling it and fitting it out yourself. But don't kid yourself about the length of time you will need for the project. It will invariably take longer than you anticipated at the outset, even for those with experience.

Assuming you decide to play it safe and go for a ready-made boat in fair condition, shop around and scan the magazine advertisements to establish a range of prices for the sort of boat you are looking for, so that you will recognise a bargain when you come across one. If you have a choice, give preference to one built by a firm with a good reputation. It will be easier to resell at a favourable price than one of dubious or unknown origin. Although it may be difficult, try to contact an earlier owner. He is more likely to give you an unbiased opinion than the vendor.

WHAT SORT OF BOAT?

Choosing the right boat to suit your purposes as well as your pocket can be one of the most important decisions you will ever have to make, because picking the wrong one might put you off boating altogether. So, before you even begin shopping around, think carefully and try to define, as clearly as you can, exactly why you want one and what you realistically expect to do with it. Power or sail? What types and sizes will be suitable? How much do you intend to spend? These are interdependent questions and not necessarily to be answered in that order.

The problem here is that it takes a certain amount of experience, sometimes bitter, to be able to make the right choice – which is all very well for those who already have it. But if you are a beginner, you

Catamaran in the Alps. With your boat on a trailer, you are free to choose your cruising area and to use it as a caravan *en route*.

won't get the experience until after you've bought the boat. So you would be well advised to buy a used rather than a new one, and avoid high depreciation. Your ideas may change in practice, and after a season or two you will probably know what you really want.

Take first the most basic decision, the choice between sail (with or without an auxiliary motor) and a fully powered craft. For those who love and respect the sea in all its moods, there can be no finer pastime than working the winds and tides with only the silent sails to drive you along. There are others, however, who are looking for fresh air and the adventure of life afloat without the hassle of sails and rigging. They want to be reasonably sure of getting from one place to another in the allotted time and are prepared to accept the fuel costs and a certain amount of noise. For them there are engine-driven craft to suit all tastes and pockets.

Temperament and to some extent physical fitness must play their part in this decision (not that it need be irrevocable). It has been said that in no other field of recreation is the cost of over-estimating one's personal capabilities so high. Out on the water, it is absolutely essential to function within the limits of oneself and the boat; to exceed them is to invite danger and even to court disaster. This may sound somewhat over the top, but it is always worth keeping at the back of one's mind.

The next consideration is the type of boating you would like to do. Will you normally be taking the boat out with your family and friends, or on your own? (Always bear in mind that you may one day have to depend on yourself, and yourself alone, to handle her.) How much time do you really expect to spend aboard? Are you thinking in terms of racing, or local pottering, or perhaps both? Will you be mostly daysailing, overnighting, or maybe adventuring further afield? A cruise, after all, just means going somewhere. And do you intend keeping her on a mooring in the summer, or even all the year round; or in a club dinghy park? Or do you plan to trail her home after every outing?

The cruising range of a small boat may, at first sight, appear extremely limited. But with a trailer you can tow it wherever you fancy and try your boat in new waters – abroad even, via a car ferry – instead of having to sail all the way. Not that you necessarily have to travel far to find adventure. More often than not there are lakes and rivers and other inland waterways within easy reach of home that can offer family fun for a modest outlay. It is perfectly practicable – within the limits of endurance set by the stamina of the crew – to navigate open waters in a small boat. This is provided you have had some practice in coastal pilotage, together with a working knowledge of tide and weather lore, and that you have adequate shelter and safety equipment. In experienced hands, even a dinghy can safely navigate the coast, provided good weather is chosen. But taking a small boat across a busy shipping lane has been likened to pushing a pram across a crowded motorway, and the tide rips that occur off the great headlands must also be avoided. There is one golden rule that must always be observed: before any trip, however short, make sure you tell someone responsible where you are going and when you expect to be back.

As we grow older, we tend to look for craft that offer a bit more comfort: a 'boat with a lid on' in the form of decking and a cabin top, or at least a cuddy. It certainly makes good sense in the case of a large family, or for any extended cruising, to go for the biggest boat you can afford to buy and maintain, and can handle, alone if need be. Alternatively, it is well worth considering the smallest boat that has the minimum necessary carrying capacity and performance, provided that expert opinion rates it sufficiently seaworthy for any conditions you could reasonably expect to encounter. There is no doubt that happy, unpretentious boating in small and simple craft can provide some very satisfying times afloat for a comparatively modest financial outlay. Camping in a small boat can also be surprisingly comfortable, given some ingenuity and a smattering of make-and-mend ship husbandry. A tidy little daysailer offers impromptu fun and a quick take-off. Getting under way in a substantial family flagship may take such a degree of organising that it may seldom be used to anything like its full potential. Indeed, if it spends too much of its life swinging around its mooring, the economics of keeping such a boat idle become a factor to be seriously reckoned with.

If your level of experience is limited, or even non-existent, or if for any other reason you are uncertain what sort and size of boat you could handle, one good way to gain experience is to try crewing on other people's boats, perhaps via a club noticeboard or through local advertising. If you have any choice, try for the type of boat that directly interests you. Getting soaked and exhausted in a fast dinghy on a reservoir might nevertheless whet your appetite for 'round-the-cans' racing, but would hardly serve as a fair introduction to motorcruising or keelboat sailing in coastal waters – which would probably seem much more enjoyable or very dull in comparison, depending on what you are looking for in your boating.

Alternatively, a holiday charter – sail or power – can give you a fair idea of the type and size of vessel you would feel confident to handle if she were yours (although the weather might mislead you). Flotilla sailing in sunny blue seas and a swimsuit could be quite unrepresentative of your average local conditions, so instead it would be well worth considering learning the ropes for a week or two at a sailing school in your area. Some firms also operate charter fleets, providing an opportunity to sample more than one boat in the course of a holiday. They advertise widely, and a browse through any of the boating periodicals will produce a useful selection of names and addresses.

WHERE TO BUY?

A study of the classified ads in two or three of these magazines over a period of several months will also give you an overall picture of the sorts and sizes of boats on the market, new and used, in your own price bracket.

Boat shows are another good way of comparing types and values, with introductory 'Try-a-Boat' rides usually available throughout the period of each exhibition, and sometimes organised at other venues in the UK during the yachting season by the British Marine Industries Federation and its equivalent in other countries.

Once you have narrowed the field sufficiently to recognise roughly what you are looking for, and rate yourself a serious prospective customer, you can gain 'hands-on' experience by making an appointment for an individual demonstration by a manufacturer's agent, or by the vendor in the case of a privately owned boat. By this stage you should of course be seriously considering buying his boat or one like it. No-one expects to clinch a sale from every demonstration, but nothing can be more annoying for the seller than the 'customer' who turns out to be just another casual time-waster looking for a free ride, with no intention of buying anything. You could also consider buying through a broker. He can be compared to an estate agent, in that he can organise and assist in a private sale, charging the seller a commission for his services – usually 8%. He may also serve as a legal and financial advisor.

Above all – and this is easy to say – try to avoid getting emotionally involved with a boat before you buy it. Always be prepared to walk away from a deal if commonsense warns you it's a bad one. And don't overspend on non-essential goodies for a boat whose value is limited, unless you are sure you can transfer them to your next one without leaving unsightly holes and blemishes.

The yachting magazines regularly publish their own tests of boats and new equipment. They are packed with hints, tips and useful advice for the newcomer, besides carrying a variety of well-informed articles on subjects ranging from basic navigation, seamanship and boat handling, to cruising experiences and the exploration of unfamiliar anchorages and rivers. All can help, in their own way, to define your personal requirements, besides broadening your overall perspective on life afloat.

If as a beginner you should feel somewhat intimidated by the sheer scale and complexity of the subject, don't worry. Even the most experienced sailors will admit to learning something every time they put to sea. All one needs at the outset is a general idea of what types of boat are available and their characteristics; how they are built, and fitted out, and where to keep them; the various forms of rigs and sails and how they work. Of course, you will need to know how to get the best out of your boating without putting undue strain on the family finances. This is what the rest of the book is all about.

2·SAILING CRAFT

For the recreational sailor, the main attraction of sail must lie not so much in its most obvious merit, that of operating economy, as in the pure romance of it: the effortlessly smooth and silent way the power is delivered to the hull, so totally in tune with nature, wasting no resources and preserving the ecology. With care, determination and a sewing machine, the yachtsman on a small budget can even make his own suit of sails, so long as they are fairly small and light (see page 101), whereas it takes a factory to produce any sort of an engine.

Another attraction is the challenge of trimming the rig to suit each fluctuation in the direction of the wind, and in handling the various sheets and halyards, actions demanding personal skill, some fine judgement and occasional muscle, together with a continual watch on the way the boat is responding. Well-found sailing craft are also inherently safer, and in heavy weather much less uncomfortable than power boats of comparable size. Also, on occasion, it has to be said, sailing boats provide more unwanted excitement than their mechanical cousins.

Without motor assistance, however, they are naturally constrained in their direction of travel relative to the wind, time-and-distance schedules are often more a matter of good fortune than of competent navigation, and they can undoubtedly be hard work in heavy weather. Sails and rigging usually need more care and maintenance than a good modern engine. By comparison, powerboats of similar length and beam are invariably more roomy and provide better accommodation than their sailing counterparts, and those with a planing hullform are capable of far higher speeds. Furthermore, there is much to be said for the steady, reassuring rhythm of reliable machinery, protected from wind and weather, and controlled by a single lever instead of some complex collection of cordage. Sea conditions permitting, such a boat will go wherever it is pointed and will maintain a predictable average speed all the way to its destination. This may explain why, in the USA for example, powerboats outnumber sailboats by something like ten to one.

Bridging the gap between these two distinct categories are the motorsailers, compromise craft combining a comparatively voluminous hull and powerful engine with a modest and easily handled rig.

They can neither sail as well as a pure sailing boat, nor motor as fast as a motorcruiser, but they can put up a very respectable performance in either mode, and offer an attractive combination of spaciousness and seaworthiness, with the added security of a back-up system if either is used on its own. Unfortunately, this duality lifts most of them right out of our price range, because they tend to be fairly large and hefty vessels with expensive diesel installations. However, a near equivalent among the budget boats we are looking at can be found in the traditionally styled open, or half-decked, sailing craft with a powerful engine. An ingenious exception is to be found on page 45.

THE LEARNING PROCESS

As I mentioned earlier, one of the best ways of getting started on this difficult and often fascinating process is to go along to your local sailing club – most of them are very friendly places. You can watch the racing and see some of the various classes of boat in action; better still, if there are vacancies, apply to join. Besides providing opportunities for crewing, which will give you an even better idea of which type of boat to consider buying (and which to avoid), you will be able to decide whether racing is likely to become your preferred style of sailing, or if the more leisurely alternative of cruising is better suited to your time and temperament. Some clubs embrace both areas of activity, and there are many boats that are suitable for either.

You could also enrol at a sailing school which uses the types of boat that interest you. Most of them run full-time courses, usually residential and lasting a week or two, as well as offering part-time instruction at weekends.

SHOAL DRAUGHT

One of the traditional pleasures of small boat sailing is that it opens up so many new cruising grounds, enabling you to explore the shallow surrounds of coastlines and islands, and the upper reaches of estuaries and rivers. Shoal draught undoubtedly adds a fresh dimension to the freedom of sailing. Most dinghies draw a mere few inches of water with raised centreboard (termed a 'centreplate' when made from sheet steel); a small cruiser less than a foot (30 cm) – although where there is insufficient depth to lower their boards, they usually need some help to windward with paddles or engine. For best performance, a centreboard takes the form of a dagger projecting vertically through the keel and sliding in a watertight trunk. On a cruiser, this runs up through the accommodation to the deckhead, much to the detriment of space in the cabin. One alternative is a ballasted plate, hinged at its forward end so that it can be swung back into a shallow recess in the hull: less efficient, but it takes up very

Fig 1 Underwater aspects: keels and draught.

1 Traditional full-length keel. Still preferred by many for blue water cruising because of the stability and easy motion it confers.

2 Fin keel. More efficient than long keel and cheaper to build. Used on the majority of modern cruisers and racers where shoal draught is not essential.

3 Daggerboard. Slides up and down in a vertical or inclined casing. Widely used in dinghies, and is the most efficient arrangement for any shoal draught boat. But it cannot kick up if grounded, and it intrudes on the accommodation space.

4 Swing keel. Kicks up if grounded, and can be housed below the cabin sole. But inaccessible, and sometimes limited by structural considerations.

5 Leeboards. Simple, accessible and inexpensive, but their appearance limits their appeal, and large ones are unwieldy.

6 Fixed shallow keel. Strong, simple and seaworthy. But the shallower it is, the less efficient it becomes. Needs deeper water than a lifting keel, and the boat is apt to heel over when taking the ground. Some have a swing keel housed inside their fixed keel.

7 Bilge keels. A popular compromise in draught between fin and lifting keel. Less efficient than either, but takes the ground comfortably. Some have an additional shallow central keel to carry the ballast.

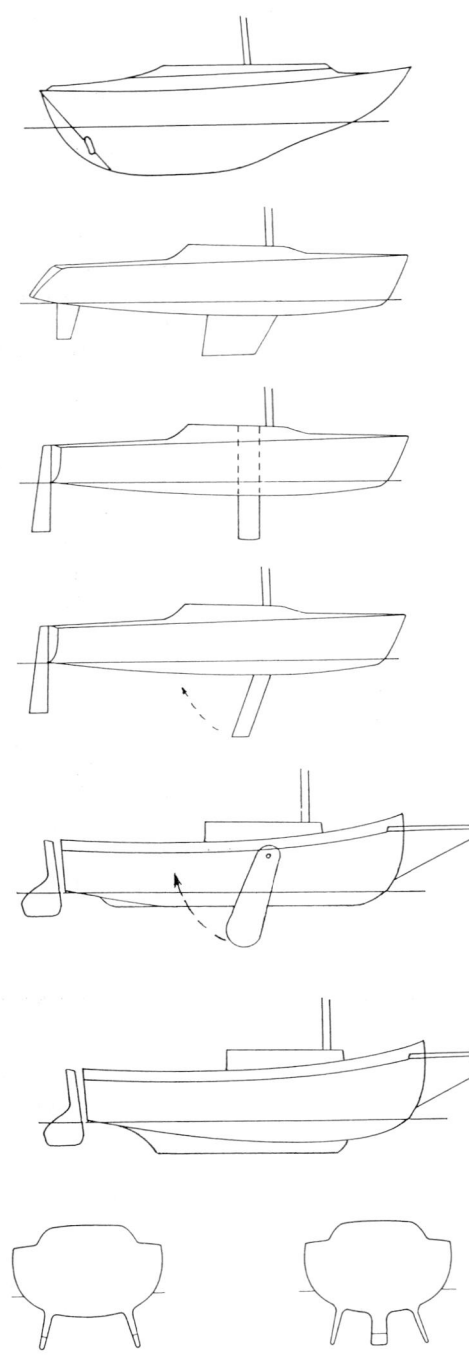

little space. Another option is to install a pair of daggerboards or swing-keels in trunks just inside the skin of the hull on either side, leaving the accommodation clear. Another attractive, though seldom seen alternative, is a pair of 'leeboards' to provide resistance to leeway, as used on the traditional Dutch working craft and the old Thames barges. These are usually hung externally, one over either side of the boat and hinged so that they can be raised or lowered. For a dinghy, a single board can suffice, simply hooked over the lee gunwhale and changed over as the boat is tacked.

Instead of lifting keels, shoal draught boats may incorporate either a very shallow fixed keel at the centre of the hull, or a pair of deeper fins, angled outwards from the turn of the bilges, which enable them to sail to windward in less than a metre of water, and on which they can sit happily when the tide has left them (provided the ground is reasonably firm and level).

Knowing that it takes so little water to keep you afloat allows you to save much valuable time, having due regard for the weather and the state of the tide, by taking short cuts across shoals and sandbanks that would otherwise have to be given a wide berth. However, in sneaking about in thin water you are more likely to run aground than the deep keelers who are obliged to stay in the recognised channels. But the majority of small boats are so light that it is often simply a matter of jumping overboard and shoving off. Except in soft mud or strong winds, it is possible to push out through quite choppy water, provided you don't mind getting wet. On the other hand, it must be said that shallow draught sometimes encourages over-confidence and the taking of unnecessary risks, such as attempting to cross shoals or harbour bars in short, steep or breaking seas.

To the delights of sailing in the shallows can be added the joy of being able to get away from the crowd, if you feel like some peace and solitude, by creeping into a secluded spot where no keeler would dare to go. The forest of masts that mark any popular anchorage can be viewed from a distance; you are on your own. You can anchor to a short cable and dry out in comfort, or put your boat aground on any stretch of clean and level bottom, or simply run up the beach, secure in the knowledge that no-one can bump into you in the night, or drag into you if it comes on to blow. Anyway, with your combination of light weight and draught, and a mostly rope cable instead of heavy chain, you are prone to sheering about at slack water or in a fluky breeze, so you would be liable to make yourself unpopular among other anchored boats.

Trouble-free grounding and being able to accept shallow moorings and mud berths also constitutes a safety factor in an emergency. If you should be caught out in really severe weather near the coast, it is comforting to know that, as a last resort, you can take refuge by deliberately running ashore. With luck and some good judgement by the helmsman, a lightweight hull with built-in buoyancy will sustain little or no damage, even in surf, and will still float if it should be holed by a rock. This is hardly a practice to be recommended, but you would probably get away with it where a keelboat would surely be wrecked.

Indeed, shoal draught has so many advantages that it is difficult to justify deep fixed keels, except where optimum performance is required for racing – when they become an essential alternative to a lifting keel of some kind – and on the larger boats designed for blue water journeying.

THE QUESTION OF SIZE

The range of boats that fall within our budget definition can conveniently be divided into four groups in terms of length, which is one of the traditionally accepted measures and probably the easiest to visualise. Nevertheless, in any boatyard line-up or boat show there will be overlaps, both in size and purpose, with one category straying into the next. Size is expensive. Length on its own can be a very misleading indicator of overall size, which effectively increases by something approaching the cube of the length rather than by the linear measurement. Beam, and the shape of the cross-sections, as much as length, define the carrying capacity. That is to say, a typical 18 ft (5.5 m) boat, which might have a beam of around 6 ft (1.8 m) and measure $2^{1}/_{2}$ ft (0.75 m) depth overall, is nearly double the size of a 14 ft (4.25 m) boat with 5 ft (1.5 m) beam and 2 ft (0.6 m) in depth.

Another way of looking at it is that small sailboats tend to just about double in weight and cost with every five-feet increase in length – a 20 footer twice that of a 15 footer, and so on – double, not just in terms of living, working and stowage space, and in general upkeep, but incorporating twice as much material, with its proportionate cost, and twice the weight to manhandle ashore or tow on a trailer. So although only a few feet in length appear to separate the majority of boats in this section of the book, their effective sizes and appearances vary widely, ranging from small dinghies and cartoppers, to a second group of open family boats, then to small fully decked cruisers; and finally to some of the larger, older boats available within our budget limit. In relative terms, the true value of sailing can best be measured by the annual cost of your boat, divided by the number of days she gives you out on the water. It pays to think small, for the less you can spend, the more you can sail and the happier the picture becomes.

Among the many designs covered by the first three categories, there are probably few, if any, that are large enough to accommodate in safety all the people who would like to go sailing with you. In order to handle a sailing boat without risking a clash of bodies when manœuvring, you need a certain minimum amount of space in which to move about and 'work the ship', and this does not become any smaller with the size of the craft. It is a constant feature. So one of the first decisions to be made is the size of crew to allow for, bearing in mind that a small boat under sail can only safely carry about half the number that can be accommodated while motoring. If it is an open boat, it should be stable enough to allow the crew to sit on the gunwhale, even in rough water, without risk of dipping it under or capsizing the craft. So a beamy hull is to be recommended – say 4 ft 8 in (1.4 m) for a 12 footer and as much as 5 ft 10 in (1.7 m) for a 16 ft dinghy. Safety considerations apart, nothing ruins a cruise more quickly than overcrowding. Matching a boat's size to its probable crew and its intended use is also essential in arriving at the all-important figure of cost.

Like so many good things in life, choosing a boat must be a soul-searching compromise between the largest you can possibly afford to buy, sail and maintain – at first glance, easily the most attractive proposition – and the smallest that can combine the minimum essential carrying capacity and performance with the lowest acceptable levels of comfort and safety in the worst conditions under which you are ever likely to use it. The latter is much the wiser option, although it is surprising how close the two can sometimes be. When they coincide, you have the enormous satisfaction of knowing you've made the best choice. But take your time about it, and always seek a second opinion – preferably an expert one – before committing yourself.

THE MATTER OF WEIGHT

If you happen to have a mathematical turn of mind, there are three statistical formulae you can use to make comparisons between sailing craft. The first is the sail area: displacement ratio, which compares the available power (sail area) with the yacht's displacement. What makes a fast boat is what makes a fast car. A heavy boat is likely to be slower than a light one, provided this can support the same amount of sail without making excessive leeway. The formula is written as SA (sq ft)/ Displacement (cu ft)$^{0.66}$, sail area being taken as the mainsail plus the foretriangle (the above-deck-area bounded by the mast and its forestay) and the displacement in tons, multiplied by 64 to give the volume in cubic feet, to the power of 2/3. Lightweight racing yachts usually give a figure of 18 to 22 and over, coastal cruisers 16 to 17, heavy offshore boats 15 to 16 and traditional motorsailers 13 to 14.

Somewhere around 18 to 19 means that the boat will be able to carry enough sail to perform reasonably well in light airs and will be easy to tow if she's a trailer-sailer, but will be heavy enough to stand up to her sail in a blow, and within the handling capabilities of the average family.

Next, the displacement:length ratio, which is a good indicator of performance, and is simply the displacement in tons divided by 0.01 times the waterline length in feet, cubed – written as $D/L = Displacement/ (0.01\ LWL)^3$. The trend among newer boats is that they are becoming lighter and faster. Generally the lower the number, the faster they are; so the D/L ratio for a traditional long-keel heavy displacement yacht might be in the region of 300–400, an average cruising boat 200–300, and a cruiser-racer 100–150, while 40 to 60 would represent a lightweight monohull racer or a multihull. A ratio of around 150 should ensure quite a lively performance and produce a good candidate for towing. Lower figures (for monohulls) mean relying to an increasing extent on crew weight to help balance the boat, whereas with 250 you could expect rather more sedate behaviour.

Finally, there's ballast ratio, in effect the righting moment, which provides a clue not only to a boat's ultimate stability, but to her ability to carry her sail without heeling to the extent that much of its power is wasted. This is the direct relationship between her displacement and the weight of her ballast, the one divided by the other. Ratios of 35 to 45% are considered normal, 50% being on the heavy side and 25 to 30% rather light. A figure in the region of 30 to 35% is good for a small cruiser. Although a higher ballast ratio would improve the motion of the boat in heavy weather and help her to shoulder her way through a steep sea, weight just for its own sake is pointless. It only means that the hull has to be that much more strongly built to withstand the stresses of increased inertia. The actual positioning of the ballast, however, has a significant effect on stability, the bottom of a deep keel or centreboard being a better location than one higher up in the bottom of the hull itself, because it lowers the centre of gravity and allows a correspondingly lower percentage figure to be acceptable. For this reason, lead is the most efficient ballast material, though unfortunately by far the most expensive. Used as internal ballast, it is also the most compact compared to, for example, pigs of iron or bags of shingle, let alone water, the most easily available and convenient of all (just open a seacock to fill or drain the tank). However, the space occupied by water is some eleven times greater than that of lead, and consequently its centre of gravity is located correspondingly higher up where it is much less effective in stabilising the boat.

ONE HULL OR TWO?
With the current increase in the popularity of multihulled sailing craft, one of the first questions, seldom considered until fairly

No parking problems with this home-built Tiki 21. She can be beached in only a foot of water. *Photo: Hanneke Boon*

recently, is whether to go for a monohull or a catamaran. That rare species, the trimaran, cannot seriously be considered for low-cost boating, because the increased weight, cost and complication of a third hull effectively rules it out of the dinghy classes, while as cruisers and racers their price – with the exception of a few older boats such as the Telstar 8 m – takes most of them far beyond the scope of this book. Which is a pity, because they deserve to be more popular.

Cats generally cost less than trimarans, but they are nevertheless more expensive than monohulls, and probably always will be, because of the amount of material and labour represented by their twin hulls and connecting structure. However, the price differential only starts to become significant at around 18–20 ft (5.5–6.0 m), amounting to around one-third more for a cruising cat than for a monohull of similar length. So that while there are many large fleets of dinghy cats in the popular racing classes, the cruisers still stand out in a crowded anchorage, representing no more than perhaps one in every ten monohulls. With a growing reputation for comfort and safety, their numbers have slowly begun to increase in recent years, but there are still relatively few budget-priced cruising cats around.

This is no doubt also due in part to their price and the limited choice of new designs available; and perhaps to a niggling worry – largely unjustified, as it happens – about the likelihood of capsize. Added to this, multihulls seem somehow to have neither the elegance of a shapely modern monohull, nor the charm and grace of a traditional one. The layout of the accommodation in small cats also takes some getting used to. But in other respects they have so much going for them that one can only hope that it will not be long before a few more manufacturers enter this, hitherto neglected, sector of the market and exploit the small multihull's advantages.

Thanks to their wide-based 'straddle stability', cats need no ballast keel or heavy centreplate to resist the heeling force of their sails, although the crew will normally position themselves on the windward side. Their hulls are also very narrow at the waterline, with the result that their wave-making resistance is less than that of the beamier monohull. Consequently, they are more easily driven in light airs. Then as the wind freshens and boatspeed increases, their lightweight hulls begin to rise due to dynamic lift, their wetted areas and corresponding drag are reduced, and speed increases still further. The normal practice with racing dinghies and the big Formula boats is then deliberately to 'fly' a hull by allowing the windward one to lift clear of the water, with still more acceleration. A manœuvre not recommended for the family cruiser! Under favourable conditions, high performance multihulls can actually sail faster than the wind, and often by a considerable margin.

With a few notable exceptions, dinghy cats are inevitably some-what heavier than their monohull counterparts. But because of their inherent transverse stability, supplemented by carrying their crew weight further out to windward, they are able to support significantly larger sail areas. The resulting power-to-weight ratio not only makes them extremely fast, with around double the top speed of the fastest conventional dinghy, and anything up to three times that of a monohull cruiser, given enough wind; it can produce some electrify-ing acceleration from a good gust. On the other hand, their light displacement and the corresponding lack of momentum also results in an inability to maintain way across localised wind shadows and the dead patches in the lee of trees and buildings along a river bank. When the wind stops, the boat stops. This applies, of course, to any lightweight dinghy, mono or multihulled, whereas a heavier keelboat will often keep moving for long enough to pick up the next puff.

When beating to windward in a seaway, successive wave strikes, which might only slow the heavy boat, may almost halt the lighter one unless, as is possible with a powerful cat, it can be kept driving fast enough to leap across the smaller crests and dance away from the big ones.

Rough weather also reduces the useable speed differential between the cruising multihull and the monohull, because even if the waves don't do it for him, the prudent helmsman will deliberately slow the boat to a more comfortable pace. Not only does this subject the rig and structure to less of a hammering, but it gives the crew a less tiring ride. If seaworthiness can be defined as the ability of a vessel to carry her crew in safety through severe weather conditions, sea-kindliness is the ability to do so in any degree of comfort. Both are strictly relative terms, for although it may be safe enough, no small boat is comfortable in heavy seas. The smaller and lighter the boat, the more exhausting its motion. Whereas a narrow boat is inclined to be too tippy, a broad-beamed one offers the waves more leverage with which to tilt it, so the cat suffers badly in this respect. She will naturally try to conform to the slope of the particular wave she is riding. In following the contours of a beam sea, and without the steadying effect of a heavy keel, the cat's motion can be quick and jerky, its light weight causing it to react almost instantaneously to the wave surfaces. Moreover, at a certain wave periodicity when beating to windward, the combination of fine bows and sterns with the pendulous momentum of the swinging mast and sails can build up into such a violent pitching motion as to bring a small cat to a virtual standstill, unless she can be eased off the wind to pick up speed and then kept driving fast through the seas.

On the other hand, the cat will probably heel no more than five or ten degrees in the sort of boisterous breeze that would lay most keelboats over to thirty or more. In addition, a fast cat's most important advantage, weather permitting, is a useful cruising speed of anything up to one-and-a-half times or even twice that of an equivalent monohull, enabling the one-day sailor to reach a favourite anchorage for lunch and be home the same evening, instead of overnighting, or to cruise that much further in the allotted time. Not that everyone buys a multihull for the sheer joy of speed on the water, for not all cats are fast. Indeed, some of the heavier and more commodious types are only marginally quicker than their monohull counterparts, though they are seldom any slower. People are equally attracted by the relatively upright sailing and the feeling of security this gives, combined with the roomy accommodation on the larger boats. It must always be borne in mind, however, that a cat's slender hulls are poor load carriers and this can cause problems, because without some restriction of stores, equipment and family paraphernalia, it is only too easy to turn a reasonably fast boat into a real clunker.

Before leaving the subject of multihulls, there is one more factor to be considered: the danger of capsize. It is debatable whether dinghy cats are any more prone to capsizing than monohulls. All dinghy sailors must be prepared occasionally to find themselves in the water when racing in gusty conditions. But more people have been put off the idea of buying a cruising multihull by the fear of turning it over than for any other reason. It is, however, almost certain to remain afloat inverted as it is not weighted with ballast, whereas the monohull is unlikely to. The primary cause of capsize is sailing with too much sail in rough or confused seas, notably on a close reach with centreboards (if any) lowered, when a sudden squall or wind shift can turn a light boat over before the sheets can be released. You can virtually always get away with it on a monohull – at the cost of some excessive heeling which slows the boat – because most of them are self-righting; a multihull is not, and because it has such great initial stability, the crew can easily be lulled into a false sense of security. But an alert skipper will be able to judge when the boat is becoming overpressed and take a reef, long before the weather hull lifts out.

Many cats have fixed, shallow keels to provide their resistance to being blown sideways. These are located close up under the hulls and hence can do little to actually trip the boat. Even with deep centreboards, provided the leeward one has been raised, whenever the cat is thrown sideways by a beam sea, it will usually skid down the face of the wave until the crest picks up the lee hull and equilibrium is restored. But for any cat with slim forward lines, there remains the danger of a diagonal capsize, when insufficient buoyancy in the bows might allow the lee one to dig in. The golden rule in sailing any multihull is to recognise and respect its operating limits and not to approach them too closely. Even when sailed with reserve, the multihull can still keep pace with the hard-driven monohull. This doesn't necessarily mean sailing slowly, merely less fast. The fast boat which is deliberately slowed down in heavy weather is much less uncomfortable than a slow one pushed to its limits. So when it begins to blow a honker, the motto should always be 'Ease back and enjoy the ride'.

SMALL DINGHIES AND CAR TOPPERS

Given the right layout and equipment, it only takes one pair of hands to sail almost anything. Large dinghies are seldom any more difficult to sail than small ones and many are actually easier for the less agile helmsman.

Experience has shown that shore handling without any kind of assistance is usually hard work with dinghies weighing much more

Privateer is a roomy 12 ft dinghy with an attractive traditional rig, available either professionally built or in the form of plans for building at home. Designed by Paul Fisher

than, say, 175 lb (80 kg), which is also about the top weight for transporting on the roof of the family car. So if you want to be completely independent of any help with launching and recovering your boat, especially up an open beach where there is no slipway, or if you want to take the boat home without having to tow a trailer you had best confine yourself to a lightly built dinghy of around 12 ft (3.7 m) in length. On the other hand, one person alone can man-handle quite a heavy boat by using a breakback trailer and winch, or a road trailer with a launching trolley (see page 115). For the habitual single-hander, a heavyweight is best kept on a mooring – if you are lucky enough to have the use of one.

Allowing sufficient space to move about in limits the crew on a 12 footer to two people, or possibly two adults and a child. Dinghies of this size are also rather on the small side for any serious cruising and are somewhat cramped, though not impossible, for sleeping aboard. But besides their low cost (there are plenty to choose from in the Group 1 price range (see page 3)) they have the advantage of being easy to right (cats less so) after a capsize, a factor always to be considered in rough water. They are also easy to manhandle ashore. Open boats even smaller than this can, of course, safely be rowed or motored with two or three passengers, but when sailing they are best confined to the helmsman alone. Safety has always to be the prime considerations – far ahead of speed, comfort or appearance. For this reason, safety harness should always be worn when sailing short-handed or in bad weather, in addition to full-buoyancy lifejackets, and of course, good quality foul weather clothing if it looks like being wet or rough.

Whatever the size or style of craft you finally choose, if it's an open boat make sure it also carries enough positive buoyancy in the form of airbags, blocks of foam, or watertight lockers to keep it and its crew afloat. Unfortunately, built-in buoyancy takes up precious space, but it is nevertheless an essential precaution against swamping or capsize. Besides, unsinkability is good for one's peace of mind in windy conditions.

Dinghy cats are a different proposition, because you sit *on* them, not *in* them, there being no accommodation in their slim hulls. These take the form of sealed, 100% buoyant floats, either one being more than capable of supporting the boat and its crew, as well as resisting the downward component of the sail forces when heeled. On account of their wide beam they can often be a bit awkward to recover following a capsize, even through 90°, let alone from a complete 180° inversion. The latter, although usually a fairly slow process due to the buoyancy of the mast and the air trapped under the sails, may bring with it the added problem, in shallow water, of the masthead fouling the river or sea bed. Then the only way to get them upright again is to apply maximum leverage from the crew, supplemented if necessary by a sack or two of water ballast, heaving on a righting line while standing on the downwind hull, or using a 'righting pole'. A conventional dinghy can simply be rolled back upright. But at least cats don't need bailing out once they are upright.

BIG DINGHIES AND OPEN FAMILY BOATS

Dealing first with monohulls, a good all-round choice for a beginner is a 14 footer (4.3 m) such as the Wanderer, a particularly safe and user-friendly cruising dinghy which has been developed with the advice of the legendary Margaret Dye. Boats like these are economical to buy (price Group 2). They are still just about light enough for easy handling ashore, plus roomy enough at a pinch for two young people or one grown-up to sleep aboard on short cruises, using a bit of ingenuity and its all-enveloping cockpit tent. If you are prepared to build a boat yourself, the 'Roamer' is a much more roomy little cruiser, and exceptionally seaworthy for its size. However, for overnight trips in a small boat it is usually more realistic to plan to pitch a tent ashore, despite the hassle of finding a suitable site, permission to use it if it happens to be private property, and struggling across a sometimes muddy foreshore with the camping gear.

If you fancy the idea of camp-cruising, moving up to 16 ft (4.9 m) makes the convenience and privacy of sleeping aboard a more practical proposition, and life afloat becomes a lot less uncomfortable. It is quite surprising how much more spacious dinghies of this size are, compared to 14 footers. Although better suited to daysailing on short trips, with perhaps the occasional coastal hop while keeping a careful watch on the weather forecast, boats of this size have nevertheless cruised far and wide. Probably the most famous example is the Wayfarer in which the indomitable Margaret Dye and husband Frank have explored coastal waters ranging from North America to the Persian Gulf. You could also consider the more recently introduced Victoria 16. But these are both nudging the top of the Group 2 price bracket, and will exceed it if you add an outboard motor and trailer.

Boats of this type are also raced as a class, as are a number of other 'moderate' designs of inherently stable and substantially built family dinghies; all of them are beamy and with plenty of freeboard. If, however, you are looking for more speed, there is a wide selection of purpose-built racers of all shapes and sizes from about 11 ft (3.3 m) upwards. Check which classes are raced locally, but be warned: most of them are highly sophisticated, powerful craft, fast and responsive, and at the same time very much less tolerant of an unskilled helmsman, demanding instant reactions in windy conditions. So if

Cruising in 14 footers. Margaret Dye (left) makes herself comfortable for a night aboard her Wanderer. Right: A home-built Roamer, unsinkable and self-righting. She may look a little boxey, but as her designer, the late Eric Coleman wrote, 'I have a theory that the appearance of a boat suddenly becomes of minor importance when one is out in deteriorating weather.'
Photo: Jeremy Beale, Dinghy Cruising Association

you are a beginner, it would be best to learn on a slower, more stable dinghy.

At 16–19 ft (4.9–5.8 m) one enters the realm of the true camping cruiser – good sea boats that are roomy enough for extended journeying in a modicum of comfort, and considerably less lively in the rough stuff than their smaller sisters. But they are rather too weighty to be beached after every trip, and require a road trailer rather than a simple trolley. Sturdily built and attractively shaped, the latest to leave the yards are glassfibre replicas of traditional types of design, some with simulated lapstrake (overlapping) planking. All of them have plenty of storage lockers and cockpit space. Someone once worked out that, on average, a smallcraft owner spends no more than one night in ten aboard. So when space is at a premium, why not settle for a boom tent instead of fixed accommodation, and a canvas dodger when you need some protection from rain and spray? After all, when you're actually sailing – in fine weather, at any rate – the cockpit is the place to be, not risking nausea in a small confined space. Cabins are for cruisers, not campers.

Typical of these larger open boats in Group 3 are two beautiful

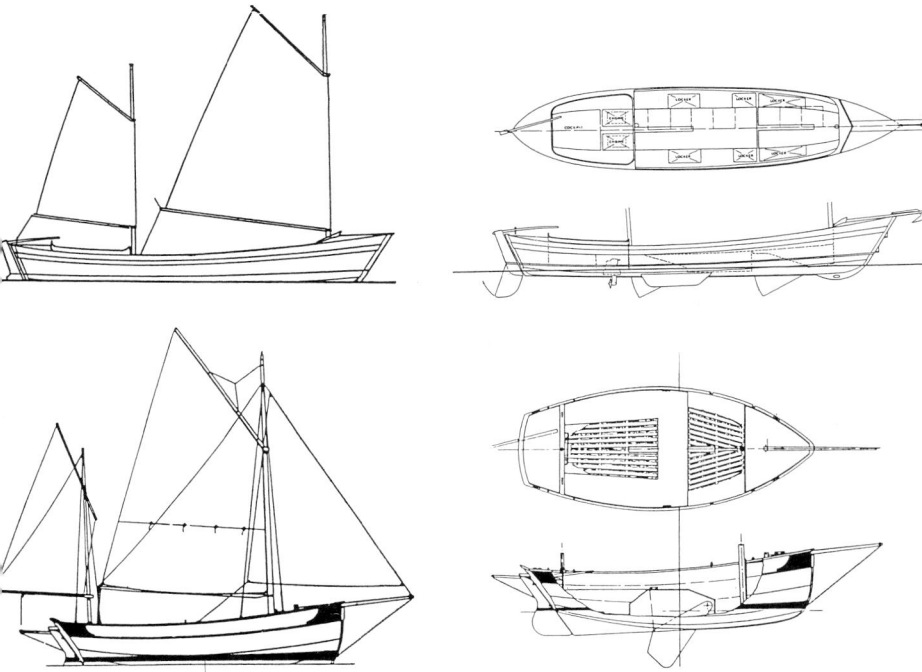

Fig 2 Two big dayboats. Top: Although Wildlife is 30 ft long, she was designed by Colin Mudie to be built quite cheaply by an amateur. Fast, on account of her waterline length and slender beam, she is unsinkable, self-righting and easily beached. This version is shown with twin outboard motors, side by side, and double centreboards.

Fig 3 Below: The chunky little Jolleyboat looks much larger than her 16 ft, with lots of space for family daysailing and plenty of 'strings' to pull. Available from a number of boatbuilders, she was designed by Laurent Giles for home construction.

cruising daysailers, the Norfolk Oyster and the Winchelsea Yawl, both built on traditional lines; and the Drascombe Lugger, among the best known and most popular of all open dayboats. One of these luggers made history by being sailed single-handed across both the Atlantic and Pacific Oceans. Such seaworthiness is reassuring when it comes on to blow during a day cruise with the family. The Lune Whammel (Group 2), which has been reproduced from a 19th century fishing boat, differs from the other three in having a full length keel instead of a centreboard, hence its draught of 2 ft

Variety in open boats. The 17 ft Norfolk Oyster (inset), well known for the exceptionally high standard of her fittings and finish, is a nimble performer with a powerful sailplan. The Winchelsea Yawl (main picture), built on the lines of the Sussex beachboats, features their distinctive 'lute' stern. Both boats provide camping space under the foredeck with the addition of a sprayhood and boom tent.

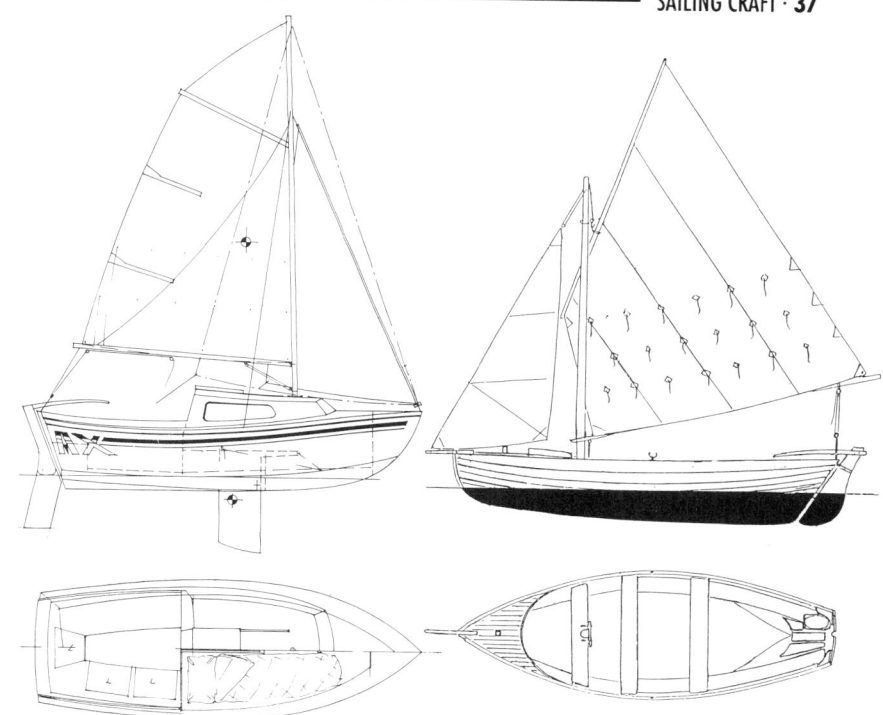

Fig 4 Left: The ultimate budget cruiser? This jaunty little West Wight Potter, 15 ft (4.5 m) long and weighing only 650 lb (295 kg), sleeps two and is priced in Group 2 range complete with engine and road trailer.

Fig 5 Right: The Lune Whammel, an exact replica of a 19th century fishing boat, carries bags of sand ballast for stability and, with no centreboard, has an unobstructed floor to sleep on.

(60 cm), making launching and recovery a little less easy, but leaving an unobstructed 8 ft (2.4 m) floor for camping. Another advantage of a long keel, carrying an integrated rudder at its after end, is that it can give a boat better directional stability than a centreboard in rough water – better even than the arrangement adopted on most modern cruisers: a short, deep fin keel with a rudder carried on a skeg some distance astern of it. From the point of view of optimum performance under normal conditions, the short keel gives much less drag through the water than a long keel, and it also makes a boat more manœuvrable in confined spaces. But if it should be thrown off course by a wave, in heavy seas and hence aerated water, the two individual foils lose some of their grip, and the helmsman has to work

The 16 ft Winkle Brig (top) being put through its paces.

50,000 miles and still going strong! Charles Stock (below) completed his budget cruiser *Shoal Waters* more than 30 years ago, and has since sailed, poled or paddled her on countless long voyages of exploration through Britain's inland waterways and coastal maze of creeks and swatchways. He doesn't believe in engines, maintaining that the winds and tides are more reliable, so he's never got around to fitting one.

harder to regain control than he would with an old-fashioned keel under his feet.

By way of contrast, dinghy cats, even the big 20 footers, are really no more than beautiful sailing machines, unequalled for their sheer sparkling speed in racing or fast day trips. Not only are they expensive (Group 3, some of them) but they are basically unsuited to overnighting, because the absence of any usable accommodation inside the hulls restricts the sleeping area to a tent across the trampoline. They are also poor load carriers and there is little stowage space for camping equipment. But what they may lack in space they certainly make up for in performance. Just imagine the thrill of planing upwind at 12 knots, or reaching at 25 knots.

SMALL CRUISING CRAFT

Although some are, in effect, no more than large dinghies with lids on them, somehow the entire character of a boat changes when it has a cosy cabin area, however cramped, in which to take shelter at the end of the day, prepare a meal, eat or sleep. Even a half-decker can provide welcome seclusion and protection from the elements. But 'going below' on a fully decked cruiser, however small, being able to close the hatch, exchange oilskins for shirtsleeves and put the kettle on the stove makes one feel totally self-contained and independent of life ashore. It is a powerful impression and one of the great joys of boating. A good example of a true mini-budget cruiser is Charles Stock's *Shoal Waters*, a 16 ft 6 in (5.0 m) wooden boat that he built himself back in 1963, and in which he has since sailed more than 50,000 miles (80,000 km) through Britain's waterways and around the coasts, with even an occasional trip to France.

Among the smallest of the decked cruisers that are available 'off the shelf', there's the evergreen Leisure 17 which has been around for nearly a quarter of a century, and the chunky little Eagle 525 with twin lifting keels, neither of them costing much more than some of the larger top-class racing dinghies. Although only 17 ft (5.2 m) long, they manage to cram in four sleeping berths, with sitting headroom in the cabin, space for a cooker and a toilet, and a self-draining cockpit. Both are in Group 3 price range including trailer. If your preference is for vintage charm and character, you can choose between some beautiful little boats of similar size and price. A typical example is the Winkle Brig, which is fitted out with three berths under a full-width cabin top, and sports a gaff topsail rig on varnished wooden spars. There are also handsome half-deckers like the Cornish Crabber 17 and Honnor Marine's Coaster, which have two bunks running under their foredecks and can be enclosed when required by a canopy over the forward end of their very spacious cockpits. In expert hands, similar small craft have made extended voyages, although the aver-

Ancient and modern: two trailer sailers at similar prices. The 16 ft Oyster-catcher (inset) is hand-built by a small Cornish company on classic lines. She positively bristles with brass, bronze and Brazilian mahogany, and is priced at the lower end of Group 4. The Legend 23.5 (main picture) is a roomy 23 ft water-ballasted cruiser/racer and costs about the same as the Oystercatcher, including outboard motor and trailer. She's mass-produced by one of America's largest yacht builders.

A pair of popular 4 berth cruisers. The Parker 21 (top) draws barely 10 in (25 cm) with centreboard raised, but is so stable that with two people standing on a side deck, and with her keel up, she will heel less than 10 degrees. Below: The Horizon 21, with no centreboard, has a more spacious cabin, but she draws 3 ft with twin bilge keels, or 4 ft if you want top performance with a single deep fin (although you cannot, of course, take the ground with this version).

age weekend sailor will find them better suited to day cruising, sleeping afloat or beached overnight. This is easily done, since they draw little more than a foot of water with centreboard lifted, and only twice that in the case of the twin bilge-keeled Leisure. As well as the advantages of shoal draft, either type of keel allows the boat to take the ground without listing over when the tide leaves her.

For anyone wishing to move to a different sailing area, none of these little cruisers weighs more than about a ton trailing weight, well within the capabilities of the average 2 litre car.

LARGER CRUISERS AND CATAMARANS

Finally, in this general category, are several larger, high-performance 4 berth, one ton yachts in Group 4. Among the best-known of these are the lifting-keel Parker 21 and the swing-keel Swift 20, and the more recently introduced Red Fox 200 (see photo on page 110) distinguished by the twin bilgeboards which project vertically above the sidedecks when raised, giving her a minimum draft of less than 8 in (20 cm) and a voluminous interior uncluttered by any keel casing. For those preferring twin fixed bilgekeels at the price of a more conventional 3 ft (0.9 m) draft, the Hunter Horizon 21 is equally roomy and, like the other three boats, features a tabernacle-hinged mast that can be quickly lowered and raised for canal cruising.

From America come some similarly deeper draughted, more heavily built but still trailerable cruisers in Group 4, such as the Compac 19 and the Catalina 22 illustrated on pages 106-7; and the beautifully equipped Legend 23.5 which displaces only 2000 lb (908 kg) after draining off the 1000 lb (454 kg) of water ballast which it relies on for its stability under sail. It has a dagger-like high aspect ratio keel that swings up into a recess in the ballast tank without encroaching on the cabin sole area. Also built in the USA is the innovative MacGregor 19, similarly water-ballasted but distinguished by its broad vee-bottomed sportsboat type hull. Powered by a 40 hp outboard motor, it has a speed of no less than 21 knots (39 kph), yet total towing weight, including a trailer and the big engine, works out at just 1500 lb (680 kg). Not surprisingly, performance under sail is not quite as good as that of a 'pure' sailing boat; but for many, its dual nature more than compensates for any shortcomings in that area.

Among the comparatively few cruising catamarans to qualify here on price (Group 4) are the Cracksman 2, a trailerable 20 footer (6.0 m) with 8 ft (2.4 m) beam, double-berth accommodation on the bridgedeck plus two singles in the hulls, and a good all-round performance under sail or power (16 knots with a 15 hp outboard motor). The sportier 24 ft (7.0 m) Strider (see page 44), has larger sails than the Cracksman and a beam of 14 ft (4.3 m). The Strider also has four berths, one forward and one aft in each of its slender

Small cruising cats. Tiki 26 (left) is a well-proven and immensely seaworthy design for home-building that has made many ocean passages in severe weather, including being raced single-handed across the Atlantic. Accommodation is fairly spartan, but you can't have everything. The Cracksman 2 (right) has 4 berths, sails well and is so easily driven that she can achieve 16 knots with only a 15 hp outboard. Her fine underwater lines can clearly be seen when she is sitting on her trailer (see page 109).

hulls, which are demountable for trailering, and a broad expanse of solid cockpit decking and storage lockers in between, covered by a camping tent when required. A trio of these little cats once cruised from England to Estonia and back, a distance of some 3000 miles. If you prefer the Polynesian look, there's the Wharram Tiki 26, also demountable and with the same type of accommodation. She is the larger sister of the Tiki 21 seen on page 27. Both are immensely seaworthy boats that have made solo Atlantic and Pacific crossings in experienced hands.

All these designs have fixed, shoal draft keels, and are factory-built in glassfibre, but the latter two can also be home-built in wood/epoxy at much lower cost. But there any similarity ends. For whereas the Strider and Cracksman are smart, thoroughly modern looking multihulls, the Tiki, as with all James Wharram's unmistakable designs, follows the traditional South Pacific pattern, with curving sheerlines and tapered sterns to match the bows. Cats such as these are capable of bursts of speed of up to 15 knots in a hard gust, and have regularly

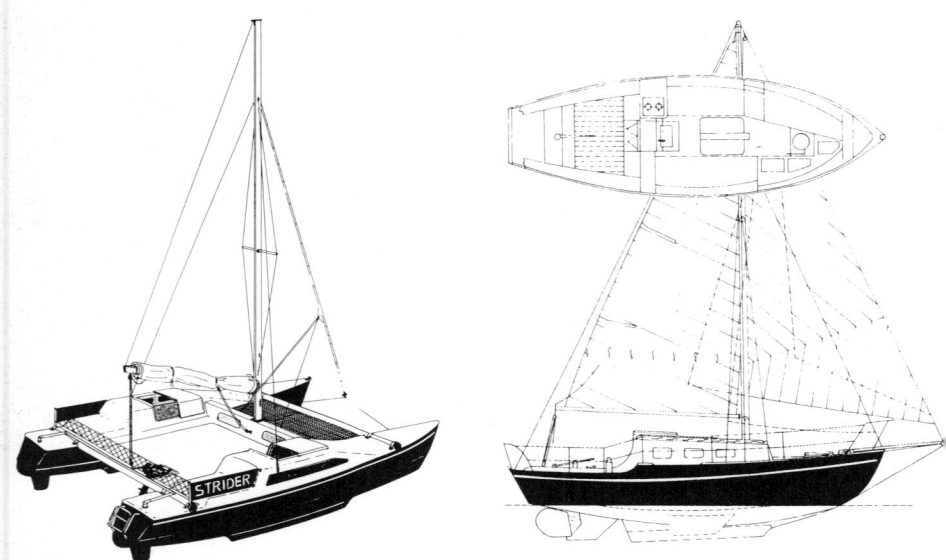

Figs 6 and 7 Catering for widely differing tastes, the only thing these boats have in common is their 24 ft length and four berths, and that both were originally designed for home-building. For whereas the Strider (left) is a popular 15 knots weekender that is regularly raced in the Micro class and can be carried around on a trailer (see page 109), Eventide (right) — designed by the renowned Maurice Griffiths — is an ageless long-distance, 5 knots cruiser, hundreds of which have been built over the past 30 years, and she displaces some 3,500 lb (1600 kg) which virtually rules her out for trailing. But you can sit comfortably on a settee berth at either side of her cabin table, instead of wedging yourself into one of Strider's slim hulls if you don't want to lounge around on her broad deck areas. It all depends on the type of sailing that appeals to you. 'Horses for courses', as the saying goes.

achieved 8–10 knots for sustained periods in force 4–5 winds. As a result, in the right weather they can almost double the day's cruising range of their monohull sisters, albeit at the expense of somewhat restricted accommodation. They are really better suited to coastal trekking and camp-cruising than to extended passagemaking, let alone ocean crossings which must have been extremely arduous, wet and uncomfortable for much of the time.

Auxiliary engine power is a matter of personal preference. None of these small boats has an inboard as standard installation, and an

A wolf in sheep's clothing, this MacGregor 19 is a true dual-nature funboat. A powerboat-shaped hull, water ballast system, swing-keel and a small, easily erected rig give you the choice of sailing at 5 knots or motoring at over 20 knots with a 40 hp motor. More pictures of her appear on page 113.

outboard motor of 4–6 hp is adequate for any of them. It is usually mounted on a lift-up bracket fitted to the stern, but an integral cockpit well is provided for it in some designs. This makes the engine easily accessible and often less noisy; but without good ventilation, exhaust fumes can be a problem.

So far, we have only been taking into account the price of a new boat, nearly all of which are nowadays built in GRP. The alternatives, of course, are to build or part-build one yourself, either in wood or GRP, or to turn to the secondhand market which opens the door to a tempting range of larger and much more elaborate designs. You then need to seriously look at the general running costs as well as the initial price, and the cost of any necessary refurbishing and repair work following the essential professional survey. With this in mind, it would be prudent to restrict yourself to about 25 ft (7.6 m) for a budget boat, unless you should happen to come across a genuine bargain in a larger one (such treasures are occasionally to be found, although they are extremely few and far between). You will need to convince yourself that its associated expenses over a prolonged period, as well as your own time with paintbrush in hand, can be offset against its seemingly low price.

Some delightful little wooden boats, such as the 24 ft (7.3 m) Eventide and the 17 ft (5.2 m) Lysander, still come on the market from time to time – indeed they are still being built from plans available from their Owners Associations – and their price is usually very affordable; but it is essential that they be surveyed for any ailments such as dry rot which can involve expensive repairs.

There are many more boats that were built in GRP which are no longer in production but are still to be found on brokers' lists and among the classified ads. None of them could be called sparkling speedsters on the water – adequate all-rounders would be a fairer description – and most of them are much too heavy and bulky for trailing. But each has a timeless character and an endearing dependability that is the mark of the good cruising yacht and over the years they may have logged countless long voyages and even have circumnavigations to their credit. Among the best known are the dear old Westerly Centaur 20 ft (7.9 m), many of which seem destined to sail on for ever if they don't fall prey to osmosis, and its catamaran equivalent, the Heavenly Twins. Both (in Group 4) have long since been superseded by more modern designs, but if you can find one to suit your pocket and in economical condition, you will have a happy cruising companion. There are also a number of good performance boats in our price range, such as the Hunter Sonata 23 (7.0 m), many of which are still raced regularly; while in Groups 2 and 3 there are plenty of other classics to choose from – for example, the Contessa 26, Virgo Voyager 23, and the Corribee 21, more than one of which has sailed across the Atlantic. All of them can be bargains at today's prices, provided that a survey reveals no major faults.

There are many people who like the idea of sailing, but, being unfamiliar with its principles, are put off by the thought of being at the mercy of the wind. They may also be more than a little uneasy at the power of a big sail, with its ability to heel the boat over until the gunwhales submerge. Sailing is truly an art that can be as simple or as complex as you choose to make it. The next chapter is intended to set a few of these fears at rest by explaining how sails work and how relatively easy they are to control.

3·RIGS AND RIGGING

It is not the purpose of this book to try to teach anyone how to handle a boat. This is best done at a sailing school, and there are a number of very good books on the subject. Nevertheless, to understand why a boat sails at all, one should be absolutely clear about the manner in which the wind acts on a rig. It is not enough to visualise it simply being blown along by the breeze, with a keel helping to prevent the hull from slipping sideways. Yet there are some people who happily continue to set sail without ever really appreciating the workings of their wonderful powerplant. With only a little further knowledge they could enjoy themselves even more, besides finding it easier to get the best out of their boat. A few diagrams and a little theorising at this stage may also serve the newcomer as a form of introduction to the silent magic of sail.

HOW SAILS WORK

With the breeze behind him, the sailor need only stand up in his boat and hold open his coat to begin sailing, and if the wind should veer towards the quarter, he can continue to make some sort of forward progress by swivelling his body accordingly. However, if the wind continues to shift, his 'sail' will become less and less effective, and long before it reaches the beam – let alone swings ahead of it – a more efficient aerodynamic shape will be needed.

The way in which the curved contour of a sail draws the boat forward is in many ways analogous to the functioning of an aircraft wing; their common purpose being to develop lift while causing the minimum of drag. But there any similarity between the two aerofoils ends. For whereas the rigid wing is designed for relatively high speed flight at a small angle of attack relative to the airflow across it, the soft sail has to be effective at very low speeds, and both its shape and the angle it presents to the wind – its incidence – must be adjustable so as to exert as much forward drive as possible with the minimum of sideways (heeling) force. Leeward drift is resisted by the keel, whose weight helps to hold the boat upright, or by a retractable centre-board.

Both forms of foil develop their lift from the difference in air pressure acting on their upper and lower surfaces – the leeward and

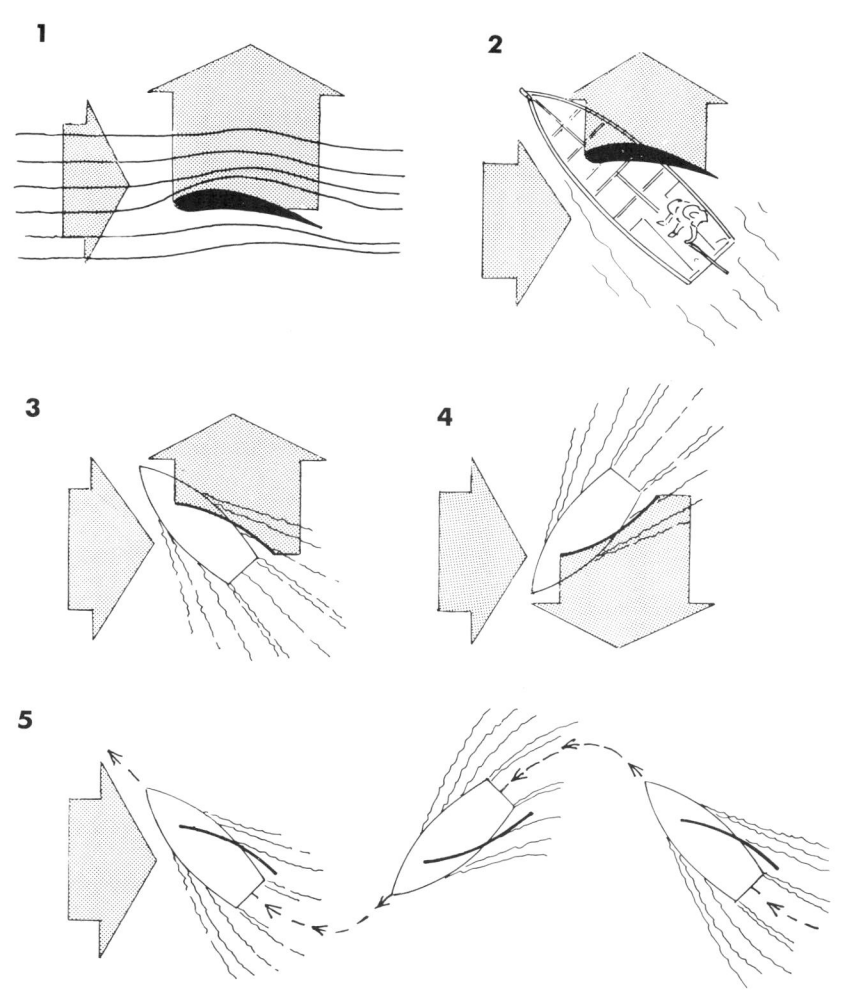

Fig 8 How sails work. **1** An aircraft wing develops a lifting force from the airstream flowing across it, and at right angle to the direction of this stream. **2** The same thing would happen if you were to plant the wing vertically on a boat. **3** and **4** Soft sails work just as well, and with a keel to prevent the boat from sliding sideways, they drive it forwards. **5** Tacking in order to make progress towards the wind.

windward ones in the case of the sailboat. That in turn is proportional to the speed of the air travelling across them. The wind flows faster on the leeward side than on the weather (windward) side accelerating as it ducks round the leading edge to pass along the back of the sail. While it is speeding up, its pressure is falling (Bernoulli's Law), causing a suction effect. Conversely, the slower air on the weather side builds up a slight positive pressure, and the resulting thrust of the sail is proportional to the pressure differential across it. The phenomenon can be strikingly demonstrated at the kitchen sink by dangling a spoon between finger and thumb and turning on a tap. As the back of the spoon is brought close to the stream of water, it will suddenly be drawn towards it as the flow is accelerated and the pressure drops.

A headsail (jib or staysail) develops its thrust in just the same way; but provided it is correctly adjusted, it also increases the drive from the mainsail by directing and smoothing the airflow across it. This allows the main to be sheeted in more closely to the centreline, which further increases its forward thrust. By a happy quirk of nature, the increased angle of the upwash that occurs naturally in the airstream ahead of it directs more of this around the lee side of the jib, thereby increasing *its* power. In this way, each sail, properly sheeted, complements the other.

Large headsails, known as genoas, develop more power than small ones on account of their sheer size. But contrary to the long-held theories about venturi suction effects, wind tunnel tests have shown that in overlapping the mainsail to create a 'slot', the big genoa does not actually increase the drive of the main any further. In fact, were it geometrically practicable – which it usually isn't, without moving the mast – to add the overlap area to that of the mainsail, or better still, to put all the area into the mainsail alone, the overall power of the rig would be that much greater, at the expense of some operational flexibility. This helps to explain the traditional popularity of 'catboats' in America (see page 57), and anyone devising their own sailplan should bear this in mind.

Where a small, non-overlapping jib is used, it can be made 'self-tacking' by leading its sheets – or single sheet if its foot is supported by some form of boom – via a traveller on a track across the deck. This is an arrangement used on many cruising boats and an invaluable aid to the short-handed sailor, enabling him to tack the boat simply by moving the tiller across, as is the case with a catboat.

The efficiency of a sail is governed, to a considerable extent, by its profile shape. As with the aircraft equivalent, where a high aspect-ratio wing, long and narrow, develops more lift than a short, broad one of the same area, so a tall, slim sail with a long luff (leading edge) in relation to its foot will normally outperform the short chunky one.

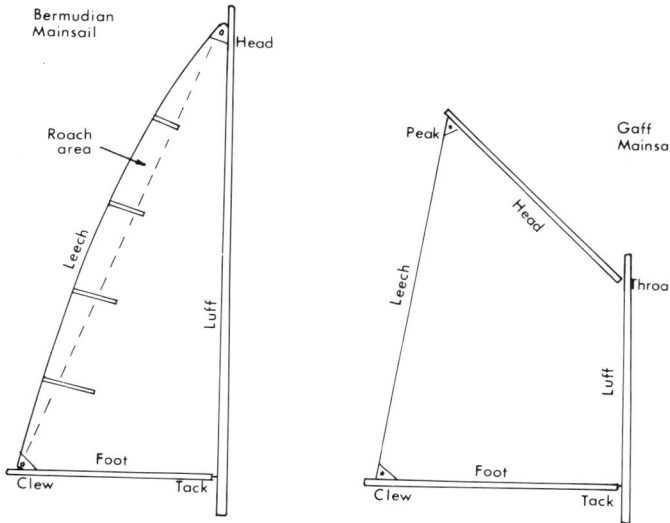

Fig 9 Parts of a sail.

That is to say, a high slender rig is generally more efficient; the broader, short-masted one rather less so, but the latter can be quite as good on a reach or running, and is also less likely to cause a capsize, because its centre of effort is comparatively low down, with correspondingly less leverage on the hull.

The performance of a sail also depends on how it has been cut by the sailmaker to give it belly, or fullness. This can be exploited by the crew, who not only adjust the angle of each sail relative to the wind and to each other, but can vary the depth and even the shape of the camber (which affects its power centre), and the degree of twist between the head and foot, which can be used to reduce the heeling force at the expense of some forward drive. Wooden or (nowadays) plastic battens are secured in pockets on the mainsail in order to support the convex area of the leech. These are normally about one-quarter the length of the boom, but, alternatively, they may run full length, not only helping to maintain the shape of the sail all the way from luff to leech, but preventing it from flogging while head to wind. If all this sounds rather complicated, in practice it is much easier done than said. Indeed it is quite surprising, and to many of us reassuring, to see just how well a good hull can still perform despite a poorly adjusted rig, any deficiency only really becoming obvious when racing or pacing one's boat against another – or in an emergency, when the amount of power available may occasionally become critical, such as when trying to claw off a lee shore.

SAILPLANS

So far as the actual layout and arrangement of sails is concerned, some types of rig are much more efficient than others, although these tend to be more complex and expensive. Just as the fastest boat is not necessarily the most enjoyable, so efficiency can sometimes seem less important than, say, a handsome appearance or the ease of handling a thoroughly practical and seaworthy rig. If we take a look at some of the many alternative sailplans and their respective merits, it may help us to decide which are the most likely to suit the kind of boating we intend to do, our personal tastes, and the size of our pocket.

Rigs vary more widely than they did a few years ago. The great nostalgia boom has led to a trend towards small cruising craft (but not, of course, on the racers) away from the dominance of the Bermudian in favour of some more interesting, traditional sail arrangements. Although there can be no doubt that a high, narrow rig like the Bermudian is best for going to windward, low rigs are not only less likely to capsize the boat, but they are easier to repair – or even to build yourself – with simple tools.

For example, in the interests of simplicity and convenience, some of them dispense with a headsail altogether, on the grounds that its 'supercharging' effect is hardly worth the extra hassle. On others the mainsail is loose-footed, with no heavy boom to bang the head of the unwary, while many feature a short mast which is connected to an upper spar or yard carrying the head of the sail. Each has its plus points and its devotees. Most of them have evolved over centuries of experience and all have successfully been applied to small craft at one time or another.

In olden times, the majority of the single-sailed vessels that plied Britain's coasts and rivers, as distinct from the great square rigged ships, were called luggers (from the word 'lug', meaning to pull or drag). A square sail hanging from its horizontal yard will take a boat downwind in fine style, and as it is braced round to form an increasingly acute angle to the hull centreline, it will drive the boat at a progressively closer angle to the wind. But only so far. Lashing the sail to a lower spar, the boom, gave it a better shape, allowing it to set more effectively close to the wind, and performance was further improved by angling the yard upwards.

Few examples of the original spar-headed rigs survived the years without the benefit of headsails, which were generally adopted to improve the manoeuvrability of these somewhat cumbersome vessels in confined waters. Several variants of the early sailplan have been scaled down and adapted to dinghies and dayboats during the past 100 years or so.

LUGSAILS

One of the most widely used and best loved is the balance lug, an easily handled rig that is particularly well suited to knock-about dinghies and the like. As can be seen from Fig 10, it comprises a short mast from the top of which the yard is suspended by the main halyard, and the boom, held down near the foot of the mast so as to tension the luff of the sail. Both yard and boom project forward of the mast to produce the 'balance' area from which the rig takes its name. The after end of the boom is controlled in the normal way by the mainsheet, adjusting its angle to the wind and at the same time tensioning the leech of the sail and preventing the yard from lifting. Added together, these features result in a geometrically stable, but deceptively simple rig, with much more to it than at first meets the eye.

When running or sailing off the wind, for example, the boom cannot rise and let the sail belly out, with the consequent risk of inducing rolling or an accidental gybe, because it is swigged down tightly beside the mast. At its forward end the sail's taut luff rope exerts an upward, 'balancing' leverage. Under these constraints, the boom also stays down and the sail remains flat during a gybe, providing an effective air cushion to absorb much of the shock towards the end of its travel from one side to the other. In gusty weather, however, the helmsman must be careful to avoid excessive heeling, because the flat sail cannot readily spill wind as the sheet is paid out and the boom, being held low, can too easily strike the water. A further advantage, shared by all short-masted rigs, is that as the sail is reefed, the yard is also lowered, leaving less aloft to catch the wind. Similarly, when lying in an exposed, rough water anchorage, having less 'tophamper' means that the boat is less likely to rock around like some demented pendulum, with consequent strain on the hull, to say nothing of its occupants. Nevertheless, a certain amount of weight aloft serves to dampen the rolling, whereas too little allows the boat to be thrown about by every passing wave.

These various virtues are all to be found in the 2000 year old Chinese lug, better known as the junk rig, but they went largely unrecognised in the West until the middle of the 19th century, when the principles were adapted by a Thames boatbuilder to produce his version of it, the balance lug. The junk itself comprises a lugsail extending forward of the mast by between a third to a sixth of its area, with rows of wooden (nowadays mostly plastic) battens running horizontally across the full width of the sail, and a sheet connected to each batten end by a span of ropes. These spread the load so evenly

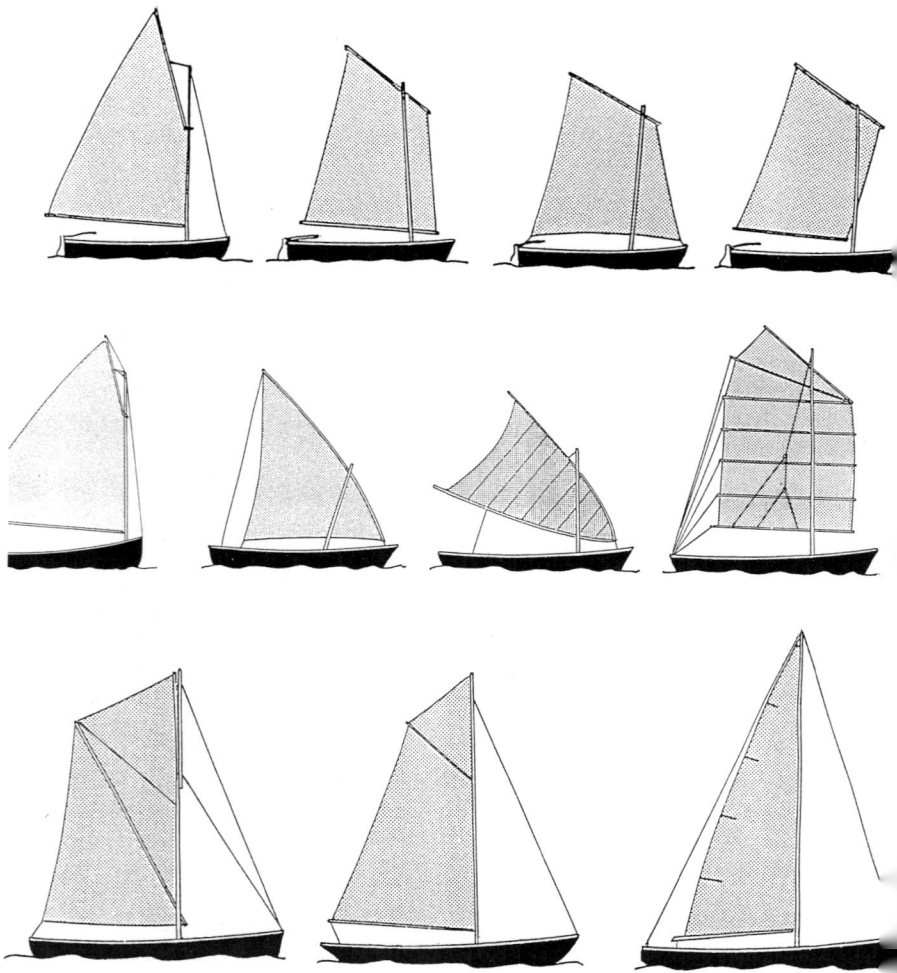

Fig 10 Una rigs and mainsail shapes. (top, left to right) gunter lug, balance lug, dipping lug, standing lug. (centre) cat rig, lateen, crab claw, junk. (bottom) spritsail, gaff, Bermudian.

across the sail that with no headsail requiring a forestay to carry it, and hence no backstay to balance the tension of the forestay, the Chinese found no need for any standing rigging to support the mast. At the same time, the battens were so effective in preventing the sail from flogging or fluttering that they were even able to use woven matting for sails instead of sailcloth, before this became widely available. The junk may look crude and ungainly to some eyes, but as a self-tending, sail-handling-without-tears rig, it is hard to beat. One or two boatbuilders offer it as an alternative to their standard sailplan, nor is it beyond the capabilities of an amateur sailmaker. Nevertheless, it has been slow to catch on in the Western world and is seldom seen on our waters.

Even more rare are the graceful lateen rig of the Mediterranean and Indian Oceans, and the Polynesian crab claw, both of which have been shown to challenge the modern Bermudian for efficiency, despite their primitive appearance. The lateen sail is triangular and boomless, distinguished by an extremely long and slender yard which is slung on a stumpy forward-raked mast with its tack hove down to the foredeck. The sheer size of the yard makes it awkward to stow in a crowded harbour (let alone on a trailer). But its bendiness is an advantage in strengthening winds, since it tends to flatten the sail as it flexes and to spill air from the peak, both of which reduce the heeling force on the boat. The crab claw behaves in a similar manner, but this features a boom as well as a yard, both of them curved, and joined at their fore ends to produce the characteristic shape.

First cousin to the balance lug, and closely related to the lateen, is the dipping lug, also boomless but having a longer mast and a shortish yard extending forward of the mast by about two-fifths of its length. This was, for many years, the traditional rig of the open naval cutter and is a wonderful 'lifting' sail, unlike the higher peaked mainsails which tend to drive the bows down by their leverage on the mast. But unfortunately, as its name implies, the yard has to be dipped round behind the mast each time the boat is tacked, which makes it rather a handful if you are on your own in rough or windy weather. (The lateen is altogether too unwieldy to be dipped, so it loses some of its efficiency on the tack that leaves the sail on the windward side of the mast.)

Much easier to control is the standing lug, so called because the yard (only slightly overlapping the mast) stays on the same side of it all the time. The boom is located entirely behind and attached to it by a metal universal joint known as a gooseneck. An attractive variant of this sets a loose-footed mainsail, usually supplemented by a tiny jib on a forestay running to the head of the short mast, making it a very easily managed rig for the beginner and the potterer, albeit with a somewhat baggy mainsail, but with no boom to bother about.

Another is the gunter lug, distinguished by its triangular sail and the way in which the yard is pulled up tight to the mast so that it is held almost vertically. With no part of this spar projecting forward of the mast, which by definition qualifies it to be called a 'gaff' rather than a yard that crosses the mast, the sail sets equally well on either tack, nor is there anything to foul the jib if one is set. From a distance it looks very like a Bermudian rig and indeed it is nearly as efficient. But like the balanced lug, it has the advantage that, as it is reefed, the yard slides down the mast, reducing the leverage of weight and wind, and its short spars can usually be stowed inside the boat.

THE CLASSIC RIGS

Now for the gaff rig. Not counting the ubiquitous Bermudian, there are more gaff-rigged boats to be seen around Europe's coastlines than all the others put together, and it has become a popular option offered by many builders of cruising boats. It consists of a four-sided sail, with its luff running in, or sewn to metal slides that themselves run in a channel up the back of the mast, the foot being similarly attached to the boom. Alternatively, it may be set loose-footed, except that its clew is tensioned from the after end of the boom, so as to be able to adjust the fullness in the sail. The boom, carried on the mast by a gooseneck, is prevented from rising when the mainsheet is freed off by a 'kicking strap' or 'vang', consisting of a tackle running diagonally between the boom and the foot of the mast. A loose-footed gaff sail can quickly be reefed to about half its size in an emergency such as a sudden squall. This is done by lowering the peak and 'tricing' or pulling up the tack with a line running from the gaff jaws – a process known as 'scandalising'. This produces an untidy bundle of cloth, but as a temporary measure it is highly effective.

Even under normal conditions, the gaff itself is less steeply peaked up than on the gunter. The resulting triangular gap is filled by a topsail which can be sent aloft on its own light spars when more drive is needed. It is a flexible and particularly handsome rig, although on some of the larger boats the complexity of the sheet and halyard arrangements can keep the single-hander uncomfortably busy at times.

An eye-catching derivative by James Wharram (see page 43), developed for his range of catamaran designs, takes the form of a loose-footed wingsail, with a deep luff pocket surrounding the mast and main halyard so as to reduce the turbulence that normally occurs behind a mast. This is surmounted by a short, and in some instances curved, gaff in the Dutch style.

One of the simplest of all these picturesque traditional sail arrangements is the sprit rig. It became a famous feature on Thames barges, the largest trading craft that could be handled by 'a man an' a boy', as the crew was referred to. Nowadays the sprit powers the diminutive 7 ft 7 in (2.3 m) Optimist dinghy on which so many thousands of children have learned to sail and to race.

Except on the Optimist dinghy, the sprit has become something of a rarity which seems a pity, for its sail and spars are fairly easy, in the small sizes, for the amateur to make. The sail is held up by a single diagonal yard, the sprit, its upper end held in a pocket at the peak of the sail and its heel by a loop of rope round the mast, known as a 'snotter'. This can be pushed upwards to tighten the belly of the sail, partially slid down so as to allow the sail to spill wind, or fully down to allow the sail to be furled by gathering it in to the mast and securing it with a few lashings ('brails', as they were called on the barges, which actually never lowered their huge heavy mainsails). The only other control is the sheet leading to the loose clew of the sail, and on the big barges, the sheets to the headsails, without which they would have been difficult to manœuvre.

On most of the simple forms of small boat rig that we have been reviewing, a jib is merely an optional extra, a useful aid to tacking, while on the Chinese junk a headsail is never carried at all. Mainsail-only boats are referred to as being una-rigged, or in America as cat-rigged. Their masts are usually stepped a correspondingly long way forward so as to put the sail's centre of effort in the right place relative to the immersed body of the hull. Despite some lack of flexibility – you have only one big sail with which to trim the power and fore-and-aft balance of the rig – there's no doubt that having just a single sheet and a tiller simplifies life for the single-hander. The most brilliant example of the modern catboat is the Freedom, conceived by Garry Hoyt in the USA and featuring high-tech carbon fibre masts, free standing like the junk with no rigging, and Bermudian shaped sails. Some Freedoms, mostly the smaller ones that fall within our Group 4 price range, have conventional booms, others use a divided wishbone boom surrounding the sail on either side and angled downwards to keep the leech tight, and sometimes combined with a wrap-around, double sided wingsail.

Many of these features can be recognised on the so-called windsurfer or sailboard rig. This consists of an isosceles-triangle shaped sail, held taut by a wishbone boom surrounding both mast and sail, and tensioned from ahead of the mast. The latter is set in a universal joint at its heel and surrounded by a pocket, sometimes zipped for convenience, running up the long side of the sail which forms the luff. The boom serves both as a support handrail and incidence control for the standing 'jockey' (who has also to act as the essential and highly mobile ballast, besides using his feet to steer the board against the straightening action of a daggerboard and aft skeg). The mast is free to rotate, so to stop the craft it is only necessary to allow the sail to weathercock freely into the wind, or to let go the boom so that the whole rig flops down into the water. The same rig can be applied to a dinghy, in which case the mast is stayed and the after end of the boom is sheeted down to the helmsman seated in the stern.

The Bermudian is foremost among modern rigs and used on the

majority of today's cruisers, as well as on virtually all racing boats for its superior aerodynamic performance to windward. This is valuable not only in competition, but in the way it affects a boat's general sailing ability. For example, in fast passage making, it can help to catch an earlier tide before it turns foul. In a real emergency, the Bermudian's fine windward ability might save the boat from grounding on a lee shore.

The Bermudian's elegant, clean, uncluttered shape will be familiar to most readers: a comparatively tall and slender mainsail, its luff and foot supported as on a gaff-rigged boat, and usually supplemented by a jib set on the forestay. This may either run to the masthead, hence the term 'masthead rig', or terminate some distance below it, when it is known as a 'fractional' rig. The latter arrangement is favoured mainly on high performance craft, where the ability to pull back the upper part of the mast by tensioning the backstay can be used in strong winds to induce a corresponding forwards bow in its lower part, flattening the sail and decreasing its power. On most cruising boats, however, the masthead rig is preferred for its overall structural security.

Tall, triangular sails are undoubtedly more efficient than short, broad ones, and are the natural choice where close-windedness is an important consideration. But as with keel configurations, one should always consider the merits of trading a certain amount of efficiency for convenience. A lofty Bermudian mast can be occasionally awkward to rig and unwieldy to lower and raise, when negotiating low bridges and for transport ashore. When the boat is on its trailer, the mast will usually overhang the hull at either end, which can be a nuisance in towing or when storage space is limited. By contrast, all the spars of the 'old-fashioned' rigs we have been considering will at least stow on or beside the boat without overlapping it, if not actually inside it. In the absence of a crane or a hinged tabernacle, stepping a short, stumpy mast on anything much larger than a dinghy is likely to be less of a struggle than staggering around with a tall one.

Fig 11 Sail plans. Top, left to right: fractional Bermudian sloop, Masthead Bermudian sloop with genoa, Bermudian cutter. Centre: Bermudian ketch, gaff yawl, Bermudian schooner. Bottom: In the past, two-masted or 'split' rigs have been used mostly on large boats in order to divide the total sail area into smaller, more easily handled sections. Despite their added complexity, however, split rigs have become increasingly popular among small boat sailors who like the look of a classic sailplan and enjoy having some extra strings to pull. These jaunty little 20 footers have been designed by Paul Fisher for home-building in plywood.

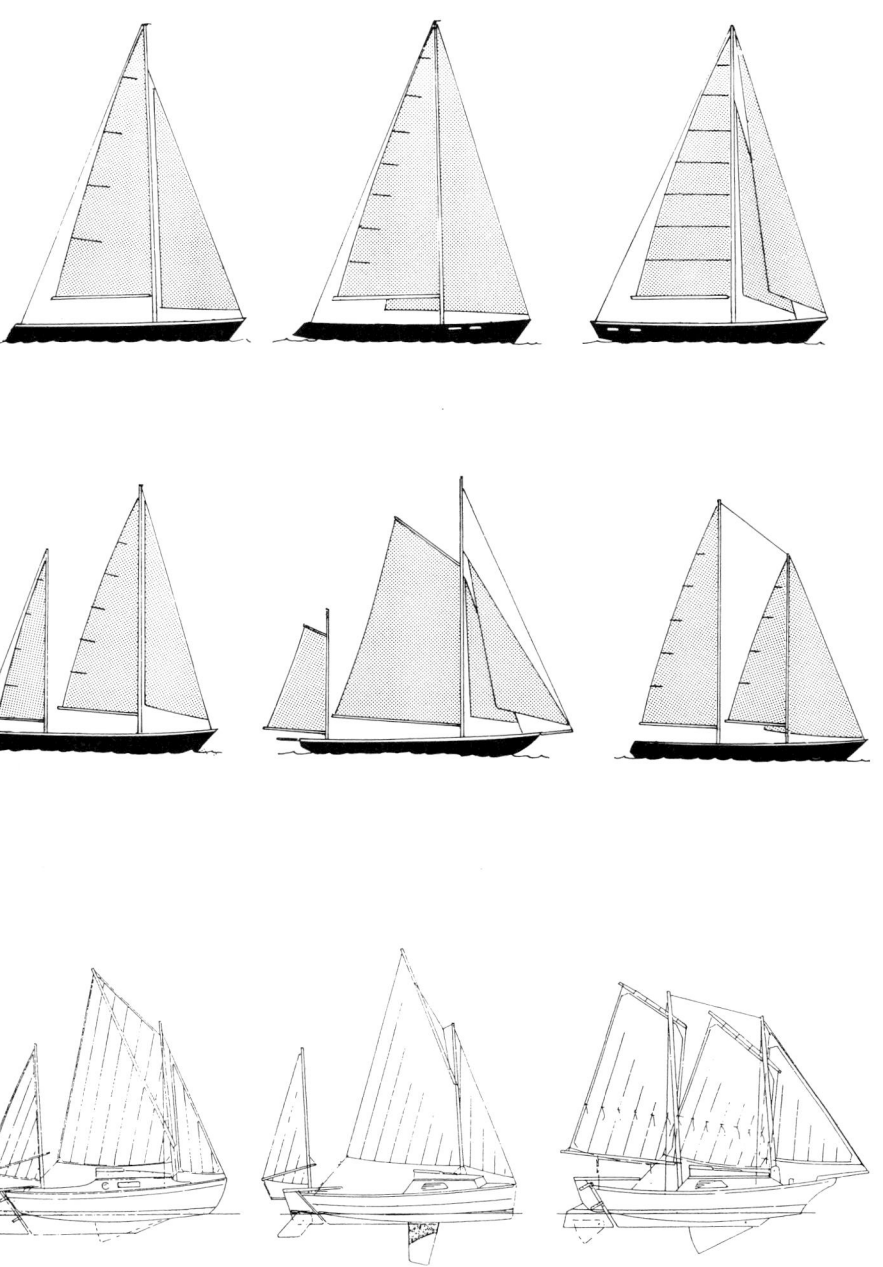

So far, we have only been considering the use of a mainsail plus single jib: the sloop rig. Setting a second headsail, termed a staysail, on another (inner) forestay, which can be made removable so as to keep the deck clear when it is not in use, turns our sloop into a cutter. For increasing the power of the rig downwind and when broad-reaching, there is the colourful billowing headsail, the spinnaker. An easier-to-use derivative is the asymmetric spinnaker, or 'cruising chute', made of lightweight nylon and set flying – that is to say, not hanked to the forestay. They do not need to be an essential part of the sail wardrobe; they are comparatively expensive on account of their sheer size. In strong winds they can sometimes be a bit of a handful for the solo sailor; but for speed and spectacle they are very hard to beat.

ONE MAST OR TWO?

With a second mast, known as a mizzen, the boat becomes either a ketch or a yawl, depending on how far aft the mizzenmast is stepped, and on its size. The traditional definition gave the ketch as locating its mizzen ahead of the rudder, the yawl abaft it, but this is no longer appropriate to many of today's designs. It is probably better to describe a yawl's mizzen as being stepped as far aft as practicable – substantially further aft than a ketch's and carrying a comparatively small sail which doesn't contribute much to the overall power of the rig, its main purpose being to balance the rig and to help when making tight turns.

The smaller the boat, the less important it becomes to sub-divide the sail area into smaller components for ease of handling. But there are certain other advantages in a two-masted rig. The prime purpose of a mizzen is to produce a well spaced-out sailplan (setting the jib from the end of a bowsprit takes it out even further) combining a low centre of effort and, correspondingly, less of a tendency to heel, with good directional steadiness, both so important in heavy weather. A mizzen sail's leverage is also valuable in close-quarters manœuvring, for as the rudder becomes less effective at very low speeds, the boat can, to a large extent, be steered by hardening in the mizzen sheet and easing the jib, and vice versa.

The yawl naturally scores over the ketch in this respect, added to which, its mizzen does not intrude on the working area of a small open boat, or into a yacht's cockpit. Conversely, it is inclined to obstruct the tiller, which has either to be specially shaped, or mechanically linked to the rudder. The mizzen may also be somewhat inaccessible, being so far out over the stern, and in consequence difficult to reach if anything should go wrong with this sail or its rigging. Indeed, the argument against any of the more complex rigs is that although they are undoubtedly more flexible and in many ways more interesting to use than the simple sloop, there is more to go wrong with them. Also, they are less efficient (the argument in favour of a large solitary mainsail), they certainly cost more to buy and to maintain; and there is not always room in a small boat to stow a large wardrobe of sails.

REEFING SYSTEMS

As we have already seen, the power of a sail can be regulated within fairly narrow limits by adjusting its shape and angle of incidence. If, however, with increasing wind strength the boat begins to show signs of becoming overpressed, or sea conditions make it desirable to slow down, the sail area needs to be reduced by 'reefing' the headsail or changing down to a smaller one, and by reefing the main itself.

One invaluable aid to reefing, though not a system in itself, is a row of 'lazyjacks', consisting of loops of light cordage hanging from the topping lift, spaced a metre or more apart and passing under the boom. Better still, these may be hung from twin topping lifts, one on either side of the sail and running from a point about two-thirds of the way up the mast, as on the Chinese junk. Their purpose is to prevent the sail, as it is lowered, from flopping all over the boat until it can be tidied up and secured; and when they are used with a fully battened sail, the entire process of reefing or stowing away becomes quite painless.

The oldest method of reefing a mainsail consists of pulling down a 'slab' of sail so as to engage a cringle in the luff with a hook on the gooseneck, lashing a matching cringle on the leech to the after end of the boom, and tying an intermediate row of reefing points down around the boom to secure the bunt of the sail. It is cheap, reliable, and still widely used. The alternatives are:

1 Another traditional method: rolling the foot of the sail round the boom, which must therefore be provided with special fittings at the attachment points for topping lift, sheet, kicking strap and gooseneck to allow it to rotate.

2 Remote slab reefing, also known as 'single-line jiffy reefing'. This is a fairly recent development, in which a single reefing line is permanently rove through both leech and luff cringles and led (via a series of turning blocks and a tackle to provide extra pulling power) to a convenient position on the boom; the additional hardware on some installations being hidden away inside the boom. Easy to use and relatively inexpensive, it is strongly recommended for the short-handed boater.

3 Rolling up the sail on a separate, geared shaft, carried inside an integral casing which forms part of either the boom or the mast itself. Both systems are extremely convenient and simple to operate, but they have been known to jam at just the wrong moment, and anyway they are as yet far too expensive for any budget boat.

Roller headsails, on the other hand, have been around in basic form, since the turn of the century, and nowadays are accepted as virtually indispensable on cruising boats, including dinghies. The sail is rolled up like a furled umbrella on a small diameter spar, rotated on the forestay by a drum at its lower end with a control line wound around it. The sail is unfurled simply by casting the control line off its cleat and hauling on one of the sheets. Traditional hanked-on sails are only really preferable to a roller system for peak performance, where changing down to a smaller sail avoids the lump of a rolled-up genoa, and a wire forestay is aerodynamically superior to a luff spar. A popular and convenient combination of the two for cruising is a roller jib or genoa, alongside a second forestay to carry a heavy storm jib; or on a cutter-rigged boat, backed by an inner – perhaps detachable – forestay for the hanked-on staysail or storm canvas.

SAIL COSTS

Prices can vary widely from one supplier to another, depending on such factors as the weight and quality of the cloth used, the standard of finishing detail, and the degree of automation employed in the loft; for example, computer-controlled laser cutting, instead of measuring tape, chalk and scissors. So it pays to shop around if you are buying a new suit of sails for your boat.

Cruising sails (except for the nylon spinnakers) are mostly made from a woven polyester cloth such as Terylene and it is the labour costs which account for rather more than half the total price. With a mainsail-plus-genoa combination for a typical 16 ft (4.9 m) dinghy costing in the region of £400 at today's prices, and those for a 21 ft (6.4 m) cruiser £700–£800 or more, you could save yourself quite a lot of money by making them yourself, as outlined later in Chapter 5. But bear in mind that whereas either of the dinghy sails could be laid out on the average livingroom floor, each of the cruiser's would require the best part of 30 ft (9 m) in each direction, and few of us have this much clean, dry, and flat floor space available. There are, however, other useful savings to be made by laundering and repairing your sails at home yourself, instead of having them professionally valeted.

Maintenance time and expense can also be minimised by treating the sails with consideration while they are in commission. Reefing the main and rolling the jib, or changing down to a smaller one in good time when it starts to blow, helps to prevent them from getting stretched and baggy. Drying off the sails whenever possible between trips avoids mildew, and stowing them away or covering them protects against the degrading effects of sunlight.

As we said earlier, such a range of alternative equipment and sail systems, and how they are supposed to work, may sound somewhat complex and even off-putting to the newcomer, but in real life it only takes an hour or two out on the water on a fine, breezy day to realise how basically simple and easy it all is. The finer points, along with a deeper appreciation of sailing, come with experience.

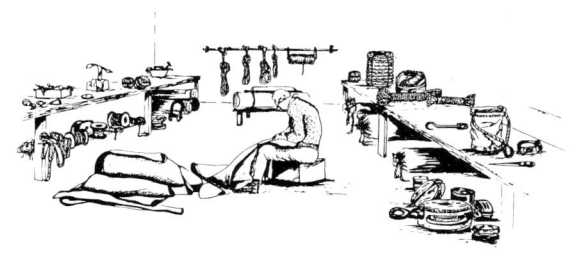

4·POWERBOATS

Some people, understandably, look for a form of boating that allows them to head more or less in the direction they want to go, regardless of wind direction and without all the hassle and upkeep of spars and canvas. They prefer a set of engine controls to a plethora of ropes demanding continual attention; and in the case of the larger motorcruisers, the voluminous accommodation uncluttered by mast supports or centreboard casings.

The ability to skim across the sea at high speed makes two uncompromising demands: a high power-to-weight ratio (ie big engines in a lightweight hull) and a suitable underwater shape. These performance boats tend, however, to be inefficient and awkward to handle when they are moving slowly. On the other hand, hulls designed to work well at low speeds may be incapable of fast cruising, no matter what engines are fitted, although they are often able to provide better accommodation and lower running costs.

Compared with sailing craft of similar length, the majority of engine-driven craft are rather more spacious and very much faster, and at modest speeds in smooth water they are no more difficult to drive than a car. They are spared the speed limitations of a sailing hull and the frustrations of light winds. So with the added weather protection of a wheelhouse or windscreen, they are undoubtedly a sensible choice for anyone who feels that sails are inclined to make a boat tippy, complicated and tiring to handle. The fast planing boats do, however, require some skilful handling when manœuvring at low speed; and being intrinsically less seakindly than sailboats, their safety in heavy weather demands a high standard of seamanship. Indeed, even moderately severe weather conditions are best avoided in most of the budget-sized motor boats we are considering, whereas in the right hands, an equivalent sailboat will remain relatively safe, if extremely uncomfortable.

HULL FORMS

Displacement hulls

The motor sailer mentioned on page 21, along with the pure sailing yacht, uses the first of the three principal underwater forms available

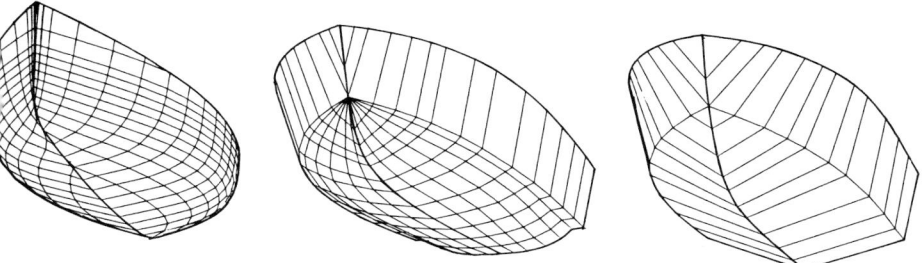

Fig 12 Hull forms. Left: Round bilge displacement hull, used for the majority of sailing craft and the slower types of powerboat. Centre: A semi-displacement hull creates more drag at low speeds but can be powered past its 'hump' speed. Right: Vee-bottomed hard-chine planing hull for fast power-boats. *Illustration: Paul Fisher*

to the designer, known as a displacement hull. This used to be easily recognisable by its classic rounded bilges – the underwater sections being shaped like half an egg – but nowadays they are rather flatter, in order to provide more usable internal space. However, the waterlines are still drawn to a point at both ends. This offers a sweet entry at the bows, without being so pinched in that they cannot hold up the boat's head when she heels to the wind. These lines also allow the water to flow freely away from the stern, which is supported just clear of the surface, with the minimum of fuss and turbulence. This helps it to slip easily through the water and to be easily driven on the limited power of its sails or small engine, as the case may be. The beam is restricted accordingly, not so bluff as to be unduly difficult to push through the water, but broad enough for the required accommodation and load carrying capacity, the sailboat tending to have finer lines than the motor sailer, which can usually call on greater engine power to overcome the extra drag.

Sails can of course be used to augment the engine power, as well as to save fuel while cruising. Bearing in mind that every 100 sq ft or 10 sq m of sail can produce roughly one horsepower in even a gentle force 3 breeze, and four times as much when windspeed doubles to a fresh force 5, the savings can rise from as much as 50% to the point in stronger winds where the engine can be shut down altogether. Sails are also very effective in steadying the boat in rough weather, common professional practice on many small fishing vessels and trawlers, with their long shallow keels providing additional roll-damping.

All this might be seen as making an irrefutable case in favour of a displacement hull, with or without sails, as the ideal all-rounder.

Virtually regardless of power, however, its top speed is limited by its length. The reason is that as speed increases beyond a certain point, a strengthening downwards suction begins to take effect in the area of the stern and this phenomenon, added to the effort of thrusting the water aside at the bows, effectively prevents the boat from ever exceeding a figure known as 'hull speed'. This can vary slightly between one design and another, but at best it is of the order of 1.4 times the square root of the waterline length, expressed in knots and feet respectively. For example, a 25 ft (7.6 m) yacht is unlikely to be able to exceed $1.4\sqrt{25} = 7$ knots (13 kph) in still water, and a truly prodigious amount of brute force would be required to surmount this barrier (indeed, double the normal cruising power might be needed even to reach its threshold in headwinds or against oncoming seas). To go any faster, you would need either a longer boat, or one with a different underwater shape; or – as Denny Desoutter once put it – a tow from a destroyer!

Semi-displacement hulls
These feature immersed and slightly flattened stern sections that act as a wedge facing the oncoming water so as to create a certain amount of lift. This in turn lowers the bows, which are themselves rather slimmer than those of a full displacement hull, enabling them to cut more sharply into the waves. The penalty to be paid for the immersed stern and level ride is the power-absorbing turbulence it creates at low speeds, which, combined with the large wetted surface area of a necessarily deep and commodious underbody, creates a considerable amount of drag. But given sufficient engine power to take this form of hull up to its 'hump speed' and beyond, the result is a reasonably fast and thoroughly competent all-round seaboat.

Planing hulls
For zipping around at still higher speeds – to put some sort of a figure on it, let's say 20 knots and over, although some semi-displacement boats can easily exceed this – it is necessary to go to a fully planing hull. This will usually be broader beamed, still with an immersed transom and squared-off waterlines aft to give plenty of buoyancy and prevent squatting, but with a nearly flat, slightly vee-shaped bottom, and a sharp corner or 'hard chine', as it is known, between the topside and bottom surfaces. The purpose of the vee is twofold: to confer a measure of directional stability – a flat tea-tray type of boat is forever tending to skid sideways with the helmsman fighting to keep it straight. More importantly, the vee provides a reasonably comfortable ride at high speeds. For this, a deadrise angle (the upward slope of the bottom either side of the centreline) of around

Shallow-vee planing hulls in action. Top: The bows lift and the stern squats as this 16 ft Maryland Cabrio begins to push through her 5 knots 'hump' speed. A 21 ft Shetland 4+2 (below) rides level while cruising at 20 knots.

15° to 20° – with a sharp entry, but flattening off towards the stern – is considered a fair compromise between the spine-jarring slamming and banging of the extremely shallow vee that is needed for the fastest boats, and the gentler motion and heavier power requirements of a deep vee with a deadrise of 25° or more. Generally speaking, the sharper the vee, the softer the ride; but the less space it can provide for accommodation.

Unlike displacement craft, the planing hull is sensitive to weight. This directly affects its speed, as does the location of its static centre of buoyancy and the weight distribution of its occupants, fuel and other movable items. The boat is also subjected to the dynamic lift created by the forward motion and to the angular thrust from its propeller(s). For proper control of the boat, all these forces have to be kept continuously in balance, and changing one force can alter the others.

Modern, high performance boats are normally offered with a variety of engine sizes, giving typical speed potentials varying from about 20 knots up to 40 knots or more, so most of these designs are optimised for around 30 knots (55 kph). Running at 20 knots, for example, or at 40, will upset the balance, which has to be corrected by adjustable trim tabs on the transom, and/or some form of power tilt mechanism of the propeller drive leg. In the case of the smaller craft with an outboard motor, this can be more simply achieved by means of permanent wedges under the stern, or altering the propeller height by raising or lowering the motor.

ENGINE TYPES

It is worth bearing in mind, when selecting an engine, that except when top speed is called for, a planing boat only needs a certain amount of power to get past the 'hump' speed and up on to the plane; after which, about two-thirds throttle is usually sufficient for cruising. Any engine more powerful than this will, of course, result in a faster boat, other factors being equal, but it will be more expensive to buy and insure, and thirstier to run if its performance is used to the full.

As a rough calculation, we can assume that it takes, at most, about 50 horsepower per ton of boat displacement to cruise at over 20 knots (37 km/hr), rather less with a few of the best modern designs. The figure goes up to over 100 hp/ton for 40 knots (75 km/hr) sportsboats and much more for the faster racers, whereas with a more modest 35–50 hp/ton the boat will be running at semi-displacement speeds of 10–20 knots (18–37 km/hr) depending on her size, while full displacement speeds of 6–10 knots (11–18 km/hr) will only require 35 hp/ton or less. Another useful rule of thumb is that the average outboard motor burns about one gallon of fuel per hour (rather less on a good modern engine) for every ten horsepower it develops. Generalisations can be misleading, none more so than in the case of marine engine fuel consumption figures, which are affected by so many factors such as the matching of the propeller diameter and pitch to the preferred cruising speed, and the state of the hull bottom surfaces. But to give some indication of what the fuel bills might run to in the course of a season, we can assume that a typical 20–25 ft (6.0–7.6 m) runabout with a 60–80 hp motor would return about three nautical miles per gallon (1.8 km/li) cruising at 20 knots (32 kph), while a frugal little 2 hp on a cruising dinghy would probably show 20 mpg (7.0 km/li) or better, at a modest 3 knots (5.5 kph). Although there are a few 4-stroke petrol and one or two diesel outboards on the market (the latter mainly for specialist applications such as working barges), most are 2-strokes. They are lighter and cheaper to buy than equivalent inboard engines, and they have the further advantages of propeller steering, which is handy in confined spaces; they can be tilted up to clear a fouled propeller, quickly unshipped and carried or wheeled ashore for servicing, and traded in for another model at most dealerships. Incidentally, a 40 hp motor, weighing around 150 lb (70 kg), is about the largest that can be started by hand – a nice feature if your battery should go dead – and is also about the heaviest that one can pick up and move around without too much difficulty.

A 4-stroke inboard engine, on the other hand, is usually more robust and should last longer. With shaft drive, it can be installed anywhere in the boat to suit the weight distribution, it can be soundproofed, and it is more accessible to work on if anything goes wrong – although it is sure to require some spanner work and lifting tackle when it has to be removed for repair or overhaul. A well-cared-for petrol inboard should not require overhauling before 1500–3000 hours of use, whereas 1000 hours is about the best that can be expected from a 2-stroke outboard. Compared with these engines, diesels of the same power are around 40% heavier, cost about twice as much to buy, and are noticeably noisier and rougher. But they seldom fail to start at the first touch of the button, they will run for 3000–5000 hours between overhauls, and they use considerably less fuel than petrol engines. For, despite their weight, which seriously affects the speed of a fast lightweight boat, they will usually return around 30% more miles to the gallon than an outboard, or as much as 50% on a slow cruiser where weight is less important; the petrol inboard comes somewhere in between the two. The savings on the occasional hour or two's use of a diesel would hardly justify its extra capital cost, but the budget boater who intends putting in plenty of sea time would do well to consider buying a used diesel boat, in preference to a new petrol-engined one.

Typical weight-to-power ratios for three 70 hp engines are 4.5 lb/hp (2.8 kg/kw) for a modern turbo-diesel; 3.2 lb/hp (2.0 kw/kg) for a

A sterndrive assembly, powered in this case by a turbocharged diesel engine. Except for an additional set of bevel gears, the drive train, external casings and propeller are similar to those of a big outboard motor.

high-speed petrol inboard, and 3.0 lb/hp (1.9 kg/kw) for the outboard including, of course, its propeller drive system. There is also a scale effect which makes all engines relatively heavier the less powerful they are, although a similar differential is maintained between the three types, eg for typical 20 hp engines, the ratios are 11.2 lb/hp (7.0 kg/kw) for the diesel (not turbo at this size); 7.0 lb/hp (4.4 kg/kw) for a petrol inboard and 5.5 lb/hp (3.4 kg/kw) for an outboard. It follows that a single-engine installation is lighter, besides being cheaper than a twin with the same total power output, the latter of course having the advantages of get-you-home reliability in the event of an engine failure, and extra manœuvrability in confined spaces.

However, the figures for the inboard engines make no allowance for the weight (and cost) of buying and installing the drive system. This may involve a conventional propeller shaft and thrust block (perhaps with a constant-velocity joint to take care of any mis-

alignment) a stern gland and a P-bracket – the traditional arrangement used on virtually all inboard-engined full-displacement
launches, working boats and motorcruisers (nowadays mostly only
the big ones); a vee-drive, with an angled-back gearbox or belt drive,
which allows the engine to be installed back-to-front above the
propshaft; or a sterndrive, which has become the accepted alternative
to an outboard on most sports boats and other fast planing craft
requiring upwards of 100hp or so. This consists of a bevel gear drive
and clutch assembly, which is usually close-coupled in unit construction with the engine, and can be swung up into the parked position,
avoiding the drag from the propeller when sailing and convenient
when beaching the boat. Outboard motors, already having this
facility, are simply clamped on without any installation costs. Taking
these into account, outboards are usually slightly cheaper overall,
and they are also only about half the weight of sterndrive power
plants. So there's much to be said for them, despite their extra noise,
thirst for fuel and shorter life.

A recent development for sterndrives, and some of the larger
outboards, is a variable pitch propeller which automatically increases
its pitch when the engine reaches its best operating speed, like the
automatic transmission on a car, giving faster acceleration combined
with lower revs and better fuel consumption at high speeds.

BOATS FOR INLAND WATERWAYS

There is one more method of propulsion which deserves serious
consideration: the electric powerplant. This has two over-riding
qualities compared with any of the others: it is almost silent, and it
doesn't pollute the atmosphere or the water. Electric power is ideal
for tranquil travelling on lakes and rivers, and for other quiet pursuits
such as fishing or bird watching. The one great disadvantage of
electric boats, unfortunately, is their very modest performance in
terms of speed and range which is dictated by battery capacity. The
batteries themselves must be of the heavy duty, deep cycle type,
designed for repeated full discharge operation. Their recharging
times are usually about eight to ten hours, and unless either an
engine-driven charger or a small outboard motor is carried, you have
to take care to be near an electrical mains supply before you run them
flat. So, for all practical purposes, an electric launch is limited to
cruising at well below its theoretical displacement speed – 4 to 5 knots
(7–9 kph) is about the best you could expect from an 18 footer
(5.5 m) – with a typical range of around 30 miles (50 km), or double
this if you don't mind carrying an additional bank of batteries (they
are very heavy).

An optional array of roof-mounted solar charging panels, currently
being experimented with on such boats, will further extend their

The Voltaire 16 (Group 3) electric launch for inland waterways can carry up to seven people and has a top speed of 5½ knots. Endurance between battery charges is about 8 hours cruising at 3½ knots, giving an effective range of 33 miles (53 km).

range, but will add considerably to the overall cost of the installation. As specialist boats produced in small numbers, it is not surprising that they are already rather expensive for their size, tending to stray high into the Group 4 price range. A cheaper alternative, if the notion of quiet electric cruising appeals to you, is to fit an electric outboard motor, with a battery and mains charger, to any suitably spacious skiff or dinghy. Whisper, for example, is a 15 ft 6 in (4.7 m) slipper launch in Group 2, with a 3 hp electric outboard which propels her at 4 knots. Being light and flat-bottomed, she can be launched and retrieved over a low bank, instead of having to use a slipway. The boat seats four passengers – two of them rather elegantly in loose cane chairs.

In a similar 'inland cruising' category, though the Group 4 limit will restrict choice to an elderly example in need of some renovation, are Britain's traditional steel narrowboats. These diesel engined, tiller-steered vessels are often gaily painted in a distinctive style not unlike that of a gypsy caravan. They either served as homes for bargee families, or have been converted from commercial canal barges. Despite their extremely limited beam, which was restricted to less than 7 ft (2.1 m) in order to enable them to negotiate the narrowest canal locks, their length of up to 70 ft (21.3 m) – some have been shortened – provides truly commodious, though elongated living accommodation complete with coal stove and central heating.

Their modern equivalent is usually built of GRP, with the beam increased to around 8 ft (2.4 m) on lengths varying from 30 ft (9.1 m) to around 65 ft (19.8 m), and can be bought second-hand. Smaller new narrowboats will be within Group 4 prices. Although restricted to using the broader locks, these boats are ideally suited to exploring, at a sedate and relaxed pace, most of the country's extensive network of waterways. If inland waterways appeal to you, there are highly developed and much wider canal systems running throughout Continental Europe, where waterborne traffic is still expanding as the roads become ever more congested. For anyone wanting to take a narrowboat abroad on holiday, there are competitive shipping rates between Britain and the Continent.

They have, of course, absolutely no pretensions to seaworthiness, and to anyone used to the agility of most powerboats, their manoeuvrability can only be described as ponderous. But they make excellent mobile houseboats, and they are extremely economical to run considering their size. There are a number of well-run charter fleets, so a week or two's holiday trial is a good way of getting to know these boats and the leisurely lifestyle that goes with them, before deciding whether or not to buy one for yourself. If you do so, you will need a licence of one type or another, depending on whether you intend using the locks, and navigating canals as well as the rivers. The fee also varies with the duration of the licence and the length of the boat. For example, a three month licence for a 25 footer would cost £70, whereas a licence for a 50 footer for a full year would work out at £180. You should also allow for mooring fees. These vary widely from one site to another, but they can add a few hundred pounds to the annual expenses on a medium sized boat. More information from British Waterways or the Inland Waterways Association (addresses on page 118).

GENERAL PURPOSE POWERBOATS

This broad classification refers to all open launches, tenders and dayboats within the size limits imposed by our restricted budget.

The rounded bilges that are a feature of these craft undoubtedly provide the most seakindly hulls. This applies to both the comparatively low powered, full displacement form with limited speed potential and to the semi-displacement type, with more engine power and substantially higher speed potential, depending on how closely the underbody approximates to that of a full planing hull. There is no hard and fast distinction between the two, which in fact serve to mark the boundaries of a useful range of hull shapes available to the designer. The fuller, more generous form will always be the best for heavy displacements, ultimate seaworthiness and slow, economic motoring, while a semi-planing profile would be chosen where speed is a major consideration, as in the majority of today's general purpose boats.

In our area of interest these are mostly around 21 ft (6.4 m) long, with a beam of 7 ft 6 in (2.3 m), capable of comfortable cruising at 16–18 knots (30–33 kph) and up to 25–28 knots (46–52 kph) top speed with a 90 hp outboard (or preferably twin 40's for peace of mind out at sea). A forward cuddy cabin with opening windows houses the helmsman's seat, controls and instruments, plus two berths for the occasional overnight trip, leaving a spacious open cockpit with side bench seating for the passengers or anglers. An excellent example is the Day Angler 21, built by Orkney Fishing Boats, and remaining just within the Group 3 limit (or Group 4 with twin outboards and a trailer). The disadvantage of a cuddy on a small boat is that the increased covered area is gained at the expense of deck space. In some designs the resulting narrow sidedecks make going forward somewhat tricky, even in smooth water and using the coachroof grabrails; certainly much too risky for young children. Smaller boats in this category can conveniently be classed as fast fishing dinghies, though they are not, of course, confined to angling, being just as suitable as runabouts and club rescue boats. Among the better known, and most popular, are the Hardy 17 (5.2 m) and the Orkney Strikeliner (16 ft (4.9 m), both with a small forward cuddy and price tags around the middle of Group 3, depending on how fully they are equipped, and including a 25 hp motor which makes them capable of around 18–20 knots (33–37 kph). Prices for 20 footers are generally towards the top of Group 3 in basic form, which takes them into the middle of Group 4 with 80–100 hp outboard motors, or right on to the top limit with an inboard diesel.

Although the latter may be preferred for reasons of economy and reliability, its weight will probably bring the top speed down from perhaps 30 knots (55 km/hr) to around 17 (31), with cruising at 12 (22). But whereas the outboard installation could be expected to return little more than two miles per gallon (0.7 km/li), the diesel would deliver at least four (1.4 km/li), so you might decide in this case to trade speed for economy. By comparison, a similar sized full-displacement hull cruising at a modest (and to some of us unacceptable) 5 knots (9 kph) would probably give as much as 10 mpg (3.5 km/li) with a diesel. This represents truly economic motoring on which you could, in a few seasons of hard use, recover the entire capital cost of the more expensive engine if the 5 knots cruising speed was acceptable.

General purpose powerboats. The Hardy Navigator (top) is a popular 18 ft motor cruiser in Group 3, with two berths, galley and toilet in the forward cabin, and a pilot's seat in the raised wheelhouse. A 50 hp outboard gives her 18 knots. Below: The 23 ft Orkney Day Angler (Group 4) features a large self-bailing cockpit and helmsman's shelter. It can maintain over 20 knots with 100 hp from either a single or twin outboards.

SPORTS BOATS

Vee-form fully planing hulls are the clear favourites for open sports boats, fast tenders and ski boats. They may either be decked across at the bows, some with a little cuddy cabin for shelter for very occasional overnighting, or they can be completely open 'bowriders', with additional seating right up in the bows ahead of the helmsman. With light weight and sufficient power, many of them are capable of an exhilarating 40–50 knots (75–90 kph), although inevitably they are liable to give you a pretty wild ride at speed in any sort of a seaway. Most of these veritable pocket rockets, such as the Ring and Invader 18 footers (5.5 m) with 120 hp outboards, or the Sea Ray with 175 hp stern drive, are Group 4 boats, whereas the 15 ft 6 in (4.7 m) Picton Royale, for example, just squeezes into Group 3 with a 70 hp motor. A small lightweight boat such as this is also reasonably economical, returning as much as 6 mpg (2.1 km/li) with restrained driving. Ski boats, incidentally, require a particularly high power-to-weight ratio, so as to provide the snap acceleration needed to pull the skiers quickly up on to the surface of the water. They also need a towing ring or post, and preferably an aft-facing seat for someone – not the helmsman, who should be looking where he is going – to keep a watchful eye on the skiers.

Although it would be wrong to label all planing hulled boats as fair weather funboats – the RIBs mentioned later are used by the coastguard and other maritime rescue services – it can be argued that they are generally best suited to sunshine and smooth water. In choppy seas, the prudent helmsman will back off the throttle sufficiently to avoid the worst of the wavetop leaping and slamming, and in really rough seas he will be obliged to slow down to below planing speed. Handling is then apt to become somewhat soggy and the boat unstable as it wallows around, where a displacement hull would remain more or less on course and relatively easily controlled.

The price of these fast and handsome funboats, many of which are imported from America, also tends to be slightly higher than that of similar sized cruisers and fishers, with 19–20 ft (5.8–6.0 m) on the upper limit of Group 4. The price does, however, include the cost of either an outboard or a sterndrive powerplant several times more powerful than those needed in the slower boats. This is usually in the range of 120–150 hp for a 16 footer (4.9 m) for example, compared with the 25–50 hp that would be sufficient for a displacement hull; and in a 20 footer (6.0 m) as much as 230 hp instead of 60–80 hp. When seen from this viewpoint, there is little to choose between them in terms of value for money. But bear in mind that powerboats of this type wear out more quickly than the slower ones, because their engines are driven harder and their hulls take a greater beating. Added to this, sportsboat styling tends to change with each new

Family sportsboats. The Welsh-built 15 ft 6 in Picton Royale has seating for four and a swim platform. With a 75 hp outboard, she has a top speed of around 40 knots but cruises economically at 25 with a skier in tow (Group 3).

model, as with cars; so their early-years depreciation is particularly heavy. Their used prices fall much more quickly than in the case of the more traditional craft, whose classic styling is more likely to survive changes in market taste. As a result, there are some real bargains to be found at little more than half their original prices after only a few years' use – although the majority can hardly be called budget boats because of their monstrous thirst for fuel.

To make best use of their power, planing craft must be built as lightly as possible, having proper regard for essential structural strength. But it is important to keep any small boat as light as possible, not only for optimum performance, but because it reduces the necessary engine size, with its attendant capital outlay and the all-important fuel consumption and running costs. So don't be lured by those thrilling figures of power and speed into buying a bigger engine than you really need, or you may find your cruising range restricted by the depth of your pocket.

Light weight makes trailering easier too. The majority of budget-sized powerboats can be brought ashore to save on mooring and berthing costs, and towed behind the family car. But bear in mind that their overall weight, ready for the road (boat + engine +

trailer) increases rapidly with boat length. A 16 footer (4.9 m) might weigh no more than, say, 1000 lb (450 kg) as a bare boat without engine, and even though this might translate into 1800 lb (800 kg) trailing weight, it remains within the capabilities of most one litre cars. Going up to a 21 footer (6.4 m), however, could well double both figures, with such boats averaging around 2100 lb (950 kg) and the corresponding road load rising to some 3500 lb (1590 kg). This will require quite a hefty car or a four-wheel-drive vehicle. (See Chapter 6.)

INFLATABLES

Inflatables have come a long way in recent years, with capabilities far removed from the early 'rubber ducks'. The smallest, in the range 7–9 ft (2.1–2.7 m), still have fabric bottoms between their surrounding buoyancy tubes; though nowadays they are usually stiffened by slatted or 'roller-shutter' interlocking floorboards. Weighing little more than 50 lb (22.7 kg), and needing only a small outboard of 2–4 hp or a sailing kit – or just a pair of oars for short trips in calm conditions – they can be deflated and stowed away in a carry bag or car boot or transported inflated on a car roof rack. Instead of being towed astern of a cruising boat (invariably a source of worry), they are also light enough to be lifted aboard and lashed on deck, still fully inflated or partially deflated and folded double, ready for instant launching. For such reasons, and also because no additional fendering is needed to protect the mother ship's topsides, they are a good choice as a yacht tender, with prices in the lower half of Group 1.

The smallest inflatables are only rated to carry a maximum of three, or in some designs four people. Moving up to the middle sizes, taking 13 ft (4.0 m) as an example, capacity increases to 5–6 passengers and weight to about 175 lb (80 kg), with prices around the Group 1–2 borderline. Some of these boats feature inflated keels to improve the handling and speed capabilities, while one or two in the Zodiac range have an ingenious inflatable, semi-rigid floor with its own vee-shaped underbody. They can take motors of 40–50 hp, and with this power many of them can plane up to 40 knots (75 kph). There are many still larger sizes of semi-rigid, but most now take the form of an RIB (Rigid Inflatable Boat) which combines the best of both worlds: a glassfibre underbody with a deep-vee bow, flattening off into broad, flat planing sections aft with automatic self-bailers; and shallow topsides terminating in large inflatable buoyancy tubes which also act as spray rails. One range of semi-professional boats, the Avon Searider, is unique in having a water ballast system within its double bottom, enabling it to take in extra weight when required for added stability. There are also RIBs as small as 9 ft (2.8 m).

The best of both worlds. Rigid inflatable boats (RIBs) combine a GRP planing hull with buoyancy tubes that make them unsinkable. The hull of Picton's Diver 595 (19 ft 6 in) is based on that of their sportsboats, resulting in a fast and roomy all-rounder, suitable for offshore use and rescue duties.

Although their appearance may be distinctly utilitarian, their performance is anything but – rivalling that of the rigid-hulled sports boats, with the advantages of 100% buoyancy and a remarkable degree of stability in rough seas. They are also considerably cheaper – on a par with fast fishers – a 15 ft (4.6 m) 6–8 passenger RIB, complete with 50 hp motor and trailer, plus all the goodies such as a sit-astride steering console and windshield, comes into Group 3. Even a 21 ft (6.4 m) 10-passenger, 120 hp rescue boat is still just inside the Group 4 band.

MOTOR CRUISERS

The demarcation between dayboat and cruiser is somewhat debatable. To merit the description, however, even the smallest true cruiser should provide sufficient amenities for a family to spend their holidays aboard in reasonable comfort – as distinct from a boat with a cuddy, a couple of seat-berths, and nothing much else. The standard is bound to vary with the size of the boat; around 18–20 ft (5.5–6.1 m) being the smallest that can offer an acceptable indoor/outdoor mix of sheltered accommodation and open cockpit space. At the same time, they are about the largest to be found inside Group 4, on account of the increased amount of material and labour involved in their superstructure, compared with the dayboat, and the more elaborate nature of the fixtures and fittings in their accommodation. Unfortunately this length inevitably limits them to only two berths, although most designs provide for two more in the cockpit, covered by some form of canopy. Good modern examples at around 19 ft (5.8 m) are the well known Hardy Sea Wings and the Yamarin Big Game from Finland, with two vee-berths forward that convert to a double, plus a toilet compartment and cooking area. Both come in at around the Group 4 limit complete with trailer and 60–70 hp outboard, giving the Yamarin a speed of over 30 knots (55 kph) and the more ruggedly built and traditionally shaped Hardy 18–20 knots (33–37 kph).

To accommodate more than two proper bunks internally, our cruiser has to be larger, which means buying it second-hand. A well used but well built oldie, such as a Freeman 23 or 24 (7.0/7.5 m) would make a good choice. Although recognisably dated by their somewhat boxy appearance compared with today's sleek profiles, boats like these provide a comfortably laid out cabin, toilet compartment and galley, and a roomy open-backed wheelhouse, with a choice of single or twin petrol or diesel inboards giving speeds of 10–14 knots (18–26 kph).

As much as by length, price is influenced by the type and size of the power unit, for on any new small boat, this represents a sizeable proportion, often more than half of the overall cost. Power, as we have already seen, costs money. With a 60 hp outboard, for example, costing roughly twice as much as one of 25 hp, it probably makes sense initially to choose a small motor option and to spend any surplus funds on the boat itself. You can always part-exchange an outboard for a more powerful one at a later date; something you cannot easily do with an inboard.

Naturally enough, size also plays a major part in seaworthiness although shape, above as well as below the waterline, is even more important. Consideration has to be given to the shape aloft, in the weight and windage of the superstructure; and below, in the way that stability and handling are affected by the sea conditions. It has to be accepted that the majority of cruisers small enough to fit our budget are primarily river craft, capable of making sheltered estuary and coastal passages in fair weather, but quite unsuited to venturing offshore if strong winds are forecast. Their violent motion in heavy seas can make them extremely difficult to control, even assuming that after several exhausting hours there is someone aboard who is still in a fit state to take the wheel.

This illustrates what is perhaps the most important of the inherent differences between motor and sailing craft of similar size: their relative behaviour under severe conditions. The weight and lateral resistance of a deep keel or centreboard tends to restrain a sailing hull from excessive rolling, helped by the pressure of the wind on the rig which pins the boat down on one side, while its driving force resists the corkscrewing effect of any cross seas. This is not to say that the sailboat won't be very wet and uncomfortable; it probably will be. But without sails, and with little or no damping effect from its vestigial keel, if it has one at all, the motorboat will be much more at the mercy of the waves, even in the hands of a skilled helmsman.

On the other hand, under the more normal conditions for which the designer intended it, it will be very much faster than the sailboat, and probably more roomy and comfortable, and it will certainly make fewer demands on its crew. Nevertheless, from a safety point of view on any long trips, and provided you get the organisation right, it makes good sense to enjoy your passage-making in the company of other boats. Cruises in company can incorporate a wide range of differing types of motorboat if their speed capabilities are similar – something that would be impracticable with sailboats.

As we said earlier, it all depends on the kind of boating that most appeals to you. Each, in its own way, is something of a challenge. All are hugely rewarding.

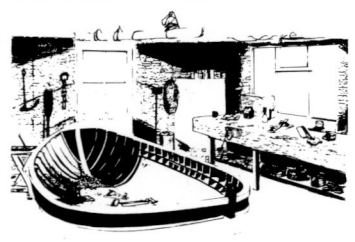

5·BUILDING YOUR OWN BOAT ———

With today's labour costs and overheads being as high as they are, and by profiting from some of the latest developments in techniques and materials, building your own boat has become by far the most effective means of getting more boat for your money. Anyone on a Group 1 budget, for example, can construct a small cruiser for little more than the price of an up-market dinghy, given the levels of skill and craftsmanship that are well within the capabilities of the average handyman.

It goes without saying, however, that such a project needs plenty of time, which many of us cannot spare, plus patience, perseverance and – let's face it – not a little courage, for even a small boat can, at times, seem like a monster in the building shed. But once any initial fears and doubts have been overcome, and you really get into the swing of a workshop routine, you may well find it less difficult and very much more enjoyable than ever you imagined it could be.

Nevertheless, such a project must be recognised at the outset as a major undertaking that should only be embarked on with a certain degree of caution. The worst mistake is to choose a design which is too big for the budget in terms of labour, quite apart from its financial cost. If it is too ambitious in either respect, it may have to be finished off in a hurry with cheap, shoddy materials and fittings; or worse still abandoned, incomplete and probably unsaleable.

Be under no illusions about the economics of DIY boatbuilding. For sure, you can save at least half the cost of the showroom product, probably more, by using your own 'free' labour if you are working in wood; rather less in GRP. But all too often, the saving is less than one hoped for, given a succession of first-timer's mistakes in budgeting on materials and particularly on fittings which can alone exceed the cost of the basic hull, or even in underestimating the size of the building shed and its heating bills. Much of the uncertainty and hassle can be avoided when the building plans are accompanied by a comprehensive set of instructions from the designer, with explanatory diagrams of awkward or important details, and a materials shopping list. However, with the huge sigh of relief at the end of what has probably felt like a mammoth task, and the enormous satisfaction and sense of achievement as the boat takes to the water, all the

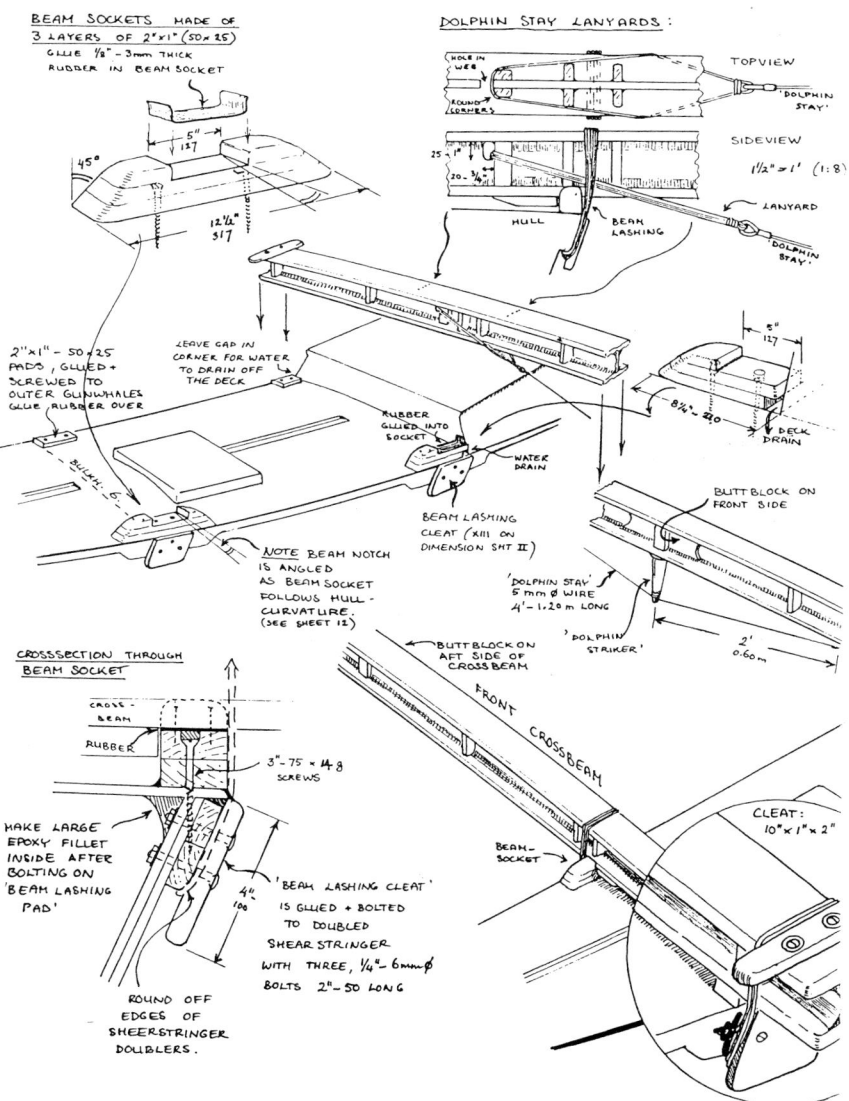

Fig 13 Much of the hassle in building a boat at home can be avoided if the plans are backed up by a comprehensive set of instructions. These are typical of catamaran designer James Wharram.

misgivings and frustrations, even the aching back, are soon forgotten.

It can be very encouraging if you get to know other home boatbuilders in your vicinity. Talking over your proposals and sharing one another's problems helps to keep you motivated, especially at times when it's all beginning to look too difficult and you are in danger of losing heart. If a number of you get together, you can also generate quite effective purchasing power, and there are some national associations with the same objectives that may be well worth joining.

For those who have never tried their hand at boatbuilding before, or have serious doubts about their capabilities – or like many of us, simply haven't the time or the determination – there are several other ways of getting afloat, although they cost more. You could hire some expert labour to help with the difficult bits and shorten the timescale or, if you can afford it, to work with you right through the entire building programme. More expensive still, you can opt for a professionally built hull, or the GRP mouldings that comprise it, and do the rest yourself. Even this will cost substantially less – possibly as little as two-thirds of the factory price.

For others unwilling to commit to such a major project, restoring an old but basically sound boat, as distinct from trying to rebuild a wreck, can be wonderfully rewarding. But when buying a second-hand boat, of whatever age, always seek a professional opinion on its condition from a surveyor, as outlined on page 14, and make your purchase offer subject to his report. You might consider his advice expensive, but it would save you from a potentially disastrous investment.

THE WORKSHOP

Don't be put off if your building conditions are not ideal. A poor workshop, badly lit and inconveniently laid out will cause you constant frustration, and you will be more liable to make silly mistakes. But boats have been built by enthusiasts on unlevel mud floors in old run-down shacks, with leaking roofs and in sub-zero temperatures. On the other hand, a good workshop is rather like having a nice sharp saw or chisel: it will make your work a whole lot easier, and enjoyable. After all, boatbuilding, like boating itself, should be fun.

You should allow yourself plenty of space in which to manœuvre lengths of timber and move large prefabricated assemblies, with a decent bench and a solid floor preferably made of chipboard or old lumber, well supported and clear of the ground. Provided the ground is firm, it can, however, simply be levelled off and covered in heavy-duty polythene sheeting.

The building must also be dry and well heated, with an area of at least twice the rectangular plan area of your boat. In other words, if the boat were to measure 20 ft (6 m) long by 8 ft (call it 2.5 m) beam, representing a rectangle of 160 sq ft (15 sq m), your workshop should cover not less than 320 sq ft (30 sq m), or more if possible – say 24 ft (7 m) by 13 ft (4 m) so as to allow walking space around the sides and ends of the hull. Even this doesn't give you much room for the essential bench. It could stand across one corner, but it would be better to increase the measurement by a few feet in whichever direction you can; and allow enough height to be able to swing components up and over without hitting the roof.

You may be able to adapt an existing structure; but if not (and if you don't want to go to the expense of a new shed), you could consider erecting a lean-to against the wall of some other building with a sloping roof, and consisting of a glued-and-nailed timber framework supporting a skin of polythene sheeting. Alternatively, a row of metal hoops with their ends firmly planted in the ground, made from waterpiping and supported by linking longitudinals, can be used to support the sheeting. This shape tends to be more rigid than a simple squared-off structure and offers less wind resistance. If you expect the project to last more than a year or so, use polythene sheet that has been ultra-violet coated to stop it from becoming brittle and cracking in sunny, windy conditions. To prevent your 'greenhouse' and its occupants from overheating in warm weather, also ensure that the ends can be swung open or rolled up for ventilation, and to allow the boat to be moved in and out easily. On a final cautionary note, do make certain that any outside electrical power connection is waterproof, and that the cable runs upwards into the building, so that rainwater cannot run down it into an unprotected junction box or socket.

TOOLS

Given perseverance and a well-organised workspace, sharp hand tools are the next most essential ingredient for successful boatbuilding. Not only are they a joy to use, but they involve no major financial outlay. The collection can be built up over a period of time, and may include some discounted or second-hand bargains. You will need some or all of the following:

Handsaws: crosscut and tenon
Coping saw
Hand drill and bits
Chisels of various sizes
Mallet
Jack plane or smoothing plane
Block plane

Spokeshave
Scrapers
Stanley knife
G-cramps (you can't have
  too many)
2 ft wooden folding ruler
Carpenter's tapes: 9 m and 2 m

Combination square   Hammers and screwdrivers
2 ft square   Putty knives and punches
Bevel gauge

Heavy-duty stationary power tools such as a table planer, band saw and table saw, though very useful pieces of equipment, are not essential. But with a few electrically powered hand tools, costing on average about £50 each, you can make light work of some otherwise time-consuming operations. Recommended are: a variable-speed drill, screwdriver, circular saw, jigsaw, planer, orbital or vibratory sander, and an angle grinder. If no main power supply is accessible, these tools will run off a portable generator of suitable output, preferably one with a slow-running 4-stroke engine, which is quieter and uses less fuel than one of the frenetic little 2-strokes.

MATERIALS FOR BOATBUILDING

Materials should be as strong and as light as possible, within the constraints of cost. The construction must be stiff, so as to resist deformation under the loads imposed by sail or engine drive system and by wave action. It must retain its strength over many years of hard use without weakening through flexing and fatigue. Steel and ferro-cement are too heavy and impracticable for small craft; aluminium is much more attractive. However it is not only expensive, but in the thin plate needed for a small boat, it tends to sag between the ribs and soon takes on a 'hungry horse' appearance. It is also vulnerable to puncture from rocks and even from beach stones. So our choice lies between GRP, wood, or a composite of the two.

GRP

Glass reinforced plastics are the combination of materials almost invariably used in commercial production, and the cheapest – provided that a sufficient number of hulls can be taken off the moulds, which are very costly pieces of tooling, and hence of no interest to the homebuilder unless, as is sometimes possible, he can hire them. A GRP laminate consists of a synthetic resin, usually polyester, reinforced with myriads of fine glass filaments – each barely one-tenth the thickness of a human hair. This glass is supplied either in the form of a mat of randomly-laid chopped strands (CSM), or as a coarse cloth woven from strings of glass threads, much stronger than CSM but unable to absorb as much resin. When all the reinforcement is made with CSM, it accounts for about a third of the weight of the hull; if all cloth (known as 'woven rovings') is used, it makes up around two-thirds of its total weight. The moulder will often use a combination of the two, according to the strength required in the various areas of the hull. A hard and glossy, pigmented outer skin, the 'gelcoat', protects the underlying laminate from absorbing water and resists abrasion.

Unlike timber, GRP is far from being a user-friendly material and it is also relatively heavy, so that it lacks positive buoyancy. What's more, it is not only a poor thermal and sound insulator, but its indifferent panel stiffness has to be corrected in key areas by additional ribs and stringers, adding weight to what may already be a heavy structure. Nevertheless, the finished hulls are tough and resilient, with – in theory – an almost indefinite life. They can also be made unsinkable by injecting foam between the hull and an inner moulding, and their surface finish can remain immaculate for many years, given a little maintenance.

A GRP hull does need periodic cleaning and polishing to remove any surface scratches, and the occasional application of a polymer sealant. Otherwise the gelcoat becomes prone to staining and susceptible to ultra violet light which causes oxidation. Once this deterioration has started, water penetration can follow and the damage soon becomes more than merely cosmetic. GRP hulls can also fall prey to osmosis, although fortunately this is less prevalent in today's hulls, thanks to improved techniques and materials. It is caused, initially, by slight porosity or local imperfections in the gelcoat, which allow water to penetrate below its surface. Here it absorbs any of the styrene or other solvents left over from the curing of the resin. The resulting pockets of fluid then draw in further water from the outside by the process known as osmosis. The result is a rash of tiny surface blisters which ultimately burst, leading to further deterioration and eventual delamination and weakening of the GRP itself. The only way to repair it is to remove the affected areas by shot-blasting, and to recoat them with polyurethane or epoxy resin.

Isophthalic resin is used in the lay-up of some top quality hulls instead of polyester. Despite its considerably higher cost, it has similar mechanical properties to those of glass and is more compatible with it, producing a significantly stronger laminate which is also more resistant to attack by osmosis.

A number of commercial boatbuilders offer bare hulls for home completion at somewhere about a half to one-third the price of a finished boat. Attractive as this may sound, you should check that essentials such as keel, deck and superstructure, hatches, internal mouldings and engine beds are included in the deal. It is usual to buy a hull with its 'lid' already fitted, because lifting the superstructure into place at home can be difficult, and it also stiffens the top of the hull to ensure that it stays the correct shape while it is being transported and unloaded. A roomy 22 ft (6.7 m) motor cruiser from Viking Mouldings, for example, can be bought at around a Group 2 price as an assembled set of bare mouldings. By the time the cruiser is ready to go to sea, it is comparable to Group 4. Similar figures apply to sailboats such as the Hunter 21, the neat little cruiser/racer mentioned earlier, whose manufacturers go a helpful step further by providing various additional kits of parts and fittings as optional extras, including furnishing items and even the spars and sails.

When buying any bare hull-and-deck, however, don't be misled by the apparently generous cost savings, since these must obviously be reflected in the amount of your labour that will be needed before the boat can be launched, and the price of the hardware which can cost twice as much as the empty shell. But the savings are none the less valuable, for without necessarily requiring the skills of a professional craftsman you should still end up with a bargain.

In praise of wood

Despite the almost universal use of moulded GRP in series production, timber, the original mariners' material, is still the best for individual or small scale boatbuilding. It is comparatively inexpensive, if you exclude the heavy hardwoods such as teak, and it is readily available in a wide variety of ready-made forms, shapes and sizes. Simple to shape and fabricate, it is essentially pleasant and satisfying to work with, non-toxic and biodegradable. It is also, without question, one of the stiffest of all structural substances for a given weight, while its strength-to-weight ratio and fatigue resistance are surpassed by only the most exotic and expensive of space age materials.

Furthermore, and perhaps even more importantly, wooden boats seem somehow to possess a character seldom found in their plastic sisters, as well as being much easier to customise (the mark of the individualist, which so many sailors are) – and to repair. What is better known about wood is its susceptibility to atmospheric moisture absorption and rot. Traditionally, wooden construction has always suffered from the bogey of damp. This not only makes it dimensionally unstable but, if allowed to get into the fabric of the timber, requires particularly good ventilation to avoid the onset of rot of one kind or another, with consequent structural deterioration. But these problems have largely been eliminated by the development of high performance adhesives and treatments (most of which *are* toxic) and techniques to take maximum advantage of these modern synthetics.

Before finally deciding on wood as your preferred material, it is important to understand the reasons for its behaviour. There are textbooks on the subject for those who would like to study it in more detail, but the following should suffice for now. The trouble with untreated timber is that its properties change with the weather; notably in the way that quite small variations in the level of humidity

Fig 14 A 15 ft micro cruiser designed by that innovative American Phil Bolger for simple construction in sheet plywood. Her accommodation includes two sleeping berths, with space for cooker and toilet. There are free-flooding wells at either end of the boat to ensure that inventory items such as outboard motor fuel, muddy anchors and warps won't contaminate the living area. A cat-yawl rig and sprit boom make her sails easy to handle and stow. *Illustration: Stephen L Davis courtesy of* Woodenboat *magazine*

cause it to swell or shrink across the grain as the fibres absorb or expel moisture through their pores. This dimensional instability, which seldom occurs evenly and often varies between adjacent pieces, in turn leads to warping and splitting due to the internal stresses, and to leaks.

Wood is also susceptible to decay by fungal growth which destroys the fibres and turns timber into a weak and crumbly sponge. It has been said that more wooden ships were lost through rot than through all the storms and naval battles of recorded history. For the fungi spores to exist, they need oxygen and warmth, and the wood itself must be at or near saturation point. Neither very dry nor totally submerged timber is likely to rot, hence the survival of so many ancient wrecks. Seawater actually kills any spores it can reach, which is why fishing boats periodically used to be sunk for 'pickling'. While a boat is afloat, however, rainwater must be kept out of the woodwork, which is not too difficult with modern paints and varnishes. Every nook and cranny must also be protected from atmospheric condensation, by means of adequate ventilation, in order to keep it stable, as well as to prevent rot.

Epoxy resin

Without good ventilation, the humid atmosphere of a cruiser's warm cabin (supplemented by evaporation from wet crew or sails in foul weather, condensation from the galley, and perhaps a little bilge water) can quickly generate a destructive 100% humidity. The only sure way to keep the moisture vapour away from the wood is to coat every piece of it with a protective film of a suitably formulated resin. This may sound tedious, but in fact it's a quick and perfectly straightforward process, provided the manufacturer's instructions on mixing and application are followed scrupulously. Epoxy is by far the best, though also the most expensive.

Conveniently, exactly the same resin, in slightly differing forms, is used for all the bonding and jointing operations. Mixed with a filler it makes a thick paste for reinforcing fillets, or a thin one for gap filling. Due to this particular characteristic, there is no need for you to be a craftsman or trained boatbuilder, or even a DIY expert. Don't worry if you are unable to make an accurate, close-fitting joint; the epoxy will fill the gap. You can dispense with the traditional wooden fillets in the construction of furniture, bunks and bulkheads (which no longer need to be a close fit to their neighbouring parts) and replace them with epoxy fillets which can be applied with a spatula and moulded to any shape, saving much time. Knowing that these internal joinery components will be securely bonded to one another, the designer will have been able to reduce much of the duplication in

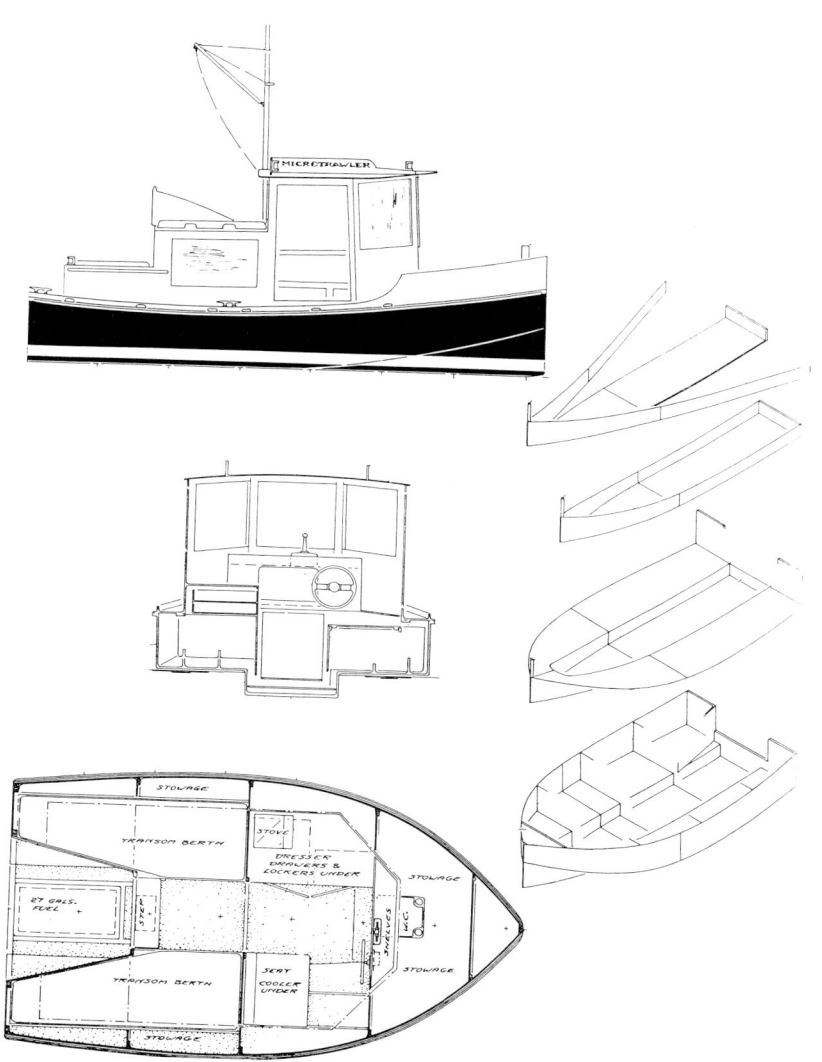

Fig 15 Another of Phil Bolger's free-thinking designs, Microtrawler, a 14 ft 6 in motor cruiser with standing headroom in the wheelhouse, helmsman's seat over the icebox, two full-length berths, galley and loo, and space for either outboard or a small inboard engine. Construction is of taped-seam plywood; the simple assembly sequence for a 'stepped sharpie' such as this is shown in the diagram on the right. Flat-bottomed boats should not be dismissed as primitive or over-simplified. They are very good load carriers, stable afloat or aground, lightweight, easily driven and, of course, comparatively easy to build.

labour and material by using many of them as structural load-bearing members.

Epoxy also provides a hard, durable surface that can be painted or varnished where necessary – for example, to shield it from sunlight, which degrades it. Saturating the timber with resin has the additional benefit, particularly with softwoods, of increasing its compressive strength. By distributing the loads on each joint over much larger areas than would be possible with mechanical fastenings such as screws or bolts, the integrity of the structure is guaranteed; every joint is then stronger than the parts that comprise it.

It certainly is a wonder material, but epoxy's disadvantages should also be recognised. Firstly, there's the health risk. Epoxy requires strict handling precautions, such as the wearing of plastic gloves and good ventilation, because its hardeners and solvents are sensitisers and irritants, and their fumes are toxic. The dust from sanding when the resin has hardened is also toxic, so face masks are essential for this part of the operation.

Like wood, it needs a warm, dry working environment in order to ensure a good bond. And it is *very* expensive, accounting for anything up to half the cost of a wooden hull. There are several other adhesives, such as polyurethane, that are much cheaper and simpler to use, non-toxic, more tolerant of working conditions, and perfectly adequate for the less highly stressed joints. But few of them have epoxy's gap-filling capability and none have its physical strength, so they require correspondingly higher standards of workmanship and like paint, which is similarly water resistant and not totally impervious, they cannot form that essential vapour barrier around wooden components.

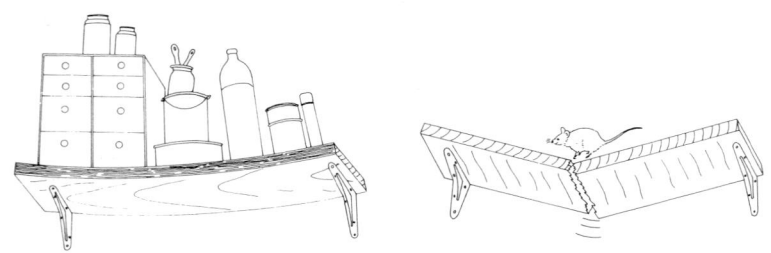

FRAME-AND-PLANK TECHNIQUE

Most of our contemporary boatbuilding techniques have evolved from the traditional frame-and-plank system that has served shipwrights for centuries and is still used on most of the largest wooden boats today. It starts with a rigid building base or strongback, built from baulks of timber levelled and squared on the workshop floor. Two timbers run the length of the planned boat, and about ten more are fastened across them at intervals corresponding to the 'stations' on the hull plan. If the floor is in good condition the strongback is unnecessary, each frame instead being supported and precisely aligned on a pair of legs, chocked to the floor to prevent them from sliding about. Attached to them (keel uppermost because for ease of working, boats are mostly built upside down) are the transverse frames which are shaped in outline to represent the hull cross-sections at each station, with the stem and sternposts standing up at either end.

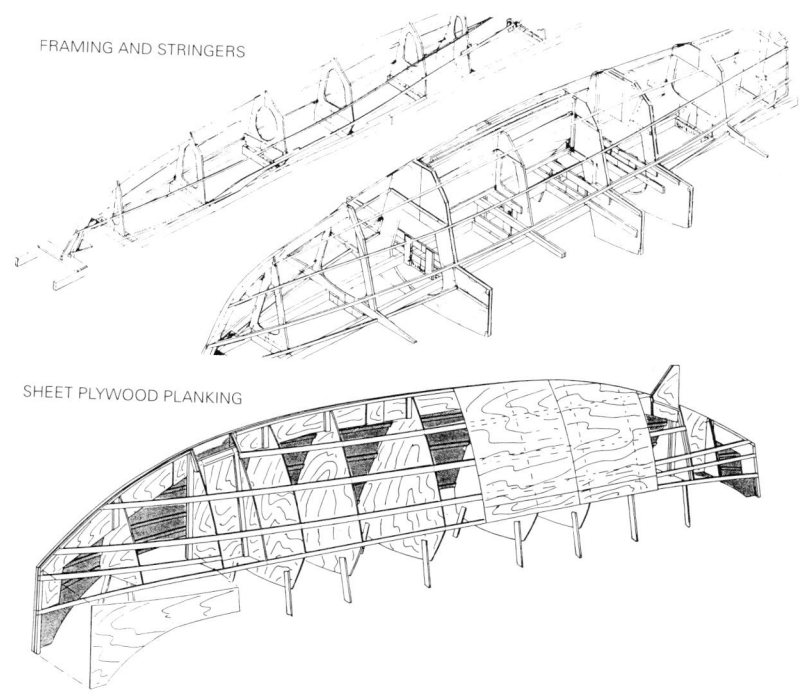

FRAMING AND STRINGERS

SHEET PLYWOOD PLANKING

Fig 16 Opposite: Timber is strong along the grain and comparatively weak across it. Plywood is comprised of bi-directional laminates which give it the same strength in both directions. Above: Construction of a typical plywood hull, showing framing, stringers and sheet planking.

Instead of the closely spaced oak timbers of the old, heavily planked vessels, many of today's wooden boats need only basic plywood formers, usually notched to accept a series of longitudinal ribs known as stringers, and an inner keel running like a backbone across the apex of the frames. With the development of epoxy, however, and the latest forms of waterproof plywood, some designs – notably those of the smaller budget boats which we are concerned with – now dispense with framework of any kind, in favour of a simple building jig which is discarded after the hull is completed; others don't even need that.

Plywood

The simplest way to plank a hull is to use marine plywood, which comes in big, handy sheets, usually 8 ft by 4 ft (244 by 122 cm). It is not inclined to warp and, unlike timber, which is strong along its grain and comparatively weak across it, ply is comprised of bi-directional laminates which give it the same strength in both directions, whichever way it is cut. Unfortunately, top grade marine ply is expensive, being made up of a multiplicity of high quality, close-grained veneers of equal thickness, whereas many of the ordinary grades, notably those of Far Eastern Meranti – and even some of the so-called 'exterior' ones – have only three laminates. These include a baulk core which sometimes contains voids that are a source of weakness and a conduit for water penetration. So despite its cost, it is best to use genuine marine ply for its superior strength and reliability.

No plywood is waterproof, however. It must be well coated with epoxy, paint or vanish, and any exterior surface of the boat liable to be walked on, or have things dropped on it, or be subject to any sort of abrasion, should be sheathed in epoxy-saturated woven glass cloth. Without this protection, any area that sustains damage will be able to absorb moisture by capillary attraction. Epoxy is just as effective in keeping water in as it is in keeping it out, so the only way moisture can escape is via the surface damage, and then only very gradually through evaporation. The result is that a large area can soon become waterlogged, weakened through delamination, and in time rotten. Any ply edges exposed to the weather, or hidden under pads or cappings where rain or seawater might collect, should be similarly protected with glass cloth or tape. Given these precautions, a well-built plywood boat should last a lifetime.

The conventional technique is to fasten the plywood to a timber framework as a cladding, looking on it as simply a skin to keep the water out, and not necessarily taking into account the strength it adds to the structure. The main benefit of this method is that the panels can be put on oversize, instead of having to be cut precisely; they are trimmed to shape after the glue has set. The resulting hull is, o

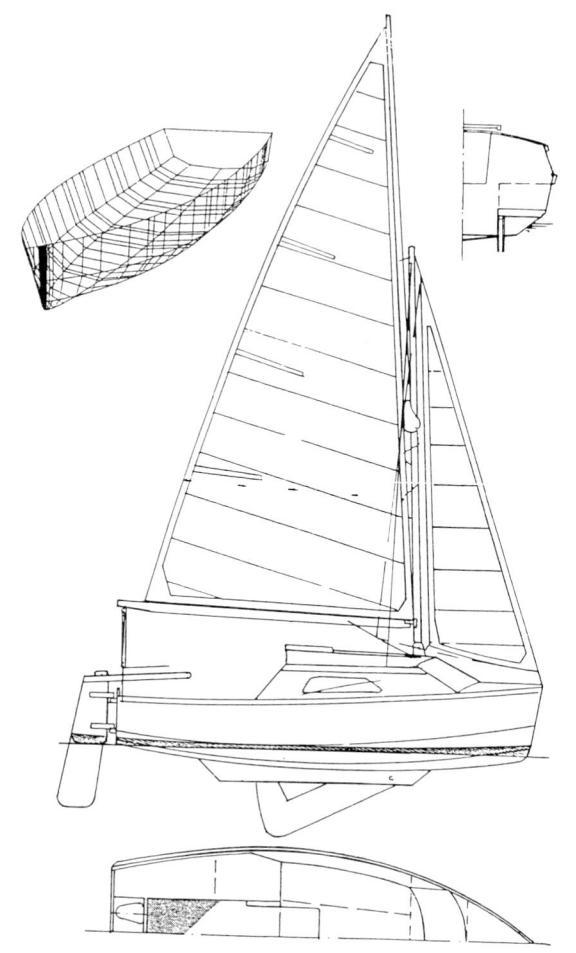

Fig 17 16 ft Lynx trailer-sailer. A design by Paul Fisher for home-building in sheet plywood. The cabin sides extend to the hull sides so as to provide comfortable sitting space and a large deck area to work on. Twin bilge plates are mounted in cases under the bunks beside a pair of water ballast tanks, leaving the cabin sole clear of obstructions. Twin skegs help her to sit securely on her trailer, and she weighs only 800 lb (360 kg). Building time is around 200 hours — call it a month's full-time work — and the cost of materials, including fittings and rig, falls inside Group 2.

course, heavier than a frameless one, and there will be bumps and hollows to be filled and sanded down to obtain a good finish. Moreover, as ply of the necessary thickness can only be bent to any extent in one plane, its shape is restricted to a straight, or at best gently rounded vee, or alternatively to a multi-chine cross section. You also have to take into account the time and material spent on the framework. But this will always remain a very attractive way of building a boat on account of its basic simplicity, and because it is not confined to small craft, unlike the next process to be described.

STITCH-AND-TAPE TECHNIQUE

When you bend plywood (or any other form of sheeting), it becomes very stiff across the direction of the bend. By making use of this property, and at the same time bonding the panel joints simply by using epoxy along their mating edges instead of holding them together via a solid timber structure, you can produce a boat which is not only lighter, stiffer, and quicker to build, but cheaper too. The 11 ft (3.3 m) Mirror pram dinghy was the first design to make use of what is known as 'stitch-and-tape' technology. Here the art of boatbuilding is akin to that of dress- or sailmaking, whose flat cloth panels with curved edges become three-dimensional when they are stitched to one another.

The process begins by making up two rectangular plywood panels of the necessary length, by means of scarfed or simple butt-strap joints, placing them on top of one another, and cutting out a pair of identical hull panels to the designed shape. Next, these are opened out, temporarily stitched together along the line of the keel with copper wire (or, at a pinch, ordinary garden wire), and then forced up into the required hull shape, using clamps and tourniquets ('Spanish windlasses'). After checking that the boat is 'square' and not twisted or otherwise out of shape, the mating edges are bonded together with epoxy. When this has cured – the term used to describe the chemical reaction between the liquid resin and the hardening agent that has been added to it – the wiring is removed, the joint is filled in with epoxy putty and the inner face of the seam reinforced with woven glass tape soaked in the resin. Very little 'fairing' should be necessary before the hull is painted or varnished, because the plywood compounds naturally into very fair curves.

There are inherent constraints on the degree of compound curvature that can be induced in this way, and hence in the range of hull types for which it is suited. The ply itself must be fairly thin, preferably not more than about 5 mm, and in reasonably short panels, otherwise the force needed to bend it becomes excessive and impractical in an amateur workshop. This in turn limits the size of boat that can be built by this method, without too much of a struggle,

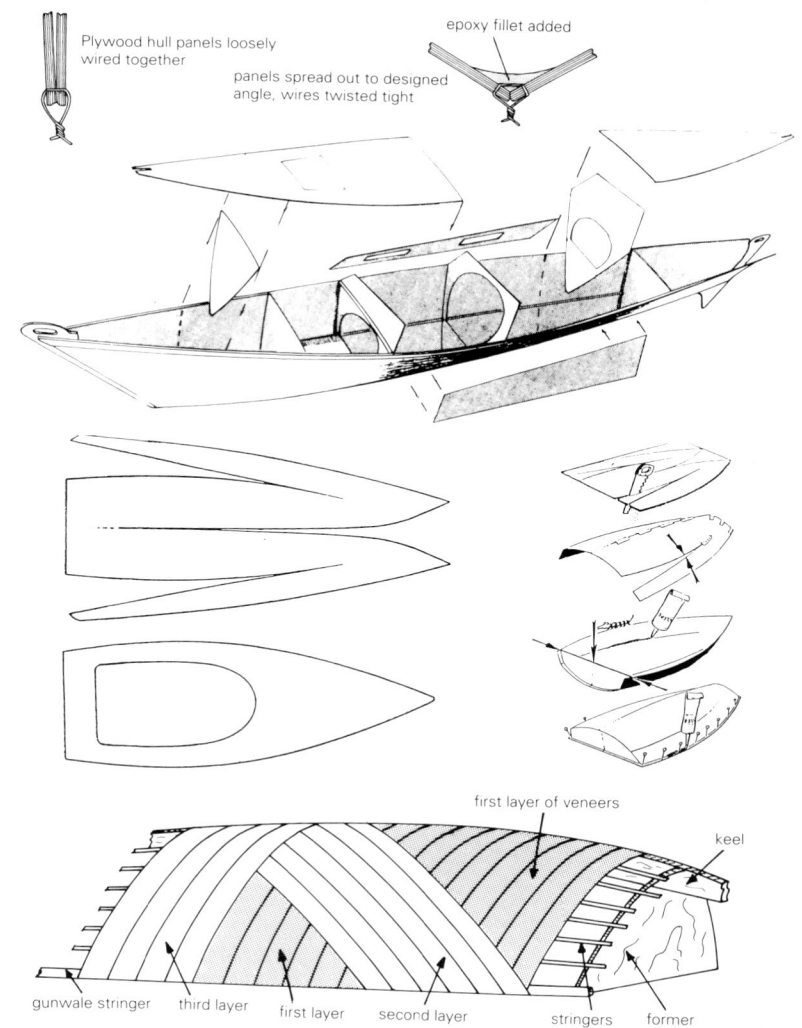

Plywood hull panels loosely wired together

epoxy fillet added

panels spread out to designed angle, wires twisted tight

first layer of veneers

keel

gunwale stringer   third layer   first layer   second layer   stringers   former

Fig 18 Top: The stitch-and-glue method. The two hull sides are wired together along the keel, and then opened out to receive the bulkheads. Centre: The Segerling dinghy is built on this principle. Try it for yourself, in miniature. Photocopy-enlarge this pattern and trace it on to card, pull into shape using modelling glue, then assemble hull on to deck, upside down, using dressmaking pins. Plans from Wendy Fitzgerald (see Appendix 4). Bottom: Laminating. Veneer strips are stapled to the stringers and edge-glued to one another. Successive diagonal layers are then bonded on and sealed with epoxy resin.

to around 18 ft (5.5 m). For larger boats, the designer sometimes combines the use of stressed ply with the earlier technique of using oversized panels in areas where their fitting is not critical.

CLINKER OR LAPSTRAKE CONSTRUCTION

A very attractive alternative way of building boats ranging from small dinghies up to cruisers as big as 36 ft (11.0 m), is to use a glued clinker or lapstrake form of construction. Clinker-built boats have been with us for hundreds of years, and there are still large numbers in service today as dinghies, fishing boats, launches and, until quite recently, as lifeboats. They were constructed from a series of slender overlapping strakes, each one individually shaped and riveted with copper nails to a row of supporting, steamed-and-bent timber frames. Lapstrake boats are still sometimes built like this for the connoisseur, but in the modern equivalent the frames are replaced by half a dozen or more fore-and-aft members known as stringers. Temporary scrap-wood or chipboard moulds act as a building frame to hold the components in place during assembly. The curved strakes are cut from plywood. One after another, beginning at the bottom, they are pinned to the moulds, epoxied to one another along their overlapping edges as well as to the stringers, and to a keelson or bottom plank forming the backbone of the boat. The 'lands' between adjoining strakes are then reinforced with thickened epoxy, and external components such as keel, bilge runners and other doubling pieces are finally added. Besides the attractive appearance of the lapstrake form on a small boat, the overlapping strakes tend to suppress spray and make for a drier ride. Moulds are sometimes taken from clinker-built wooden craft to simulate lapstrake on GRP hulls, where the corrugated effect adds considerably to the panel stiffness without increasing the weight.

This form of frameless building is particularly strong and resilient for its weight, for its allows the hull to flex under load, easing out any potential high stress points. As designer Colin Mudie puts it, a frame can act as the knee across which you break sticks. For the same reason, the athwartships components such as seats, mast supports and deck beams are best carried on the stringers instead of directly on the hull sides. Freed of the geometrical restrictions imposed by sheet panel cladding, the designer also has more scope to achieve graceful, sweeping sheerlines. But lapstrake construction is considerably more time-consuming, and it takes patience and a certain amount of practice to translate the design drawings and dimensions into the full-sized strakes and to assemble them successfully. It is a process that cannot be rushed and, except perhaps in the case of the smallest pram dinghies, is better suited to the ambitious amateur prepared to take the extra time and accept some delays, than to the beginner

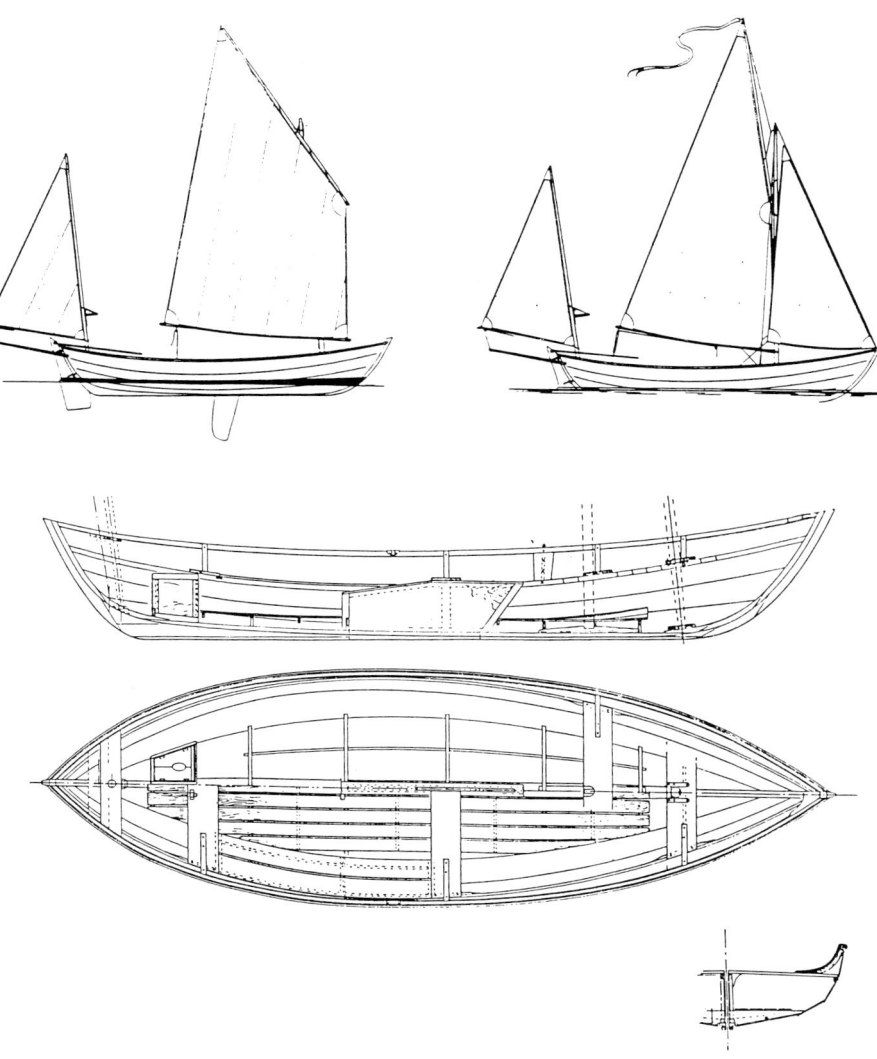

Fig 19 This 19 ft Caledonia Yawl designed by Iain Oughtred is a handsome example of lapstrake plywood construction, without any frames or stringers. There is enough room for two to sleep on overnight cruises under a cockpit tent; the bottom boards can be raised to give a flat and level floor for this purpose. Building time is about 200 hours; materials including rig are in the Group 2 range.

doubtful of his skills and anxious to see results before the project begins to lose its initial impetus.

LAMINATING AND STRIP PLANKING

Before leaving the subject of wood, two more methods of using it in boatbuilding should be mentioned, although both are even more time-consuming, and will probably only appeal to the more ambitious amateur. The first is termed laminating, in which the stringers, a large number of them, are closely spaced across some temporary framework so as to define the hull shape as precisely as possible, and very thin strips of ply – sometimes even of single veneers – are stapled diagonally across them. The more severe the curvature, the narrower the strips have to be, and each one must be painstakingly tapered towards its ends so that it can lie snugly alongside its neighbour, allowing for the compound nature of the curve. This is followed by several successive layers, epoxied and stapled at right-angles to the preceding one. It is altogether a very laborious process, as you can imagine, but it produces a light, strong and resilient semi-monocoque shell that makes a particularly handsome sight when varnished, as for example in the case of sculling boats such as the racing 'fours' and 'eights'.

The second technique to take a quick look at is strip planking. Transverse frames or bulkheads, linked by a keel and a few stringers, are planked from bow to stern with narrow strips of a lightweight stable timber such as Western red cedar, edge-glued together and skinned externally with epoxy-saturated glass cloth. This not only provides the necessary stiffness, but resists abrasion and lessens the risk of damage from impact. Being transparent, it can also be varnished if this is preferred to painting, given a high enough standard of visible workmanship. The further apart the two load-bearing skins and the greater the consequent thickness of the sandwich, the stiffer it becomes, the principal purpose of the core being to increase the thickness without adding significantly to its weight. Certain synthetic materials, such as closed cell foam, can be used for the core in place of wood, although they tend to crush more readily and consequently require heavier skins.

On the whole, sandwich hulls are light and strong, whilst providing a considerable degree of both sound and thermal insulation, and positive buoyancy in the event of flooding – though not well enough to sustain the weight of a heavy engine or lead keel. Compared with all-wooden construction, however, they take considerably longer to build, cost more in materials, and are more difficult to repair in the event of impact damage. Furthermore, there is a scale effect which progressively reduces their weight and strength advantage the smaller the hull becomes. A dinghy built like this, for example, aside from being unnecessarily complicated, would actually be heavier than a solid wooden one. So neither of the last two methods can really be recommended for a budget boat, despite their other undeniable advantages.

GRP KIT PANEL CONSTRUCTION

There is, however, one more system which may appeal to those with a preference for 'everlasting' plastics in place of treewood, and who would like to try their hand at building in this material without the need for special moulds. It is known as the GRP kit panel system. Instead of cladding a wooden framework with plywood, you cover it with home-made panels of GRP, prefabricated on a mould table made from kitchen-type melamine faced chipboard. This is first coated with a release agent to prevent the panel from sticking to it, followed by a coating of coloured resin for the gelcoat outer skin. As soon as it has partially cured, one or more layers of glass cloth saturated in polyester (or one of the other resins) are applied, worked in with a roller, and left to cure. Foam sandwich panels can be made up in the same way. When they are taken off the table, they will have acquired the melamine's mirror finish and need no further surface treatment, or painting. They are also sufficiently flexible to be sprung into a gentle radius, though not into compound curves. The panels are then assembled against the frames as if they were pieces of ply, bonded to any that are to remain in place. The corners (chines) are filled with resin putty – or by sections of compound-curved 'corner mouldings' made in a similar way on thin ply formers. The basic materials needed for this method of construction cost much the same as buying the plywood sheets, and you certainly save on the finishing and painting; the rest – the labour in making the panels – is extra.

SAILMAKING

Like boatbuilding, home sailmaking can be immensely satisfying, besides saving money, and in its simpler forms requires no special talents. Yet while many people nowadays build their own boats, comparatively few aspire to making their own sails. To most of us, there appears to be more than a touch of professional magic in a well-cut suit of sails; but in fact the magic lies not so much in the making as in their design. In the case of the high-tech racers this has become a science in its own right, using a range of specialist materials. Such sails are best left to the professional lofts, but there's nothing particularly tricky about making sails for a small cruising boat.

Armed with a set of drawings, which the boat's designer can usually supply if they don't already form part of his DIY package, all you need is care, a generous measure of determination, and most important of all, plenty of space in which to work on and around the sails. This means commandeering a large, flat area that will accommodate the largest sail, full size, preferably with a wooden surface so that the individual cloths can be laid out and held in place with spikes (thumb tacks or map pins if you object to leaving holes in the living room floor).

The most essential piece of equipment is the sewing machine – an ordinary domestic model that can do zig-zag is perfectly satisfactory for small boat sails up to about 20 m^2 in area. In addition you will require:

- A sharp knife and a pair of large dressmaking scissors.
- An electric soldering iron for heat-sealing the raw edges of cloth and rope ends.
- A hand-sewing palm, which is made of thick leather and worn on the hand for protection when pushing the needle through the sailcloth.
- A selection of sailmaker's needles in sizes from 10 to 15.
- A collection of spikes. You can make them from cheap screwdrivers, sharpened to a point (or thumb tacks/map pins). 2 kg weights will also do the job, but you will need plenty of them.
- A 10 m metal tape measure.
- A bendy wooden batten for marking out the curved lines.
- A fid, which is a tapered spike made of hardwood, used for opening the lay of a rope when making a splice.
- Chalk and string for marking out the floor and the cloth.

The materials consist of polyester (Terylene or Dacron) sailcloth of the specified weight – 150 gm/m^2 for an ordinary dinghy, for example, and say 200 gm for a small cruiser's mainsail – allowing about 25% more than the area of the sails for making accessory items such as sail batten pockets, and the reinforcement pieces at the corners and edges, (and some 20 gm ripstop nylon if you are going to make a spinnaker). You will also need waxed polyester twine (1 or 2 kg) for hand seaming; medium polyester thread for the sewing machine (nylon for the spinnaker); some rolls of double-sided sticky tape; pre-stretched polyester rope and tape; and the various accessories shown on the plan, such as slides, rings, hooks and thimbles.

You start by drawing the shape of the sail, full size, on the floor, spiking each corner and stretching the string tightly around them from one to the next. Then from the plan, measure the depths of curvature along the edges and chalk these points at intervals on the floor, and draw a line through the points with the bendy batten. Finally, draw another line 2 cm or so outside this one to allow for the tabling (hem) along the leech and foot, and about 4 cm for the rope or tape reinforcement on the luff (and between the throat and peak of a four-sided sail).

Next, there's the actual cutting. Woven cloth will stretch and begin to fold if it is pulled at an angle to its threadlines, but remains stable when the tension is along the weft or the warp (try it on your handkerchief). Most sails are cut horizontally, with the threadlines running more or less at right angles to the leech, which is usually under stress and where stretch must be avoided. This results in the cloth meeting the boom on the bias, and the designer uses this as a means of inducing some fullness, or 'flow', into the sail, depending on its shape and size, and how he wants it to perform. There is a variety of different cuts that can be used – mitre, vertical, radial, cross-cut, etc – but the horizontal cut is the simplest and most common. So in this case you begin by laying and cutting a foot panel at 90° to the leech. Pin it in position before you lay the next one, allowing for a seam overlap of about 1 mm for every 10 gm/m^2 cloth weight, running parallel and then broadening out as it approaches the luff on most sails (above dinghy size), depending on where the designer wishes to introduce flow into the flat shape. Number each panel as you cut it, sticking it to the previous panel with the double-sided tape to prevent it from creeping up on the next one, and removing the pins as you progress.

The sail is now ready for stitching. Position the sewing machine close to the floor with plenty of space around it for handling the large pieces of cloth. Starting with the first two panels, sew from leech to luff, keeping close to the outer edge along the seam. Then turn the material over and sew a second row along the other edge. When all the panels are joined in this way, lay the resulting sail back on the floor over the chalked plan and pin down the corners, stretching it just sufficiently to remove the wrinkles. You can now turn back and crease the material along the chalk line, seal the raw edges with the soldering iron, lay in place the leechline and any drawstrings that may be needed later for pulling a rope through the tabling, and sew down the edges. Next come the batten pockets, cut so that their threadline runs in the same direction as it does on the sail, and approximately half as wide again as the battens themselves. Finally, there's the all-important and painstaking process of hard sewing the various reinforcement strips and patches, slides or hanks, cringles, grommets eyelets and reef points, any luff or headropes, and the headboard when one is specified.

Like boatbuilding itself, sailmaking is a major subject in its own right, and this sketchy outline is only included here in order to give the reader some idea of what is involved. Before deciding whether to have a go at it yourself, you would be well advised to study one of the specialist books on the subject. It may all sound like rather an ambitious programme, especially if it follows the building of an entire boat, but in fact it's not such a lengthy process as it may at first appear. The result will then be there for all to see, to be remembered and admired every time the sails are hoisted; and at least the making of them will have been a refreshing change from working for weeks in wood or plastics.

Whichever way you choose to build your boat, and in whatever materials, there is so much to enjoy in the process that it is not surprising that some people find they enjoy building them as much as they do sailing them. At the launching, there can be no one prouder than the person who has created her with his own hands. Setting out on the water in a boat you have built yourself is a dream that has been shared over the years by countless aspiring sailors, and nowadays, for the majority, it can be realised.

PLANS FOR HOME-BUILDERS

If you would like a list of suppliers of plans for home-builders, please send a stamped addressed envelope to the publishers at the address given on page ii.

6·WHEELS UNDER YOUR KEEL

Whether you build a boat or buy one, power or sail, you are likely to be faced with the problem of where to keep her economically, and a trailer could provide the ideal solution.

TRAILER SAILING

Not so very long ago, only dinghies and small dayboats could be stored ashore when not in use, and simply put into the water when they were required. Larger boats usually spent their lives on an open water mooring between trips. You reached it in your dinghy, or were ferried out by the club or boatyard launch. Nowadays, as we have seen, boat parking is big business. Faced with the difficulty of renting a private mooring or finding a site where you may lay one of your own, you are all too often left with only one alternative to paying for a convenient but prohibitively expensive berth in a marina: part-voyaging by road, taking your vessel to the water on a trailer.

Dry-sailing brings many other benefits besides economy to the small craft owner. The concept is now widely accepted as a logical and extremely attractive alternative to having any kind of moored or marina-based boat whose weekend cruising range will, in all likelihood, seldom exceed thirty or forty miles, even under ideal circumstances. Let's face it, for all their convenience when cruising, there's an uninspiring sameness about most marinas, each one looking exactly like the one you just left. Instead, using the family car to tow the boat, you are free to choose your cruising ground, attend events or spend holidays far from your home port. You can go abroad if you wish, taking a car ferry, with no worries about the weather. You can also use the boat itself as a caravan during the journey. Admittedly, a small craft has only limited accommodation and creature comforts, but your opportunities for exploration will broaden considerably.

There is, of course, the unavoidable chore of launching and recovery which occasionally, on awkward terrain or in bad weather, can become something of a hassle. There's also, regrettably, still a shortage of launching sites in some parts of Britain, although pressure is increasing on local authorities to improve

FEATURES

1 Rudder blade clamp – holds well but you have to lean over the transom to adjust and lock blade in position.

2 Outboard mounted on transom bracket is easily lifted from water.

3 Fuel tank stows neatly in cockpit locker adjacent to engine position.

4 Bilge pump conveniently mounted in side of cockpit well.

5 Deep galley stowage bin. Useful place for stowing tins.

6 Pop-top with large companionway hatch lifts to give 5 ft 7 in headroom and is enclosed by canvas hood.

7 Stowage locker for anchor and warp, but no bow roller as standard.

8 One of the many stowage lockers.

9 Rigid water tank can be easily lifted out for filling and cleaning.

10 Chemical toilet stows unobtrusively in forecabin area.

11 Spirit stove, an optional extra.

12 Tee bolt to clamp centre plate down to stop it vibrating under sail.

13 Centreplate pivot bearing.

14 Lift-out cool box doubles as companionway step.

15 Centreplate projects below hull when swung into the up position.

16 Battery housed in cockpit locker.

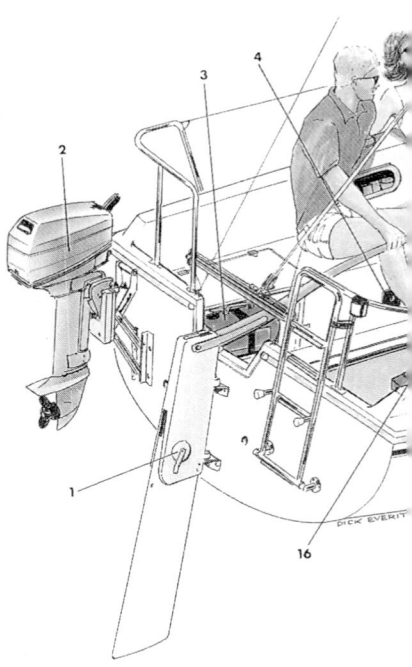

their waterside facilities. On the other hand, you will have free parking for the boat, sitting on her trailer in the security of your own driveway or garden, and readily accessible for maintenance or odd jobs whenever you feel like tackling them. In addition, you will avoid the boatyard's considerable charge for haul-out and winter storage, and for putting her back in the water at the start of the season. But without the long periods afloat, and provided you give the bottom a periodic wash to remove any algae that may be starting to form, you will be saved the annual expense and chore of applying antifouling paint, which is not only costly but is invariably messy to apply. A further bonus is that your decks will remain clear of bird fouling, which can at times be a nuisance in coastal areas.

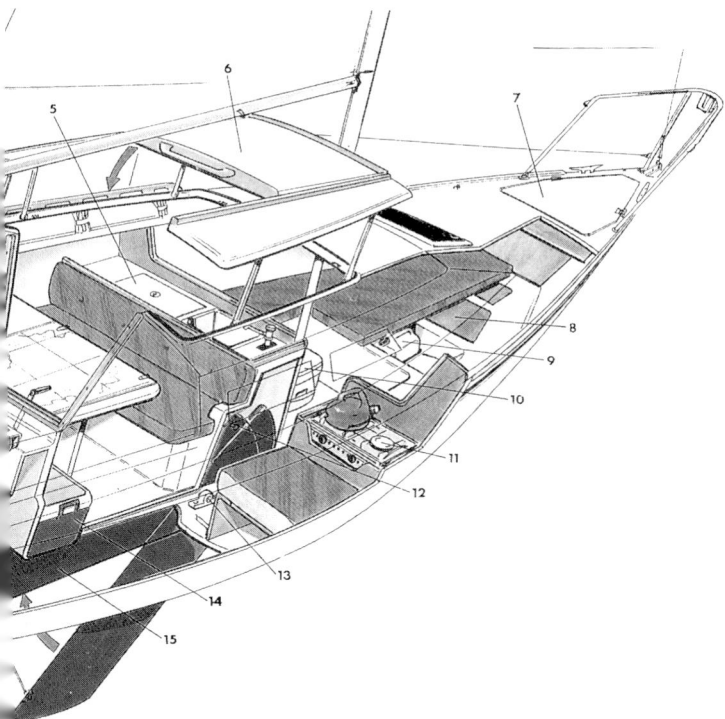

Fig 20 The anatomy of a good trailer-sailer, the Catalina 22. The lighter the boat, the smaller the car it takes to tow her; and the shallower her draught, the less the depth of water she will need to float clear of the trailer. *Drawing: Dick Everitt courtesy of* Practical Boat Owner *magazine*

WHAT SORT OF BOAT FOR TRAILING?

Almost any small powerboat can be trailed, provided it meets the regulations that govern, among other things, the total weight and width of the load behind your car. The same applies to sailboats, but in their case there is a big difference between a legally trailerable boat and what can be classed as a true trailer-sailer. There are many types that you can, for example, take with you on a week or fortnight's holiday. But there are few that can be launched and retrieved easily enough in a single weekend and allow you a worthwhile period afloat; day trips are normally impractical. There are some clever designs, however, in which you can be afloat in just a matter of minutes. These are the ones that will give you the least toil and the most sailing time over the season. Catamarans incidentally, for all their other virtues, do not show up particularly well in this respect (with the exception of the few designs with fixed bridgedeck accommodation, such as the Cracksman). With most of them, their two hulls, stowed side by side on a telescopic or wide flat-bed trailer, involve the extra time needed to drag them apart and fit their crossbeams and cockpit decking before they can be launched. The whole procedure has to be carried out in reverse before you can head back home.

If you build the boat yourself, you can choose the design accordingly. If you are shopping for a ready-made boat, it is worth paying close attention to certain primary features, notably weight. Lightness is one of the keys to success in any trailer boat, power or sail. It dictates not only the size and type (and cost) of buying and running the tow car, but the ease of manhandling the boat on the slipway. This latter consideration even applies to dinghies on their rudimentary launching trollies, a light pram or little racer being, quite literally, child's play; whereas a solidly built 14 footer can prove very hard work for anyone without a helper. Many dinghy slips are not directly accessible to a car with a winch-equipped trailer.

Powered dayboats and small cruisers generally present no problems. Once you have decided which category to go for, it is just a matter of matching the weight of any particular model that takes your fancy to the towing capacity of the car, or vice versa. Powerboats undoubtedly lend themselves to spur-of-the-moment boating decisions. They need only a bit of practice in manoeuvring them on and off the trailer. Rigging a sailboat, on the other hand, can take a lot of additional time and muscle unless its geometry is specifically aimed at minimising hassle on the slipway. A tall, unwieldy spar can have you staggering around as if you were trying to toss the caber, unless it is pivoted near deck level in a 'tabernacle' and equipped with some form of detachable strut (such as the spinnaker pole guyed out at either side). A purpose-built A-frame to enable it to be raised or lowered, using a rope attached to the forestay and taken round a winch.

The alternative is to choose a gaff or gunter rigged boat with a short mast that can simply be pushed up while someone else heaves on the forestay. In either case, a detachable support for the mast near the stern will help overcome the strain of the initial lift when it is nearly horizontal. If the chainplates are at the same height as the mast pivot, the shrouds can remain lightly tensioned to provide the sideways support.

The critical measurement for the hull is the height of the boat's waterline from the road, as she sits on the trailer. Shallow draught, combined with a low-slung trailer, means that you won't have to take the outfit into deep water. You can even launch some of them without getting the wheel bearings wet. Owners of the heftier boats, however,

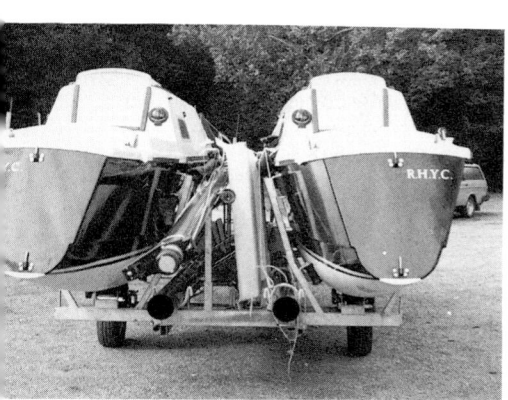

Top: A Strider catamaran, hulls demounted on a telescopic trailer. Right: Once assembled, she can be launched single-handed from a small slipway. Below: Launching and recovery takes less time with fixed bridgedeck designs such as this Cracksman 2, seen here ready to slide off the trailer which stays almost clear of the water.

Drawing barely 8 in (20 cm) of water, the Red Fox 200 floats off her trailer without even getting the wheel bearings wet. See page 42 for more about this 4-berth cruiser.

may tell you that a decent amount of draught and weight is a blessing in windy weather, as it helps prevent the boat from being blown about just when you are trying to line it up with the trailer. Boats with fixed keels, even twin-keelers, are at some disadvantage here, needing comparatively deep water before they can float clear. If you want to avoid wading in up to your chest with one of these, you will need to have it craned in and out from the quayside, but this is often expensive. Even a 16 footer can cost you as much as £50 for each lift (in or out), so it pays to do your own launching wherever you can.

Good examples of an easy-to-handle trailer sailer, in addition to the lifting keel boats mentioned in Chapter 2, are the Etap (French) and Dehler (German) 22 footers, drawing some 15 in (40 cm) or so, and the Swift 18 which manages to float in a bare 6 in (15 cm) of water. Like the others, they are well-equipped Group 4 boats, with four berths, easily managed rigs and their own mast raising equipment. If these are not affordable, there is invariably an attractive selection of similar cruising craft on the second-hand market at little more than half their new prices. If you are looking for the ultimate bargain, there are some excellent dayboats such as the Dockrell 17 and Bass Boat 16 to be found down in the Group 2 and 3 price range.

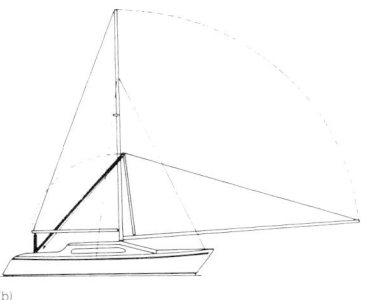

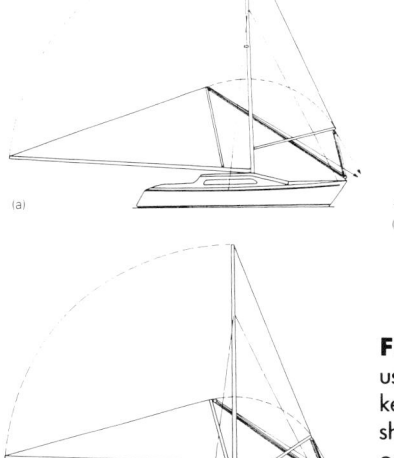

(a)

(b)

(c)

Fig 21 Raising and lowering the mast, using (a) the reversed boom or a spinnaker pole as a strut, (b) boom and mainsheet tackle, (c) an A-frame, its feet hinged on either·sidedeck. In this example, the mast is stepped in a tabernacle.

Below: A lightweight mast is easily raised with a second crewmember to steady it by taking up the slack in a line attached to the forestay.

Open boats and dinghies were, of course, the original 'trailer sailers' long before this label was invented.

THE LAW ON YOUR TRAIL

Before choosing either the boat or the tow car, it is worth taking a look at the principal regulations that are aimed at making them compatible and which affect the design of their common denominator, the trailer itself. These regulations can vary in detail between one country and another (in the USA even between neighbouring states). So although the regulations are common throughout the European Community, you should check with one of the motoring organisations or a national yachting authority such as the RYA in Britain for any differences if you intend venturing further abroad. Most police forces have the authority to 'stop and search' if for any reason they suspect you are breaking their local rules on size and loading, quite apart from speeding.

Towing speeds and size restrictions

Speed and size are simple matters. The almost universal speed restrictions while towing are 60 mph (96 kph) on motorways and 'split' highways, and 50 mph (80 kph) on all other roads except where a lower limit applies, such as in built-up areas. On a long journey, you should have no difficulty in averaging at least 35 mph (say 55 kph) excluding overnight stops. Size is also fairly straightforward. The trailer width is limited to 7 ft 6 in (2.3 m), but the boat may overhang it by a foot or 30 cm either side, resulting in a maximum permissible beam, including any projecting bits and pieces, of 9 ft 6 in (2.9 m). Length, as such, doesn't present a problem, because there is no specific restriction on it, but by the time a boat reaches, say, 28 ft (8.5 m) it will almost certainly be too heavy to tow.

Weight

The law says that if the gross towing weight (trailer + load) is more than 750 kg (1650 lb), the trailer must be fitted with brakes. Without brakes, the towing weight must be less than half that of the car. The legal limit with hydraulic auto-reverse or over-run brakes, as they are termed, is 3500 kg (7700 lb) which is much more than most cars can pull. Experience has shown that 1:1 is the maximum safe and sensible weight ratio between the trailer and a car with 2-wheel-drive. If you want to be conservative restrict it to 85%, or 1.5:1 for four-wheel-drive vehicles. The lighter the load in relation to the permitted maximum, the easier the driving will be.

Exceeding that maximum is not only illegal but could well invalidate the trailer warranty, to say nothing of your insurance in the

Four-wheel-drive is an advantage on a steep or slippery launching ramp.

event of an accident. The gross and unladen weights of the trailer and its serial number, together with the name and address of its manufacturer must be displayed on it. The car's kerb weight should be on a window sticker, so that the police can quickly check that you are within the legal limits. Also remember that front-wheel-drive cars lose a certain amount of traction on steep gradients as the weight distribution shifts from the front wheels to the back ones. So always check the manufacturer's recommendations in the handbook. They usually base them on the car's ability to restart on a 12% gradient.

The same goes for the weight of the boat bearing down on the tow hitch of the trailer. Insufficient nose weight invariably leads to snaking, which is not only dangerous but likely to attract the attention of the police. There is no actual legal requirement governing nose weight, but for stable towing it must always be positive – say five to ten percent of the total load. You can measure it on the bathroom scales, and adjust it either by moving the trailer axles, or by shifting one or two heavy items such as anchors or the outboard motor fore and aft in the boat (making sure that they are securely wedged or tied down afterwards). Don't forget to add the weight of these to the builder's figures for boat and trailer, together with all the rest of your cruising inventory, which can easily amount to several hundred pounds. Alternatively, load them aboard and visit the local weighbridge. Carry as much as you can in the boot of the car, in order to minimise the trailer load. If your boat has removable internal ballast, transferring it to the car will similarly improve the towing ratio by loading the latter and lightening the trailer.

WHICH TYPE OF CAR?

Generally speaking, most boats up to about 18 ft (5.5 m) can be trailed satisfactorily behind the average 1600 cc family saloon or utility. For sizes of 18 to 20 ft (5.5–6.1 m), a larger engine will be needed and for anything over 20 ft you will need a car or pick-up with a powerful engine or four-wheel-drive. A vehicle's weight alone is no guarantee of its suitability for towing; neither is its stated maximum power output which, in the case of high compression, fast revving sporty cars, is usually far too peaky to be of much practical use for towing. You need a good hefty torque response at reasonably low rpm for effective pulling. If you have to thrash the engine for much of the journey, especially in hilly country, to get the power you want, this will cause excessive wear and tear on it, and its transmission, not to mention the car's occupants.

Assuming that you have chosen the boat and are now buying the car, knowing the minimum weight and size you will need to tow it, it's best to ignore the horsepower figures and instead to look for one with a fairly big engine that develops plenty of torque low down in the rev range. Diesel engines are good in this respect, besides being economical on fuel, but unless they are of comparatively large capacity, or turbocharged, their performance can be a bit too sluggish.

As regards the rest of the vehicle, there are a number of desirable features worth having if you can afford them. Automatic transmission on a tow car certainly justifies its extra fuel consumption. It will enable you to move off smoothly from a standstill, even uphill, without worrying about having to slip the clutch and without snatching the trailer or inviting wheelspin. Similarly, the ABS system available on some cars stops any one wheel from locking when you brake on a slippery surface. Firm springing, preferably assisted by a set of load levellers and heavy duty shock absorbers, gives a more stable ride than a softer, more luxurious suspension that would be inclined to wallow around with a trailer behind it. Even better is one of the self-levelling systems, as fitted on the more expensive Citroën and Mercedes models, while power steering makes life much easier when you are manœuvring a car and trailer combination.

Finally, there's four-wheel-drive. This is well worth its cost if you plan to frequently tow your boat to slipways and haul out on steep and slippery slopes. Avoid buying the small engined off-the-road buggy with insufficient weight and a very short wheelbase; this will be inclined to produce a choppy ride and a correspondingly jerky tow. The larger specialist vehicles such as the Land and Range Rovers are much to be preferred, together with the big Nissans and Toyotas. Four-wheel-drive has become increasingly available on mid-range family cars like the Ford Sierra and Vauxhall Cavalier, which make excellent tow cars, besides being quiet and comfortable.

THE RIGHT TRAILER

Most manufacturers' catalogues show a basic range of trailers from which they produce tailor-made variants to suit some of the most popular boats. If yours is not among them, your enquiry should specify its overall length and beam, and the all-up weight including engine, battery and a full tank of fuel, as well as all the other gear you will be loading aboard. In the case of a small sportsboat with a powerful engine, for example, these extras could easily double its bare weight, much less so for a sailboat. Prices, as you might expect, vary widely according to the size and type of trailer and the complexity of its equipment, from a simple dinghy trailer for a few hundred pounds to a well specified twin-axle outfit costing as much as a Group 1 boat. So avoid buying anything more sophisticated than you need.

The frames of most good-quality trailers are made from hot-dipped galvanised steel. Aluminium trailers are lighter – you could expect to save perhaps 50 kg on a small one, as much as 200–300 kg on a large one – and they certainly last longer than steel ones, which are reckoned to begin rusting within 10–15 years where they are immersed in seawater. Unfortunately, however, aluminium trailers cost some 30–40% more, so it is not surprising that demand for them is fairly limited.

Next, there's the choice to be made between two wheels or four.

Two-wheeled trailers, besides being significantly cheaper than the twin-axled variety, are easier to manœuvre in a restricted space. The cost of a twin-axled trailer can be justified on long or frequent journeys by its superior stability. An added advantage is that, in the event of a burst tyre, there is another on the same side to steady the load while you slow down. Having decided on this, there are two basic forms of trailer to be considered, A-framed or T-framed, each with a choice between multiple sets of self-aligning, swinging arms carrying multiple rubber rollers to support the keel and hull, or – less expensive – a single set of keel rollers to take the weight, with a supportive 'bunk' or cushioned rail at either side to cradle the hull. A-frames have the advantage that the supports, and hence the boat, can be carried low down between the wheels. This in turn lowers the centre of gravity of the combined load and improves its stability under tow, and also allows the boat to float off or be winched back on to the trailer in shallower water than is the case with most T-frames.

Some of these have either a 'break-back' facility that lets part of the trailer tilt so that the boat slides off more readily, restrained if necessary with the winch wire; or a separate piggy-back, 4-wheeled launching trolley, running on ramps on the main chassis (and securely clamped to it while on the road). This carries the boat down into the

Fig 22 Laying your own temporary mooring – useful for picnics ashore when you don't want the boat stranded as the tide goes out.

water, leaving the road trailer with its vulnerable wheel bearings and brakes ashore in the dry. The trolley itself can be fitted with buoyancy collars so that it floats with the boat, making it very easy to recover.

Some manufacturers fit pressurised hubs to keep the water out of the bearings, and there are add-on hub caps that work on the same principle. There's nothing you can do, however, about wet brakes except to dowse them in fresh water and let them dry out, keeping them well serviced between trips. If you find yourself obliged to go in over the axles, at least wait for a few minutes after you arrive for the bearings to cool down; warm ones will suck in the salt water.

Adjustable trailer legs, or some other type of quick action ratchet jacks are essential to stop the whole outfit from rocking about or tipping up when you are clambering about on it. You will also need a boarding ladder for getting in and out of the boat; wheel chocks as a back-up to the handbrake when parked on a slope; and wheel clamps plus a lockable tow hitch to deter thieves whenever it is left unattended. Wheel covers will protect the tyres if you are lucky enough to experience some long spells of hot sunshine. A useful tip for keeping road grime and car exhaust deposits off your boat on long journeys is to wipe over the frontal areas with washing-up liquid a day or so before starting out. This gives it time to dry, leaving a protective film which is easily rinsed off while you are launching. Be sure to carry a spare wheel and a jack powerful enough to lift the trailer with the boat on it. Remember to clip on the 'break-away' wire or safety chain which should link the trailer to the car; this automatically applies the parking brake if for any reason they should become detached from one another while under way.

The little jockey wheel at the front of the trailer makes it easy to move around by hand, but it's a good idea to replace it with twin wheels or one of the jumbo balloon tyred variety if you will be traversing sand or soft ground; they sink in less.

LAUNCHING TIPS

Always carry two good lengths of light rope that can be made fast to the stem and stern of the boat to control it in the water after the primary restraint, the winch cable, has been cast off. If there's an onshore breeze or a crosswind, and you can make fast to something nearby, take the stern line out to it to prevent the boat from being blown back on to the launching site; or start the engine as soon as the prop is in the water, so that you can back off immediately you are afloat. On your return, the same lines can be used to line up the boat with the cradle. It helps if a pair of docking arms are fitted to the trailer (or trolley) standing up at either side at the point of maximum beam and marked with the required depth of water.

Another good idea is to lay your own temporary mooring, using the dinghy and a heavy, flat-bottomed weight (known as a 'frape') – or an anchor if there's no possibility of fouling some other line – with a stand-up pulley block attached to it. Through this block you run a long line with its end taken ashore, led round a post or stake, and tied together. The boat's painter is then made fast to the frape line, and as soon as it has been launched it can simply be hauled out into deep water and left securely moored while someone parks the car and trailer. The same system works well for picnics ashore, the frape being dropped and the line paid out as you motor or drift on to the beach, and the boat pulled back out after the crew has jumped ashore. It saves launching the dinghy, or even getting your feet wet if the bank is steep. But don't drop the mooring too far out, or the dinghy may lift it at high water and drift away.

There are many other neat dodges that you will come across among your fellow trailer-sailors, or read about or that you will devise to suit your own particular way of going about things. One of the attractions of boating is the incentive and the opportunity to exercise the natural inventiveness and self-reliance that seems to be inherent in the nature of all seafarers. Such ideas do more than save you time or money; when they work well, you will find that they can also work wonders for your ego.

HELPFUL ORGANISATIONS

British Inflatable Boat Owners
  Association
Patrick Bryans
Hatton House
Leven, Fife KY8 5QD
0333-320218

British Marine Industries Federation
Meadlake Place
Thorpe Lea Road
Egham, Surrey TW20 8HE
0784-472222

British Waterways
Willow Grange
Church Road
Watford WD1 3QA
0923-226422

Cruising Association
Ivory House
St Katharine Dock
London E1 9AT
071-481 0881

Dinghy Cruising Association
David M Jones
56 Grebe Crescent
Horsham, West Sussex RH13 6ED
0403-66800

Electric Boat Association
Ms Gillian Nahum
Mill House
Mill End
Henley on Thames, Oxon RG9 3AY
0491-578870

Inland Waterways Association
114 Regent's Park Road
London NW1 8UQ
071-586 2510

Junk Rig Association
373 Hunts Pond Road
Titchfield
Fareham, Hants PO14 4PB
0329-842613

Maritime Information Centre
The National Maritime Museum
Greenwich, London SE10 9NF
081-858 4422

National Federation of Sea Schools
Straddlestones
Fletchwood Lane
Totton, Southampton SO4 2DZ
0703-869956

Royal Yachting Association
RYA House
Romsey Road
Eastleigh
Hampshire SO5 4YA
0703-629962

Trail Sail Association
David Evans
Scape Haven
22 Grand Stand
Scapegoat Hill
Golcar
Huddersfield HD7 4QN
0484-653998

Yacht Brokers', Designers' and
  Surveyors' Association
Wheel House
Petersfield
White Hill
Borden, Hampshire GU35 9BU
0420-473862

BOATBUILDERS & IMPORTERS

Avon	Avon Inflatables, Dafen, Llanelli, Dyfed SA14 8NA
Cabrio	Mayland Marine, Steeple Road, Lower Mayland, Chelmsford, Essex CM3 8BE
Catalina 22	Catalina Yachts, Room 24, Hamble Point Marina, School Lane, Hamble, Southampton SO3 5NB
Coaster	Honnor Marine Ltd, Drascombe Works, Dartington, Totnes, Devon TQ9 6DP
Compac 19	Island Packet Yachts, Moat House, Dorsington, Stratford-upon-Avon, Warwickshire CV37 8AX
Crabber 17	Cornish Crabbers Ltd, Rock, Wadebridge, Cornwall PL27 6PH
Cracksman 2	Modular Mouldings Ltd, Lower Quay, Gweek, Helston, Cornwall TR12 6UD
Day Angler/Strikeliner	Orkney Boats Ltd, Ford Lane Industrial Estate, Arundel, Sussex BN18 0DF
Dehler 22	Dehler Yachts UK, Hamble Point Marina, School Lane, Hamble, Southampton SO3 5NB
Drascombe Lugger	Honnor Marine Ltd, Drascombe Works, Dartington, Totnes, Devon TQ9 6DP
Eagle 525	Moreton Marine Products Ltd, Moreton, Swinderby, Lincoln LN6 9HT
First 210	Beneteau UK Ltd, Hamble Point Quay, School Lane, Hamble, Hampshire SO3 5JD
Hardy 17 & 18	Hardy Marine Ltd, North Walsham, Norfolk NR28 0AN
Horizon 21	Hunter Boats Ltd, Sutton Wharf, Rochford, Essex SS4 1LZ
Invader 18	Quaycraft Ltd, Quay House, Bridge Road, Swanwick, Hampshire SO3 7EB
Jolleyboat	Charles Beddingfield, 9 Sheringham Close, Upton, Wirral, Merseyside L49 4LJ
Legend 23.5	Opal Marine, Camper & Nicholsons Marina, Mumby Road, Gosport, Hampshire PO12 1AH
Leisure 17	Boating Scene, High Road, Laindon, Basildon, Essex SS15 6DS
Lune Whammell	Character Boats, 21 Church Grove, Overton, Nr Morecambe, Lancashire LA3 3HZ
MacGregor 19	MacGregor Yachts International Ltd, Unit 2, Visick Engineering Works, Devoran, Truro, Cornwall TR3 7NB

Norfolk Oyster	Shotley Point Marina, Shotley Gate, Ipswich IP9 1QJ
Oystercatcher 16	Mayfly Classic Boats, The Boat Yard, Gweek Quay, Helston, Cornwall TR12 6UF
Parker 21	G W Parker & Son Ltd, Horseshoe Lane, Kirton, Boston, Lincolnshire PE20 1LW
Picton Royale and 595	Picton Boats Ltd, Brynmenyn Industrial Estate, Bridgend, Glamorgan CF32 9TD
Privateer	Long Island Boats, 1 Spring Street, Wool, Wareham, Dorset BH20 6DB
Red Fox 210	Red Fox Yachts, Castleton House, High Street, Hamble, Hampshire SO3 5HA
Ring 18	Ring Powercraft, Unit W, Riverside Industrial Estate, Littlehampton, West Sussex BN17 5DF
Shetland 4+2	Shetland International Boats Ltd, Redgrave Common, Redgrave, Diss, Norfolk IP22 1RZ
Strider	Fantasy Yachts, Bridwell Lane North, St Brideaux, Plymouth PL5 1AB
Swift 20	Marlin International Ltd, Chartwood House, Breamore, Hampshire SP6 2FF
Tiki 21 and 26	Imagine Multihulls, 3 Trevol Business Park, Torpoint, Cornwall PL11 2TB
Victoria 16	Victoria Marine Ltd, Shore Road, Warsash, Hampshire SO3 6FR
Viking	Viking Mouldings, Unit 11, Ongar Road, Trading Estate, 20 Ongar Road, Great Dunmow, Essex CM3 1EU
Voltaire 18	The Thames Electric Launch Co, PO Box 3, Goring-on-Thames, Reading, Berkshire RG8 0HQ
Wayfarer and Wanderer	Anglo Marine Services Ltd, Wade Road, Goose Lane Industrial Estate, Clacton-on-Sea, Essex CO15 4LT
West Wight Potter	Martin Pook Design, 11 Greenhill Close, Colehill, Wimborne, Dorset BH21 2RQ
Whisper	Conrad Natzio, The Old School, Brundish Road, Raveningham, Norwich NR14 6QB
Winkle Brig	Eric Bergqvist, Ferry Boatyard, Fiddlers Ferry Yacht Haven, Penketh, Cheshire WA5 2UJ
Yamarin Big Game	Bob Spalding Ltd, Suffolk Yacht Harbour, Levington, Ipswich, Suffolk IP10 0LN
Zodiac	Zodiac UK Ltd, 2 Edgemead Close, Round Spinney, Northampton NN3 4RG

INDEX

A-frame 115
airflow 48
Annual Percentage Rate 10
automatic transmission 114

balance lug 53
ballast ratio 26
Bass boat 110
berthing 12
Bermudian rig 57, 58
bilge keel 23
boatbuilding materials 86
Bolger, Philip C. 89, 91
break-back trailer 115
British Marine Industries Federation 18
brokerage 19
buoyancy 32

Caledonia Yawl 99
camping cruiser 33
capsize 30, 32
car topper 32
catboat 57
cat rig 54
Catalina 22 42, 106
catamarans 26
Centaur 46
centreboard 21
Certificate of Competence 6
Chinese lug 53
clinker 98
Coaster 39
Compac 19 42
compound curvature 100
Contessa 26 46
Cornish Crabber 39
Corribee 46
crab-claw rig 55

credit terms 10
Cracksman 2 42, 109
crew 21, 25
cruising cats 42
cutter 58

daggerboard 23
Day Angler 74
daysailer 35
deadrise 66
Dehler 22 110
depreciation 13
diesel engines 69
dipping lug 55
displacement hull 65
displacement: length ratio 26
DIY 15
Dockrell 17 110
Drawcombe Lugger 35
draught 23
dry rot 90
Dye, Frank & Margaret 33

Eagle 525 39
electric propulsion 71
epoxy 90
essential equipment 7
Etap 22 110
Eventide 44

Finance 10
Fisher, Paul 31, 59, 65, 95
four-wheel-drive 114
framing 93
Freedom 57
Freeman 23 80
fractional rig 58
fuel consumption 69
furling gear 61

gaff rig 56
gelcoat 87
genoa 50
GRP 86
Griffiths, Maurice 44
gunter lug 55

Hardy 17 18, 74
hard chine 66
Heavenly Twins 46
hire purchase 12
Horizon 21 41
hull forms 64
hull speed 66

inboard engines 69
inflatables 78
inland waterways 5, 73
insurance 9
interest rates 10
Invader 18 76
inventories 7, 8, 9
isophthalic resin 87

Jolleyboat 35
junk rig 53

keels 22
ketch 60
kit panel 101

laminating 100
lapstrake 98
lateen rig 55
launching trolley 32, 108, 115
lazyjacks 61
leeboard 23
Legend 23.5 40
Leisure 17 39
licensing 6
lifting keel 22
loans 10
lugsail 53

Lune Whammel 35, 37
Lynx 16 95
Lysander 46

MacGregor 19 42
maintenance 10
marinas 11, 13
marine mortgage 10
masthead rig 58
Mayland Cabrio 67
Mirror 96
motor cruisers 79
motor sailers 20
moorings 13
Mudie, Colin 35, 98

narrowboats 72
Norfolk Oyster 36
nose weight 113

outboard motors 69
operating costs 9, 13, 69
Optimist 56
osmosis 14, 87
Oughtred, Iain 99
overall length 24
Oystercatcher 40

Parker 21 41
partnership 13
planning hull 66
Picton Royale 77
plywood 94
price grouping 3
Privateer 31

reefing 60
Red Fox 42, 110
registration 6

RIBs 78
Ring 18 76
Roamer 33, 34
roller reefing 61
rot 90
round bilge 65
Royal Yachting
    Association 6, 112

sail area: displacement
    ratio 25
sail battens 51
sailboard 57
sail parts 51
sail plans 53
sailing clubs 17, 18, 21
schooner 59
second-hand boats 13
Searider 78
Segerling 97
self-tacking 50
Shetland 4+2 67
shoal draught 21
Shoal Waters 39
size 24
slab reefing 61
sloop 58
ski boat 76
Sonata 46
speed 28, 33, 66, 74, 76
sportsboat 76
sprit rig 56
stability 26, 28
standing lug 55
sterndrive 71
stitch-and-tape 96
Stock, Charles 38
Strider 42, 44, 109
straddle stability 28

Strikeliner 74
strip planking 100
surveys 14
Swift 20 42
swing keel 22

tabernacle 108
T-frame 115
Telstar 27
Tiki 21/26 27, 43
tools 85
trailers 115
trailer-sailers 11, 16, 105
trimarans 27

Una rig 57

VAT 6
vee-drive 71
Victoria 16 33
Viking Mouldings 87
Virgo Voyager 46
Voltaire 72

Wanderer 33
water ballast 26, 42, 45,
    95
weight: power ratio 25
Wayfarer 33
Wharram, James 43, 83
weight 25, 112
West Wight Potter 37
Winchelsea Yawl 36
Wildlife 35
Winkle Brig 38, 39
Workshop 84

yawl 60

Self-Catering Holidays

in Britain

2010

- Cottages, farms, apartments and chalets
- Over 400 choices of places to stay

Cutkive Wood Holiday Lodges, St Ive, Liskeard, Cornwall (page 18)

HG Guides Ltd, 2010
ISBN 978-1-85055-423-3

Maps: ©MAPS IN MINUTES™ / Collins Bartholomew (2009)

Typeset by FHG Guides Ltd, Paisley.
Printed and bound in China by Imago.

Distribution. Book Trade: ORCA Book Services, Stanley House,
3 Fleets Lane, Poole, Dorset BH15 3AJ
(Tel: 01202 665432; Fax: 01202 666219)
e-mail: mail@orcabookservices.co.uk
Published by FHG Guides Ltd., Abbey Mill Business Centre,
Seedhill, Paisley PA1 ITJ (Tel: 0141-887 0428 Fax: 0141-889 7204).
e-mail: admin@fhguides.co.uk

Self-Catering Holidays in Britain is published by FHG Guides Ltd,
part of Kuperard Group.

Cover design: FHG Guides
Cover Picture: with thanks to Fisherground Farm, Keswick. See p267 for full details.

symbols

⊘	Totally non-smoking	🐕	Pets Welcome
🐎	Children Welcome	**SB**	Short Breaks
♿	Suitable for Disabled Guests	♖	Licensed

Contents

Editorial Section   1-6
Tourist Board Ratings   298
Directory of Website Addresses   299
Index of Towns/Counties   315

SOUTH WEST ENGLAND

7

Cornwall and Isles of Scilly, Devon, Dorset, Gloucestershire, Somerset, Wiltshire

SOUTH EAST ENGLAND

69

Berkshire, Buckinghamshire, Hampshire, Isle of Wight, Kent, Oxfordshire, Surrey, East Sussex, West Sussex

EAST OF ENGLAND

85

Cambridgeshire, Hertfordshire, Norfolk, Suffolk

MIDLANDS

100

Derbyshire, Herefordshire, Lincolnshire, Nottinghamshire, Shropshire, Staffordshire, Warwickshire, Worcestershire

YORKSHIRE

116

East Yorkshire, North Yorkshire

NORTH EAST ENGLAND

129

Durham, Northumberland

NORTH WEST ENGLAND

141

Cumbria, Lancashire

CHANNEL ISLANDS

160

SCOTLAND

Aberdeen Banff & Moray   165
Argyll & Bute   166
Ayrshire & Arran   181
Borders   184
Dumfries & Galloway   188
Dunbartonshire   191
Edinburgh & Lothians   192
Fife   194
Highlands   195
Lanarkshire   205
Perth & Kinross   206
Stirling & The Trossachs   211
Scottish Islands   212

WALES

Anglesey & Gwynedd   221
North Wales   228
Carmarthenshire   230
Ceredigion   231
Pembrokeshire   233
Powys   239
South Wales   243

IRELAND

Co. Clare   244

CARAVANS & CAMPING

245

Pet Friendly Accommodation   259

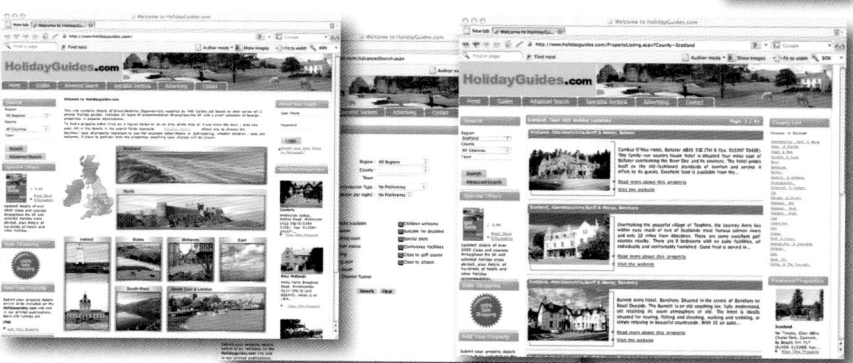

England and Wales · Counties

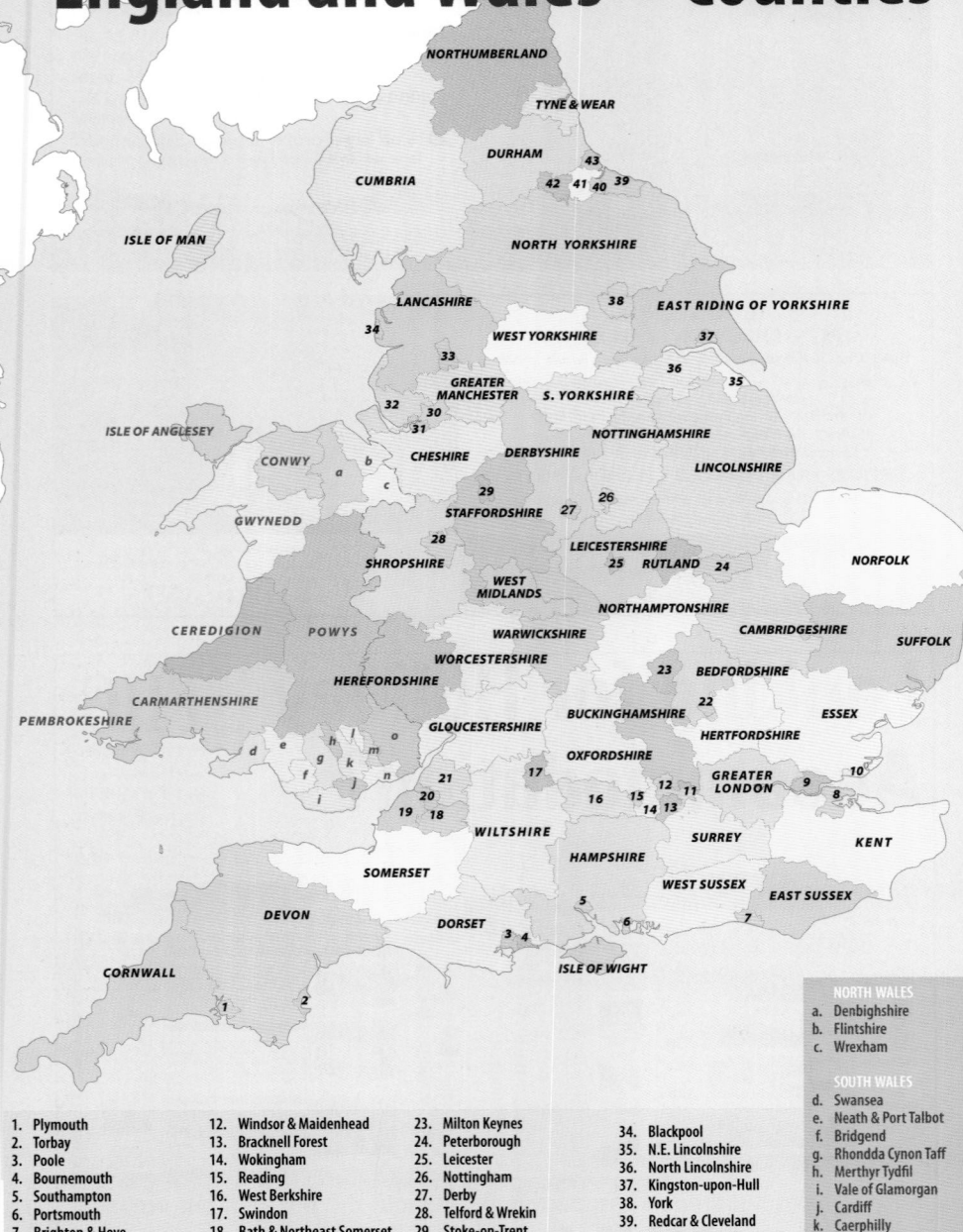

NORTHUMBERLAND

TYNE & WEAR

DURHAM

43

CUMBRIA   42 41 40 39

ISLE OF MAN

NORTH YORKSHIRE

LANCASHIRE   38   EAST RIDING OF YORKSHIRE

34   WEST YORKSHIRE   37

33   36

GREATER   35
MANCHESTER   S. YORKSHIRE
32   30
31   CHESHIRE   DERBYSHIRE   NOTTINGHAMSHIRE

ISLE OF ANGLESEY   LINCOLNSHIRE

CONWY   a   b
c   29   STAFFORDSHIRE   27   26

GWYNEDD   28   LEICESTERSHIRE
SHROPSHIRE   25   RUTLAND   24   NORFOLK
WEST
MIDLANDS
NORTHAMPTONSHIRE

CEREDIGION   POWYS   WARWICKSHIRE   CAMBRIDGESHIRE   SUFFOLK
WORCESTERSHIRE
HEREFORDSHIRE   23   BEDFORDSHIRE
CARMARTHENSHIRE   22   ESSEX
PEMBROKESHIRE   GLOUCESTERSHIRE   BUCKINGHAMSHIRE   HERTFORDSHIRE
d   e   h   l   m   o
f   k   n   OXFORDSHIRE   GREATER   10
i   j   21   17   LONDON   9
20   16   15   12 11   8
19   18   14 13
WILTSHIRE   SURREY   KENT
SOMERSET   HAMPSHIRE   WEST SUSSEX   EAST SUSSEX
5   6   7
DEVON   DORSET
3 4   ISLE OF WIGHT
CORNWALL
1   2

1. Plymouth
2. Torbay
3. Poole
4. Bournemouth
5. Southampton
6. Portsmouth
7. Brighton & Hove
8. Medway
9. Thurrock
10. Southend
11. Slough
12. Windsor & Maidenhead
13. Bracknell Forest
14. Wokingham
15. Reading
16. West Berkshire
17. Swindon
18. Bath & Northeast Somerset
19. North Somerset
20. Bristol
21. South Gloucestershire
22. Luton
23. Milton Keynes
24. Peterborough
25. Leicester
26. Nottingham
27. Derby
28. Telford & Wrekin
29. Stoke-on-Trent
30. Warrington
31. Halton
32. Merseyside
33. Blackburn with Darwen
34. Blackpool
35. N.E. Lincolnshire
36. North Lincolnshire
37. Kingston-upon-Hull
38. York
39. Redcar & Cleveland
40. Middlesborough
41. Stockton-on-Tees
42. Darlington
43. Hartlepool

NORTH WALES
a. Denbighshire
b. Flintshire
c. Wrexham

SOUTH WALES
d. Swansea
e. Neath & Port Talbot
f. Bridgend
g. Rhondda Cynon Taff
h. Merthyr Tydfil
i. Vale of Glamorgan
j. Cardiff
k. Caerphilly
l. Blaenau Gwent
m. Torfaen
n. Newport
o. Monmouthshire

IVYLEAF BARTON SELF-CATERING COTTAGES are well equipped and sleep between 2 and 8 people. They are available all year round and some take pets by arrangement. Prices include bed linen and electricity.

All seven cottages have both TV/video/DVD and CD/radio/ DAB players. Guests have the use of an all-weather tennis court and the cottages are adjacent to a 9-hole golf course/driving range/ mountain board slope.

The Cottages make an ideal safe location for families. Just 3 miles from Bude, they enjoy an elevated position with stunning views over both the coast towards Bude Bay and in the distance to Trevose Head and also the north Cornish countryside to Bodmin. The well known surfing beaches at Sandymouth Bay and Summerlease beach are both 10 minutes' drive away. *Details from Robert B. Barrett.*

Short breaks available Oct to May excl. Bank Holidays

Ivyleaf Barton HOLIDAY COTTAGES

**Ivyleaf Hill, Bude EX23 9LD • 01288 321237/07525 251773
e-mail: info@ivyleafbarton.co.uk • www.ivyleafbarton.co.uk**

Coombe Cottages

Paul & Helen Seez, Coombe Cottages,
Crackington Haven, Bude EX23 0JG
Tel: 01840 230664

Crackington Haven is a small unspoilt cove overlooked by 400 foot cliffs, with rock pools and a sandy beach at low tide – ideal for swimming or surfing.

Coombe Cottages are situated within this Area of Outstanding Natural Beauty, only 300 yards from the beach, coastal path or pub.

Little Coombe sleeps two, *Rivercoombe* sleeps four and both cottages have their own fenced gardens with picnic table and BBQ. Inside, they are well equipped and have open fires for those more chilly evenings.

Along the private drive there is a laundry room, and easy off-road parking is available outside each cottage.

symbols

 Totally non-smoking

 Children Welcome

 Suitable for Disabled Guests

 Pets Welcome

SB Short Breaks

Licensed

Falmouth

Raven Rock and Spindrift
Contact: Mrs S. Gill, Bodrigy,
Plaidy, Looe PL13 1LF
Tel: 01503 263122

- Two bungalows adjacent to Plaidy Beach. Spindrift has en suite bedroom, sleeps two; Raven Rock has two bedrooms and sleeps four. Own parking spaces, central heating, wheelchair accessible. Semi-detached bungalows are fully furnished, well equipped and have sea views. Set in peaceful surroundings at Plaidy. Open plan lounge-diner-kitchen. Colour TV. Patio garden. Electricity and gas included in rent. Pet by arrangement. Personally supervised. No smoking.
- Looe is a fishing port with a variety of shops and restaurants and is only a few minutes by car or a 15 to 20 minute walk.
- Weekly terms: Spindrift from £260 to £350
　　　　　　　　Raven Rock from £305 to £465
- Out of season short breaks (three days minimum)

The Perfect Cornish Country Cottage

THE OLD BARN is located in a small hamlet of renovated farm buildings, situated in the hills above the pretty coastal town of Looe, South East Cornwall. It enjoys magnificent views across the valley and has a completely enclosed garden. Within easy reach of the coast, the Eden Project, and the Lost Gardens of Heligan.
- Sleeps 6.
For further details, ring
Carolyn & Richard - 01503 265739
www.oldbarnholidays.net

SB

Fox Valley Cottages
Lanlawren, Trenewan, Looe PL13 2PZ

Set in beautiful countryside
For a peaceful and relaxing holiday
A warm welcome from Andy & Linda, who are two of the partners who live on site.
- Indoor heated pool, spa and sauna • Cleaned to a high standard, warm, comfortable and well equipped
- Log fires for those cosy winter nights • A field where your dog can have a good run around • Just three miles from Polperro, with country and coastal walks nearby
- We are open all year round, including Christmas.
- Short breaks, long weekends or midweek breaks out of season.

Tel: 01726 870115 • e-mail: foxvalleycottages@btconnect.com • www.foxvalleycottages.co.uk

Talehay Holiday Cottages
Pelynt, Near Looe PL13 2LT
A Quiet Haven in the Countryside near the Sea

Beautiful, traditional cottages with many original features retained provide superb holiday accommodation on 17C non-working farmstead.

Set in 4 acres of unspoilt countryside offering peace and tranquillity with breathtaking coastal and country walks on your doorstep. This is an ideal location for dogs and their owners alike. Close to the Eden Project.

Tel: Mr & Mrs Dennett • 01503 220252
e-mail: infobookings@talehay.co.uk • www.talehay.co.uk

Once part of a Duchy of Cornwall working farm, now farmhouse and farm buildings converted to a high standard to form a nine cottage complex around former farmyard. Sleeping from two to ten. All cottages are well furnished and equipped and prices include electricity, bed linen and towels. Most cottages have a garden. Five acre grounds, set in delightful wooded valley, with tennis, putting, children's play area, fishing lake, animal paddock, games room with pool and table tennis. Gym & Spa pool. Separate bar. Laundry. Barbecue. Railcar from Liskeard to Looe stops at end of picnic area. Have a 'car free' day out. Children and well behaved dogs welcome (no dogs in high season, please). Prices from £120 per week.

Badham Farm, St Keyne, Liskeard PL14 4RW
Tel: 01579 343572
e-mail: badhamfarm@yahoo.co.uk • www.badhamfarm.co.uk

SB

Trevarthian Holiday Homes • Marazion

High quality Victorian Cottages and Apartments in the prime Mounts Bay Location. Superb views of St Michael's Mount, Mousehole, Newlyn, Penzance.
A selection of the finest self-catering accommodation available.
One minute walk to safe, sandy beach. Playground, pubs, restaurants, galleries, shops, bus routes for Land's End, St Ives, Penzance.
Sleep 1-5 • Low Season £170-£320 per week,
High Season £420-£830 per week • Open all year • NO SMOKING

Contact Mr Sean Cattran, Trevarthian Holiday Homes, West End, Marazion TR17 0EG
Tel: 01736 710100 • Fax: 01736 710111 • info@trevarthian.co.uk • www.trevarthian.co.uk

MENAGWINS is situated on the edge of Gorran village, one mile from the coast and within easy reach of beaches, fishing, and the Coastal Footpath. The picturesque fishing port of Mevagissey is 3 miles away; Lost Gardens of Heligan 3 miles, Eden Project 14 miles.

Cottage sleeps up to five: three bedrooms, bathroom with bath and shower, fitted kitchen, separate lounge and dining room. Large garden with barbecue area. Linen and towels provided.

Well behaved pets welcome.

For details contact: MRS M.R. BULLED, MENAGWINS,
GORRAN, ST AUSTELL PL26 6HP • 01726 843517

Looking for holiday accommodation?
for details of hundreds of properties
throughout the UK including
comprehensive coverage of all areas of Scotland try:
www.holidayguides.com

GREENBANK

is detached, standing in a large lawned garden within 270 yards of Porth's sandy beach. The flats are fully equipped for two to six persons, with colour TV, fridge, electric cooker and razor point. Hot water and bed linen included in the tariff.

Suitable for couples and families, with cots and high chairs supplied. Laundry room with automatic washing machine and tumble dryer. Guests' telephone. Car park. Open all year. No dogs.

Personally supervised by resident proprietor, Lesley Dutton.

GREENBANK HOLIDAY FLATS

Greenbank Cottage, 25 Porth Way, Porth, Newquay TR7 3LW
Tel: 01637 872546
e-mail: enquiries@greenbankholidayflats.co.uk

Holiday Accommodation in Constantine Bay - Cornwall's most relaxing holiday location

SB

GARDEN COTTAGE HOLIDAY FLATS

are located in beautiful Constantine Bay close to Padstow in North Cornwall.

Our three comfortable flats are surrounded by a large grassy garden area, and conveniently situated just 200 yards from the golden sands of Constantine Beach.

The land surrounding the property adjoins Trevose Golf Course, and the area is full of opportunities for walking, cycling, water sports, and relaxation.

There is a good village shop half a mile from the flats and there are more shops, pubs, restaurants and a garage at St. Merryn which is two miles away. At Trevose Golf Club there is also a swimming pool, tennis courts, and as well as the championship 18 hole course there is a short 9 hole course for beginners with another 9 full size holes. And all this is just at the end of Garden Cottage Flats' back field.

Three beautifully appointed flats: *Tamarisk, Trevose View, and Treliza*, set in their own grounds with grassy lawns, ample parking and a barbeque and picnic area.

• Electricity included in the rent.

• Well behaved pets are welcome at an additional charge of £25 per week

• There is ample parking on site.

• All are equipped with electric cooker, microwave, fridge, kettle, toaster, iron and ironing board. There is a full range of crockery and cooking utensils, as well as vacuum cleaners and cleaning equipment.

Liz and Russell Harris
Garden Cottage Holiday Flats
Constantine Bay, Padstow, Cornwall PL28 8JJ
01841 520262 • www.gardencottageflats.co.uk
e-mail: liz@gardencottageflats.co.uk

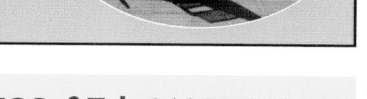

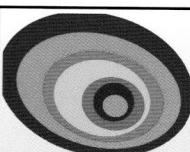

Please note

All the information in this book is given in good faith in the belief that it is correct. However, the publishers cannot guarantee the facts given in these pages, neither are they responsible for changes in policy, ownership or terms that may take place after the date of going to press. Readers should always satisfy themselves that the facilities they require are available and that the terms, if quoted, still apply.

Devon

Ashburton

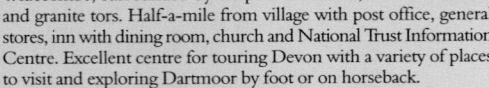

SB

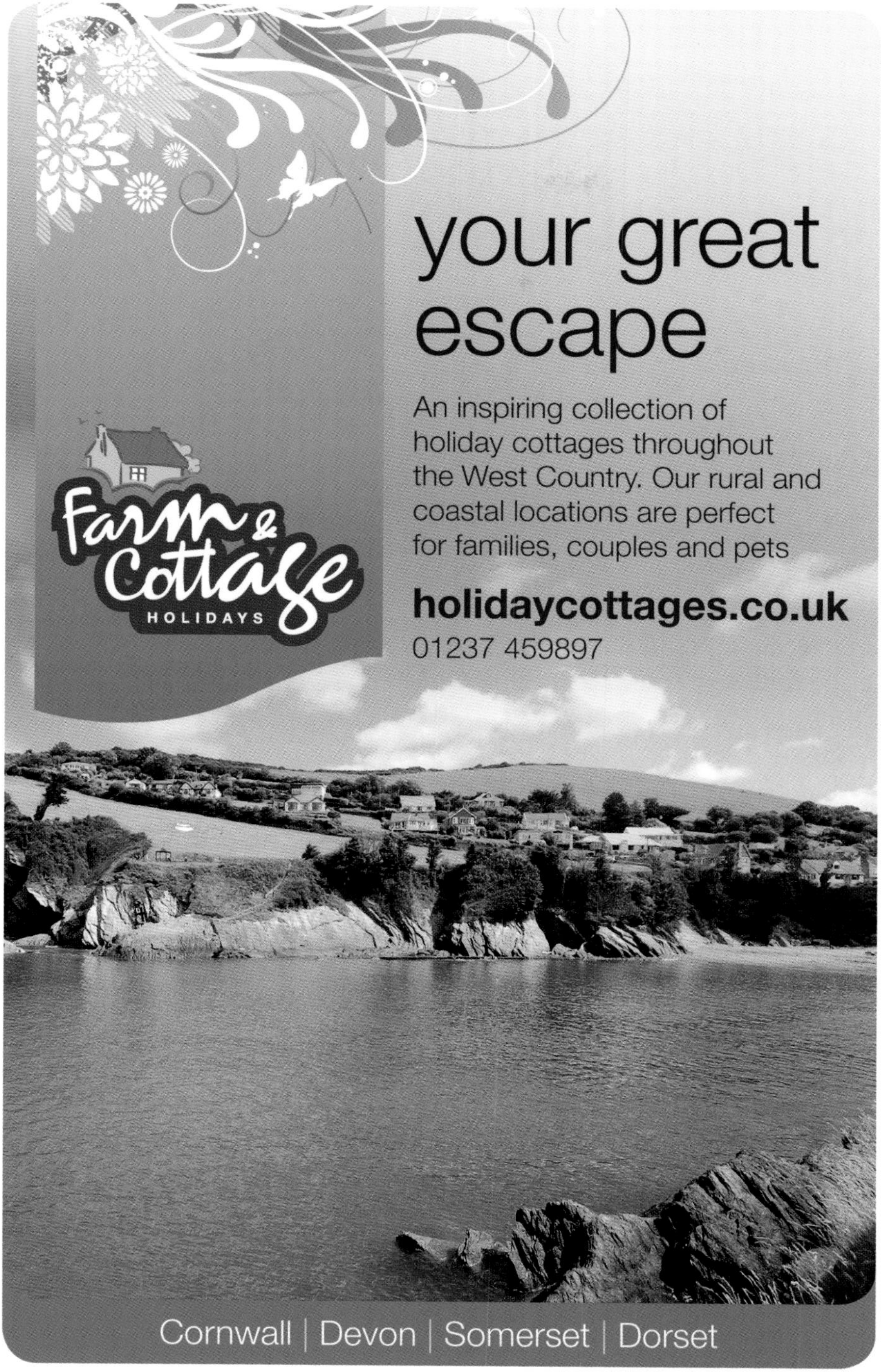
your great escape
An inspiring collection of holiday cottages throughout the West Country. Our rural and coastal locations are perfect for families, couples and pets
holidaycottages.co.uk
01237 459897
Farm & Cottage
HOLIDAYS
Cornwall | Devon | Somerset | Dorset

Brixham, Broadwoodwidger, Chulmleigh

DEVONCOURT HOLIDAY FLATS

BERRYHEAD ROAD, BRIXHAM, DEVON TQ5 9AB

Devoncourt is a development of 24 self-contained flats, occupying one of the finest positions in Torbay, with unsurpassed views. At night the lights of Torbay are like a fairyland to be enjoyed from your very own balcony.

MasterCard VISA

EACH FLAT HAS:
Heating
Sea Views over Torbay
Private balcony
Own front door
Separate bathroom and toilet
Separate bedroom
Bed-settee in lounge
Lounge sea views over Marina
Kitchenette - all electric
Private car park
Opposite beach
Colour television
Overlooks lifeboat
Short walk to town centre
Double glazing
Open all year
Mini Breaks October to April

SB

Tel: 01803 853748
(or 07802 403289 after office hours)
website: www.devoncourt.info

West Banbury Farm Cottages...where relaxation is a way of life

SB

Come to West Banbury and you'll discover a rural haven where you can unwind and relax. We are near Broadwoodwidger, West Devon, ideally located for exploring Devon and Cornwall, including the north and south coasts. Plenty of family attractions are within easy reach. We have ten charming cottages, each spacious and very comfortable, set around two courtyards with stunning views to Dartmoor. The cottages sleep 2 to 8. Large indoor heated pool, sauna, games room, children's play area, fun pitch and putt, and a grass tennis court. Open all year. Dogs welcome. Short breaks available.

For more information call Anna-Rose on 01566 780423

w w w . w e s t b a n b u r y . c o . u k

Northcott Barton Farm Cottage

Beautifully equipped, spotlessly clean three bedroom cottage with large enclosed garden. A walker's and country lover's ideal: for a couple seeking peace and quiet or a family holiday. Very special rates for low season holidays, couples and short breaks. Near golf, riding, Tarka trail and R.H.S. Rosemoor. Character, comfort, beams, log fire, *"Perfick"*. Pets Welcome, no charge.

SB

For availability please contact Sandra Gay,
Northcott Barton, Ashreigney, Chulmleigh, Devon EX18 7PR
Tel/Fax: 01769 520259
e-mail: sandra@northcottbarton.co.uk
www.northcottbarton.co.uk

Partridge Arms Farm

Yeo Mill, West Anstey, South Molton, North Devon EX36 3NU

Times gone by...For those who want to enjoy a break in more unusual circumstances, Partridge Arms Farm has a converted, self-catering railway carriage. The carriage is situated on the old Taunton to Barnstaple railway line and, as well as being fully equipped, it sleeps up to 6 people. Children are welcome to stay in the carriage, as are dogs. The railway line offers a delightful and fascinating walk. Visitors can also explore at their leisure the 200 acres of surrounding farmland, which is situated in the Southern foothills of Exmoor. Prices start from £490 per week (no hidden extras). Daily rates available.

Now a working farm of over 200 acres, four miles west of Dulverton, "Partridge Arms Farm" was once a coaching inn and has been in the same family since 1906. Genuine hospitality and traditional farmhouse fare await you. Comfortable accommodation in double, twin and single rooms, some of which have en suite facilities. There is also an original four-poster bedroom. Children welcome. Animals by arrangement. Residential licence. Open all year. Fishing and riding available nearby. FARM HOLIDAY GUIDE DIPLOMA WINNER *Bed and Breakfast from £25 • Evening Meal from £15.*

For further information contact Hazel Milton
Tel: 01398 341217 • Fax: 01398 341569
bangermilton@hotmail.com

West Millbrook

SELF CATERING

ADJOINING EXMOOR. Two fully-equipped bungalows and one farmhouse annexe (properties sleep 2/8) in lovely surroundings bordering Exmoor National Park. Ideal for touring North Devon and West Somerset including moor and coast with beautiful walks, lovely scenery and many other attractions. North Molton village is only one mile away. All units have electric cooker, fridge/freezer, microwave and digital TV; two bungalows also have washing machines/dryers. Children's play area; cots and high chairs available free. Linen hire available. Games room. Car parking. Central heating if required. Electricity metered. Out of season short breaks. Weekly prices from £100 to £480. Colour brochure available.

Mike and Rose Courtney, West Millbrook, Twitchen, South Molton EX36 3LP
Tel: 01598 740382 • e-mail: wmbselfcatering@aol.com
www.westcountrynow.com • www.westmillbrook.co.uk

---

symbols

 Totally non-smoking

 Children Welcome

 Suitable for Disabled Guests

 Pets Welcome

SB Short Breaks

Licensed

SB

LANGSTONE MANOR HOLIDAY PARK

SILVER

AA
▶▶▶
HOLIDAY, TOURING
& CAMPING PARK

*S*et amongst delightful mature grounds in a sheltered wooded valley on the favoured south-west edge of Dartmoor, Langstone Manor offers the perfect escape for those seeking to explore and enjoy the wide range of interests and activities the adjacent moorland has to offer. We offer a range of self catering holiday accommodation, from a newly refurbished manor house apartment and holiday homes with full facilities to spacious, well appointed cottages. Level, well-drained pitches are available for camping, with toilet, shower and laundry facilities all close to hand. The Langstone Bar, with a woodburning stove, terrace, games room and evening meals, is perfect to relax and unwind at the end of the day.

No loud music, no traffic noise, stunning starry skies, peace and quiet and of course, a friendly atmosphere.

We are well placed for exploring Dartmoor, Devon and Cornwall, with Dartmoor as the back garden and the exciting and vibrant market town of Tavistock (with swimming pool, waterslides and cinema) just down the road. Then there is the beautiful south Devon coast a car ride away, with spectacular coastal walks and cosy fishing harbours nestled amongst sandy beaches and rock pools.

Our various facilities cater for long or short breaks to suit all tastes and budgets.

Moortown, Tavistock, Devon PL19 9JZ
Tel & Fax: 01822 613371
jane@langstone-manor.co.uk
www.langstone-manor.co.uk

WEST PUSEHILL FARM COTTAGES

SB

Resident proprietors, The Violet Family have been welcoming visitors to West Pusehill Farm for over twenty years, and many return time and time again.

Ideal for family summer holidays, restful spring/winter breaks, or a perfect base to explore Devon's outstanding coast and countryside and many outdoor activities.

West Pusehill Farm Cottages not only give you the freedom and independence of a self-catering holiday, but the local area offers a wide range of excellent restaurants and cafes, so your holiday can be enjoyed by every member of the family.

- ❖ Located in an Area of Outstanding Natural Beauty
- ❖ Eleven sympathetically converted cottages
- ❖ BBQ area
- ❖ Children's playground
- ❖ On-site heated outdoor pool
- ❖ Laundry room
- ❖ Golf, fishing, walking, exploring, shopping
- ❖ Family attractions

West Pusehill Farm
Westward Ho!
North Devon EX39 5AH
Tel: 01237 475638/474622
e-mail: info@wpfcottages.co.uk
www.wpfcottages.co.uk

CHICHESTER HOUSE HOLIDAY APARTMENTS

SB

Quiet, relaxing, fully furnished apartments. Opposite Barricane Shell Beach – central seafront position with outstanding sea and coastal views.

Watch the sun go down into the sea from your own balcony.

• Open all year • Free parking • Pets by arrangement.

SAE to resident proprietor, Joyce Bagnall.

Off-peak reductions. Short Break details on request.

The Esplanade, Woolacombe EX34 7DJ
Tel: 01271 870761

Looking for holiday accommodation?

for details of hundreds of properties
throughout the UK including
comprehensive coverage of all areas of Scotland try:

www.holidayguides.com

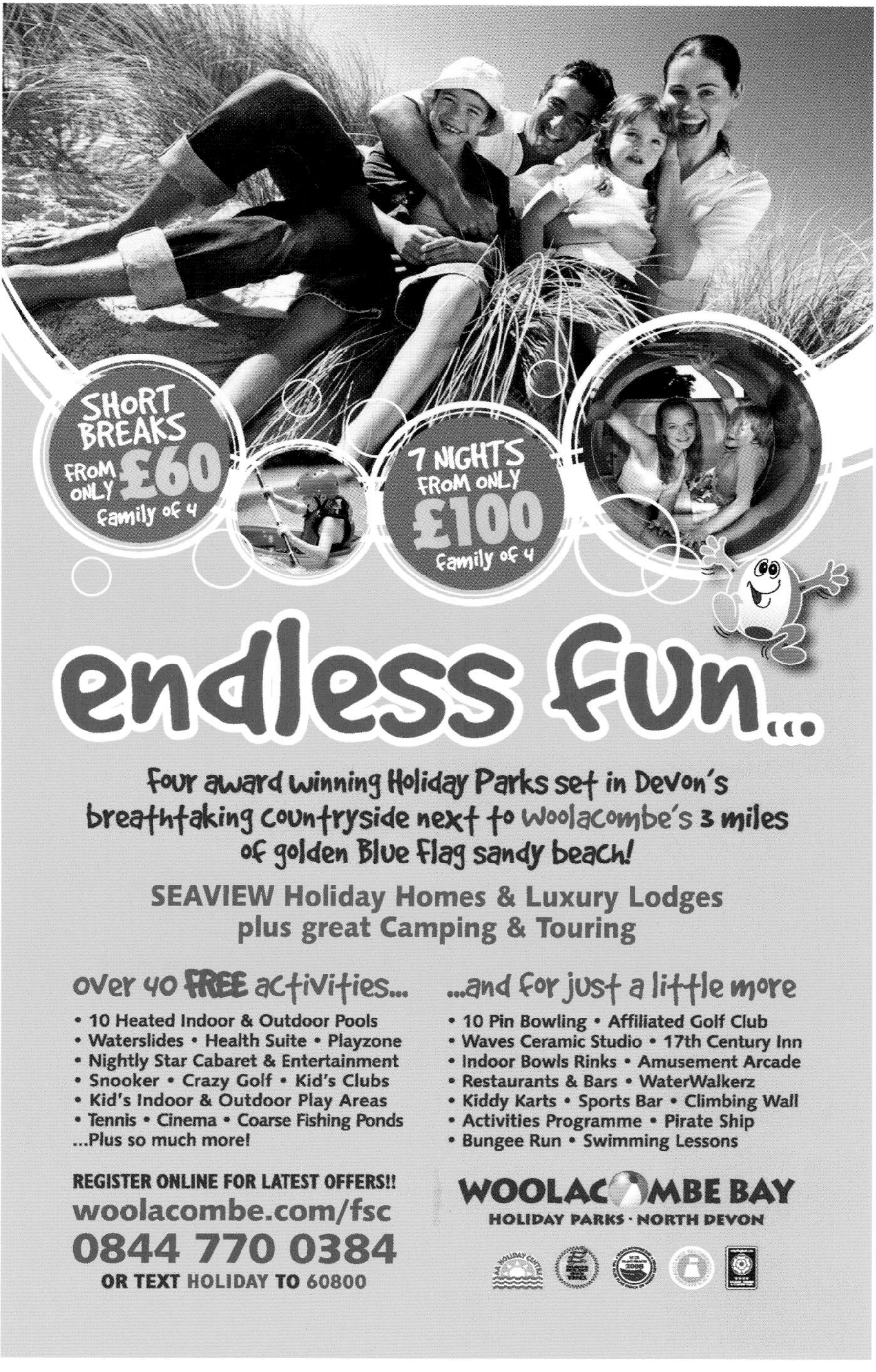
SHORT BREAKS FROM ONLY £60 family of 4
7 NIGHTS FROM ONLY £100 family of 4
endless fun...
Four award winning Holiday Parks set in Devon's breathtaking countryside next to Woolacombe's 3 miles of golden Blue Flag sandy beach!
SEAVIEW Holiday Homes & Luxury Lodges plus great Camping & Touring
over 40 FREE activities...
• 10 Heated Indoor & Outdoor Pools
• Waterslides • Health Suite • Playzone
• Nightly Star Cabaret & Entertainment
• Snooker • Crazy Golf • Kid's Clubs
• Kid's Indoor & Outdoor Play Areas
• Tennis • Cinema • Coarse Fishing Ponds
...Plus so much more!
...and for just a little more
• 10 Pin Bowling • Affiliated Golf Club
• Waves Ceramic Studio • 17th Century Inn
• Indoor Bowls Rinks • Amusement Arcade
• Restaurants & Bars • WaterWalkerz
• Kiddy Karts • Sports Bar • Climbing Wall
• Activities Programme • Pirate Ship
• Bungee Run • Swimming Lessons
REGISTER ONLINE FOR LATEST OFFERS!!
woolacombe.com/fsc
0844 770 0384
OR TEXT HOLIDAY TO 60800
WOOLACOMBE BAY
HOLIDAY PARKS · NORTH DEVON

Dorset

Bridport, Burton Bradstocl, Charmouth

17thC FROGMORE FARM

Frogmore is a 90-acre grazing farm situated tranquilly in beautiful West Dorset, overlooking the Jurassic Coast of Lyme Bay, and away from the crowds. Ideal for walking, our land is adjacent to National Trust land to the cliffs, (Seatown 1½ miles) and the South West Coastal Path. The cottage is fully equipped for five people. Downstairs - lounge/kitchen with dining area. Upstairs - double en suite bedroom, twin bedroom, large sun room with single bed, bathroom. Bed linen provided. The immediate walking area is rugged and very hilly and the cottage has steep stairs and outside steps (unfortunately not suitable for the disabled or very young children). *Well behaved dogs very welcome* • *Open all year* • *Car essential* • *Brochure and terms free on request* • *B&B also available* • *Contact Mrs Sue Norman.*

Frogmore Farm, Chideock, Bridport DT6 6HT　•　Tel: 01308 456159
www.frogmorefarm.com　•　e-mail: bookings@frogmorefarm.com

Mimosa

The Fossil & The Cross

Granary Lodge

Tamarisk Farm

Beach Road, West Bexington, Dorchester DT2 9DF
Tel: 01308 897784　Mrs J. Pearse

★★★★★★
SELF CATERING

On slope overlooking Chesil beach between Abbotsbury and Burton Bradstock.
Three large (Mimosa is wheelchair disabled M3(i) and Granary Lodge M1 is disabled-friendly) and two small cottages. Each one stands in own fenced garden.
Glorious views along West Dorset and Devon coasts. Lovely walks by sea and inland. Part of mixed organic farm with arable, sheep, cattle, horses and market garden (organic vegetables, meat and wholemeal flour available). Sea fishing, riding in Portesham and Burton Bradstock, lots of tourist attractions and good markets. Good centre for touring Thomas Hardy's Wessex. Safe for children and excellent for dogs. Very quiet. Terms from £260 to £980.

e-mail: holidays@tamariskfarm.com　www.tamariskfarm.com/holidays

Cardsmill
Farm Holidays

**Whitchurch Canonicorum,
Charmouth, Bridport,
Dorset DT6 6RP
Tel & Fax: 01297 489375
e-mail: cardsmill@aol.com
www.farmhousedorset.com**

★★★
SELF
CATERING

Stay on a real working family farm in the Marshwood Vale, an Area of Outstanding Natural Beauty. Enjoy country walks to the village, coast and around farm and woods. Watch the daily milking, see baby calves and lambs, and seasonal activities here on this 590 acre farm. En suite family, double and twin rooms available, with CTV, tea/coffee trays. *B&B £26-£36pppn.* ETC ★★★

Also available, three large, rural, quiet farmhouses. Each has private garden, double glazed conservatory and ample parking.

• TAPHOUSE has 6 bedrooms, 4 bathrooms, lounge, 22'x15' kitchen/diner.
• COURTHOUSE COTTAGE and DAIRY each have 3/4 bedrooms and 2 or 3 bathrooms. Games room, parking, separate gardens. All have C/H, dishwasher, washing machine and very well equipped kitchen/diner/lounge.
All available all year for long or short stays.
Brochure available, or check the website.

Grade II Listed Cottage with 3 bedrooms, 2 bathrooms, approx. one minute walk to beach, close to harbour.

VB ★★★

Other properties available weekly or short breaks.

Weymouth has a lovely sandy beach and picturesque harbour with pavement cafes. There is plenty to do all year round.

Phone: 01305 836495 • Mobile: 0797 1256160
e-mail: postmaster@buckwells.plus.com
www.holidaycottagesweymouth.co.uk

Gloucestershire

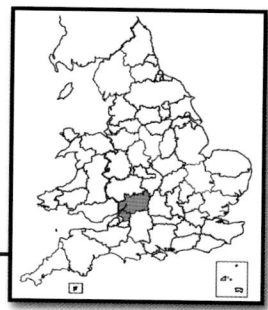

ROYLANDS FARM COTTAGE

is a comfortable home-from-home situated within a working farm, with classic styling to blend in with its rural surroundings. Rooms are spacious, bright and welcoming with all usual en suite and private facilities, lounge and kitchen. One single, one twin and a double bedroom, all with full English breakfast, towels, TV and tea and coffee making facilities. Uniquely guests can take advantage of their own lounge, or relax and take in the beautiful views of the Severn estuary and the surrounding countryside from the adjoining conservatory or large country garden. Ample secure and secluded off-road parking.

Fernhill, Almondsbury, Bristol, Gloucs BS32 4LU
Tel: 07791 221102
Mobile: 07768 286924

e-mail: jane@roylandfarmcottage.co.uk
www.roylandfarmcottage.co.uk

Roylands Farm Cottage

symbols

	Totally non-smoking		🐕	Pets Welcome
	Children Welcome		SB	Short Breaks
	Suitable for Disabled Guests		⚲	Licensed

HARTWELL FARM COTTAGES
Ready Token, Near Bibury, Cirencester GL7 5SY

Two traditionally built cottages with far reaching views, on the southern edge of the Cotswolds. Both are fully equipped to a high standard, with heating and woodburning stoves; large private enclosed gardens. Stabling for horses; tennis court. Ideal for touring and horse riding. Glorious walks, excellent pubs. Non-smoking. Children and well-behaved dogs welcome. Sleep 3-4.

Contact: Caroline Mann: Tel: 01285 740210
e-mail: ec.mann@btinternet.com • www.selfcateringcotswolds.com

---

Two Springbank, 37 Hopton Road, Upper Cam GLII 5PD

Fully equipped mid-terraced cottage (sleeps 4 + cot) in pleasant village about one mile from Dursley which has a swimming pool and sports centre.
Superb base for Cotswold Way, touring Severn Vale and Forest of Dean.
Few miles from Slimbridge Wildfowl Trust, Berkeley Castle and Westonbirt Arboretum and within easy reach of Gloucester, Bristol, Bath and Cirencester.
Ground floor: sitting room with TV/DVD and electric fire, dining area, fitted kitchen with fridge/freezer, electric cooker and microwave. Utility room with washing machine; lawn and patio. **First floor:** two bedrooms (one double, one twin), bathroom with shower. Electricity, linen and towels included, also cot and highchair if required.
Prices: Low season: £204-£252 per week. High season: £252-£285 per week.

Sorry no pets or smoking

Mrs F.A. Jones, 32 Everlands, Cam, Dursley, Gloucs GLII 5NL • 01453 543047
e-mail: info@twospringbank.co.uk • www.twospringbank.co.uk

Looking for Holiday Accommodation?

for details of hundreds of properties throughout the UK, visit our website

www.holidayguides.com

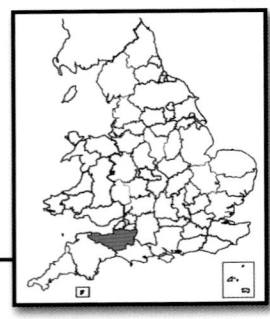

Somerset

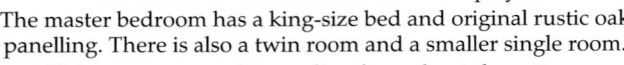
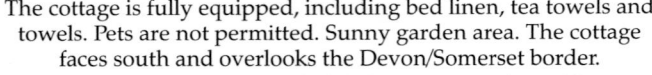

Please note

All the information in this book is given in good faith in the belief that it is correct. However, the publishers cannot guarantee the facts given in these pages, neither are they responsible for changes in policy, ownership or terms that may take place after the date of going to press. Readers should always satisfy themselves that the facilities they require are available and that the terms, if quoted, still apply.

Wiltshire

SB

SB

symbols

🚭	Totally non-smoking	🐕	Pets Welcome
🎠	Children Welcome	**SB**	Short Breaks
♿	Suitable for Disabled Guests	🍷	Licensed

London & South East England

The Houses of Parliament as seen from the London Eye

The focus of the South East of England is the capital, London, a thriving metropolis, with shops, theatres, concerts, museums and sporting events attracting visitors from all over the world. Away from the city, the seaside resorts in Kent, Sussex and Hampshire provide traditional family fun and sandy beaches, as well as all kinds of water-based sports, while further inland both in these counties and in Oxfordshire, Buckinghamshire and Berkshire there are market towns, stately homes, country parks and nature reserves to explore and enjoy.

London has everything to offer! With a wide range of accommodation at prices to suit every pocket, it's easy to spend a weekend here or a take a longer break. Among the most popular places for visitors are the museums and art galleries. The National Gallery houses one of the largest art collections in the world, while the Tate Modern concentrates on the work of artists from the beginning of the 20th century. Except for some special exhibitions, entry to both is free, and this also applies to the Natural History Museum and the Victoria and Albert Museum. To see what's going on all over London, take a trip on the London Eye, the world's highest observation wheel, or meet celebrities (or at least their wax doubles) at Madame Tussauds.

Kent, a county of gentle, rolling downland, long known as the 'Garden of England',

provides opportunities for all kinds of outdoor pursuits. The North Downs Way makes its way through an Area of Outstanding Natural Beauty stretching from Kent through Sussex to Surrey, starting at Dover, including a loop to Canterbury along the Pilgrim's Way. In the White Cliffs area there are a number of heritage walks and trails to follow, while a stay in the downland villages offers an excellent opportunity to explore the many local paths. With easy access from London, the shingle and sandy beaches at resorts such as Deal, Ramsgate, Margate, Broadstairs and Herne Bay have long been an attraction.

West and East Sussex share with neighbouring Kent an attractive coastline with cliffs and sandy beaches, and the countryside of the High Weald and the North Downs.There are endless possibilities for walking, cycling, horse riding, golf, and if you're looking for something more adventurous, hang gliding and paragliding! Don't forget the castles, like Bodiam near Hastings, and the historic ruins at Pevensey and Lewes, or Arundel, one of England's most important stately homes, in West Sussex. The best known resort is Brighton, with its pebble beach, classic pier, Royal Pavilion and Regency architecture. For a shopping day out visit the designer shops, art galleries and antique shops in The Lanes.

Whether you prefer an active break or a quiet country holiday, **Hampshire** offers plenty of choices.There are gardens and country parks, historic houses and wildlife parks, museums and castles, and with its location on the Channel coast, all the activities associated with the seaside. There's plenty to do outdoors in Hampshire: walking, cycling and horse riding on the heathland and ancient woodlands of the New Forest National Park, and for more thrills, paragliding and hang gliding at the Queen Elizabeth Country Park on the South Downs.

All kinds of watersports are available along the coast, but of course the **Isle of Wight**, only a short ferry ride away from the mainland, has award-winning beaches, water sports centres, seakayaking, diving, sailing and windsurfing. For land-based activities there are over 500 miles of interconnected footpaths, historic castles, dinosaur museums, theme parks and activity centres, while the resorts like Sandown, Shanklin, Ryde and Ventnor offer all that is associated with a traditional seaside holiday. There is a thriving arts community, and of course two internationally renowned music festivals held every year.

Less than an hour from London, **Surrey** is the most wooded county in the UK, and an extensive network of footpaths for walkers covers the chalk downs, woods and heathland of the Surrey Hills and North Downs. Alternatively wander through the traditional villages and historic market towns, and stop for lunch at a traditional pub or restaurant. Walk along the Thames towpath to Runnymeade Meadow where the Magna Carta was signed in 1215, or take a leisurely boat trip through the traditional English countryside. Families will enjoy a visit to a working farm, cycling or horse riding, or for more excitement, try the thrilling rides at one of the theme parks.

Whatever your interests, whether in the countryside or the town, **Berkshire** has much to offer. In the east of the county, just a short train ride away from central London,

is Windsor Castle, the largest inhabited castle in the world. Racegoers will find plenty of action in Berkshire, with both Ascot and Royal Windsor in the east, and Newbury to the west, where you can also take a tour of the stables at Lambourn and watch the early morning gallops.

Oxford, the 'city of dreaming spires', has attracted visitors for centuries, and in contrast to lively city life, the **Oxfordshire** countryside is ideal for a relaxing break. Stretching from Oxford to the Cotswolds, the mysterious Vale of the White Horse is named after the oldest chalk figure in Britain, dating back over 3000 years. The historic market towns like Abingdon and Wantage make good shopping destinations, or visit the pretty villages, stopping for lunch in one of the many traditional English pubs. Follow the village trail at Kidlington, the largest village in England, or visit the nature reserve at Adderbury Lakes.

Only half an hour from London, the rolling hills and wooded valleys of the **Buckinghamshire** countryside provide a wonderful contrast to city life. There are fascinating historic towns and villages, including West Wycombe, owned by the National Trust, which also has many other interesting properties in the area. These include the stunning gardens at Cliveden, former home of the Astors and focus of the early 20th century social scene.

Photo courtesy Thanet District Council

Berkshire

Please note

All the information in this book is given in good faith in the belief that it is correct. However, the publishers cannot guarantee the facts given in these pages, neither are they responsible for changes in policy, ownership or terms that may take place after the date of going to press. Readers should always satisfy themselves that the facilities they require are available and that the terms, if quoted, still apply.

Buckinghamshire

Old Stone Barn

Mr & Mrs Garry Pibworth,
Home Farm, Warrington,
Olney MK46 4HN
Tel: 01234 711655
Fax: 01234 711855

The Old Stone Barn is peacefully positioned on an arable farm 1½ miles from the beautiful market town of Olney where there is a wide variety of shops, cafes, bars and restaurants. The accommodation is a charming combination of old character and modern facilities, and consists of 7 spacious self-contained apartments (sleep 1-6), centrally heated and equipped with colour TV and payphone. Linen and towels are provided, and there is a laundry room with washing machines and a tumble dryer. Computer room and wifi available.

Guests can relax in the gardens, make use of the outdoor heated swimming pool, or take day trips to Oxford, Cambridge, London or the Cotswolds.

Terms from £240 to £560 per week.

e-mail: info@oldstonebarn.co.uk
www.oldstonebarn.co.uk

SB

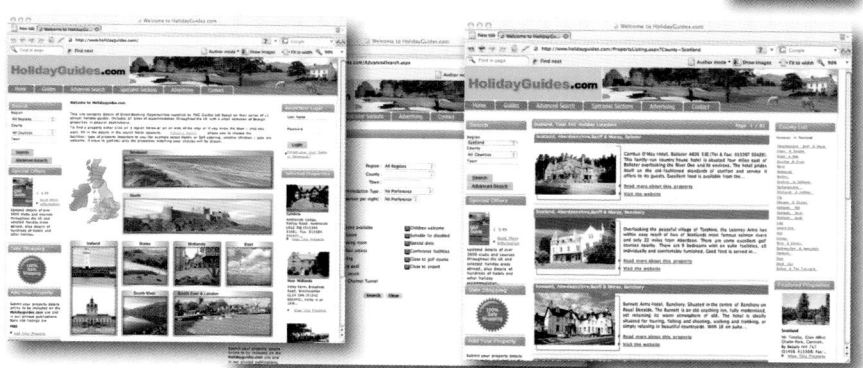

Hampshire

Newly built architect designed "ecobuild" in peaceful location on working farm.

East Cottage *sleeps 7 and attached* **West Cottage** *sleeps 3. The two cottages can be interconnected. Single storey accommodation. Each bedroom has its own bathroom. Open plan living/kitchen areas. Woodchip heating and log burner.*
• guest membership to nearby 9-hole parkland golf course • ideal countryside base to explore the historic Hampshire area or for cycling/walking in the Itchen Valley • adjacent to the famous Avington Trout Lakes • "ecobuild" • pets welcome • golf and fishing

Contact: Robert Stent, Park Farm Office, Avington, Winchester SO21 1BZ
Tel: 01962 779955
robert@avingtonholidays.co.uk
www.avingtonholidays.co.uk

symbols

 Totally non-smoking

 Children Welcome

 Suitable for Disabled Guests

 Pets Welcome

SB Short Breaks

 Licensed

'PENNYPOT'

sleeping two, is a nicely furnished, peaceful apartment adjoining Ha'penny House (a ★★★★★ Guest House offering luxury bed and breakfast accommodation). Set in a quiet area of the unspoilt village of Milford-on-Sea and just a few minutes' walk from both sea and village, it is ideally situated for touring the New Forest, Bournemouth, Salisbury and the Isle of Wight.

The apartment has its own separate entrance, a double bedroom, lounge with TV and DVD, diningroom, fully equipped kitchen and bathroom, use of a large garden and summer house.

Heating, power, linen and towels are included
• Private parking • Non-smokers only
• Sorry no pets
• Friday to Friday bookings
from £220 to £360 per week.

Carolyn Plummer, Ha'penny House,
16 Whitby Road, Milford-on-Sea,
Lymington SO41 0ND • Tel: 01590 641210

info@hapennyhouse.co.uk • www.hapennyhouse.co.uk

The Old Stables

Fritham Farm, Fritham, Lyndhurst SO43 7HH
e-mail: frithamfarm@btinternet.com
www.frithamfarm.co.uk
Contact John & Penny Hankinson
Tel: 023 8081 2333

Relax in the peace - perfect peace - of this detached cottage on our farm in the heart of the New Forest. Spacious and comfortable lounge/dining room. Separate en suite bedroom with double or twin bed. French windows lead from each room to a private patio. Colour TV in both rooms. Central heating. Well-equipped galley kitchen.

Set in An Area of Outstanding Natural Beauty, Fritham Farm is a working stud farm of 51 acres, producing the well known "Fritham" ponies. A wonderful centre for walking, cycling, riding and touring.

Tariff
£275 to
£325

Isle of Wight

The Coach House

is a self-contained apartment in the grounds of Frenchman's Cove, with delightful views of Tennyson Down.

It offers self catering accommodation for a family of four/five, with a well appointed kitchen area with microwave, fridge/freezer, electric cooker, kettle, toaster, cafetière etc. The lounge/dining area has comfortable seating and a TV, DVD and CD/radio/cassette player. The master bedroom has an en suite bathroom with bath and shower over, WC and washbasin. The ground floor has a lobby and utility room complete with a washing machine, tumble dryer etc. plus a WC and washbasin. A door leads to a sleeping area with 2'6" bunk beds (suitable for children only), and stairs leading to the rest of accommodation which is on the first floor. No pets.

Please contact Sue or Chris Boatfield for details.
Frenchman's Cove, Alum Bay Old Road, Totland, Isle of Wight PO39 0HZ
Tel: 01983 752227 • www.frenchmanscove.co.uk

TOTLAND BAY. 3 Seaview Cottages, Broadway, Totland Bay.
This well-modernised cosy old coastguard cottage holds the Farm Holiday Guide Diploma for the highest standard of accommodation. It is warm and popular throughout the year. Located close to two beaches in beautiful walking country near mainland links. It comprises lounge/ dinette/kitchenette; two bedrooms (sleeping five); bathroom/toilet. Well furnished, fully heated, TV, selection of books and other considerations.
Rates: Four day winter break from £60; a week in summer £290.
• Sleeps 5. • Non-smokers only.
Mrs C. Pitts, 11 York Avenue, New Milton, Hampshire BH25 6BT (01425 615215).

Kent

Country cottages and detached pine lodges set in bluebell woods overlooking four acres of water, with a panoramic view of fields, woods and the nearby unspoilt village.

Eight detached PINE LODGES beautifully situated by the water's edge, with views across the water to the village of Woodchurch a mile or so away. Sleep up to 6.
attractive living/dining areas • lakeside terrace • sun decks • fully equipped pine kitchens • one double bedroom, two twin bedrooms • bathroom

ROUGHLANDS BUNGALOW, with its own large garden, set well back from the quiet country road between Appledore and Woodchurch. Sleeps up to 5.
attractive kitchen/dining area • fully equipped pine kitchen • one bedroom with double and single bed, one twin bedroom • large garden • off-road parking

Three terraced COTTAGES with views across the fields to the church. Sleep up to 5.
attractive kitchen/dining areas • fully equipped pine kitchens • one double bedroom, one twin bedroom, one single bedroom • off-road parking

**ASHBY FARMS LTD, PLACE FARM,
KENARDINGTON, ASHFORD TN26 2LZ**
Tel: 01233 733332 • Fax: 01233 733326
e-mail: info@ashbyfarms.com
www.ashbyfarms.com

Hawthorn Farm Cottages

In the delightful rural setting of Ware, near Canterbury, in four acres of gardens surrounded by orchards, Hawthorn Farm comprises our home and four self-catering cottages. All our holiday cottages offer single storey accommodation and sleep 4/5. PILGRIMS COTTAGE is suitable for disabled wheelchair users. CHAUCER, MILLER AND PILGRIMS COTTAGES are in a terrace of three, and FRIARS COTTAGE stands alone.
Ideally situated for touring, cycling, walking, relaxing and exploring the Kent coastline. All bed linen and towels provided. Children's play field and equipment. Ample parking. Pets welcome by arrangement.

ETC ★★★/★★★★

Steve and Doreen Ady, Hawthorn Farm Cottages
Corner Drove, Ware, Near Ash, Canterbury, Kent CT3 2LU
Tel: 01304 813560 • www.hawthornfarmcottages.co.uk
e-mail: hawthornfarmcottages@dsl.pipex.com

Reach Court Farm Cottages, St Margaret's Bay

Situated in the heart of a family-run, working farm, surrounded by open countryside, these five luxury self-contained cottages are very special. They are set around the old farm yard in an attractive setting of lawns and shrubs with open views from the front or rear. The cottages sleep from two to six plus cot, and the accommodation is of the highest standard, giving them a relaxing country feel, with the kitchens equipped with ovens, fridges, microwaves, toasters, coffee makers, etc. There is also a washing machine and tumble dryer in an adjoining laundry room.
Reach Court Farm is the nearest farm to France and was known as the "Front Line Farm" during World War II. St Margaret's is a rural village with shops and public houses offering a range of eating facilities. Dover, Folkestone, Canterbury and Sandwich are all within easy reach.
Mrs J. Mitchell, Reach Court Farm,
St Margaret's-at-Cliff, St Margaret's Bay, Dover CT15 6AQ
Tel & Fax: 01304 852159
e-mail: enquiries@reachcourtfarmcottages.co.uk • www.reachcourtfarmcottages.co.uk

symbols

⊗	Totally non-smoking	🐕	Pets Welcome
🎠	Children Welcome	**SB**	Short Breaks
♿	Suitable for Disabled Guests	♀	Licensed

Oxfordshire

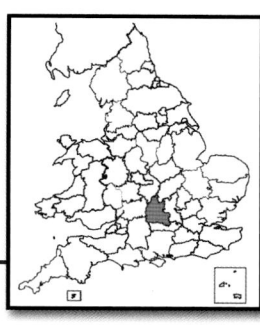

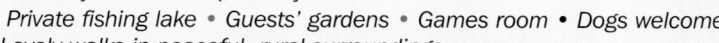

Kingston-Upon-Thames

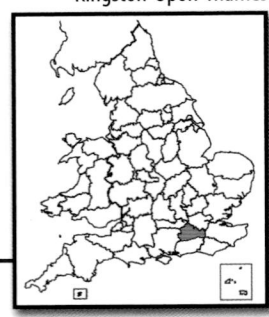

Surrey

East Sussex

An Award winning holiday park with luxury log cabin accommodation. A magnificent heated pool complex with children's paddling area, Jacuzzi, steam room, sauna, gymnasium with cardiovascular and resistance training equipment, beauty therapies, fitness classes, tennis court, children's play area, restaurant, bars, clubhouse and holiday home sales. All this plus beautiful 1066 Country on your doorstep and the Sussex coast just five miles away. Call today for a brochure or visit our award winning website.

01424 773344

**Crowhurst Park, Telham Lane,
Battle, East Sussex. TN33 0SL**
www.crowhurstpark.co.uk
enquiries@crowhurstpark.co.uk

CROWHURST PARK
Holiday Village

Heathfield

Cannon Barn, a Sussex wheat barn built in 1824, has been sympathetically converted to provide modern comforts. Boring House is a small working farm with sheep. There are ponds and a stream on the farm, and plenty of footpaths in the area, including one which crosses the farm, giving plenty of choice for walkers.

Tel: 01435 812285

Locally, there is a good selection of pubs for meals, and also a great variety of things to do and places to visit for all the family.

Please visit our website for photographs and further information.
Short Breaks available out of season. Sleeps 8-10. Prices £190-£900.

Contact: Mrs A. Reed, Boring House Farm,
Nettlesworth Lane, Vines Cross, Heathfield TN21 9AS
e-mail: info@boringhousefarm.co.uk
www.boringhousefarm.co.uk

West Sussex

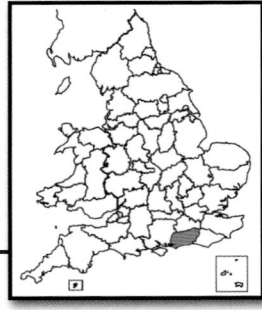

Henfield

New Hall Holiday Flat and Cottage

New Hall, New Hall Lane, Small Dole, Henfield BN5 9YJ • www.newhallcottage.co.uk/

New Hall, the manor house of Henfield, stands in three-and-a-half acres of mature gardens, surrounded by farmland with abundant footpaths. The holiday cottage is the original 1600 farmhouse. It has one en suite bedroom, a large living room, dining room with two folding beds and kitchen; a door opens into the walled garden. The holiday flat is the upper part of the dairy wing. Its front door opens from a Georgian courtyard and it has three bedrooms sleeping five, lounge/diner, kitchen and bathroom. Both units are fully equipped and comfortably furnished. Children welcome. Open all year.

Terms from £300 to £480 per week.

For details and availability please telephone
Mrs M.W. Carreck (01273 492546)

Photo courtesy Leighton Buzzard Railway Ltd

Leighton Buzzard Railway, Bedfordshire

Stretching inland from the North Sea, a peaceful rural landscape of downland, fens, ancient forest and heathland covers the counties of Norfolk, Suffolk, Essex, Cambridgeshire, Hertfordshire and Bedfordshire, while along the coast there are sandy beaches, cliffs and rockpools, sleepy villages, quiet seaside towns and busy family resorts. This is the area to visit for anyone who loves the outdoors. Long subject to the influence of Europe, remains exist from the times of the Romans, Anglo-Saxons and Normans and the countryside is dotted with medieval towns and villages.

Along the **Norfolk** coast from King's Lynn to Great Yarmouth the broad, sandy beaches, grassy dunes, nature reserves, windmills, and pretty little fishing villages are inviting at all times of year. Following the routes of the Norfolk Coastal Path and Norfolk Coast Cycle Way, walk or cycle between the picturesque villages, stopping to visit the interesting shops and galleries, or to enjoy the seafood at a traditional pub or a restaurant. An important trade and fishing port from medieval times, the historic centre of King's Lynn is well worth a visit, and take a break at Great Yarmouth for family entertainment, 15 miles of sandy beaches, traditional piers, a sea life centre and nightlife with clubs and a casino. On the low-lying Fens, the Norfolk Broads or through the ancient pine forests and heathland of The Breck there are walking, cycling and horse riding trails, and market towns and villages to explore. In contrast to the quiet and calm of coast and country, in the medieval city of Norwich with its historic streets and half-timbered houses, cathedral, Norman castle and museums you'll find not only history, but opera, ballet, theatre, music and restaurants .

Suffolk's 40 miles of unspoilt World Heritage coastline is perfect for a seaside holiday. Wander through the coastal forests or along the shingle and sandy beaches admiring the scenery, or hire bicycles for a family bike ride. Eat oysters at Orford or follow the Suffolk Coastal Churches Trail. Fishing is particularly popular on the Waveney as well as many on other rivers and golfers have a choice of short local courses and some of championship standard. Horse racing enthusiasts can't miss Newmarket, whether for a fun day out, to visit the National Horseracing Museum or to take a guided tour round the National Stud. However you choose to spend the day, the wonderful choice of locally produced food served in one of the many pubs, restaurants and cafes will provide the perfect end to your stay.

From the historic port of Harwich in the north to the Thames estuary in the south, the 300 miles of coastline and dry climate of maritime **Essex** have attracted holiday makers since early Victorian times. There are fun family resorts with plenty of action like Clacton, on the Essex sunshine coast, and Southend-on-Sea, with over six miles of clean safe sand and the world's longest pleasure pier. Along the coast there are quiet clifftop walks, sheltered coves, long beaches, mudflats, saltmarshes and creeks. Previously the haunt of smugglers, these are now a great attraction for birdwatchers, particularly for viewing winter wildfowl. Walkers and cyclists will enjoy the gently rolling landscape of the Essex countryside. Explore the medieval towns and villages like Thaxted and Saffron Walden, where long ago saffron was produced for the textile industry, the Norman keep at Colchester, England's oldest town and the grand stately homes like Ingatestone Hall and Audley End. All this within an hour of London!

Cambridgeshire immediately brings to mind the ancient university city of Cambridge, lazy hours punting on the river past the imposing college buildings, students on bicycles, museums and bookshops. This cosmopolitan centre has so much to offer, with theatres, concerts varying from classical to jazz, an annual music festival, cinemas,

Maldon, Essex

Photo courtesy Essex County Council

botanic gardens, exciting shops and to round it all off, restaurants, pubs and cafes serving high quality food. In the surrounding countryside historic market towns, pretty villages and stately homes wait to be explored. Visit Ely with its magnificent cathedral and museum exhibiting the national collection of stained glass, antique shops and cafes. Elizabethan Burghley House and Elton Hall with its beautifully restored rose garden are among the stately homes and historic houses in the county, and there's a wide choice of art galleries to visit too.

Hertfordshire's situation just north of London means that visitors based here have the advantage of easy access to all the city's facilities while staying in a pleasant rural environment. This is a county of small, historic market towns and villages with interesting shops, pubs and restaurants serving wonderful food, art galleries and museums. Despite its magnificent Gothic appearance Knebworth hides an original Tudor mansion, and is well worth a visit both for the exterior architecture and the treasures it contains. Perhaps it is best known now as the 'Stately Home of Rock' and is famous worldwide for the concerts held in the grounds. Hatfield House too has Tudor origins and a wing still survives of the Royal Palace of Hatfield where Elizabeth I spent her childhood. The present Jacobean mansion is surrounded by 1000 acres of parkland with trails marked out for pleasant country walks.

Whatever the weather, in **Bedfordshire** there's a wide choice of activities and places to visit. For a family day out, go on safari to find the 'big five' at ZSL Whipsnade, near Dunstable, one of Europe's biggest wildlife conservation parks or at Woburn Safari Park. Visitors interested in gardening history will enjoy the formal gardens modelled on Versailles laid out in the early 18th century at Wrest Park near Bedford and a later Regency design at the Swiss Garden at Biggleswade, and everyone will have fun finding the way round the Hoo Hill Maze at Shefford.

Great Yarmouth, Happisburgh, Hunstanton

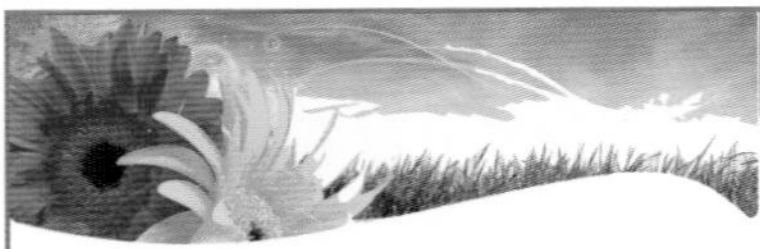

Sunwright Holidays

Sundowner Holiday Park

Newport, Hemsby, Near Great Yarmouth

Fully furnished and equipped self-catering chalets, sleep up to 6. Two bedrooms, kitchen with all your cooking needs, lounge with TV, bathroom with shower over bath. Close to beach, Norfolk Broads and many attractions. Pets most welcome!

★★ CHALET

Contact: Mrs Michelle Browne, 50 Mariners Compass, Gorleston, Great Yarmouth, Norfolk NR31 6TS • 01493 304282 • e-mail: sunwrightholiday@aol.com

www.sunwrightholidays.com

Ollands Farm Barn

Short Lane, Happisburgh NR12 0RR

Lovingly restored to a very high standard, this 18thC barn features a beamed cathedral ceiling, wood-burning stove, quaint paddle stairs, central heating, comfortable king-size bed in galleried bedroom, sofa-bed downstairs, fully fitted kitchen, shower room.

Well behaved dogs are welcome and receive a special treat when they come to stay. We are proud owners of two lurchers and two deerhounds, also two cats and small flock of chickens.

Tel: 01692 652280 • e-mail: mastuart@talk21.com

www.ollandsfarmbarn.co.uk

SB

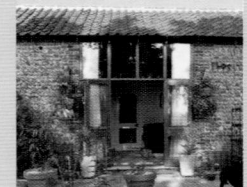

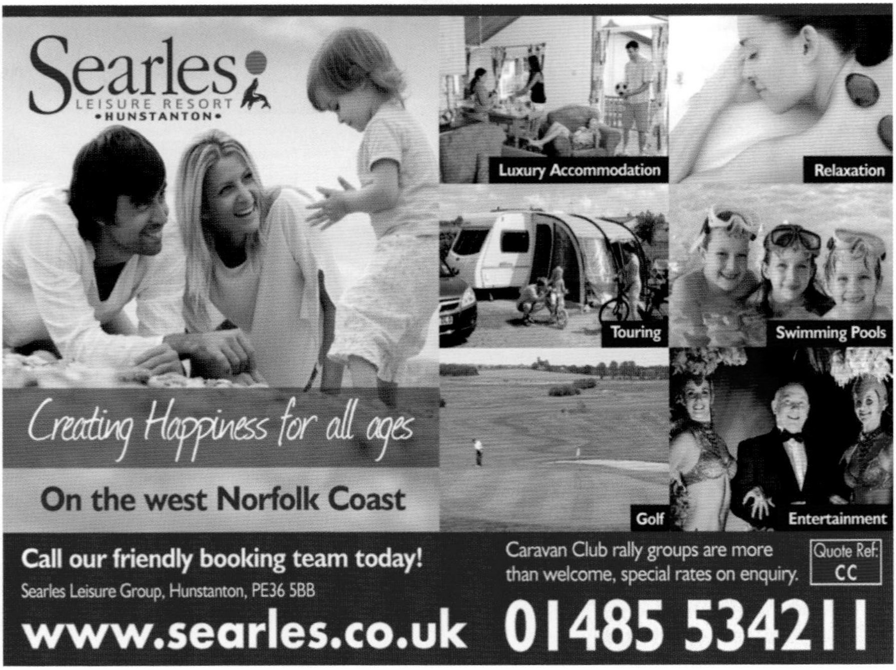

Call our friendly booking team today!

Searles Leisure Group, Hunstanton, PE36 5BB

Caravan Club rally groups are more than welcome, special rates on enquiry.

Quote Ref: CC

www.searles.co.uk 01485 534211

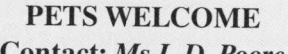

SB

STONE HOUSE FARM • *LYNG, NORFOLK*   *sleeps 5+cot*

PRICES FROM
£320-£485

◆ Free fishing on site ◆ Linen, towels and electricity included ◆ Short Breaks ◆ Good cycling & walking
This traditional brick and flint cottage, with its own enclosed garden and parking, nestles beside a willow-clad mixed coarse fishing lake in the picturesque village of Lyng, in Wensum Valley, which is steeped in history and legends. The cottage sleeps 5 + cot and has three bedrooms (one double, one twin, one single), widescreen TV, DVD, stereo/CD player, electric/gas cooker, fridge/freezer, microwave and washing machine. It is situated 13 miles from Norwich and is ideally positioned to visit the North Norfolk coast. Shop, post office, pub, garage, public telephone, small touring caravan park, riding stables and a nature reserve are all within a 5 minute walk. Places to visit include The Dinosaur Park, steam railways, stately homes, garden and craft centres, the Norfolk Broads, mediaeval city of Norwich, Pensthorpe Waterfowl Park, and Wensum Valley and Barnham Broom Golf Clubs.

Free brochure available • Contact Suzan Jarvis • Tel: 0044(0)1603 870812
e-mail: info@utopia-paradise.co.uk • www.utopia-paradise.co.uk

Holiday Properties (Mundesley) Ltd
6a Paston Road, Mundesley, Norwich NR11 8BN

We are a small family business that has been established over 50 years.

We have a choice of landscaped chalet sites that are close to the beach and village amenities.

Our chalets are heated and well equipped with all the essentials and include a comfortable lounge area, a fitted kitchen, 2 bedrooms and a bathroom. They are graded from 1 to 3 stars with the East of England Tourist board.

Also available are our Manor Court Bungalows. These are newly built. Spacious accommodation with en suite facilities, a large fully equipped kitchen and luxuries such as 32" Flat Panel TV, dishwasher and washing machine. They have good access and parking and each one has their own private courtyard.

Phone: 01263 720719
www.holidayprops.co.uk
info@holidayprops.co.uk

Weybourne

Suffolk

Bungay

Please note

All the information in this book is given in good faith in the belief that it is correct. However, the
publishers cannot guarantee the facts given in these pages, neither are they responsible for
changes in policy, ownership or terms that may take place after the date of going to press.
Readers should always satisfy themselves that the facilities they require are available
and that the terms, if quoted, still apply.

symbols

 Totally non-smoking

 Children Welcome

 Suitable for Disabled Guests

Pets Welcome

SB Short Breaks

Licensed

Lodge Cottage
Laxfield, Suffolk

Pretty 16C thatched cottage retaining some fine period features. Sleeps 4. Pets welcome. Fenced garden. One mile from village. 30 minutes to Southwold and coast. Rural, quiet and relaxing. For brochure phone Jane:

01986 798830 or 07788 853884 or e-mail: janebrewer@ukonline.co.uk

WINNER BEST SELF CATERING ESTABLISHMENT TOURISM IN SUFFOLK AWARDS 2007

Gladwins Farm *Cottages in Constable Country*

Set in 22 acres of rolling Suffolk countryside, Gladwins Farm offers a selection of accommodation. Guests staying in any of our 4★ or 5★ self-catering cottages (sleeping 2-8) can enjoy our heated indoor pool, sauna, hot tub, the hard tennis court and playground. There is coarse fishing in our lake and farm animals to entertain the children. Pets welcome in most cottages and loads of dog walking! Riding, golf and beach within easy reach. *On-line booking through our website,*

SB

If a quiet holiday in a charming area of Olde England is on your agenda, call Pauline or Robert Dossor on 01206 262261 and arrange a memorable stay. See us on the internet at www.gladwinsfarm.co.uk or call for our colour brochure and DVD. Winners, Suffolk Self-Catering Holiday of the Year 2007.

e-mail: gladwinsfarm@aol.com
Gladwins Farm, Harper's Hill, Nayland, Suffolk CO6 4NU

The Midlands

View towards Scotland Bank, Herefordshire

Photo courtesy Herefordshire Tourism

Extending eastwards across the centre of England from the Welsh borders to the North Sea coast and the Wash, the Midlands includes Derbyshire, Herefordshire, Leicestershire and Rutland, Lincolnshire, Northamptonshire, Nottinghamshire, Shropshire, Staffordshire, Warwickshire, West Midlands and Worcestershire. The heart of England and birthplace of the industrial revolution, the landscape varies between quiet farmland, dramatic, windswept moors and tors and gently rolling hills. For outdoor lovers there's a tremendous variety of activities, from watching the seals on the Lincolnshire coast to rock climbing in the Peak District. There are magnificent stately homes to visit, castles steeped in history, beautiful gardens and of course, endless shopping of every kind. The towns and cities offer a wide choice of nightlife, theatres and concerts.

The **West Midlands**, with Birmingham its hub, is the focus of all transport networks in central England so that access is easy by road, rail and air. In Birmingham's vibrant centre there's plenty to do. Shopping has to be high on the agenda and there are art galleries, and art, dance and music festivals to go to, as well as major international events and exhibitions to appeal to everyone.

Herefordshire, on the on the border with Wales, will appeal equally to outdoor lovers and enthusiasts for the arts, crafts and literature, as well as to all food lovers! There

are endless opportunities for all kinds of outdoor activities, with footpaths and bridleways through countryside rich in wildlife. The Black and White Village Trail takes visitors through beautiful countryside to pretty little villages and towns, each with its own individual characteristics and shops. The climate and fertile soil has resulted in wonderful local produce, particularly fruit and vegetables, beef and dairy products.

If you're looking for a break from the pace of life today, but with plenty to do and see, and with a choice of superb food to round off your day, Ludlow in South **Shropshire** is the place to visit. The annual Ludlow Festival, with classical music and jazz, Shakespeare performances, dance and fireworks is just one major event in the town's calendar. There are over 30 castles all over Shropshire, as well as stately homes and all kinds of gardens. For more recent events visit the ten museums at the Ironbridge Gorge where you can learn all about the early inventions leading to the start of the Industrial Revolution.

Worcestershire, stretching south-east from the fringes of Birmingham, is a county of Georgian towns, Cotswold stone villages, Victorian spas, former industrial centres and wonderful walking country. In the Malvern Hills choose between gentle and more strenuous exercise to appreciate the superb views of the surrounding countryside, or take a more restful look at the countryside on a ride on the Severn Valley Railway between Bromsgrove and Kidderminster.

Think of **Warwickshire**, and Shakespeare and Stratford-on-Avon immediately come to mind. A great way to see round this interesting town of black and white, half-timbered buildings is to take a guided walking tour, or better still, hire a bike. Round off the day at the newly rebuilt Royal Shakespeare Theatre next to the river. As well as Sir Basil Spence's Coventry Cathedral and two other churches designed by him, Coventry is home to Warwick Arts Centre, the largest in the Midlands, and there's an Art Trail to follow alongside Coventry Canal.

Northamptonshire may appear a quiet, rural county, but it's very much a place for action and family fun. Everything you would expect to find in the countryside is here – walking, cycling, fishing, wildlife, beautiful villages and traditional inns and pubs. Motorsports enthusiasts will be more than satisfied, with stock car racing at the Northampton International Raceway, Santa Pod, the home of European Drag Racing.

Coast or country, the choice is yours for a holiday in **Lincolnshire**. With award-winning beaches, miles of clean sand, theme parks, kite surfing, wake boarding and water skiing, there's action and excitement for everyone along the Fun Coast and at Cleethorpes on the Humber estuary. At Skegness, as well as all the fun on the beach, children will love watching the seals being fed at the seal sanctuary. In Lincoln walk round the battlements at the Castle, explore the cobbled streets lined with medieval buildings and visit the imposing Gothic cathedral, one of the finest in Europe.

Set in the centre of the Midlands, the rolling countryside, canals, forests, beautiful villages, interesting market towns and history make **Leicestershire and Rutland** well worth a visit. Spend a peaceful hour or two cruising along the Ashby Canal in a narrowboat past Bosworth Battlefield where the Wars of the Roses ended in 1485. With over 1000 different species there's plenty to see at Twycross Zoo at Hinckley, or take a walk through Burbage Wood to see the native fauna. Rutland is England's smallest county with the largest man-made lake in Europe. Cycle round the shoreline, cruise on the water, walk round the lake, while the really energetic can take the walkers' route, Round Rutland, all of 65 miles long.

Nottinghamshire's historic and literary connections make it a highly interesting area to spend a short break or longer holiday. Whether you prefer taking part in sport or just enjoy watching, there's a great variety available. Watch cricket at Trent Bridge, horse racing at Nottingham and the all-weather course at Southwell, and ice hockey at Nottingham's National Ice Centre, or try ice skating yourself. The city of Nottingham, with its links to the legend of Robin Hood, is also a wonderful place to shop - don't miss the traditional Lace Market.

For walking, climbing, mountain biking and caving visit **Derbyshire**. There are activities available at every level and courses to suit everyone. From the gently rolling farmland and National Forest in the south to the rugged demanding landscape of the Dark Peak in the north there are trails for cyclists and walkers to follow, many along old railway lines. Buxton was a spa from Roman times, but the main attractions now are concerts, theatre and the annual literary and music festival. Visit the market town of Chesterfield to see the church with the crooked spire, and for a step back in time go to Crich Tramway Village.

Situated right in the middle of England, **Staffordshire** is a county of open spaces and ancient woodlands, exciting theme parks, stately homes and castles, miles of canals and the largest street-style skate park in Europe at Stoke-on-Trent. There are thrills and fun for every age group at the theme parks. As well as the heart-stopping rides, walk through the Ocean Tank Tunnel at Alton Towers to watch the sea creatures from all the world's oceans and make a big splash in the Waterpark.

Derbyshire

Fleet Cottage
Belper, Derbyshire   enjoy**England** ★★★★

Newly renovated 18th century Grade II listed two bedroom cottage, beamed throughout. Ideal base for the Peak District. Lovely walks and views.

Fleet Cottage, 66 The Fleet, Belper DE56 1NW
Tel: 01773 823240 • Mobile: 0786 626 5446
e-mail: info@thefleetcottage.co.uk
www.thefleetcottage.co.uk

SB

Self contained in Derbyshire

Beautifully renovated Victorian stables providing 7 self-contained en-suite apartments, each sleeping 4-5, with Lounge Area, Gallery Bedroom and Fully Fitted Kitchen.

Grassy Lane, Burnaston,
Derbyshire DE65 6LN
Tel: 01332 510000
www.stableslodge.co.uk

Stables Lodge

 Overnight Accommodation
Holiday Accommodation · Weekend Breaks

SB

PRIORY LEA HOLIDAY FLATS

Beautiful situation adjoining woodland walks and meadows. Cleanliness assured; comfortably furnished and well equipped. Colour TV. Bed linen available. Full central heating. Sleep 2/6. Ample private parking. Close to Poole's Cavern Country Park. Brochure available from resident owner. Open all year. Terms from £115 to £295. Short Breaks available

Mrs Gill Taylor, 50 White Knowle Road, Buxton SK17 9NH • Tel: 01298 23737
e-mail: priorylea@hotmail.co.uk
www.priorylea.co.uk

Looking for holiday accommodation?

for details of hundreds of properties
throughout the UK including
comprehensive coverage of all areas of Scotland try:

www.holidayguides.com

Wolfscote Grange
Farm Cottages
Hartington, Near Buxton, Derbyshire SK17 0AX
Tel & Fax: 01298 84342

Charming cottages nestling beside the beautiful Dove Valley in stunning scenery.

Cruck Cottage is peaceful 'with no neighbours, only sheep' and a cosy 'country living' feel.

Swallows Cottage offers comfort for the traveller and time to relax in beautiful surroundings. It sparkles with olde worlde features, yet has all modern amenities including en suite facilities and spa bathroom.

The farm trail provides walks from your doorstep to the Dales. Open all year. Dogs by arrangement only

Weekly terms from £180 to £490 (sleeps 4) & £180 to £600 (sleeps 6).

e-mail: wolfscote@btinternet.com
www.wolfscotegrangecottages.co.uk

TADDINGTON. Judith Hawley, Ash Tree Barn, Taddington, Near Buxton SK17 9UB (01298 85453).
Ash Tree Barn offers comfortable accommodation in a self-contained wing of a newly converted nineteenth century barn in a quiet, unspoilt village midway between the famous spa town of Buxton and the ancient market town of Bakewell. Taddington makes an ideal base for exploring the Peak District and has many wonderful local walks. The accommodation comprises living room with exposed beams and log burning stove; bright kitchen with electric cooker, microwave, fridge and ironing facilities; spacious hallway, one double bedroom with en suite bath/shower room; off-road parking.
Rates: from £220 to £350 per week incl. heating/electricity/linen/towels.
e-mail: jah@ashtreebarn.fsnet.co.uk

  SB

SB

Woodland Hills Court
Holiday Cottages

We have 5 brick built holiday cottages.
Four have two double/ twin bedrooms, one of
which is wheelchair-friendly. The fifth cottage
has one bedroom with a 4-poster bed and a
bathroom with a roll-topped bath.
All five cottages have an open-plan, well
equipped kitchen, dining room and lounge
with colour TV and DVD player.
The four two-bedroom cottages have a
modern, good-sized wet room. There are
gardens and patios for each cottage for added
privacy, and full use of a drying and laundry
room for our guests.

• All linen and towels are provided.
• A child's cot is available on request.
• Electricity is extra, each cottage having its own meter.
• There is ample off road parking.

*South Derbyshire offers lots of entertainment for all ages, Donington Park
motor racing, Alton Towers, Calke Abbey, Kedleston Hall, Twycross Zoo, and
lots more in the new National Forest, including horse riding.*

A starter pack will be placed in your cottage;
flowers and/or chocolates arranged on request.

Price from £350 to £500 per week

Short stays subject to availability.

**Woodland Hills Court
Ivy House Farm
Stanton by Bridge
Derby DE73 7HT
Tel: 01332 863152
info@ivy-house-farm.com
www.woodlandhillscourt.co.uk**

Herefordshire

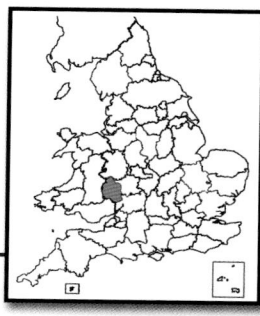

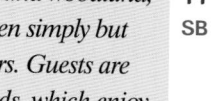

SB

WHITNEY-ON-WYE • HEREFORDSHIRE
The Studio

Set in large gardens which look out to the Black Mountains and Hay Bluff, the Studio is an ideal base from which to explore the beautiful Hereford/Welsh border and Wye Valley. Nearby is the famous book town of Hay-on-Wye. Comfortable self-contained ground floor accommodation sleeping 2-3. Fitted kitchen-diner, sitting room with bed settee, shower room, double bedroom and sun room leading to patio.

Terms: £245 per week, electricity and bed linen included, cot available. Ample parking.

Our speciality is fishing breaks.
We offer an opportunity during your holiday to fly fish for trout on the owner's pools nearby.

Mrs V. Pennington, Greenacre, Whitney-on-Wye, Herefordshire HR3 6EJ
Tel: 01497 831665 • e-mail: valmai@tiscali.co.uk • www.greenacrehereford.co.uk

Lincolnshire

Alford, Barnoldby-Le-Beck

SB

WOODTHORPE HALL COUNTRY COTTAGES

Very well appointed luxury one and three bedroomed cottages, overlooking the golf course, all with central heating, colour TV, microwave, washer, dryer, dishwasher and fridge freezer. Woodthorpe is situated approximately six miles from the coastal resort of Mablethorpe and offers easy access to the picturesque Lincolnshire Wolds. Adjacent facilities include golf, fishing, garden centre, aquatic centre, snooker, pool and restaurant with bar and family room. ETC ★★★★. For further details contact:

Woodthorpe Hall, Woodthorpe, Near Alford, Lincs LN13 0DD • Tel: 01507 450294
• Fax: 01507 450885 • enquiries@woodthorpehallleisure.co.uk • www.woodthorpehallleisure.co.uk

SB

Three well appointed cottages and riding school situated in the heart of the Lincolnshire Wolds.

GRANGEFARM
COTTAGES & RIDING SCHOOL

The tasteful conversion of a spacious, beamed Victorian barn provides stylish and roomy cottages, one sleeping 6, and two sleeping 4 in one double and one twin bedroom, comfy sittingroom and diningroom. Fully equipped kitchen. Bathroom with bath and shower.

You don't need to ride with us, but if you do....

The Equestrian Centre offers professional tuition, an all-weather riding surface, stabling for guests' own horses, and an extensive network of bridle paths.

GRANGE FARM COTTAGES & RIDING SCHOOL

Waltham Road, Barnoldby-le-Beck, N.E. Lincs DN37 0AR

For Cottage Reservations Tel: 01472 822216 • mobile: 07947 627663

www.grangefarmcottages.com

Nottinghamshire

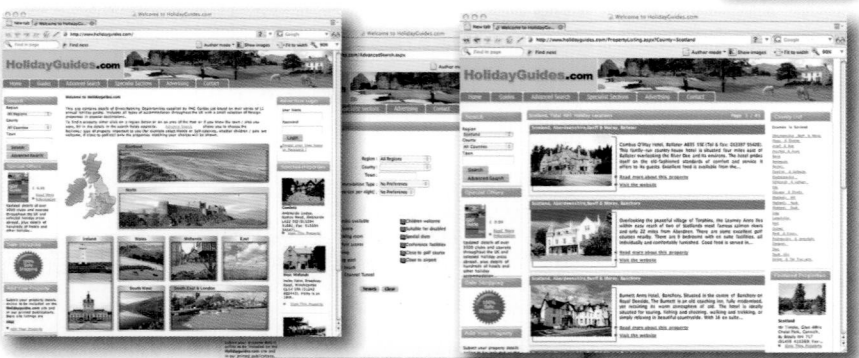

Shropshire

Horseshoe Cottage Clun Valley

Private self-catering cottage situated in the beautiful gardens of a 17th century Listed house in Clunbury, a village of archaeological interest in a designated Area of Outstanding Natural Beauty – A.E. Housman countryside. Completely furnished and equipped; suitable for elderly and disabled persons.

The Welsh Border countryside is rich in medieval history, unspoilt villages and natural beauty. Enjoy walking on the Long Mynd and Offa's Dyke, or explore Ludlow and Ironbridge.

SB

Colour TV.
Children and pets welcome;
cot available.
Ample parking.
Terms £145 to £200 per week.
Please write or phone for
further details.

Mrs B. Freeman, Upper House, Clunbury, Craven Arms SY7 0HG
Tel: 01588 660629

Ravenscourt Manor • SELF-CATERING COTTAGE

Renovated to an extremely high standard whilst retaining all its character, the lovely cottage at Ravenscourt Manor is an historic timber framed building, near good pubs, restaurants and National Trust properties. Superb area for walking or touring in the Shropshire Hills. Historic Ludlow is only three miles with its many festivals, amazing architecture and famous restaurants. The cottage is superbly equipped and furnished (sleep 2/5). Warm welcome and welcome pack.
Hereford 15 miles • Leominster 8 miles • Stratford 50 miles.

SB

01584 711905

Mrs E. Purnell, Ravenscourt Manor, Woofferton, Ludlow SY8 4AL
e-mail: elizabeth@ravenscourtmanor.plus.com
www.smoothhound.co.uk •••• www.virtual-shropshire.co.uk

Ludlow

Staffordshire

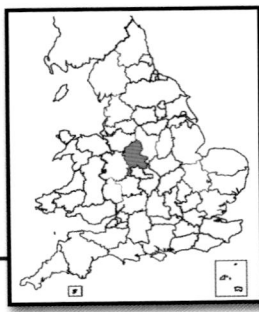

Leek

Warwickshire

symbols

⊘	Totally non-smoking	🐕	Pets Welcome
🎠	Children Welcome	SB	Short Breaks
♿	Suitable for Disabled Guests	♈	Licensed

Great Malvern, Malvern

Worcestershire

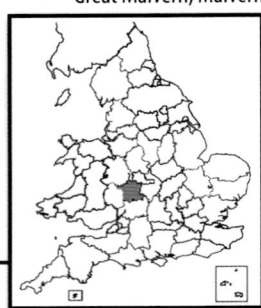

Photo courtesy Scarborough Borough Council

South Bay, Scarborough, North Yorkshire

Seaside with cliffs and golden beaches, wild moorland, rolling hills and dales, castles and abbeys, museums, wildlife, lively cities, busy market towns, wonderful food, great shopping, Yorkshire has it all! From gliding to wind surfing to steam trains, there's an activity for everyone. Situated in north east England, and historically divided into North, West and East Ridings, each of the regions in this guide, North, South, East and West, has its own characteristics, but together they still have much in common.

East Yorkshire is all about fun and action outdoors. From building sandcastles on the award-winning beaches along the North Sea coast in the east to walking in the Wolds inland, all the family will find an activity to enjoy. The Blue Flag beaches at Bridlington and Hornsea are ideal for children and if they tire of the sun and sand there's plenty of traditional entertainment too. Water sports aren't confined to the seaside, with windsurfing at Dacre Lakeside Park and jet skiing at Fossehill near Driffield, an ideal centre from which to explore both coast and country, and for golfers there's a choice of clifftop links and parkland courses inland and on the coast. For a taste of city life visit Hull, with its lovely waterfront, explore the Old Town while following the sculptures of the Seven Seas Fish Trail, enjoy modern drama at the Truck Theatre, and jazz, sea shanty and literature festivals, or watch football and rugby at the KC Stadium. Wherever you go, countryside, seaside or city, you're sure of an interesting and fun time.

Not only does **South Yorkshire** have a considerable industrial heritage to offer, but its situation at the eastern gateway to the Peak District National Park makes it an ideal destination for anyone looking for an outdoor break. Have fun and learn at the same time at the Magna Science Adventure at Rotherham, where the interactive displays are based on the four elements, air, earth, fire and water, or for a day outdoors picnic in the peaceful grounds of the nearby historic Roche Abbey in the beautifully landscaped valley of Maltby Beck, while listening to the birdsong. As well as the abbey ruins, there are interesting churches and chapels to visit, and Doncaster has fine examples of Georgian architecture. Children will love getting really close to wild and farm animals from all over the world at the nearby Yorkshire Wildlife Park, or if the weather isn't so good, there's swimming, ice skating and a climbing wall at Doncaster Dome.

West Yorkshire is a mix of wild moorland and towns and cities with a long industrial heritage. Spend time in one of the many fascinating museums of past working life, then stride out over the moors, taking in the dramatic scenery, before a shopping spree or a wonderful afternoon tea. There's a model Victorian village for mill workers at nearby Saltaire, where Salts Mill has been transformed into the Hockney Gallery, with a restaurant and everything from musical instruments to carpets for shoppers to browse and buy. From there, wander along the banks of the Leeds-Liverpool Canal, so vital for trade in a past age, and perhaps watch the Five Rise Locks in action. Leeds is the destination for a lively city break. Theatres, ballet, opera, festivals, restaurants, clubs, and of course, one of the best shopping experiences in the country, all are here to provide entertainment and a memorable stay. Visit the exclusive shops in the Victoria Quarter and find sought after brands in the new developments at The Light and Clarence Dock on the waterside. If all this is too much for some family members, Harewood House with its wonderful interior, gardens, and adventure playground is nearby, as well as the Yorkshire Planetarium.

The city of York in **North Yorkshire** is full of attractions for the visitor. View it gently floating through the air on a balloon trip, or if you prefer to keep your feet on the ground take a walk round the ancient walls, to get a first glimpse of the compact urban centre dominated by the magnificent York Minster, the largest medieval Gothic cathedral in northern Europe. Have fun finding your way through the the the Snickelways, the maze of hidden alleyways, and enjoy a morning – or longer – in the interesting independent little shops and boutiques as well as all the top high street stores. Explore York's long past at Jorvik, the recreation of the original Viking city from 1000 years ago or become an archaeologist for the day at Dig! and excavate for yourself items from Viking, Roman, medieval and Victorian times. Outside the city the vast open stretches of the North York Moors and the Yorkshire Dales National Parks and the golden sandy beaches of the coast are perfect for an active holiday. Walking, riding, cycling, horse riding, or just enjoying the great outdoors, North Yorkshire provides an ideal destination. Every standard of fitness and ability is catered for, whatever the sport or activity. Walkers will find gentle short circular routes centred on interesting, historic stone villages and busy market towns, and more arduous long distance trails, like the Cleveland Way, the Pennine Trail and the Dales Way, or the really challenging Yorkshire Three Peaks in Ribblesdale.

Photo courtesy Scarborough Borough Council

Whitby Abbey

Photo courtesy National Railway Museum

All aboard at the National Railway Museum

Bridlington, Flamborough

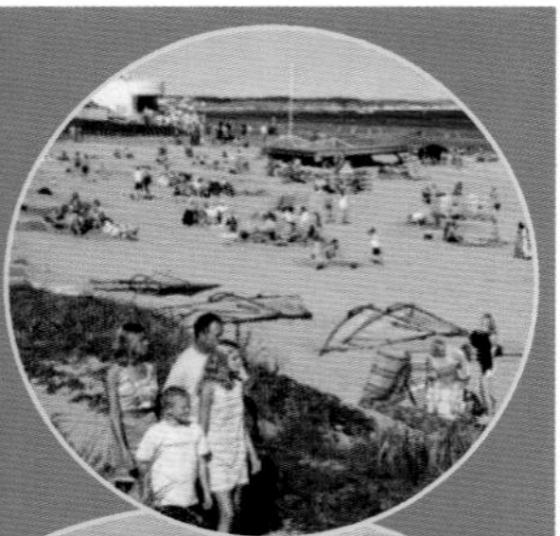

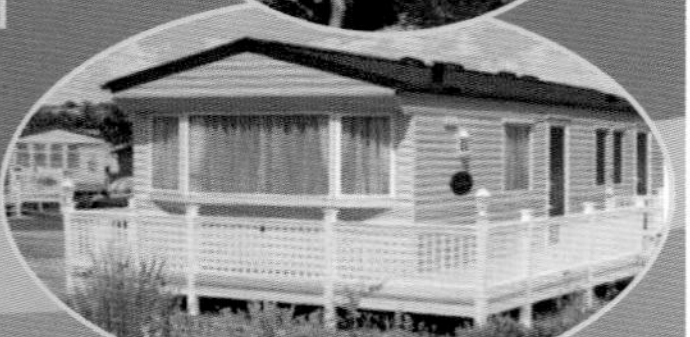

East Yorkshire

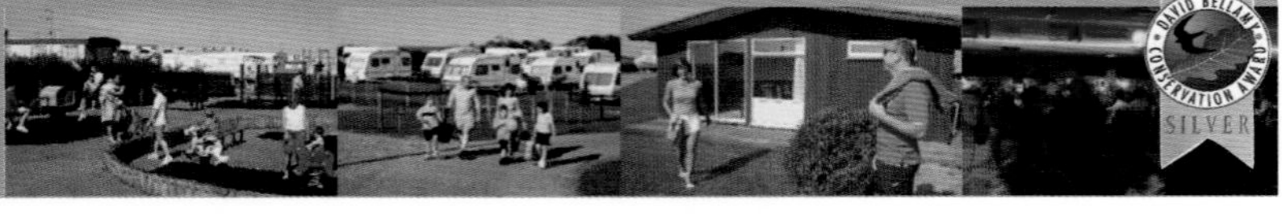

Mowbray Stable Cottages
Stockton Road, South Kilvington YO7 2LY
Mrs M. Backhouse - 01845 522605

Situated within a mile of Thirsk and the village of South Kilvington, these recently converted cottages provide an ideal base for exploring the North Yorkshire Moors, Yorkshire Dales, and within easy reach of York, Durham, and the east coast. COTTAGE NO. 1 sleeps four. One double bedroom, one twin, a large shower room, combined living/kitchen/dining room. Ramped access for wheelchairs, wider doors throughout, handrails etc. in shower room. COTTAGE NO. 2 sleeps two. One double bedroom, en suite shower room, living room, separate kitchen/dining room. Not suitable for wheelchair users. Both cottages are equipped with an electric oven/hob, fridge, microwave, colour TV, shaver point and gas central heating. Linen, but not towels, are included in price. Pets welcome by arrangement. Car essential. No smoking. **Cottage No.1 £50 per night • Cottage No.2 £35 per night • Min. 2 nights**

Rose Cottage Farm Holiday Cottages
Sutton-under-Whitestonecliffe, Thirsk YO7 2QA
Tel: 01845 597309
www.rose-cottage-farm.co.uk

Enjoy a stay in our self-catering holiday cottages in the heart of Herriot Country, with superb scenery and wonderful walking. Within easy reach of Thirsk, Helmsley, York, Scarborough, Harrogate, Malton, the North York Moors and the Yorkshire Dales.

Each sleeps two (twin or king-size bed) • All linen, towels, welcome pack and heating included in price
Laundry facilities available • Shared patio area and secluded lawn
Short breaks available (minimum 3 nights) • Well behaved pets accepted by arrangement.

www.greenhouses-farm-cottages.co.uk Set in the tiny hamlet of Greenhouses and enjoying splendid views over open countryside, three cottages offering a very quiet and peaceful setting for a holiday. The cottages have been converted from the traditional farm buildings and the olde world character has been retained in the thick stone walls, exposed beams and red pantile roofs. All are well equipped, and linen, fuel and lighting are included in the price. There are ample safe areas for children to play. Sorry, no pets. Prices from £295 to £645 per week. Winter Breaks from £200.

Nick Eddleston, Greenhouses Farm Cottages, Greenhouses Farm, Lealholm, Near Whitby YO21 2AD • 01947 897486

White Rose Holiday Cottages
Whitby• Sleights• Sneaton
Quality cottages and bungalows offering a warm and friendly welcome. Sleeping 1-9. Private parking. Ideal for coast and country.
B&B also available in double en suite room with lounge area.
June & Ian Roberts, 5 Brook Park, Sleights, Near Whitby, North Yorkshire YO21 1RT
Enquiries: Tel: 01947 810763
www.whiterosecottages.co.uk

Durham

Laneside, a luxury cottage for up to 6 persons, situated in the Area of Outstanding Natural Beauty in Upper Teesdale, is a haven of tranquillity, combining the best features of traditional Dales life with modern facilities. This former farmhouse occupies an elevated position and enjoys breathtaking south-facing panoramic views of the Upper Raby Estate. It is situated on a carpet of ancient meadows with botanical species and supporting an array of wildlife.

Prices from £290.00 per week. For further details please contact:

Raby Estates Office, Staindrop, Co Durham DL2 3AH
Tel: 01833 660207 • lynda.currie@rabycastle.com

Greenwell Hill Farm Cottages

Traditional farm buildings sensitively converted to attractive sandstone cottages offering high standard self-catering accommodation.
TV/DVD • En suite bathrooms
Modern kitchens with fridge/freezer, microwave etc.
Situated in an Area of Outstanding Natural Beauty, within easy reach of many attractions. Ideal for family holidays.
The Stables (sleeps six plus one), The Byre (sleeps two plus two), The Granary (sleeps eight),
Barn (sleeps 13), The Gin Gan (sleeps five) and Greenwell Hill Farmhouse (accommodation for ten or more)

Karen Wilson, Greenwell Farm, Tow Law, Co. Durham DL13 4PH
Tel: (01388) 527247 • e-mail: enquiries@greenwellhill.co.uk • www.greenwellfarm.co.uk

symbols

⊘	Totally non-smoking	★	Pets Welcome
🏇	Children Welcome	**SB**	Short Breaks
♿	Suitable for Disabled Guests	♉	Licensed

Northumberland

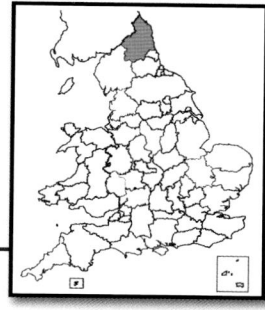

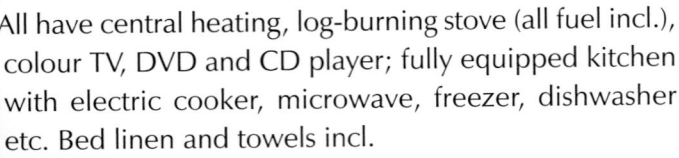

WAREN LEA HALL

Waren Mill, Bamburgh

*Luxurious Self-Catering
Holiday Accommodation
for families, parties and friends.*

Wonderful SHORT BREAKS on the beautiful Northumberland coast.

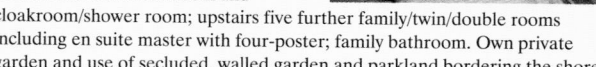

Standing on the shore of beautiful Budle Bay, an Area of Outstanding Natural Beauty and a Site of Special Scientific Interest for its birdlife, lies spectacular WAREN LEA HALL. This lovely, gracious old Hall, set in 2 ½ acres of shoreline parkland and walled gardens, enjoys breathtaking views across the bay and sea to Lindisfarne. In addition to THE HALL there are two entirely self-contained apartments, GHILLIE'S VIEW and GARDEN COTTAGE.

THE HALL *(for up to 14 guests, with 6 bedrooms)*

Beautifully furnished to complement its Edwardian grandeur, with high ceilings, chandeliers, sash windows, fireplaces and polished wooden

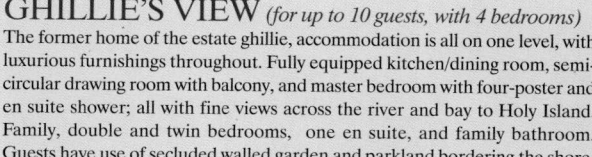

floors. Breathtaking views from every room. Large drawing and dining rooms opening on to floodlit terrace; large, fully equipped kitchen/breakfast room. Ground floor twin bedroom and cloakroom/shower room; upstairs five further family/twin/double rooms including en suite master with four-poster; family bathroom. Own private garden and use of secluded, walled garden and parkland bordering the shore.

GHILLIE'S VIEW *(for up to 10 guests, with 4 bedrooms)*

The former home of the estate ghillie, accommodation is all on one level, with luxurious furnishings throughout. Fully equipped kitchen/dining room, semi-circular drawing room with balcony, and master bedroom with four-poster and en suite shower; all with fine views across the river and bay to Holy Island. Family, double and twin bedrooms, one en suite, and family bathroom. Guests have use of secluded walled garden and parkland bordering the shore.

GARDEN COTTAGE *(for up to 4 guests, with 2 bedrooms)*

The terrace wing of Waren Lea Hall, reached through its own entrance from the garden. All the light and sunny rooms are prettily furnished with high quality fabrics, pine furniture and polished wooden floors throughout, and face the lovely gardens which guests can use. The well equipped kitchen/dining room, lounge, double and twin bedrooms, one en suite, and family shower room are all on one level.

For further information please contact the owners:
Carolynn and David Croisdale-Appleby
Abbotsholme, Hervines Road
Amersham, Buckinghamshire HP6 5HS
Tel: 01494 725194 • Mobile: 07901 716136
e-mail: croisdaleappleby@aol.com
www.selfcateringluxury.co.uk

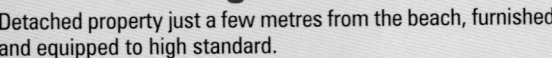

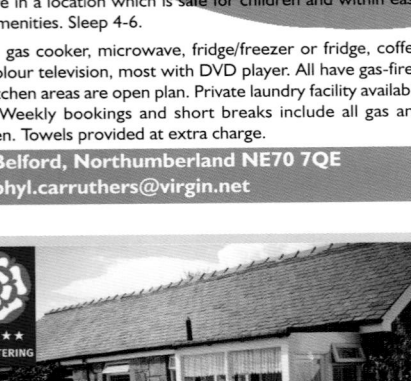
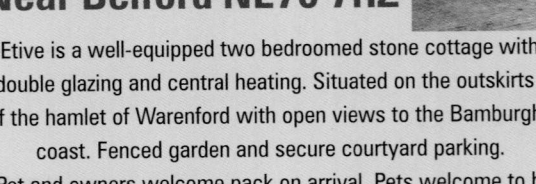

Bockenfield Self-catering Holiday Lodges

- 10 luxury lodges in a rural woodland setting near the A1, between Alnwick and Morpeth
- Stylish interiors with modern fully fitted kitchens
- Sleep 4/6 • Open 11 months a year
- Patio doors leading onto exterior decking
- Small launderette on site • Shops etc in nearby Felton
- Easy access to spectacular Northumberland Heritage Coastline

www.cwelchshomes.com

For details contact: Ms L. Blewitt, Felton, Near Morpeth, Northumberland NE65 9QJ
Tel: 01670 787643 • Fax: 01670 783283 • e-mail: bockenfield@welchshomes.com

Stables Cottage

is a self-catering holiday cottage located in the village of Gunnerton near Hexham, with car parking and easy access to the main road. It sleeps 4 in a double bedroom and twin bedroom; sun lounge, bathroom, well equipped kitchen. The cottage is centrally heated and there is a log burner for those cosy evenings. There is a patio area for eating outside, or just to relax. The village of Gunnerton is just 9 miles from the market town of Hexham and is an ideal location for exploring Hadrian's Wall, Kielder, Newcastle upon Tyne and many more places of interest.

SB

Contact: Susan & David Reay, The Stables Cottage, Coal Road, Gunnerton, Hexham NE48 4EA
Tel: 01434 681852/689942
http://stablescottagelet.co.uk

Milecastle Inn Cottages

These cottages have excellent views to Hadrian's Wall and are ideally situated next to a traditional pub/restaurant, renowned for its good food and well kept ales. The cottages provide an excellent base for walkers/cyclists/golfers, or indeed anyone visiting the many attractions in the area.

- *Each sleeps 3 • No children under 12 years*
- *Non-smokers only • Minimum stay 3 nights*

Contact: Mrs C. Hind, Milecastle Inn, North Road, Haltwhistle NE49 9NN • Tel: 01434 321372
e-mail: clarehind@aol.com • www.milecastle-inn.co.uk

High Dalton Cottage

SB

Cosy and comfortable cottage on a family-run working farm set in 270 acres of beautiful scenery and wildlife. The cottage has been converted from stables and has two double rooms and one twin, each with en suite bath/shower room. The cottage is in an area of Northumberland's most picturesque and interesting countryside and has private parking and an enclosed garden with patio. The quaint Roman towns of Hexham and Corbridge are nearby. The award-winning championship golf courses of Slaley Hall and Matfen Hall are a short distance away; other attractions include Newcastle, Kielder Water and Gateshead Metro Centre.

For details contact Mrs J. Stobbs, High Dalton Farm, Hexham NE46 2LB
e-mail: stobbsjudy@aol.com • tel: 01434 673320

North West England

Photo courtesy Cars of the Stars Museum

Cars of the Stars Museum, Keswick, Cumbria

Bright lights and vibrant city nightlife, thrills and entertainment at the seaside, quiet coastal resorts and countryside, and awe-inspiring upland scenery are all to be found in England's North West. From non-stop action in Manchester and Liverpool, the stately homes and glorious gardens of Cheshire, the lively Lancashire seaside and the wonderful walks and climbs of the western Pennines and Cumbria, this region is perfect for a weekend getaway or a longer family holiday.

Manchester and the surrounding area is the place to go for shopping and nightlife, art, music and industrial heritage, and of course, sport. With two famous football teams, international cricket, rugby and all the facilities from the 2002 Commonwealth Games there's plenty to keep sports fans fully occupied. The Arndale Centre in the city, the Trafford Centre just a few miles away and the Lowry Outlet Mall in Salford will ensure that shoppers are happy too. The newly renovated Manchester Art Gallery full of wonderful paintings, MOSI, the Museum of Science and Industry with hands-on exhibitions for all age groups, the Imperial War Museum North and Urbis, a new concept in museums, concentrating on all aspects of contemporary city life are there to browse through and explore.

In **Cheshire**, just south of Manchester, combine a city break in historic Chester with

a day or two at one of relaxing spas either in the city itself or in one of the luxury resorts in the rolling countryside. Time your visit to the historic Georgian mansion at Tatton Park to coincide with one of the wide choice of events held there throughout the year, including the annual RHS Flower Show. Chester, with its wonderful array of Roman, medieval and Georgian buildings is a fascinating place to visit. Walk round the most complete example of city walls in the whole country, past the beautiful cathedral, before browsing through the wonderful range of shops, art galleries and museums.

The region now known as **Cumbria**, in England's north west, has been attracting tourists since the end of the 17th century, and the number of visitors has been increasing ever since. The area is a walkers' paradise, and whether on foot, in a wheelchair or a pushchair there's a path and trail for everyone. There are magnificent views from the lakesides as well as from the hill and mountain tops, so whether you're following one of the 'Miles without Stiles' on relatively level, well laid tracks around the towns and villages, climbing in the Langdales or tackling Scafell Pike, the highest mountain in England, you won't miss out on all the Lake District has to offer. The busy market town of Keswick is the ideal centre for exploring the north Lakes, including the historic port of Whitehaven, the former centre for the rum trade. Stay in Penrith, Appleby-in-Westmorland or Kirkby Lonsdale to explore the western Pennines or Silloth-on-Solway to discover the Solway Firth coast. Finally don't miss out Carlisle and its cathedral and castle, the stronghold involved in so many battles with the Scots, the Jacobite rebellions and the Civil War.

Liverpool, an exciting multicultural city built on a history of trade with the Americas, Africa and Asia, is still an important port, but now the emphasis is on art, music and drama and the city's multicultural heritage. Contrasting with this is the tranquil surrounding countryside and coast of the **Merseyside** region, stretching into the counties of Cheshire and Lancashire, where there are ample opportunities for outdoor activities in country parks and nature reserves and on more than 30 miles of coastline and beaches. In Liverpool itself there are theatres, art galleries and museums, cathedrals and endless possibilities for shopping, almost all right in the city centre. Not far from the centre the wonderful interiors and gardens at Speke Hall, a Tudor manor house cared for by the National Trust, are well worth a visit, while back at the Albert Docks the Bugworld

Experience, the UK's first insectarium, is just the place to find out all about all kinds of creepy crawlies! Further afield enjoy the views and sea breezes at the Wirral Country Park and beach, and if you're feeling energetic take a walk along the 12 miles of the Wirral Way. City, coast and country, there's plenty to keep the family occupied for an interesting holiday break.

Generations of excited holiday-makers have visited **Lancashire's** coastal resorts, and amongst them Blackpool stands out as the star attraction. For seaside fun, amusements and entertainment it's difficult to beat, but the quieter resorts along the coast with traditional seaside attractions have their own appeal. There's fun for all ages in Blackpool, Britain's most popular resort, from the Big Wheel on Central Pier, the thrilling rides at the Pleasure Beach, and the Winter Gardens with award-winning shows, jazz and rock concerts, to the tropical sharks and reef fish at Sealife, the Sandcastle Waterpark, and a ride in a historic tram along the newly renovated Central Promenade, not forgetting sand, sea and donkey rides. Take a ride to the top of the most famous feature of all, Blackpool Tower, to see the wonderful views and celebrate the arrival of autumn with the annual the spectacle of the Blackpool Illuminations. Further north at Morecambe take part in the Catch the Wind Kite Festival held on the sands in July, just one of a number of events in the town each year. From Clitheroe, with its castle and specialist shops, explore the beautiful Forest of Bowland in the centre of the county, wandering along the lowland riversides or tramping over the moorland hills. Follow the circular Lancashire Cycleway from north to south along sleepy roads through interesting little villages, or test your mountain biking skills in Gisburn Forest where there are trails for everyone from beginners to the highly experienced. Preston, with everything from high street names to farmers' shops and markets, is the destination for shopping, as well as the National Museum of Football.

Photo courtesy Blackpool Tourism

Stanley Park, Blackpool, Lancashire

Cumbria

Burnside Park

www.burnsidepark.co.uk

Now part of the Hapimag Holiday World !

Burnside Park has a selection of 44 one and two bedroom cottages and apartments just 300m from the centre of Bowness and Lake Windermere, offering top quality self catering accommodation and leisure facilities, all year round.

Burnside Park
Kendal Road-Bowness
Cumbria LA23 3EW
08700 46 86 24
stay@burnsidepark.co.uk

43A Quarry Rigg, Bowness-on-Windermere

Ideally situated in the centre of the village close to the Lake and all amenities, the flat is in a new development, fully self-contained, and furnished and equipped to a high standard for owner's own comfort and use. Lake views, ideal relaxation and touring centre. Close to Beatrix Potter Museum. Accommodation is for two/three people. Bedroom with twin beds, lounge with TV, video and DVD; convertible settee; separate kitchen with electric cooker, microwave and fridge/freezer; bathroom with bath/shower and WC. Electric heating. Parking for residents.
Rates: Low season £180 to £240; High Season £240-£350
• *Weekends/Short Breaks also available.* • *Sleeps 2/3* • *Sorry, no pets.*
SAE, please, for details to E. Jones, 45 West Oakhill Park,
Liverpool, Merseyside L13 4BN

Tel: 0151-228 5799
e-mail:
eajay@btinternet.com

symbols

Totally non-smoking		**SB**	Pets Welcome
Children Welcome		**SB**	Short Breaks
Suitable for Disabled Guests			Licensed

SB

Ash Gill Cottages
Torver, Near Coniston Cumbria

Set amidst the rolling hills surrounding Coniston Water, in an area of outstanding natural beauty, two adjoining houses, both sleeping six and appointed to the highest standard. Entrance hall with downstairs toilet, and expansive lounge/dining room and a well equipped kitchen. Double-bedded room on first floor with en suite facilities, two comfortable twin-bedded rooms with bathroom. Central heating throughout for the cooler months. Bed linen and towels provided. Ample parking, gardens and patios. Excellent base for walking, touring, watersports and pony trekking. Open all year for weeks and breaks.
Terms from £375 to £600 per week. Sorry, no pets.
Brochure and details from Mrs D. Cowburn, "Lyndene", Pope Lane, Whitestake, Near Preston, Lancashire PR4 4JR • 01772 612832
e-mail: dorothy@ashgillcottages.co.uk   website: www.ashgillcottages.co.uk

---

DENT VILLAGE

Character cottage for four
www.dentcottages.btinternet.co.uk
e-mail: dentcottages@btinternet.com
Tel: 015396 25294

Situated in the centre of the attractive old village of Dent with its narrow cobbled streets and surrounded by marvellous scenery. This delightful 17th century cottage is a Grade ll Listed building and has been restored with care. The accommodation is comfortably furnished and is situated opposite Dent Church. This lovely holiday home enjoys an outlook over the surrounding countryside to the hills beyond and makes an ideal base for touring the Dales, or as a walking centre with open fells close at hand.

2 bedrooms - 1 double and 1 twin (with vanity unit), lounge with dining area, kitchen, and bathroom with toilet. Services: Electric fire in lounge, night storage heaters – all electricity included in the rent. Colour TV, shaver point, microwave oven. Large basement garage.

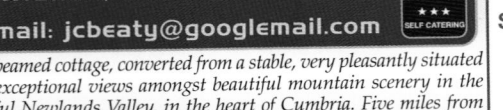

SB

Howscales was originally a 17th century farm. The red sandstone buildings have been converted into five self-contained cottages, retaining many original features.

Set around a cobbled courtyard, the cosy, well-equipped cottages for 2-4, are surrounded by award-winning

NATIONAL ACCESSIBILITY SCHEME: CATEGORY 2	★★★★ SELF CATERING

gardens and open countryside. Shared laundry facilities.
Cared for by resident owner. Ideal base from which to explore the Eden Valley, Lakes, Pennines and Hadrian's Wall.

Please contact us or see our website for details.

- **£220 to £550 weekly** • **Sleep 2/4**
- **Non-smoking** • **Open all year**
- **Short breaks available**
- **Well-behaved pets welcome by arrangement**

Liz Webster, Howscales, Kirkoswald, Penrith CA10 1JG
Tel: 01768 898666 • **Fax: 01768 898710**
e-mail: liz@howscales.co.uk • **www.howscales.co.uk**

SB

Only one mile from Ullswater, our four detached log cabins have a peaceful fellside location in 25-acre grounds with two pretty lakes. Ducks, moorhens, red squirrels and wonderful birdlife. Doggy heaven! Sleep 2-5.

Land Ends Cabins
Watermillock, Near Ullswater CA11 0NB
Tel: 017684 86438
e-mail: infolandends@btinternet.com
www.landends.co.uk

★★★ SELF CATERING

symbols

	Totally non-smoking		Pets Welcome
	Children Welcome	SB	Short Breaks
	Suitable for Disabled Guests		Licensed

Lancashire

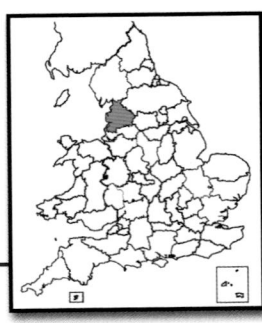

Clitheroe

Aberdeen, Banff & Moray

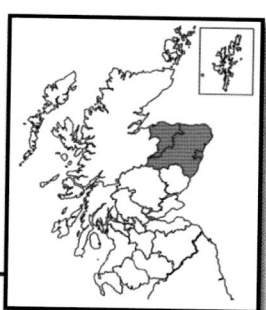

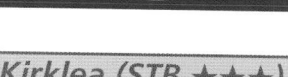

Argyll & Bute

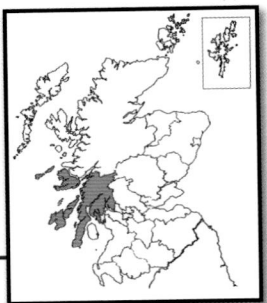

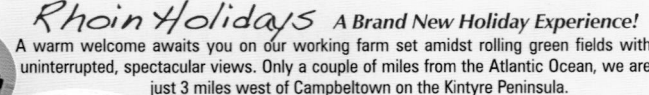

symbols

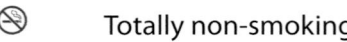

 Totally non-smoking

Children Welcome

Suitable for Disabled Guests

Pets Welcome

SB Short Breaks

Licensed

Garden Cottage

Inistrynich

Dalmally

Argyll PA33 1BQ

Two cottages overlooking Loch Awe surrounded by beautiful scenery, the perfect retreat for a peaceful holiday

- **Garden Cottage (sleeps 8)**
- **Millside Cottage (sleeps 4)**

Dalmally 5 miles, Inveraray 11 miles, Oban 28 miles.

Millside Cottage

Both have garden area, convector heaters in all rooms, open fire in living rooms, electric cooker, fridge, immersion heater, electric kettle, iron, vacuum cleaner, washing machine, colour TV. Cot and high chair by request. Dogs allowed by arrangement. Car essential, ample parking. Ideal for touring mainland and Inner Hebrides. Good restaurants, hill walking, forest walks, fishing, boat hire, pony trekking, National Trust gardens and golf within easy reach. Open Easter to November.

Rosneath Castle Park

SELF-CATERING HOLIDAYS • HOLIDAY HOMES • PARK HOMES
WATERSPORTS CENTRE • ADVENTURE PLAYGROUND • RESTAURANT • FISHING TACKLE SHOP

So near, yet so far away

It could scarcely be possible to imagine a more attractive setting for a holiday park than nature has provided for Rosneath Castle.

Known locally as the 'Green Isle', its many visitors over the years have taken that name away with them, along with many fond memories of their stay.

Although not much more than an hour's drive from Glasgow, the spectacular scenery en route to Rosneath Castle Park will have you believing you're a million miles away. When you arrive, you will find yourself - in more ways than one - at a 5 star park recognised by VisitScotland.

The wooded policies that play an important role in the privacy and seclusion of Rosneath Castle, play host to Park Homes, Holiday Homes and Self-Catering Holiday Homes.

So whether you are here to unwind the main sail or to chill out at the water's edge, at Rosneath Castle your expectations can never be set too high.

Scottish
TOURIST BOARD
★★★★★
HOLIDAY
PARK

01436 831208
www.rosneathcastle.co.uk
Rosneath Castle Park, Rosneath, Near Helensburgh, Argyll G84 0QS

Located in an unspoilt area of outstanding beauty and abundant wildlife, Ardachearnbeg Cottages provide everything required for a wonderful holiday in glorious Glendaruel.

Ardachearnbeg Cottages

Whether visitors wish for adventure or to steep themselves in history, to be active, to watch the birds and wildlife, to walk, cycle or sail, or simply to relax, the cottages provide a comfortable and warm base for doing so.

All properties have ample parking, are centrally heated, double glazed, offer TV, DVD & CD players, all white goods, garden furniture and outdoor barbecue facilities. Pets are welcomed by arrangement.

Ardachearnbeg Cottages
Glendaruel, Argyll PA22 3AE
Tel: 01369 820272
e-mail: info@ardachearnbeg.co.uk
www.ardachearnbeg.co.uk

Scottish
TOURIST BOARD
★★★★★
SELF
CATERING

19th century Minard Castle beside Loch Fyne is a peaceful location for a quiet break. Stroll in the grounds, walk by the loch, explore the woods, or tour this scenic area with lochs, hills, gardens, castles and historic sites.

THE LODGE • a comfortable bungalow with small garden and view through trees to the loch, sleeps 4-6.

THE MEWS APARTMENT • sleeps 4-5.

• Well equipped; central heating, hot water, linen and towels included.
• Terms £140 to £390 per week. Open all year.

Also Four Star B&B in Minard Castle;
from £60pppn, open April-Oct.

Minard Castle
SELF-CATERING
Minard, Inveraray PA32 8YB
Tel & Fax: 01546 886272
reinoldgayre@minardcastle.com
www.minardcastle.com

Duntrune Castle Holiday Cottages

Five traditional self-catering cottages set in the spacious grounds of 12th century Duntrune Castle, which guards the entrance to Loch Crinan. All have been attractively modernised and accommodate two to five persons.

The estate comprises 5000 acres and five miles of coastline. Without leaving our land, you can enjoy easy or testing walks, sea or river fishing, and watching the abundant wildlife. Nearby are several riding establishments, a bicycle-hire firm, and a number of excellent restaurants.

Prices from £250 to £500 per week.

Pets are welcome.

For further details please contact:
**Robin Malcolm,
Duntrune Castle, Kilmartin,
Argyll PA31 8QQ
01546 510283
www.duntrune.com**

Darroch Mhor Chalets

Carrick Castle, Loch Goil, Argyll PA24 8AF

Chill out in Scotland's first national park. Five self catering chalets nestling on the shores of Loch Goil, each with superb lochside views and offering a peaceful and relaxing holiday in the heart of Argyll Forest Park. Each chalet has two bedrooms, living room with colour TV, fitted kitchen with fridge, freezer, microwave, toaster etc. and bathroom with bath and overhead shower. Car parking by each chalet. Great hill walking.

Ideal for pets, genuinely pet-friendly • Open all year – weekly rates £140-£295. Weekend & short breaks available all year, reductions for 2 persons. One pet free.

Tel: 01301 703249 • e-mail: mail@argyllchalets.com • www.argyllchalets.com

Inchmurrin Island

SELF-CATERING HOLIDAYS

Inchmurrin is the largest island on Loch Lomond and offers a unique experience. Three self-catering apartments, sleeping from four to six persons, and a detached cedar clad cottage sleeping eight, are available.

The well appointed apartments overlook the garden, jetties and the loch beyond. Inchmurrin is the ideal base for watersports and is situated on a working farm.

Terms from £407 to £850 per week, £281 to £560 per half week.

A ferry service is provided for guests, and jetties are available for customers with their own boats. Come and stay and have the freedom to roam and explore anywhere on the island.

e-mail: scotts@inchmurrin-lochlomond.com
www.inchmurrin-lochlomond.com
Inchmurrin Island,
Loch Lomond G63 0JY
Tel: 01389 850245 • Fax: 01389 850513

COLOGIN – a haven in the hills

If you've just got married or just retired, have toddlers in tow or dogs you can't bear to leave at home, or you just want to get away for a break with all the freedom of a self-catering holiday, then we may have just what you are looking for. Our cosy chalets and well appointed lodges offer everything you need for a relaxing country holiday.

One of the most appealing features of Cologin is its peace and tranquillity. With 14 lodges, 4 chalets, Cologin Farmhouse and Cruachan Cottage at Cologin we have plenty of different accommodation options. Choose from a cosy one-bedroom chalet or the larger two-bedroomed lodges, or sleep up to 10 adults and 4 children in our traditional Scottish farmhouse.

Our award-winning family-friendly pub and restaurant, *The Barn,* is within easy reach of all our properties. It's a perfect place to unwind and relax. With its unique atmosphere and friendly staff it is the reason why many of Cologin's guests return year after year.

If you love the great outdoors come rain or shine and want to escape from the routine of city life, Cologin is for you. With 17,000 acres of waymarked forest trails above the farm you can enjoy nature at its finest, with glorious scenery and breathtaking views from the summit over Oban Bay to the islands beyond.

Contact us for colour brochure:
Jim and Linda Battison – resident owners
Cologin, Lerags Glen, Oban, Argyll PA34 4SE
Telephone: 01631 564501 • Fax: 01631 566925
e-mail: info@cologin.co.uk
www.cologin.co.uk

COLOGIN
a haven in the hills
STB ★★★–★★★★
Self Catering

Ayrshire & Arran

SB

Kilmory Lodge Bunkhouse is in a beautiful and tranquil setting on the Isle of Arran, off the west coast of Scotland. It is a modern, comfortable bunkhouse, purpose-built to accommodate groups, to a maximum of 23, and ideal for work groups, families and all group holidays. There are ample toilet and shower facilities and bed linen is supplied, but guests have to provide their own towels. There is a fully equipped kitchen/dining area with tables and chairs for relaxation, and a large drying/airing cupboard.The building is attached to Kilmory Village Hall. Groups using the bunkhouse have the option of using the extra facilities that the Hall offers.

Kilmory Lodge Bunkhouse, Kilmory, Isle of Arran KA27 8PQ
Telephone: 01770 870345
e-mail: enquiries@kilmoryhall.com • www.kilmoryhall.com

Noddsdale House, Largs • *Bell Loft and East Wing*

Peaceful surroundings with stunning views • Plenty of places to explore - islands, castles, gardens
Many golf courses in the area • Tennis court in the garden • We welcome children 10 years old and over.

SB

The Bell Loft, the former staff wing, has been completely renovated to provide luxurious accommodation for 4 people, whilst **The East Wing**, which retains the charm of the old guest wing, is ideal for 2. Both wings have their own front door, and are full of character.

They are part of Noddsdale House, a B Listed Arts and Crafts Country House just outside Largs on the Firth of Clyde, with easy access to the Islands. It is a very special place to stay, and provides the perfect setting for a peaceful and relaxing holiday. Terms £400-£850. Short Breaks available. STB ★★★/★★★★

Jane Evans, Noddsdale Estate, Brisbane Glen, Largs, Ayrshire KA30 8SL
Tel: 01475 673757 / 672382 • www.ayrshirecountryholiday.co.uk

---

  **1 Guildford Street, Millport, Isle of Cumbrae**
e-mail: b@1-guildford-street.co.uk • www.1-guildford-street.co.uk

SB

Five flats and one house - comfortable modern, QualityAssured - to cater for 2 - 10 persons. Ideal for extended families. Superb sea views. Close to shops, pubs, restaurants and the beach. Small garden. Rates include heating. Sorry no pets.

Only a 15 minute ferry crossing from Largs, the Isle of Cumbrae is a small, friendly, unspoilt island, with cycling, golf, walking, bowling, sailing and birdwatching. Open all year.

Terms from £155 to £675 per week.

Mrs Barbara McLuckie, Muirhall Farm, Larbert, Stirlingshire
FK5 4EW • Tel: 01324 551570 • Fax: 01324 551223

Please note

All the information in this book is given in good faith in the belief that it is correct. However, the publishers cannot guarantee the facts given in these pages, neither are they responsible for changes in policy, ownership or terms that may take place after the date of going to press. Readers should always satisfy themselves that the facilities they require are available and that the terms, if quoted, still apply.

Melrose

Dumfries & Galloway

Castle Douglas

CASTLE DOUGLAS. Cala-Sona, Auchencairn, Castle Douglas.
A stone-built house in centre of Auchencairn village, near shops, Post Office and garage. To let, furnished. Linen supplied. Two bedrooms (one double bed; two single beds); cot available. Bathroom, bedroom with double bed, livingroom and kitchenette with electric cooker, fridge and geyser. Auchencairn is a friendly seaside village and you can enjoy a peaceful holiday here on the Solway Firth where the Galloway Hills slope down to the sea. Many places of historic interest to visit, also cliffs, caves and sandy beaches. A haven for ornithologists. SAE brings prompt reply. Car essential - parking.
• Sleeps 6.
Mrs Mary Gordon, 7 Church Road, Auchencairn, Castle Douglas DG7 1QS (01556 640345).

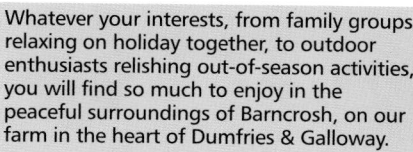

Dunbartonshire

Edinburgh & Lothians

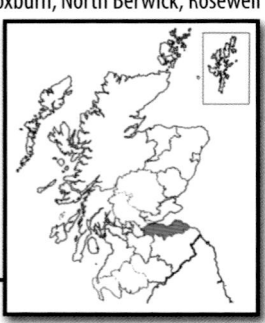

Fife

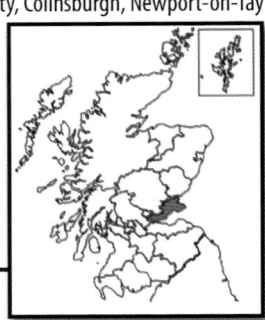

Highlands

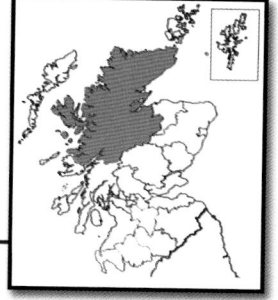

SPEYSIDE LEISURE PARK

Self-Catering Holidays in the Heart of the Highlands

The park is situated in a quiet riverside setting with mountain views, only a short walk from Aviemore centre and shops. We offer a range of warm, well equipped chalets, cabins and caravans, including a caravan for the disabled. Prices include electricity, gas, linen, towels and use of our heated indoor pool and sauna. There are swings, a climbing frame and low level balance beams for the children. Permit fishing is available on the river. Discounts are given on some local attractions.

Families, couples or groups will find this an ideal location for a wide range of activities including:

- *Horse riding • Golf • Fishing • Hillwalking*
- *RSPB Reserves • Mountain and Watersports • Reindeer herd*
- *Steam railway and the Whisky Trail*

Only slightly further afield you will find Culloden Moor, the Moray Firth dolphins and of course, the not to be missed, Loch Ness.
Accommodation sleeps from 1-6, and we offer a reduced rate for a couple or one single person. Short Breaks are available.
Sorry, no pets, except guide and hearing dogs. No tents or camper vans.

Speyside Leisure Park
Dalfaber Road, Aviemore,
Inverness-shire PH22 1PX
Tel: 01479 810236
Fax: 01479 811688
e-mail:
fhg@speysideleisure.com
www.speysideleisure.com

Craigmore

Glenurquhart House Hotel
Drumnadrochit • Loch Ness • Glen Affric

On a wooded hillside in the grounds of a country house hotel in beautiful Glenurquhart, this attractive bungalow is 5 miles from Drumnadrochit. Tastefully decorated and comfortably furnished, the property is well-appointed, spacious and bright and all rooms are on one level. The house faces south with views down the glen and has a lovely conservatory and a mature enclosed garden. Private parking. The hotel is a short walk away and offers meals and bar facilities.

Glenurquhart runs from Drumnadrochit on the shores of Loch Ness deep into the mountain wilderness area of Glen Affric, which is renowned for rare plants and wild life and offers excellent walking, climbing and cycling. The loch provides angling, cruises, water sports and sailing. Inverness, 20 miles away, has an international airport, quality shops, restaurants and excellent leisure facilities. Within an easy day trip are the Great Glen, Ben Nevis, Glencoe and the Black Isle. The village has shops, riding centre and visitor centres including the fascinating Urquhart Castle.

One room with king-size double (cot available), One twin bedroom, one bunk bedroom, spacious lounge with double sofa bed and multi-fuel stove, dining room, conservatory, large kitchen, utility, shower room, bathroom. All electric plus stove. American-style fridge/freezer, dishwasher, washing machine, dryer, microwave, television, video, DVD, CD player. Bed linen and towels supplied. The property is being upgraded for 2009 with new luxury bathroom and kitchen.

Carol and Ewan Macleod
Glenurquhart House Hotel
Marchfield, Drumnadrochit, Inverness IV63 6TJ
Telephone: 01456 476234
e-mail: info@glenurquhart-house-hotel.co.uk
www.glenurquhart-lodges.co.uk

Peaceful tranquillity

LOCHCARRON. The Cottage, Stromecarronach, Lochcarron West, Strathcarron.
The small, stone-built Highland cottage is fully equipped and has a double bedroom, shower room and open plan kitchen/living room (with open fire). It is secluded, with panoramic views over Loch Carron and the mountains. River, sea and loch fishing are available. Hill-walking is popular in the area and there is a small local golf course. Nearby attractions include the Isle of Skye, Inverewe Gardens, the Torridon and Applecross Hills and the historic Kyle Railway Line. For full particulars write, or telephone.
• Working croft.• Sleeps 2. • Dogs welcome, under control at all times.
Mrs A.G. Mackenzie, Stromecarronach, Lochcarron West, Strathcarron IV54 8YH (01520 722284).
www.lochcarron.org

SB

Readers are requested to mention this FHG guidebook when seeking accommodation

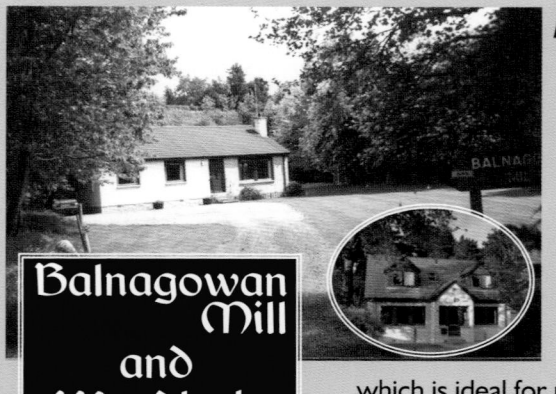

Lanarkshire

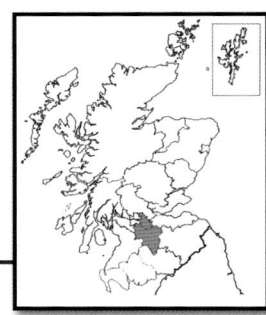

Biggar (Clyde Valley)

Perth & Kinross

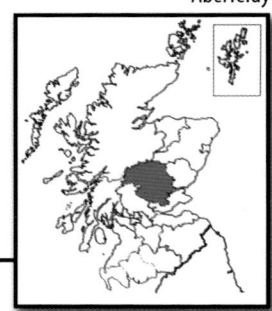

LOCH TAY LODGES

Acharn, By Aberfeldy

This stone-built terrace houses six self catering lodges - three lodges sleep up to 4, two lodges sleep up to 6, one sleeps up to 8. They are fully equipped with colour television, washing machine, microwave, electric cooker & oven, and fridge. Bed linen, duvets and towels are all provided, electric blankets are also available. A separate drying area is available to hang up wet clothes or store bicycles. On the loch side 150 yards from the lodges there is access to a boat house to store sail boards, diving equipment and the like. A "starter pack' of groceries can be ordered from the village shop and will be delivered to your lodge prior to your arrival. Each lodge has own enclosed garden. Cots and highchairs available. Rates £225-£610.

SB

Tel: 01887 830209
Fax: 01887 830802
e-mail: remony@btinternet.com
www.lochtaylodges.co.uk

Scottish Tourist Board ★★★ SELF CATERING

Blairgowrie, Perthshire   STB ★★★★

- *Fully equipped kitchen:* electric hob and oven, dishwasher, washing machine, fridge freezer and microwave.
- *Bathroom:* with electric shower over bath.
- *Lounge:* colour TV with Freeview, CD and DVD player.
- *Bedroom:* Double bedded room; all bed linen is included.
The apartment is gas centrally heated throughout but also has an electric fire in the lounge area. It is attached to the main house but has its own private entrance and parking area. Guests are invited to make use of the patio area and garden.

Coupar Angus Road, Rosemount, Blairgowrie PH10 6JT
Tel/Fax: 01250 870700 • www.heathparkhouse.com

Heathpark House Apartment

SB

AUCHAVAN STABLES, GLENISLA PH11 8QW

Contact: MRS GAMMELL, ARDARGIE FARMS,
LAGUNA HOUSE, MURTHLY, PERTH PH1 4HE

Four Star stable conversion set in a quiet Highland glen, offering a very comfortable base to explore this peaceful area. Ideally placed to ski at Glenshee or for hillwalking or cycling from the doorstep in the Cairngorms National Park. Balmoral, Glamis and Blair Castles are a short drive as are no less than six fine golf courses. Shop and pub seven miles away. The house is non-smoking and comprises a spacious living room with open fire, large family room with open-plan dining and kitchen, utility room, 3 bedrooms (total of 8 beds), bathroom and shower room. Oil, electricity and firewood along with bed linen and towels are included. Sat TV/ DVD/CD in both main rooms. Dog by arrangement. Prices £381-£772 weekly, Saturday to Saturday.

SB

Tel: 01738 710440 • e-mail: sarah.gammell@btconnect.com

Photo courtesy Cardiff County Council

Cardiff Castle, South Wales

Anglesey & Gwynedd is rich in archaeological and historical heritage, and is home to a diversity of wildlife which inhabit the cliffs, estuaries, heaths and rich farmland. Tourists love the unspoilt beaches and extensive sands, and the popular seafront at Benllech offers miles of clean golden sands, safe bathing, boating, fishing and windsurfing activities, as well as the usual ice cream kiosks, seaside shops, and food. Snowdonia to the west attracts climbers and walkers, but the less active will enjoy the 9 mile return journey on Bala Lake Railway which runs alongside Llyn Tegid, or Bala Lake as it also known, and through the beautiful Snowdonia National Park to the market town of Bala. The small, peaceful seaside village of Aberdovey within Snowdonia National Park is a popular resort with a thriving little harbour and very popular with those who enjoy a more active holiday. All kinds of watersports, including sailing, sailboarding, fishing, and boat trips, are available, and there is also an 18-hole championship golf course. The Llyn Peninsula also boasts some of the best sailing and surfing beaches in North Wales and its capital, Pwllheli, has an impressive marina which berths over 400 boats and has space for overnight mooring. No holiday in the area can be complete without a visit to the Royal town of Caernarfon with its wonderful views across the Menai Straits, and the mountains of Snowdonia in the background. The majestic Caernarfon Castle, one of Europe's greatest medieval fortresses famous for the investiture of Prince Charles as Prince of Wales in 1969, houses the Royal Welsh Fusiliers Regimental Museum.

In **North Wales** there are charming towns and villages to explore, soft sandy beaches and rugged coastline, and as many castles, stately homes, gardens, parks, craft centres, museums and steam trains as anyone could desire. Better book a long holiday to start the grand tour, and then come back again to catch up with all that you will surely have missed. Betws-y-Coed, North Wales' most popular inland resort, houses The Snowdonia National Visitor Centre with its craft units and thrilling video presentations – always worth a visit. For fun filled family holidays try Llandudno, where a whole host of summer events and activities can be enjoyed, or Rhyl with its Children's Village on the Promenade, plus amusements, boating ponds and fairground. Walkers and cyclists will revel in the breathtaking scenery of the Prestatyn hillside and the Clwydian

Range and will find all the information that they need at Offa's Dyke Visitor Centre. Most people would enjoy a break in Llangollen with its variety of attractions. The town hosts many different international events each year, including the famous Eisteddfod Music Festival which attracts visitors from all over the world. Throughout North Wales there can be found a variety of good restaurants, cafes and traditional country pubs, so eating out is never a problem, and the abundance of shops and open-air markets, as well as the many quality craft shops, ensure that you return home with those special little gifts for your family or friends.

Carmarthenshire is surely the best region for an activity or leisure break, with activities for everyone from cycling to bird watching, and from walking to sailing and fishing. The region also boasts many good golf courses , offering affordable golf to players of all abilities. The Millennium Coastal Park is one of the most popular tourist attractions in

Conwy Castle, North Wales

Britain, with breathtaking views of the Gower Peninsula, and a unique variety of attractions stretching from Pembrey Country Park with its acres of beautiful parkland, and one of the best beaches in the UK, as well as many excellent family attractions. Visitors will enjoy exploring the many interesting little villages, and there is an endless choice of places to eat and drink, including pubs, restaurants, inns and cafes.

Although it is one of the largest counties within Wales, **Ceredigion** is one of the least populated. There is plenty of variety and spectacular coastal and countryside scenery to be enjoyed. The Cambrian Mountains are only some half an hour's drive from most coastal areas and the coast is similarly accessible to inland areas. Aberaeron's most notable feature is its architecture - one house in every four is listed as being of special architectural or historical interest. Beyond Cardigan, to the south, are the high hills of the Preseli mountains and the Pembrokeshire Coast National Park whilst inland lies the Teifi Valley - offering marvellous angling - and Cenarth's famous falls. Tresaith is one of the locations most favoured by visitors to Ceredigion. It is almost a picture-book seaside village and offers a wonderful sandy beach, ideal for families, with clean sands, clear waters, and rocks to climb. There are many species of bird to be seen along the coastline including Red Kite, and you may be able to spot dolphins and seals in the waters.

Pembrokeshire's entire coastline is a designated National Park, with its sheltered coves and wooded estuaries, fine sandy beaches and some of the most dramatic cliffs in Britain. The islands of Skomer, Stokholm and Grasholm are home to thousands of seabirds, and Ramsey Island, as well as being an RSPB Reserve boasts the second largest grey seal colony in Britain. Pembrokeshire's mild climate and the many delightful towns and villages, family attractions and outdoor facilities such as surfing, water skiing, diving, pony trekking and fishing make this a favourite holiday destination.

Powys is situated right on England's doorstep and boasts some of most spectacular scenery in Europe. It is ideal for an action-packed holiday with fishing, golf, pony trekking, sailing and canal cruising readily available, and walkers have a choice of everything from riverside trails to mountain hikes. Offa's Dyke Path runs for 177 miles through Border country, often following the ancient earthworks, while Glyndwr's Way takes in some of the finest landscape features in Wales on its journey from Knighton to Machynlleth and back to the borders at Welshpool. There are border towns with Georgian architecture and half-timbered black and white houses to visit, or wander round the wonderful shops in the book town of Hay, famous for its Literary Festival each May. There are Victorian spa towns too, with even the smallest of places holding festivals and events throughout the year.

Brecon Beacons, South Wales

As well as being an ideal holiday destination in its own right Swansea Bay is a perfect base for touring the rest of **South Wales**. A great place for all sorts of watersports such as sailing canoeing, fishing and waterskiing, or you may prefer such land based activities as walking, cycling and horse riding. Just a short journey from the City you will find the beautiful Glamorgan Heritage Coast, overlooked by dramatic cliffs. Especially popular with walkers and hikers this area is also ideal for long, leisurely strolls in the secluded coves and inlets along the coast. There are more than 15 golf courses here including the famous Royal Porthcawl. For something different visit the Wye Valley and the Vale of Usk with awesome castles, breathtaking scenery and a rich and colourful history. The area is steeped in industrial heritage, and at Blaenavon World Heritage Site visitors can go underground with a miner and uncover real stories about people from the past. The 13th century castle of Caerphilly

is the largest in Wales and home to the ghostly Green Lady who haunts its halls. Many staff at Rhondda Heritage Park claim to have seen a phantom miner, or the ghost of a woman with two young children, and the legendary King Arthur is also reputed to have connections to the valleys. The area is popular for leisurely walks, or serious hikes and there are dedicated paths, challenging bike trails and, of course, plenty of opportunities for a game of golf.

Cardiff is one of the UK's top shopping venues, with malls, quaint arcades and markets, as well as independent chain stores and boutiques. The architecture is a blend of the old and the new, from the 2000 year old Cardiff Castle, one of Wales's leading tourist attractions with its enchanting fairytale towers and splendid interior, to the impressive and ultra-modern Wales Millennium Centre.

Wales
Great Days Out: Visits and Attractions

Henblas Country Park
Bodorgan, Anglesey • 01407 840440
Lots of fun for all the family - tractor tours, shearing demonstrations, indoor adventure playground, farm animals, crazy golf, tearoom.

Anglesey Sea Zoo
Brynsiencyn, Anglesey • 01248 430411
www.angleseyseazoo.co.uk
Meet the fascinating creatures that inhabit the sea and shores around Anglesey; adventure playground, shops and restaurant.

Ewe-phoria
Corwen, North Wales • 01490 460369
www.adventure-mountain.co.uk
Fascinating insight into the work of the shepherd and his sheepdog. Sheepdog and sheep shearing demonstrations, meet the lambs and puppies.

Sygun Copper Mine
Beddgelert, North Wales • 01766 890595
www.syguncoppermine.co.uk
Award-winning attraction with underground audio-visual tours. See stalagmites and stalactites formed from ferrous oxide.

Vale of Rheidol Railway
Aberystwyth, Ceredigion • 01970 625819
www.rheidolrailway.co.uk
An unforgettable journey by narrow gauge steam train, climbing over 600 feet in 12 miles from Aberystwyth to Devil's Bridge. There are many sharp turns and steep gradients, and the journey affords superb views of the valley.

Magic of Life Butterfly House
Aberystwyth, Ceredigion • 01970 880928
www.magicoflife.org
Hundreds of colourful butterflies, giant caterpillars and bizarre insects, plus collections of rare and endangered plants. Woodlands, walks and waterfalls nearby.

Folly Farm
Kilgetty, Pembrokeshire • 01834 812731
www.folly-farm.co.uk
In the heart of the countryside, with six fantastic zones - an award-winning attraction with a zoo, fungair, indoor/outdoor play areas and refreshments.

Manor House Wild Animal Park
Near Tenby, Pembrokeshire • 01646 651201
www.manorhousewildlifepark.co.uk
Set in landscaped grounds round an 18th century manor. Lots of animals, including a 'close encounters' unit, plus daily falconry displays.

King Arthur's Labyrinth
Machynlleth, Powys • 01654 761584
www.kingarthurslabyrinth.com
Sail along an underground river deep into the Labyrinth and far into the past.... into a world of mystery, legends and storytelling. Tales of King Arthur and other ancient Welsh legends unfold in this dramatic underground setting.

Centre for Alternative Technology
Machynlleth, Powys • 01654 705950
www.cat.org.uk
World-renowned centre demonstrating practical and sustainable solutions to modern problems. Water-powered cliff railway, dynamic displays of wind and solar power, and organic gardens.

Rhondda Heritage Park
Trehafod, South Wales • 01443 682036
www.rhonddaheritagepark.com
One of the top heritage and cultural attractions in South Wales. The Black Gold Tour is guided by ex-miners and gives a vivid idea of what their working life was like.

Caldicot Castle & Country Park
Near Chepstow • 01291 420241
www.caldicotcastle.co.uk
Explore the castle's fascinating past with an audio tour, and take in the breathtaking views of the 55-acre grounds from the battlements. Children's activity centre, play area; tearoom.

Your place in the country...

Discover the magical beauty of South Wales, Gower, Mumbles and exciting Swansea Bay.

Stay in one of our huge selection of excellent self-catering accommodation and enjoy the freedom of having your very own place in the country.

We are the agency with the widest range of superior holiday cottages, houses and apartments in Gower, Mumbles and the Maritime Quarter of Swansea.

Whether you want to experience the sheer beauty and breathtaking scenery of the area, partake in some of the activities on offer or visit one of the many attractions there is so much to do and see come rain or shine.

Visit Wales
Croeso Cymru

homefromhome.com
relax unwind enjoy...

42 Queens Rd, Mumbles, Swansea, SA3 4AN
Telephone +44 (0) 1792 360624
Email enquiries@homefromhome.com
Website www.homefromhome.com

Self Catering Holiday Accommodation in Swansea Bay, Mumbles, Gower & South West Wales

Anglesey & Gwynedd

ABERSOCH. Around the magnificent Welsh Coast. Away from the madding crowd. Near safe sandy beaches. A small specialist agency offering privacy, peace and unashamed luxury. First Wales Tourist Board Self Catering Gold Award Winner. Residential standards - Dishwashers, Microwaves, Washing Machines, Central Heating, Log Fires, No Slot Meters. Linen provided. Pets welcome free. All in coastal areas famed for scenery, walks, wild flowers, birds, badgers and foxes. Free colour brochure.
S.C. Rees, "Quality Cottages", Cerbid, Solva, Haverfordwest, Pembrokeshire SA62 6YE (01348 837871).
website: www.qualitycottages.co.uk

SB

Ingledene Bach

"Ingledene Bach", our holiday cottage is to the rear of the main house which is run as a B&B. Originally the servants' quarters, the cottage, which sleeps 2 adults and 2 children, is light and airy and close to the beach, providing a perfect base for a traditional seaside holiday. Downstairs: fully fitted kitchen, dining area, sitting room and bathroom. Upstairs: double bedroom and children's room with bunk beds (both rooms with sea views). Bedding and towels provided. Outside, guests have use of the garden and barbecue area with ample parking and room for boats.
Prices from £175 - £495 per week. Non-smoking. Sorry, no pets.

Richard and Shirley Murphy, Ingledene Bach, Ravenspoint Road, Trearddur Bay LL65 2YU
Tel: 01407 861026
e-mail: info@ingledene.co.uk • www.ingledene.co.uk

❖ Ty Gwyn ❖

Tel: 01678 521267

SB

• **TY GWYN** • Static six-berth luxury caravan with two bedrooms, shower, bathroom, colour TV, microwave, etc. on private grounds.

Situated two miles from Bala in beautiful country area. Ideal for walking, sailing, fishing and canoeing. 30 miles from nearest beach. Pets welcome

Contact: **MRS A. SKINNER, TY GWYN, RHYDUCHAF, BALA LL23 7SD**

Readers are requested to mention this FHG guidebook when seeking accommodation

SB

OGWEN VALLEY
HOLIDAYS
★★★ ★★★★

**1 PENGARREG, NANT FFRANCON,
BETHESDA, BANGOR LL57 3LX**

Spectacular Snowdonia

Ty Pengarreg Cottage Flat for two, £169-£329pw.
Pen y Graig Old Farm Cottage for six, £259-£609pw.
Comfortable and welcoming with spectacular views.

Tel: 01248 600122

e-mail: jilljones@ogwensnowdonia.co.uk   www.ogwensnowdonia.co.uk

BEAUMARIS. Around the magnificent Welsh Coast. Away from the madding crowd. Near safe sandy beaches. A small specialist agency offering privacy, peace and unashamed luxury. First Wales Tourist Board Self Catering Gold Award Winner. Residential standards - Dishwashers, Microwaves, Washing Machines, Central Heating, Log Fires, No Slot Meters. Linen provided. Pets welcome free. All in coastal areas famed for scenery, walks, wild flowers, birds, badgers and foxes. Free colour brochure.
S.C. Rees, "Quality Cottages", Cerbid, Solva, Haverfordwest, Pembrokeshire SA62 6YE (01348 837871).
website: www.qualitycottages.co.uk
SB

• Comfortable three-bedroom dormer bungalow with enclosed garden

• Safe for children and dogs (welcome!)

• Near excellent beaches, forest, coastal footpath

• Birdwatching area

• Snowdonia approximately 30 minutes' drive.

• Fully equipped; bedding and electricity inclusive

• Colour TV/DVD player, microwave

• Off-road parking

Croeso

Wales Cymru
★★★

£235 to £435 per week

**MRS J. GUNDRY, FARMYARD LODGE,
BODORGAN, ANGLESEY LL62 5LW
Tel: 01407 840977**

FHG Guides publish a large range of well-known accommodation guides.
We will be happy to send you details or you can use the order form
at the back of this book.

CRICCIETH. Around the magnificent Welsh Coast. Away from the madding crowd. Near safe sandy beaches. A small specialist agency offering privacy, peace and unashamed luxury. First Wales Tourist Board Self Catering Gold Award Winner. Residential standards - Dishwashers, Microwaves, Washing Machines, Central Heating, Log Fires, No Slot Meters. Linen provided. Pets welcome free. All in coastal areas famed for scenery, walks, wild flowers, birds, badgers and foxes. Free colour brochure.

SB **S.C. Rees, "Quality Cottages", Cerbid, Solva, Haverfordwest, Pembrokeshire SA62 6YE (01348 837871).** website: www.qualitycottages.co.uk

HARLECH. Around the magnificent Welsh Coast. Away from the madding crowd. Near safe sandy beaches. A small specialist agency offering privacy, peace and unashamed luxury. First Wales Tourist Board Self Catering Gold Award Winner. Residential standards - Dishwashers, Microwaves, Washing Machines, Central Heating, Log Fires, No Slot Meters. Linen provided. Pets welcome free. All in coastal areas famed for scenery, walks, wild flowers, birds, badgers and foxes. Free colour brochure.

SB **S.C. Rees, "Quality Cottages", Cerbid, Solva, Haverfordwest, Pembrokeshire SA62 6YE (01348 837871).** website: www.qualitycottages.co.uk

PORTHMADOG. Around the magnificent Welsh Coast. Away from the madding crowd. Near safe sandy beaches. A small specialist agency offering privacy, peace and unashamed luxury. First Wales Tourist Board Self Catering Gold Award Winner. Residential standards - Dishwashers, Microwaves, Washing Machines, Central Heating, Log Fires, No Slot Meters. Linen provided. Pets welcome free. All in coastal areas famed for scenery, walks, wild flowers, birds, badgers and foxes. Free colour brochure.

SB **S.C. Rees, "Quality Cottages", Cerbid, Solva, Haverfordwest, Pembrokeshire SA62 6YE (01348 837871).** website: www.qualitycottages.co.uk

Gwynfryn, an organic farm near Pwllheli, with Abersoch, Portmeirion and Snowdonia less than 30 minutes' drive.

On Lleyn various family interests are available: walking, cycling, fishing or relaxing on sandy beaches. Chester and Shrewsbury, Manchester and Liverpool airports are 2 to 2½ hours away from our quality self-catering cottages.

GWYNFRYN FARM HOLIDAYS
PWLLHELI LL53 5UF
Tel: 01758 612536 • Fax: 01758 613771

• Every Monday evening (weather permitting) Alwyn & Sharon host a BBQ - all are welcome. The BBQ facility is also available for guests to use from Tuesday to Sunday. For those rainy days, there is a fantastic games room with soft play area for the under-fives, pool table, table tennis, air hockey,

darts etc. On the upper floor there is table football and a PS2 games console with a 58" television.

For the energetic, you may want to visit our fitness room. With Life Fitness and Body Solid gym equipment you are guaranteed a good workout, and to relax those aching limbs visit our indoor heated swimming pool with sauna and Jacuzzi.

All houses have microwave, fridge/freezer, dishwasher, TV., video, CD/radio, hair dryer, crockery and utensils. All bedding, heating & electricity are included.

• Free use of the Laundry (two washing machines and two tumble dryers)
• A payphone and an internet enabled PC are also available.

www.gwynfrynfarm.co.uk
gwynfrynfarm@btconnect.com

North Wales

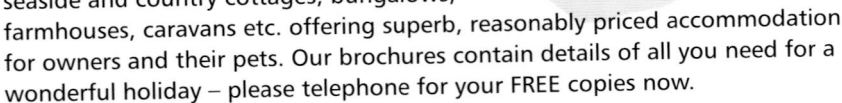

Llandona, Morfa Nefyn

LLANDDONA. Around the magnificent Welsh Coast. Away from the madding crowd. Near safe sandy beaches. A small specialist agency offering privacy, peace and unashamed luxury. First Wales Tourist Board Self Catering Gold Award Winner. Residential standards - Dishwashers, Microwaves, Washing Machines, Central Heating, Log Fires, No Slot Meters. Linen provided. Pets welcome free. All in coastal areas famed for scenery, walks, wild flowers, birds, badgers and foxes. Free colour brochure.
SB **S.C. Rees, "Quality Cottages", Cerbid, Solva, Haverfordwest, Pembrokeshire SA62 6YE (01348 837871).**
website: www.qualitycottages.co.uk

MORFA NEFYN. Around the magnificent Welsh Coast. Away from the madding crowd. Near safe sandy beaches. A small specialist agency offering privacy, peace and unashamed luxury. First Wales Tourist Board Self Catering Gold Award Winner. Residential standards - Dishwashers, Microwaves, Washing Machines, Central Heating, Log Fires, No Slot Meters. Linen provided. Pets welcome free. All in coastal areas famed for scenery, walks, wild flowers, birds, badgers and foxes. Free colour brochure.
SB **S.C. Rees, "Quality Cottages", Cerbid, Solva, Haverfordwest, Pembrokeshire SA62 6YE (01348 837871).**
website: www.qualitycottages.co.uk

Carmarthenshire

Bronwydd Arms

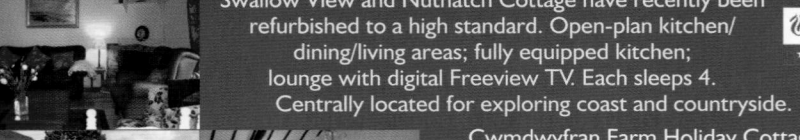

CWMDWYFRAN FARM HOLIDAY COTTAGES

Swallow View and Nuthatch Cottage have recently been refurbished to a high standard. Open-plan kitchen/dining/living areas; fully equipped kitchen; lounge with digital Freeview TV. Each sleeps 4. Centrally located for exploring coast and countryside.

Wales Cymru ★★★★

Cwmdwyfran Farm Holiday Cottages
Cwmdwyfran, Bronwydd Arms,
Carmarthenshire SA33 6JF
Tel: 01267 281419
e-mail: info@cwmdwyfran.co.uk
www.cwmdwyfran.co.uk

symbols

	Totally non-smoking		Pets Welcome
	Children Welcome	SB	Short Breaks
	Suitable for Disabled Guests		Licensed

Ceredigion

ABERPORTH. Around the magnificent Welsh Coast. Away from the madding crowd. Near safe sandy beaches. A small specialist agency offering privacy, peace and unashamed luxury. First Wales Tourist Board Self Catering Gold Award Winner. Residential standards - Dishwashers, Microwaves, Washing Machines, Central Heating, Log Fires, No Slot Meters. Linen provided. Pets welcome free. All in coastal areas famed for scenery, walks, wild flowers, birds, badgers and foxes. Free colour brochure.
S.C. Rees, "Quality Cottages", Cerbid, Solva, Haverfordwest, Pembrokeshire SA62 6YE (01348 837871). SB
website: **www.qualitycottages.co.uk**

Readers are requested to mention this FHG
guidebook when seeking accommodation

Parc Farm
Holiday Cottages
Oakford, Near Llanarth
Ceredigion SA47 0RX

Cardigan Bay and the harbour town of Aberaeron are just 3½ miles away from these comfortable stone cottages situated amidst beautiful farmland and quiet wooded valleys close to the sea.

With lovely gardens to enjoy and relax in, overlooking trout ponds and set in picturesque village in 14 acres of land.

New Quay, 5½ miles away, boasts a sandy beach with slipway water sports, tennis and boat trips for fishing or watching the dolphins offshore. Also many beautiful spots and sandy coves to explore and enjoy. Inland, less than an hour's drive away, lies spectacular mountain scenery. Ideal for walking, cycling, birdwatching and horse riding.

Mr and Mrs Dunn • 01545 580390

LLANGRANNOG. Around the magnificent Welsh Coast. Away from the madding crowd. Near safe sandy beaches. A small specialist agency offering privacy, peace and unashamed luxury. First Wales Tourist Board Self Catering Gold Award Winner. Residential standards - Dishwashers, Microwaves, Washing Machines, Central Heating, Log Fires, No Slot Meters. Linen provided. Pets welcome free. All in coastal areas famed for scenery, walks, wild flowers, birds, badgers and foxes. Free colour brochure.

SB   **S.C. Rees, "Quality Cottages", Cerbid, Solva, Haverfordwest, Pembrokeshire SA62 6YE** (01348 837871).
website: **www.qualitycottages.co.uk**

Pembrokeshire

Valley View Cottages
Newchapel, Pembrokeshire

01239 841850

SB

Luxury holiday cottages set in an idyllic location

Recently converted luxury cottages set in the delightful and unspoilt rolling countryside of Pembrokeshire with far-reaching views over the surrounding hills, farmland, woodlands and the famous river **Teifi Valley**, renowned for its fishing and scenery. Our dog-friendly, self-catering holiday cottages, in a superb location, provide a tranquil retreat from the hustle and bustle of modern day living. The cottages provide excellent accommodation for 1 - 6 people and are fully equipped for all year comfort. Each cottage has its own enclosed garden with patio furniture and BBQ.

Located 10 minutes from the town of Cardigan. Enjoy beautiful beaches, walking, bird watching and much more. Good local food and pubs.

All bedding, towels, electricity and heating are provided free of charge. A stair gate, cot and highchair are available on request at no extra charge.

WTB ★★★/★★★★★

Valley View Cotttages, Bwthyn Alltgoch, Newchapel,
Boncath, Pembrokeshire SA37 0HH
Tel: 01239 841850 • Mob: 07702 557673
info@valleyviewcottages.co.uk
www.valley-view-cottages.co.uk

BOSHERTON. Around the magnificent Welsh Coast. Away from the madding crowd. Near safe sandy beaches. A small specialist agency offering privacy, peace and unashamed luxury. First Wales Tourist Board Self Catering Gold Award Winner. Residential standards - Dishwashers, Microwaves, Washing Machines, Central Heating, Log Fires, No Slot Meters. Linen provided. Pets welcome free. All in coastal areas famed for scenery, walks, wild flowers, birds, badgers and foxes. Free colour brochure.

SB **S.C. Rees, "Quality Cottages", Cerbid, Solva, Haverfordwest, Pembrokeshire SA62 6YE (01348 837871).** website: www.qualitycottages.co.uk

Readers are requested to mention this FHG
guidebook when seeking accommodation

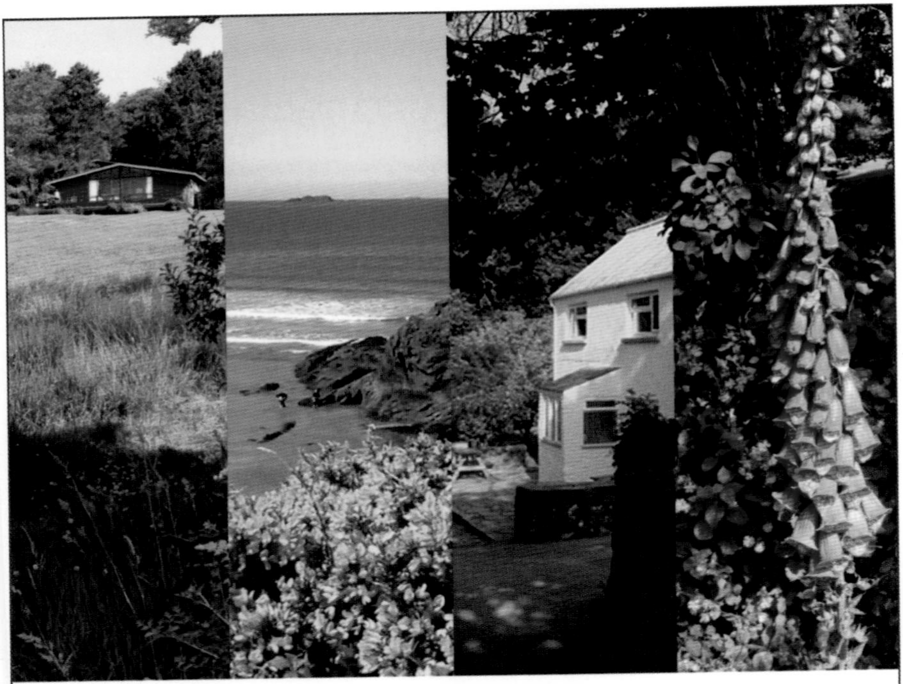

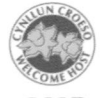

TIMBER HILL

SELF CATERING CEDAR LODGES

You will find Timber Hill nestling in beautifully landscaped grounds on south facing slopes overlooking a secluded, wooded valley in the heart of the Pembrokeshire Coast National Park... **this is Pembrokeshire at its best!**

• Superbly appointed and equipped, cosy cedarwood lodges • Idyllic self-catering cottage • Ideal for families - couples, and individuals • Five minutes drive to two safe sandy beaches and a short walk to the Pembrokeshire Coast Path • Excellent fishing in our well stocked, private lake • An abundance of wildlife

Recipients of the annual David Bellamy Environmental Gold Award for 10 years!

Brochure from the resident proprietors. John and Annette Bauer, Timber Hill, Broad Haven, Nr Haverfordwest, Pembrokeshire SA62 3LZ

08452 306090 Email: info@timberhill.co.uk

www.timberhill.co.uk

★★★★★
★★★
★★

THE NATURAL HOLIDAY HIDEAWAY

CYNLLUN CROESO WELCOME HOST
GOLD

Newgale, Newport, St Davids

NEWGALE. Around the magnificent Welsh Coast. Away from the madding crowd. Near safe sandy beaches. A small specialist agency offering privacy, peace and unashamed luxury. First Wales Tourist Board Self Catering Gold Award Winner. Residential standards - Dishwashers, Microwaves, Washing Machines, Central Heating, Log Fires, No Slot Meters. Linen provided. Pets welcome free. All in coastal areas famed for scenery, walks, wild flowers, birds, badgers and foxes. Free colour brochure.
S.C. Rees, "Quality Cottages", Cerbid, Solva, Haverfordwest, Pembrokeshire SA62 6YE (01348 837871). **SB**
website: www.qualitycottages.co.uk

NEWPORT. Around the magnificent Welsh Coast. Away from the madding crowd. Near safe sandy beaches. A small specialist agency offering privacy, peace and unashamed luxury. First Wales Tourist Board Self Catering Gold Award Winner. Residential standards - Dishwashers, Microwaves, Washing Machines, Central Heating, Log Fires, No Slot Meters. Linen provided. Pets welcome free. All in coastal areas famed for scenery, walks, wild flowers, birds, badgers and foxes. Free colour brochure.
S.C. Rees, "Quality Cottages", Cerbid, Solva, Haverfordwest, Pembrokeshire SA62 6YE (01348 837871). **SB**
website: www.qualitycottages.co.uk

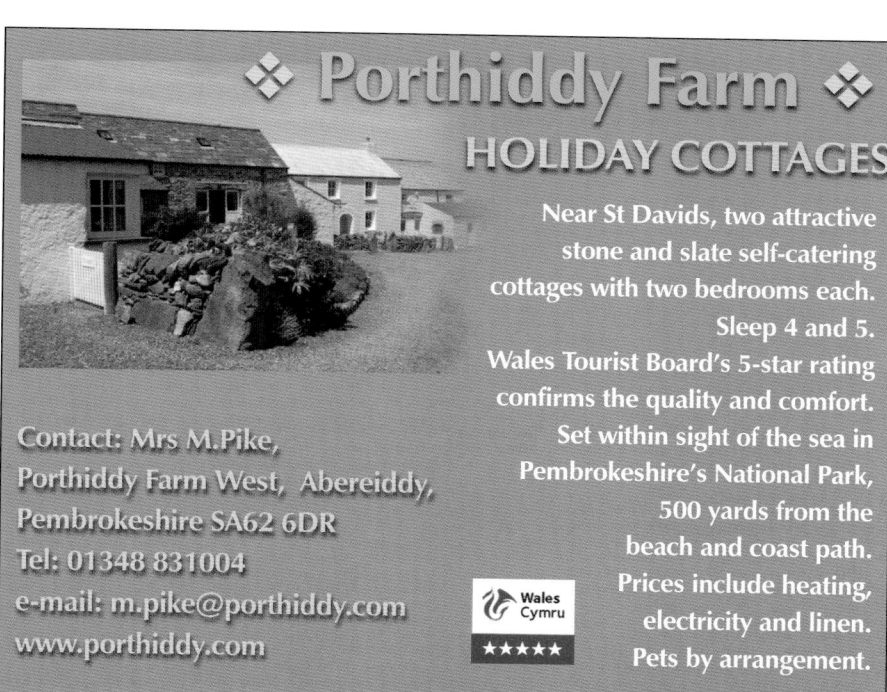

❖ **Porthiddy Farm** ❖
HOLIDAY COTTAGES

Near St Davids, two attractive stone and slate self-catering cottages with two bedrooms each. Sleep 4 and 5. Wales Tourist Board's 5-star rating confirms the quality and comfort. Set within sight of the sea in Pembrokeshire's National Park, 500 yards from the beach and coast path. Prices include heating, electricity and linen. Pets by arrangement.

Contact: Mrs M.Pike,
Porthiddy Farm West, Abereiddy,
Pembrokeshire SA62 6DR
Tel: 01348 831004
e-mail: m.pike@porthiddy.com
www.porthiddy.com

Wales Cymru ★★★★★

ST DAVIDS. Around the magnificent Welsh Coast. Away from the madding crowd. Near safe sandy beaches. A small specialist agency offering privacy, peace and unashamed luxury. First Wales Tourist Board Self Catering Gold Award Winner. Residential standards - Dishwashers, Microwaves, Washing Machines, Central Heating, Log Fires, No Slot Meters. Linen provided. Pets welcome free. All in coastal areas famed for scenery, walks, wild flowers, birds, badgers and foxes. Free colour brochure.
S.C. Rees, "Quality Cottages", Cerbid, Solva, Haverfordwest, Pembrokeshire SA62 6YE (01348 837871). **SB**
website: www.qualitycottages.co.uk

www.holidayguides.com

SOLVA. Around the magnificent Welsh Coast. Away from the madding crowd. Near safe sandy beaches. A small specialist agency offering privacy, peace and unashamed luxury. First Wales Tourist Board Self Catering Gold Award Winner. Residential standards - Dishwashers, Microwaves, Washing Machines, Central Heating, Log Fires, No Slot Meters. Linen provided. Pets welcome free. All in coastal areas famed for scenery, walks, wild flowers, birds, badgers and foxes. Free colour brochure.
S.C. Rees, "Quality Cottages", Cerbid, Solva, Haverfordwest, Pembrokeshire SA62 6YE (01348 837871). website: www.qualitycottages.co.uk

TENBY. Around the magnificent Welsh Coast. Away from the madding crowd. Near safe sandy beaches. A small specialist agency offering privacy, peace and unashamed luxury. First Wales Tourist Board Self Catering Gold Award Winner. Residential standards - Dishwashers, Microwaves, Washing Machines, Central Heating, Log Fires, No Slot Meters. Linen provided. Pets welcome free. All in coastal areas famed for scenery, walks, wild flowers, birds, badgers and foxes. Free colour brochure.
S.C. Rees, "Quality Cottages", Cerbid, Solva, Haverfordwest, Pembrokeshire SA62 6YE (01348 837871). website: www.qualitycottages.co.uk

Powys

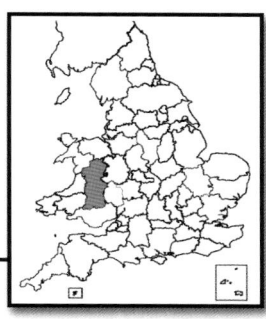

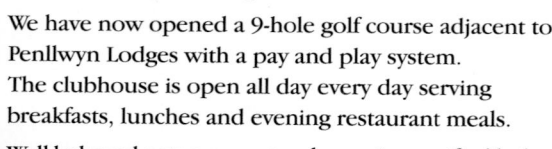

SB

MADOG'S WELLS
Llanfair Caereinion, Welshpool, Powys SY21 0DE
Beautiful, peaceful valley with lots of wildlife.
Three bungalows, wheelchair accessible. Free gas,
electricity and linen. Cot/highchair available on
request. Games room and children's play area.
Daily rates available out of main school holidays. Two three-bedroom
bungalows (WTB 4/5 Stars) from £140 to £530. Two bedroom
bungalow (WTB 3 Stars) £100 to £300. Open all year.

Contact Michael & Ann Reed for further details • Tel/Fax: 01938 810446
e-mail: info@madogswells.co.uk www.madogswells.co.uk

South Wales

Ireland

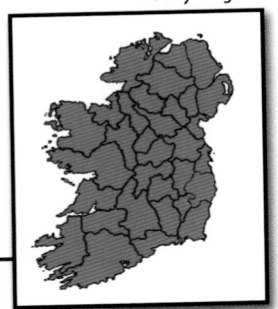

symbols

	Totally non-smoking		Pets Welcome
	Children Welcome	**SB**	Short Breaks
	Suitable for Disabled Guests		Licensed

Bude, Crackington Haven

symbols

🚭	Totally non-smoking		Pets Welcome
🐴	Children Welcome	**SB**	Short Breaks
♿	Suitable for Disabled Guests		Licensed

SB

Greenhowe Caravan Park
Great Langdale, English Lakeland.

Greenhowe is a permanent Caravan Park with Self Contained Holiday Accommodation. Subject to availability Holiday Homes may be rented for short or long periods from 1st March until mid-November. The Park is situated in the heart of the Lake District some half a mile from Dungeon Ghyll at the foot of the Langdale Pikes. It is an ideal centre for Climbing, Fell Walking, Riding, Swimming, or just a lazy holiday.

Please ask about Short Breaks.

LODGES ALSO AVAILABLE

Greenhowe Caravan Park

Great Langdale, Ambleside Cumbria LA22 9JU

For free colour brochure
**Telephone: (015394) 37231
Fax: (015394) 37464
www.greenhowe.com**

Newby Bridge

A well tended, uncrowded and wooded site set amidst picturesque fells between the Cartmel peninsula and the southern tip of Lake Windermere.

On-site facilities; flush toilets
- *❖ hot showers*
- *❖ laundry facilities*
- *❖ hair dryers ❖ deep freeze*
- *❖ gas on sale*

Tourers (30 pitches) £16 per night (incl. electricity & VAT).
Tents (30 pitches) £14 - £16 per night.
Auto homes £16 .
All prices for outfit,
plus 2 adults and 2 children.

Open March 1st to October 31st.
Oak Head Caravan Park, Ayside, Grange-over-Sands LA11 6JA

Cullompton, Seaton

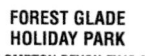

SB

Gruinard Bay Caravan Park

Situated just a stone's throw from the beach, Gruinard Bay Caravan Park offers the perfect setting for a holiday or a stopover on the West Coast of Scotland. Family-owned and personally operated, the park boasts magnificent views across Gruinard Bay.

• Sea front touring pitches • Electric hook-ups
• Camping pitches • Free toilet and shower facilities
• Gas available on site • Laundry facilities
• Static Holiday Homes available
• Pets welcome (not in Holiday Homes)

Tony & Ann Davis,
Gruinard Bay Caravan Park,
Laide, Wester Ross IV22 2ND
Tel/Fax: 01445 731225
www.gruinard.scotshost.co.uk

Dunroamin
Caravan Park
Main Street, Lairg IV27 4AR

Lew Hudson, his wife Margaret and their family welcome you to Dunroamin Caravan Park. A small family-run park situated in the picturesque village of Lairg by Loch Shin, this is the ideal base for touring the whole of Sutherland and Caithness. Fishing and walking nearby, with golf just 15 miles away. Outstandingly well maintained grounds with Crofters licensed restaurant on site. Electric hook-ups. 200 yards from pub, bank, shops, post office, etc. Holiday caravans for hire, tourers and tents welcome.

Tel: 01549 402447
enquiries@lairgcaravanpark.co.uk
www.lairgcaravanpark.co.uk

Looking for holiday accommodation?
for details of hundreds of properties
throughout the UK including
comprehensive coverage of all areas of Scotland try:

www.holidayguides.com

West Lodge Caravan Park

Comrie PH6 2LS • 01764 670354

Two to six berth caravans for hire fully equipped with gas cooker, running water, toilet, electric fridge, lighting, colour TV and gas fire. Crockery, cutlery, cooking utensils, blankets and pillows are provided. Sheets and towels can be hired. All caravans have toilets and showers. Pitches available for tents, tourers, motor homes. One modern shower block on site, with showers and hot and cold running water; electric hook-ups; modern launderette and dish washing area, shop. Fishing, golf, tennis, bowling, hill-walking and canoeing all within easy reach. Watersports available on nearby Loch Earn. Ideal for touring, 23 miles north of Stirling and 23 miles west of Perth. Open 1st April to 31st October.

From £39 to £49 nightly, £225 to £290 weekly; VAT, electricity and gas incl. Tents and tourers £10-£20 nightly.

www.westlodgecaravanpark.co.uk

Scottish TOURIST BOARD ★★★★ HOLIDAY PARK

Kilvrecht Caravan Park

Secluded campsite on a level open area in quiet and secluded woodland setting. There is fishing available for brown trout on Loch Rannoch. Several trails begin from the campsite.

Please write, fax or telephone for further information.
Loch Rannoch, Perthshire PH8 0JR
Tel: 01350 727284
Fax: 01350 727811
e-mail: douglas.halliday@forestry.gsi.gov.uk

symbols

    Totally non-smoking

    Children Welcome

    Suitable for Disabled Guests

🐕   Pets Welcome

SB   Short Breaks

    Licensed

The Pines Caravan Park

Small, peaceful, family-run park, with views in glorious mid-Wales. Situated on A470 four miles south of Rhayader – a good central position for exploring the Elan and Wye Valleys. A bird watchers' paradise, with many varieties of birds including the Red Kite.

Luxury modern holiday homes for hire and for sale. Fully equipped with shower, flush toilet, hot and cold water, cooker, fridge, microwave, colour TV. Weekly hire terms from £220 per week.

Mid-week bookings accepted. Shop and cafe close by. Pets welcome. Wheelchair accessible caravan available for hire. Please send for brochure. Philip and Sally Tolson.

**Doldowlod,
Llandrindod Wells LD1 6NN
Tel/Fax: 01597 810068**
www.pinescaravanpark.co.uk
email: info@pinescaravanpark.co.uk

Lauragh

Creveen Lodge

SB

Immaculately run small hill farm overlooking Kenmare Bay in a striking area of County Kerry. Reception is found at the Lodge, which also offers guests a comfortable sitting room, while a separate block has well-equipped and immaculately maintained toilets and showers, plus a communal room with a large fridge, freezer and ironing facilities. The park is carefully tended, with bins and picnic tables informally placed, plus a children's play area with slides and swings.

There are 20 pitches in total, 16 for tents and 4 for caravans, with an area of hardstanding for motor caravans. Electrical connections are available. Fishing, bicycle hire, water sports and horse riding available nearby. SAE please, for replies.

*Mrs M. Moriarty, Creveen Lodge, Healy Pass Road, Lauragh
00 35364 83131 • 00 353 64 66 83131 from June 2009
e-mail: info@creveenlodge.com • www.creveenlodge.com*

FHG Guides

publish a large range of well-known accommodation guides.
We will be happy to send you details or you can use the order form
at the back of this book.

Pet-Friendly Accommodation

A selection of self-catering properties where pets are welcome.
Each entry includes brief details of facilities on offer eg enclosed garden,
access to beach etc, and whether there is a charge for pets.

Counties are arranged in A-Z order within each country.

Cornish Character Cottages

Quality Cornish Cottages sleeping from 1 to 8, at a price you can afford. Situated in peaceful wooded valley leading to the beach. Perfect location for walking, touring or just relaxing. 14 acres of fields/woodlands to exercise your dog. Open all year.
Featured in The Good Holiday Cottage Guide.

**Mineshop, Crackington Haven EX23 0NR.
Phone Charlie or Jane (01840 230338)
e-mail: info@mineshop.co.uk
www.mineshop.co.uk**

• *enclosed garden* • *exercise area* • *walks nearby*
• *beach nearby* • *£17 per pet per week*

CREEKSIDE HOLIDAY HOUSES

• Spacious houses, sleep 2/4/6/8 • Peaceful, picturesque water's edge hamlet • Boating facilities • Use of boat
• Own quay, beach • Secluded gardens
• Near Pandora Inn • Friday bookings • Dogs welcome.

**PETER WATSON, CREEKSIDE HOLIDAY HOUSES,
RESTRONGUET, FALMOUTH TR11 5ST • 01326 372722
www.creeksideholidayhouses.co.uk**

• *exercise area* • *walks nearby*
• *access to beach* • *pets £15 per week*

Cornwall - Falmouth
SELF-CATERING BUNGALOW

Sleeps 6. Walking distance of harbour and town.
Dogs welcome. ETC ★★★

For prices and availability contact
**MRS J.A. SIMMONS (01277 654425)
or see our website
www.parklandsbungalow.co.uk**

• *enclosed garden* • *exercise area* • *walks nearby*
• *pets £10 per week*

Fowey Harbour Cottages

We are a small Agency offering a selection of cottages and flats situated around the beautiful Fowey Harbour on the South Cornish Coast. Different properties accommodate from two to six persons and vary in their decor and facilities so that hopefully there will be something we can offer to suit anyone. All properties are registered with VisitBritain and are personally vetted by us. Short Breaks and weekend bookings accepted subject to availability (mainly out of peak season but sometimes available at "last minute" in season). Brochure and details from:

**W. J. B. Hill & Son, 3 Fore Street, Fowey PL23 1AH
Tel: 01726 832211 • Fax: 01726 832901
e-mail: hillandson@talk21.com
www.foweyharbourcottages.co.uk**

• *enclosed garden* • *walks nearby* • *no charge for pets*

WRINGWORTHY COTTAGES•LOOE

Our 8 traditional stone cottages are set amongst unspoilt Cornish hills in 4 acres of space. Wringworthy is minutes from Looe with its stunning coastal path and sandy beaches. Walks from our door; dog-friendly beaches within a short drive. Sleeping 2-8, each cottage layout is unique but all are fully equipped with fridges, washing machines, DVD/video, microwaves, linen, towels etc. Green Acorn Award holders. ETC ★★★★ Self-catering.

Tel: 01503 240685 • www.wringworthy.co.uk
pets@wringworthy.co.uk

• *enclosed garden* • *exercise area* • *walks nearby*
• *access to beach* • *pets £18 per week*

Greenmeadow Cottages

Near Perranporth • ETC ★★★

Highly praised luxury cottages. Sleep 6. Superbly clean, comfortable and spacious. Open all year. Short Breaks out of season. Pets welcome in two of the cottages. Non-smoking. Ample off-road parking. For brochure and bookings

Tel: 01872 540483
www.greenmeadow-cottages.co.uk

• *enclosed garden* • *walks nearby*
• *access to beach* • *pets £25 per week*

Classy Cottages

Two cottages just feet from the beach in Polperro + three other coastal cottages. Out of season all cottages priced for two people. Cottages sleep 2-16. Access to indoor pool, well equipped gym and tennis courts. Very high quality cottages with open log fires. Pets very welcome. Please contact:
Fiona and Martin Nicolle on 01720 423000
e-mail: nicolle@classycottages.co.uk
www.classycottages.co.uk

• *enclosed garden* • *exercise area* • *walks nearby*
• *access to beach* • *pets £12 per week*

VIEW FROM THE PROPERTIES

POLPERRO

Affectionately let for 30 years for good old-fashioned family holidays, as well as for friends and couples to enjoy, where pets and children are most welcome. Comfortable holiday cottages, built around 250 years ago, full of character and charm, sleeping from 2-14, with sunny terraced gardens, giving a Mediterranean-type setting. From £175-£595 per cottage per week. Pets come free. Private parking free. For brochure please telephone Graham Wrights offices.

01579 344080

• *enclosed garden* • *exercise area* • *walks nearby*
• *access to beach* • *no charge for pets*

BOSINVER FARM COTTAGES

Bosinver's individual farm cottages are so nice our guests often don't want to leave. Here you can relax in real comfort, with 30 acres of wildflower meadows to walk your dog, and a short stroll to the village pub. Located near St Austell and the sea, Bosinver is a great base for glorious walks, Heligan Gardens and the Eden Project. Ideal all year round, particularly spring, autumn and winter when the crowds are gone, the colours are changing and the cottages are as warm as the welcome. **ETC ★★★★**

Best Self-Catering Establishment 2005-7 Cornwall Tourism Awards
Mrs Pat Smith, Bosinver Farm, Trelowth, St Austell PL26 7DT
Tel: 01726 72128 • reception@bosinver.co.uk • www.bosinver.co.uk

• *exercise area* • *walks nearby* • *pets £30.00 per week*

If it's views you want, this is the place for you!

The Links Holiday Flats

Lelant, St Ives, Cornwall TR26 3HY

Magnificent location alongside and overlooking West Cornwall Golf Course, Hayle Estuary and St Ives Bay. Both flats have lovely views. Wonderful spot for walking. We are five minutes from the beach and dogs are allowed there all year round. Two well-equipped flats which are open all year.

Your hosts are Bob and Jacky Pontefract
Phone or fax 01736 753326

• *exercise area* • *walks nearby* • *access to beach*

Sandbank Holidays
ST. IVES BAY

SANDBANK HOLIDAYS

St Ives Bay, Hayle, Cornwall TR27 5BL
Tel: 01736 752594
www.sandbank-holidays.co.uk

High quality Apartments and Bungalows for 2-6 persons. Peaceful garden setting close to miles of sandy beach, acres of grassy dunes and SW Coastal Path. Dogs welcome. Fully equipped for your self-catering holiday. Heated, Colour TV, Microwave etc. Spotlessly clean. All major debit and credit cards accepted.

• *enclosed garden* • *exercise area* • *walks nearby*
• *access to beach* • *pets £14 to £21 per week*

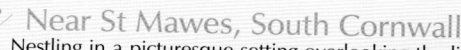

Sea Pink Near St Mawes, South Cornwall

Nestling in a picturesque setting overlooking the little bay of St Just-in-Roseland, Sea Pink is ideally located for exploring the coast and attractions. Recently refurbished, there is a spacious lounge, dining area opening on to sun terrace and lawned garden; three bedrooms. Brochure available.

Contact Judy Juniper • Tel: 01872 863553
e-mail: cottageinfo@btconnect.com
www.luxury-holiday-cottages.com

• *enclosed garden* • *exercise area* • *walks nearby*
• *access to beach* • *pets £15 per week*

Greenhowe is a permanent Caravan Park with self-contained holiday accommodation. Subject to availability Holiday Homes may be rented for short or long periods from 1st March until mid-November. The Park is situated in the Lake District half-a-mile from Dungeon Ghyll at the foot of the Langdale Pikes. It is an ideal centre for climbing, fell walking, riding, swimming. Please ask about Short Breaks. ETC ★★★★ New Lodges now available.

Greenhowe Caravan Park, Great Langdale, Ambleside, Cumbria LA22 9JU. For free colour brochure: Telephone: (015394) 37231 • Fax: (015394) 37464 www.greenhowe.com

• *walks nearby* • *pets £6 per night, £30 per week*

NEW PALLYARDS

HETHERSGILL, CARLISLE CA6 6HZ
Tel: 01228 577308 • www.4starsc.co.uk
Serviced and self-catering accommodation, located approximately 12 miles north east of Carlisle, an ideal location for visiting Hadrian's Wall, the Lake District, Kielder Forest, Gretna and the Scottish Borders.
New Pallyards is a small farm of 65 acres, and the accommodation comprises a converted farmhouse and self-catering cottages.
Dogs/pets by arrangement. See website specials.

• *enclosed garden* • *exercise area* • *walks nearby*

The Coppermines &
Coniston Lakes Cottages
70 unique Lakeland cottages for 2-30 of quality and character in stunning mountain scenery. Log fires, exposed beams.
Weekends and Short Breaks. ★★★ to ★★★★
Book online: www.coppermines.co.uk
Tel: 015394 41765 • Pets very welcome!

• *enclosed garden* • *exercise area* • *walks nearby*
• *pets £25 per week*

Fisherground Farm, Eskdale, Cumbria
Fisherground is a lovely traditional hill farm, with a stone cottage and three pine lodges, sharing an acre of orchard. Ideal for walkers, nature lovers, dogs and children, we offer space, freedom, peace and tranquillity. We have a games room, a raft pool and an adventure playground. Good pubs nearby serve excellent bar meals.

Ian & Jennifer Hall, Orchard House, Applethwaite, Keswick, Cumbria CA12 4PN • 017687 73175 holidays@fisherground.co.uk • www.fisherground.co.uk

• *exercise area* • *walks nearby* • *access to beach*
• *no charge for pets*

Peaceful woodland setting next to the River Walkham in the Dartmoor National Park. Ideally placed to explore the beauty of Devon. Purpose-built lodges available all year round, sleeping 2-7, tastefully blending into the surroundings. Interior specification and furnishings to a high standard - including fully fitted kitchen with oven, microwave and dishwasher. 3 golf courses a short drive away. Easy walk to village and shops Scenic walks, fishing. Dogs accepted. Horse riding nearby. Small, select touring area for caravans, tents and motor caravans. Launderette. On A386 Plymouth-Tavistock road.

For free brochure: Dept PW, Dartmoor Country Holidays, Magpie Leisure Park, Horrabridge, Yelverton, Devon PL20 7RY (01822 852651) or visit our website: www.dartmoorcountryholidays.co.uk

• *exercise area* • *walks nearby* • *£2.50 per pet per week*

Station Lodge, Doddiscombsleigh, Exeter

Comfortably furnished apartment In the beautiful Teign River valley. Ideal for exploring Devon's moors, coasts and villages. Kitchen, lounge/diner, en suite bedroom with double bed. Private garden, extensive grounds. Pubs, shops and walks nearby, golf, fishing, horseriding, tennis and swimming pools within 10 miles. Central heating. Colour TV. All linen provided. Parking. Non-smokers only. Well behaved dogs welcome. From £200 per week. Short Breaks welcome. For further details contact:

Ian West, Station House, Doddiscombsleigh, Exeter EX6 7PW
Tel: 01647 253104
e-mail: enquiries@station-lodge.co.uk • www.station-lodge.co.uk

• *enclosed garden* • *exercise area* • *walks nearby*
• *no charge for pets*

Perfect location for dogs and their owners.
Six stone cottages with country views.
Wildlife nature trail for 'walkies' on site.
Dog-friendly beaches and pubs nearby.
Woodburners and private gardens.
Short Breaks off season. Open all Year

Dittiscombe Holiday Cottages, Slapton
Near Kingsbridge, South Devon TQ7 2QF
Tel: 01548 521272
www.dittiscombe.co.uk

• *enclosed garden* • *exercise area*
• *walks nearby* • *pets £20.00 per week*

CRAB COTTAGE

Charming fisherman's cottage, 50 yards from the quay on the River Yealm. Watch the boats on the river from the cottage gardens and window seats. Delightful, quiet village in an area of outstanding natural beauty. Fantastic walks, beaches and dog-friendly pubs on the doorstep. Walk across to village shops in Newton Ferrers at low tide
Close to the South Devon Coastal Path. Sleeps 5

Noss Mayo, South Devon   Tel: 01425 471372
e-mail: 07enquiries@crab-cottage.co.uk
www.crab-cottage.co.uk

• *enclosed garden* • *walks nearby*
• *pets £25 per week, per pet*

The Pet Holiday Specialist

Bolberry Farm Cottages

Bolberry, Near Salcombe, Devon TQ7 3DY • 01548 561384
Luxury two and three bedroom barn conversion cottages. Private gardens. Shared orchard. Views across valley. Gas, coal, open fires. Parking. Finished to a very high standard. Linen and towels included. Central heating. Close to coastal path and pet-friendly beaches. Dog wash. Short Breaks out of season. Superb meals available at our nearby Port Light Inn & Hotel.
e-mail: info@bolberryfarmcottages.co.uk
www.bolberryfarmcottages.co.uk

- *enclosed garden* • *walks and beaches nearby*
- *no charge for first pet*

Cutaway Cottage

Thurlestone

Cutaway Cottage
Thurlestone, Kingsbridge TQ7 3NF
Self-catering cottage within fenced garden in the middle of the village, on private road.
5 minutes to pub and shop.
20 minutes' walk to beaches and sea
Ideal for children, dog walkers and bird watchers.
Pets free of charge
Phone Pat on 01548 560688

- *enclosed garden* • *walks nearby*
- *access to beach* • *no charge for pets*

NEWHOUSE FARM COTTAGES

Superior Quality Self-catering Accommodation
Eight beautifully converted, well equipped, Grade II Listed stone barns, with a choice of accommodation ranging from a one-bedroom cottage with four-poster bed through to our spacious five-bedroom barn sleeping 10. Take a stroll through 23 acres of flower-filled meadows and woodland, or simply relax in our heated indoor swimming pool and games room. For long or short breaks and more information, please call us on **01884 860266**
or visit our website at www.newhousecottages.com
Newhouse Farm, Witheridge, Tiverton, Devon EX16 8QB

- *enclosed garden* • *exercise area* • *walks nearby*
- *no charge for pets*

Please note
All the information in this book is given in good faith in the belief that it is correct. However, the publishers cannot guarantee the facts given in these pages, neither are they responsible for changes in policy, ownership or terms that may take place after the date of going to press. Readers should always satisfy themselves that the facilities they require are available and that the terms, if quoted, still apply.

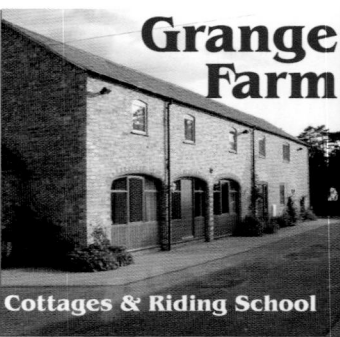

Grange Farm

Three well appointed cottages and riding school situated in the heart of the Lincolnshire Wolds. Stylish and roomy cottages, one sleeping 6, and two sleeping 4 in one double and one twin bedroom, comfy sittingroom and diningroom. Fully equipped kitchen. Bathroom with bath and shower. ETC ★★★★.
The Equestrian Centre offers professional tuition, an all-weather surface, and stabling for guests' own horses.
Waltham Road, Barnoldby-le-Beck, N.E. Lincs DN37 0AR
For Cottage Reservations Tel: 01472 822216
Mobile: 07947 627663 • www.grangefarmcottages.com

Cottages & Riding School

• enclosed garden • exercise area • walks nearby
• pets £20 per week

POACHERS HIDEAWAY HOLIDAY COTTAGES
Flintwood Farm, Belchford, Horncastle LN9 5QN
Tel: 01507 533555
Award-winning self catering cottages set in 150 acres of wildflower meadows, fishing lakes and woodland. Sleep 2-24. Miles of private pathways, direct access onto Viking Way footpath. Sauna, jacuzzi and massages available. Linen and towels provided. Stunning views, peaceful and relaxing. ETC 4/5 Stars.
e-mail: info@poachershideaway.com
www.poachershideaway.com

• 40-acre exercise area • walks from your door
• pets £10 per week • kennels available

Grange Farmhouse
MALTBY-LE-MARSH, ALFORD LN13 0JP
Tel: 01507 450267
Farmhouse B&B and self-catering country cottages set in 15 idyllic acres of Lincolnshire countryside. Peaceful base for leisure and sightseeing. Two private fishing lakes. Many farm animals. Pets welcome. Brochure available.
Contact Mrs Graves.
www.grange-farmhouse.co.uk
• walks nearby
• pets £5 per night B&B, £30 per week SC

SAND DUNE COTTAGES

Superior brick-built, tiled roof cottages
Newly fitted double glazing throughout
Adjacent golf course • Lovely walks on dunes and coast
2-4 night breaks early/late season
Terms from £69 to £355.
SAND DUNE COTTAGES, TAN LANE, CAISTER-ON-SEA, GREAT YARMOUTH NR30 5DT
Tel: 01493 720352 • mobile: 07785 561363
e-mail: sand.dune.cottages@amserve.net
www.eastcoastlive.co.uk/sites/sanddunecottages.php

• exercise area • walks nearby
• access to beach • pets £15 per week

Bolding Way Holidays

Weybourne, North Norfolk

BIDDLES COTTAGE (Self Catering), sleeps 2.
TACK ROOM (room only), sleeps 2.
Breakfast is NOT included in the price!
Well behaved pets are welcome in both. Open throughout the year.
Weybourne is located in An Area of Outstanding Natural Beauty and on The Heritage Coast. Both have fenced gardens and excellent local walks. Use of owners' hot tub.
The Barn, Bolding Way, Weybourne, Holt, Norfolk NR25 7SW
Tel: 01263 588666 • e-mail: holidays@boldingway.co.uk
www.boldingway.co.uk

• *enclosed garden* • *walks nearby*
• *beach 10 mins walk* • *no charge for pets*

A selection of modern superior fully appointed holiday chalets in a choice of locations near Great Yarmouth. Enjoy panoramic views of the sea from WINTERTON, a quiet and picturesque 35-acre estate minutes from the beach, while CALIFORNIA has all the usual amenities for the more adventurous holidaymaker, with free entry to the pool and clubhouse. Pets very welcome at both sites.

For colour brochure please ring 01493 377175
or write to 15 Kingston Avenue,
Caister-on-Sea, Norfolk NR30 5ET
www.wintertonvalleyholidays.co.uk

• *walks nearby* • *access to beach*
• *pets £20.00 per week*

Swinhoe Farm Cottages & Riding Centre, Belford

Three properties, all comfortably furnished and with fully equipped kitchens. Dove and Pine Cottages sleep six and Cuthbert's Cottage sleeps four. All properties have electric blankets and duvets, and linen is provided. At the rear of the properties is a large grass playing area with shared furniture and barbecue. Pets welcome by arrangement; horse riding lessons and trekking available on farm.
Valerie Nixon, Swinhoe Farm House, Belford NE70 7LJ
Tel: 01668 213370 • www.swinhoecottages.co.uk
valerie.nixon@farming.co.uk / valerie@swinhoecottages.co.uk

• *enclosed garden* • *exercise area* • *walks nearby*
• *no charge for pets*

Etive Cottage

Warenford, Near Belford NE70 7HZ
Tel: 01668 213233
e-mail: janet.thompson1@homecall.co.uk

Etive is a well-equipped two bedroomed stone cottage with double glazing and central heating. Situated on the outskirts of the hamlet of Warenford with open views to the Bamburgh coast. Fenced garden and secure courtyard parking. Pet and owners welcome pack on arrival - Pets welcome to bring along well behaved owners. Secure parking.   For brochure contact Jan Thompson.
Regional Winner - Winalot 'Best Place to Stay'

• *enclosed garden* • *walks nearby* • *no charge for pets*
• *local beaches accessible all year round to dogs*

Artists, photographers, birders, walkers, cyclists, fishermen, golfers and especially families, find Berwick an architectural gem, an ideal centre for basing their holiday. On a clear day you can see no fewer than three magnificent castles, suggesting exciting days out, from the ramparts which surround the old part of the town and which form an excellent source for enjoyable walks. Our secluded quality maisonette and studio flat (first and second floors, sleeping up to 12) offer a comfortable choice of accommodation, within a few minutes' easy walk of shops, restaurants, golf course, beaches etc.

**2 The Courtyard, Church Street, Berwick-upon-Tweed TD15 1EE
Tel: 01289 308737 • www.berwickselfcatering.co.uk**

• *walks nearby* • *access to beach* • *no charge for pets*

Mocktree Barns

Holiday Cottages

A small group of comfortable self-catering cottages around a sunny courtyard. Well-equipped. Sleeping 2-6. Two cottages with no stairs. Friendly owners. Open all year. Short breaks. Pets and children welcome. Lovely views. Excellent walks from the door through farmland and woods. Hereford, Cider Country, Black & White villages, Shropshire Hills, Shrewsbury, and Ironbridge all an easy drive. Ludlow seven miles. Good food and drink nearby. Brochure available. VisitBritain ★★★

**Clive and Cynthia Prior, Mocktree Barns,
Leintwardine, Ludlow SY7 0LY (01547 540441)
e-mail: mocktreebarns@care4free.net
www.mocktreeholidays.co.uk**

• *walks nearby* • *no charge for pets*

Toghill House Farm

**Toghill, Wick, Near Bath BS30 5RT
Tel: 01225 891261 • Fax: 01225 892128
www.toghillhousefarm.co.uk**

Situated just four miles north of Bath and within a few miles of Lacock, Castle Combe, Tetbury and the Cotswolds. The 17th century farm buildings have been converted into luxury self-catering cottages with well equipped kitchens. Ample car parking. Pets welcome. Separate laundry room and all bed linen, towels etc. included. B&B also available in warm and cosy 17th century farmhouse.

• *exercise area* • *walks nearby* • *pets £12 per week*

Primrose Hill

offers spacious, comfortable accommodation in a terrace of four bungalows. Private gardens with panoramic views over Blue Anchor Bay, Dunster Castle and Exmoor. A dog-friendly beach is a 10-minute walk away, with other lovely walks from your doorstep. Fully wheelchair accessible. Winner Accessible Somerset Awards 2008. Exmoor Excellence Awards, Self Catering Holiday of the Year 2006/7 Enjoy England★★★★

**Primrose Hill Holidays, Wood Lane, Blue Anchor TA24 6LA
Tel: 01643 821200 • info@primrosehillholidays.co.uk
www.primrosehillholidays.co.uk**

• *enclosed garden* • *walks nearby* • *access to beach*
• *pets £15 per week, assistance dogs free*

WESTWARD RISE HOLIDAY PARK
Brean, Near Burnham-on-Sea TA8 2RD

Highly recommended luxury 2/6 berth Chalet-Bungalows on a small quiet family-owned Park adjoining sandy beach. 2 double bedrooms, shower, toilet, colour TV, fridge, cooker. Duvets and linen. Open all year. Centrally heated during winter months. Laundry on Park. Caravan sales available. Shops, clubs, amusements & restaurants nearby. Dogs welcome

Call now for a FREE BROCHURE

Tel & Fax: 01278 751310 • www.westwardrise.com

• *exercise area* • *walks nearby* • *access to beach*
• *£15 per dog per week (max. 2 dogs)*

CHEDDAR - SUNGATE HOLIDAY APARTMENTS
Church Street, Cheddar, Somerset BS27 3RA
Tel: 01934 842273/742264
enquiries@sungateholidayapartments.co.uk
www.sungateholidayapartments.co.uk

Delightful non-smoking apartments in Cheddar village, each fully equipped. Sleep two/four. Laundry facilities. Private parking. Family, disabled and pet friendly.
Contact: Mrs M. M. Fieldhouse for brochure.
ETC ★★

• *walks nearby* • *pets - please ask for quote*

Beside River Exe - Centre of Exmoor National Park -
Close to coast. Four charming self-catering cottages. Dogs and horses welcome. Stabling available.
VisitBritain ★★★★

Riscombe Farm Holiday Cottages
Exford, Somerset TA24 7NH
Tel: 01643 831480
www.riscombe.co.uk

• *enclosed garden* • *exercise area* • *walks nearby*
• *pets £15 per week*

Holiday Cottages - Exmoor National Park

Quality cottages in the grounds of a former hunting lodge. Wonderful moorland location. Totally peaceful with superb views. Shop and pub 300 metres. Excellent walking straight from your cottage. Log fires. Very well appointed. Dogs & horses welcome. Individual gardens. Sleep 2-6. Internet access. Open all year. Short breaks available. ETC ★★★★

Tel/Fax: 01643 831302 • www.westerclose.co.uk
Val & Mike Warner, Westerclose House, Withypool, Somerset TA24 7QR

• *enclosed gardens* • *exercise area*
walks everywhere • *pets £12 per week per dog*

Exmoor
The Pack Horse

Allerford, Near Porlock, Somerset TA24 8HW
Tel: 01643 862475 • www.thepackhorse-exmoor.co.uk
e-mail: holidays@thepackhorse-exmoor.co.uk

Our self-catering apartments and cottage are situated in this unique location within a picturesque National Trust village which has local amenities. The Pack Horse sits alongside the shallow River Aller, overlooking the famous bridge. Enjoy immediate access from our doorstep to the beautiful surrounding countryside, pretty villages, spectacular coast, and Exmoor. **ETC ★★★/★★★★**

• *exercise area* • *walks nearby*
• *£15.00 per pet*

Croft Holiday Cottages
The Croft, Anchor Street, Watchet TA23 0BY
Tel: 01984 631121 • ETC ★★★★

Courtyard of six cottages/bungalows situated in a quiet backwater of the small harbour town of Watchet. Parking, central heating. TV, DVD, washing machine, fridge/freezer, microwave. Use of heated indoor pool. Sleep 2-6 persons. £195-£695 per property per week. Contact: Mrs K. Musgrave.
e-mail: croftcottages@talk21.com
www.cottagessomerset.com

• *enclosed garden* • *walks nearby*
• *beach nearby* • *pets £15 per week*

Annie's Cottage

The converted wing of Hill Farmhouse, retaining a wealth of period features, located in peaceful countryside, yet with good access to Southwold, Norwich, the Norfolk Broads, and the Waveney Valley. Two bedrooms (sleeps 4). Large lounge/dining room with wood-burning stove (logs provided). Enclosed private garden with picnic table and barbecue. Linen, towels and electricity included.

**Contact: Lynne Morton, Hill Farm Holidays,
Ilketshall St John, Beccles, Suffolk NR34 8JE
Tel: 01986 781240 • www.hillfarmholidays.com**

• *enclosed garden* • *exercise area* • *walks nearby*
• *no charge for pets*

Kessingland Cottage

An exciting 3-bedroom semi-detached cottage situated on the beach, 3 miles south of sandy beach at Lowestoft. Fully and attractively furnished with colour TV. Delightful sea and lawn views from floor-to-ceiling windows of lounge. Accommodation for up to 6 people. Well-equipped kitchen with electric cooker, fridge, hot and cold water; electric immersion heater. Electricity by £1 coin meter. Bathroom with bath and shower. No linen or towels provided. Only a few yards to beach and sea fishing. One mile to wildlife country park with mini-train. Buses ¼-mile and shopping centre ½ mile. Parking, but car not essential. Available 1st March-7th Jan. From £95 Low Season-£375 High Season.

SAE to Mr. S. Mahmood, 156 Bromley Road,
Beckenham, Kent BR3 6PG • Tel & Fax: 020 8650 0539
e-mail: jeeptrek@kjti.co.uk • www.k-cottage.co.uk

Kessingland Beach

• *walks nearby* • *access to beach* • *pets £25 per week*

Gladwins Farm Cottages

in Constable Country

Set in 22 acres of Suffolk countryside, Gladwins Farm offers a selection of accommodation. Guests in our self-catering cottages (sleeping 2-8) can enjoy the heated indoor pool, sauna, hot tub, the hard tennis court and playground. There is coarse fishing in our lake plus farm animals to entertain the children. Pets welcome in most cottages and loads of dog walking! Riding, golf and beach within easy reach. Book online. ETC 4/5 Stars. Winners, Suffolk S/C Holiday of the Year 2007.

Gladwins Farm, Harper's Hill, Nayland, Suffolk CO6 4NU
e-mail: gladwinsfarm@aol.com • 01206 262261
www.gladwinsfarm.co.uk

* *enclosed garden* • *exercise area* • *walks nearby*
* *£20 per dog per week*

The Barn, Hampton Wick

An attractive and economical alternative to London hotels...
Ideal for the discerning traveller, whether for business or pleasure, this recently restored barn conversion offers all the necessities of modern life in a self-catering setting while retaining its original charm. The Barn is in Hampton Wick just 30 minutes from central London. There is a comfortable cottage-style sitting room, spacious kitchen with all modern amenities, three bedrooms (one en suite) and two bathrooms. At our nearby hotel, Chase Lodge, we have a fully licensed bar and restaurant.

For details contact: Chase Lodge Hotel, 10 Park Road, Hampton Wick, Kingston-upon-Thames Surrey KT1 4AS • Tel (020) 8943 1862 e-mail: info@chaselodgehotel.com • www.chaselodgehotel.com

* *enclosed garden* • *exercise area* • *walks nearby*
* *no charge for pets*

Chiddingly, East Sussex. Adorable, small, well-equipped cottage in grounds of Tudor Manor. Two bedrooms, sleeps 4-6. Full kitchen and laundry facilities. Telephone. Use of indoor heated swimming pool, sauna/jacuzzi, tennis and badminton court. Large safe garden. Pets and children welcome. ETC ★★★
From £420 – £798 per week incl. Short Breaks £258-£375

Apply: Eva Morris, "Pekes", 124 Elm Park Mansions, Park Walk, London SW10 0AR

Tel: 020-7352 8088 • Fax: 020-7352 8125
e-mail: pekes.afa@virgin.net • www.pekesmanor.com

* *enclosed garden* • *walks nearby*
* *two dogs free, extra dogs (max 2) £7 per week*

CROSSWOODHILL FARM HOLIDAY COTTAGES • near Edinburgh
Award-winning? Well-equipped? Spacious? Family, pet and disabled friendly? Yes to all these questions. And so much more…. explore our livestock farm, relax in front of a blazing fire with a book, let the kids loose on the toy and games cupboards once home from a wealth of exciting days out. Or play outside. Spoilt for choice with both the area and with 3 very different properties. Each sleeps up to 6.
Winner of 2008 VisitScotland Thistle Award for Accommodation: Customer Care STB Green Tourism Gold Award • STB 3/4/5 Stars • ASSC.
www.crosswoodhill.co.uk or www.fivestarholidaycottage.co.uk
or enjoy our blog on www.edinburgh-holiday-cottages.co.uk
Contact: Geraldine Hamilton, Crosswoodhill, West Calder EH55 8LP
Tel. 01501 785205 • e-mail: cottages@crosswoodhill.co.uk
• *exercise area* • *walks nearby* • *pets £20 per week*

Rheindown
Beauly
Tel: 01463 782461

Two self-catering chalets situated above and overlooking the village of Beauly with outstanding views of the river and surrounding hills. The chalets sleep two/six in two bedrooms, and a put-u-up in the living room. Fully equipped with full-sized cooker, fridge, microwave oven. Rheindown is a small working farm with breeding cows, sheep and poultry, and our friendly collie dog, Nell. Lots of country and hill walks. From £190-£270 per week. STB ★
**Mrs M. M. Ritchie, Rheindown, Beauly IV4 7AB
e-mail: mm.ritchie@btopenworld.com**
• *garden* • *exercise area* • *walks nearby*
• *no charge for pets*

Telford & Fraser
Self Catering Cottages

**Nick & Patsy Thompson,
Insh House, Kincraig, near Kingussie PH21 1NU**
Two traditional stone and timber cottages with modern comfort and convenience in a superb rural location. Ideal for many outdoor activities and good touring base. Totally non-smoking. Children and dogs welcome.
STB ★★★
Tel: 01540 651377
e-mail: inshhouse@btinternet.com
website: www.kincraig.com/inshhouse
• *walks nearby* • *access to loch shore*
• *no charge for pets*

MONDHUIE CHALETS & B&B
NETHY BRIDGE, INVERNESS-SHIRE PH25 3DF
Tel: 01479 821062
Situated in the country between Aviemore and Grantown-on-Spey, two comfortable, self-catering chalets, or you can have Dinner, B&B in the house. A warm welcome awaits you. Pets welcome. Red squirrels seen daily. Free internet access.
e-mail: david@mondhuie.com
www.mondhuie.com
• *enclosed garden* • *exercise area* • *walks nearby*
• *no charge for pets*

Kilvrecht Caravan Park

Secluded campsite on a level open area in quiet and secluded woodland setting. There is fishing available for brown trout on Loch Rannoch. Several trails begin from the campsite.

Please write, fax or telephone
for further information.

Loch Rannoch, Perthshire PH8 0JR
Tel: 01350 727284
Fax: 01350 727811
e-mail: hamish.murray@forestry.gsi.gov.uk

- exercise area • walks nearby
- no charge for pets

Ty Gwyn

•**TY GWYN**• two-bedroomed luxury caravan in private grounds. Situated just two miles from Bala in beautiful country area, ideal for walking, sailing, fishing and canoeing. Only 30 miles from seaside.

MRS A. SKINNER, TY GWYN
RHYDUCHAF, BALA LL23 7SD
Tel: 01678 521267

- enclosed garden • exercise area
- walks nearby • no charge for pets

Croeso

- *Comfortable three-bedroomed house*
- *Enclosed garden • Near beaches, common, forest*
- *Fully equipped; bedding and electricity inclusive*
- *Colour TV/DVD player, microwave*
- *Dogs and children welcome.*

WTB ★★★

MRS J. GUNDRY, FARMYARD LODGE,
BODORGAN,
ANGLESEY LL62 5LW
Tel: 01407 840977

- enclosed garden • walks nearby
- access to beach • no charge for pets

PARC WERNOL PARK
Chwilog, Pwllheli LL53 6SW

Panoramic views, peaceful and quiet. Ideal for touring Lleyn and Snowdonia; 4 miles Criccieth and Pwllheli; 3 miles beach. Cycle route. Free coarse fishing lake, safe children's play area, games room. Footpaths; dog exercise field. 1,2 & 3 bedroom cottages. 2 and 3 bedroom caravans and chalets. Colour brochure.
Personal attention at all times and a truly Welsh welcome.

01766 810506 • www.wernol.co.uk
e-mail: catherine@wernol.co.uk

- exercise area • walks nearby
- *£15 per dog per week*

17th century farmhouse in the heart of Kilvert country, rural Radnorshire, only five miles from Hay-on-Wye, the famous centre for secondhand books. You will find peace and tranquillity in this wonderful walking country. Within easy reach of the Brecon Beacons National Park, Herefordshire and even the Welsh coast. Two self-catering apartments; sleeping 2-11 in comfort, which easily combine for a larger party. WTB ★★★

**MRS E. BALLY, LANE FARM, PAINSCASTLE,
BUILTH WELLS LD2 3JS**
Tel & Fax: 01497 851605 • e-mail: lanefarm@onetel.com

• *exercise area* • *walks nearby* • *no charge for pets*

The Rock Cottage
Huntington, Kington

Secluded, stone-built, character cottage overlooking picturesque farm and woodlands near Offa's Dyke footpath. Ideal for touring, birdwatching, golf and pony trekking. Sleeps 4/6. Two bedrooms, fully equipped kitchen, lounge with wood-burner. Central heating. Spacious garden with patio area. Children and pets welcome.

Mrs C. Williams, Radnor's End, Huntington, Kington HR5 3NZ
Tel: 01544 370289 • www.the-rock-cottage.co.uk

• *exercise area* • *walks nearby*
• *no charge for pets*

The Park House Motel
Crossgates, Llandrindod Wells LD1 6RF

Set in 3 acres of beautiful Welsh countryside and close to the famous Elan Valley. Accommodation includes static caravans, touring pitches and fully equipped motel units which have either a twin or double bedroom, shower room, and kitchen with a dinette that converts to a double bed. Sleeping up to 3, they can be booked for either self-catering or B&B. On-site facilities include restaurant and bar. Well behaved pets are very welcome.

Tel: 01597 851201 • www.parkhousemotel.net

• *exercise area* • *walks nearby* • *no charge for pets*

MADOG'S WELLS Llanfair Caereinion, Welshpool, Powys SY21 0DE

Beautiful, peaceful valley with lots of wildlife. Three bungalows, wheelchair accessible. Free gas, electricity and linen. Cot/ highchair available on request. Games room and children's play area. Daily rates available out of main school holidays. Two three-bedroom bungalows (WTB 4/5 Stars) from £140 to £530. Two bedroom bungalow (WTB 3 Stars) £100 to £300. Open all year.

Contact Michael & Ann Reed for further details
01938 810446
e-mail: info@madogswells.co.uk • www.madogswells.co.uk

• *enclosed garden* • *exercise area* • *walks nearby*
• *pets £10-£15 per week*

Whitehall Cottage. Cosy cottage in lovely Border countryside. 2 miles from Offa's Dyke. Central heating, washing machine, microwave, dishwasher, colour TV, inglenook, woodburner, linen included; power shower over bath. Sleeps 4 plus cot. Ample parking. Sun-trap garden. On working farm in peaceful hamlet. Children and pets welcome.

MRS R. L. JONES, UPPER HOUSE,
KINNERTON, NEAR PRESTEIGNE,
POWYS LD8 2PE
Tel: 01547 560207

• enclosed garden • walks nearby
• no charge for pets

Discover the beauty of Wales
on board one of our excellent narrowboats

Cruising along the Monmouth and Brecon Canal, through the Brecon Beacons National Park, you can take a weekend, midweek break or longer.

We have boats for 2-8 people and pets are welcome.
Four seater day boats also available.
Visit our website for up to date availability.
www.castlenarrowboats.co.uk
or call 01873 830001 for a brochure
Castle Narrowboats, Church Road Wharf, Gilwern, Monmouthshire NP7 0EP

One, four or more dogs welcome FREE. Three self-catering units in well converted stone Welsh Longhouse, set in old hilltop fort in 20 acres with fine views across to mountains. Quiet area with good access to many places of interest. Good walking. Open all year. **WTB ★★★**. Brochure from:

Sue & John Llewellyn, Cwrt-y-Gaer, Wolvesnewton,
Chepstow, Monmouthshire NP16 6PR
Tel: (01291) 650700
e-mail: john.llewellyn11@btinternet.com
www.cwrt-y-gaer.co.uk

• exercise area • walks nearby
• no charge for pets

Cwrt-y-Gaer
in the
Vale of Usk and
Wye Valley

Looking for holiday accommodation?
for details of hundreds of properties
throughout the UK including
comprehensive coverage of all areas of Scotland try:
www.holidayguides.com

Ratings & Awards

For the first time ever the AA, VisitBritain, VisitScotland, and the Wales Tourist Board will use a single method of assessing and rating serviced accommodation. Irrespective of which organisation inspects an establishment the rating awarded will be the same, using a common set of standards, giving a clear guide of what to expect. The RAC is no longer operating an Hotel inspection and accreditation business.

Accommodation Standards: Star Grading Scheme

Using a scale of 1-5 stars the objective quality ratings give a clear indication of accommodation standard, cleanliness, ambience, hospitality, service and food, This shows the full range of standards suitable for every budget and preference, and allows visitors to distinguish between the quality of accommodation and facilities on offer in different establishments. All types of board and self-catering accommodation are covered, including hotels, B&Bs, holiday parks, campus accommodation, hostels, caravans and camping, and boats.

VisitBritain and the regional tourist boards, enjoyEngland.com, VisitScotland and VisitWales, and the AA have full details of the grading system on their websites

The more stars, the higher level of quality

★★★★★
exceptional quality, with a degree of luxury

★★★★
excellent standard throughout

★★★
very good level of quality and comfort

★★
good quality, well presented and well run

★
acceptable quality; simple, practical, no frills

National Accessible Scheme

If you have particular mobility, visual or hearing needs, look out for the National Accessible Scheme. You can be confident of finding accommodation or attractions that meet your needs by looking for the following symbols.

 Typically suitable for a person with sufficient mobility to climb a flight of steps but would benefit from fixtures and fittings to aid balance

 Typically suitable for a person with restricted walking ability and for those that may need to use a wheelchair some of the time and can negotiate a maximum of three steps

 Typically suitable for a person who depends on the use of a wheelchair and transfers unaided to and from the wheelchair in a seated position. This person may be an independent traveller

 Typically suitable for a person who depends on the use of a wheelchair in a seated position. This person also requires personal or mechanical assistance (eg carer, hoist).

DIRECTORY OF WEBSITE AND E-MAIL ADDRESSES

A quick-reference guide to holiday accommodation with an e-mail address and/or website, conveniently arranged by country and county, with full contact details.

Self-Catering
Hoseasons Holidays Ltd, Lowestoft, Suffolk NR32 2LW
Tel: 01502 502628
• website: www.hoseasons.co.uk

•LONDON

Hotel
Athena Hotel, 110-114 Sussex Gardens, Hyde Park, LONDON W2 1UA
Tel: 020 7706 3866
• e-mail: athena@stavrouhotels.co.uk
• website: www.stavrouhotels.co.uk

Hotel
Gower Hotel, 129 Sussex Gardens, Hyde Park, LONDON W2 2RX
Tel: 020 7262 2262
• e-mail: gower@stavrouhotels.co.uk
• website: www.stavrouhotels.co.uk

B & B
Hanwell B & B, 110a Grove Avenue, Hanwell, LONDON W7 3ES
Tel: 020 8567 5015
• e-mail: tassanimation@aol.com
• website: www.ealing-hanwell-bed-and-breakfast.co.uk/new/index

Hotel
Queens Hotel, 33 Anson Road, Tufnell Park, LONDON N7 0RB
Tel: 020 7607 4725
• e-mail: queens@stavrouhotels.co.uk
• website: www.stavrouhotels.co.uk

B & B
S. Armanios, 67 Rannoch Road, Hammersmith, LONDON W6 9SS
Tel: 020 7385 4904
• website: www.thewaytostay.co.uk

•BERKSHIRE

Guest House
Clarence Hotel, 9 Clarence Road, WINDSOR Berkshire SL4 5AE
Tel: 01753 864436
• e-mail: clarence.hotel@btconnect.com
• website: www.clarence-hotel.co.uk

•CAMBRIDGESHIRE

B & B
Mrs Hatley, Manor Farm, Landbeach, CAMBRIDGE, Cambridgeshire CB25 9FD
Tel: 01223 860165
• e-mail: vhatley@btinternet.com
• website: www.manorfarmcambridge.co.uk

•CORNWALL

Self-Catering
Cornish Traditional Cottages, Blisland, BODMIN, Cornwall PL30 4HS
Tel: 01208 821666
• e-mail: info@corncott.com
• website: www.corncott.com

Self-Catering
Mineshop Holiday Cottages, CRACKINGTON HAVEN, Bude, Cornwall EX23 0NR
Tel: 01840 230338
• e-mail: info@mineshop.co.uk
• website: www.mineshop.co.uk

Self-Catering
Mr P. Watson, Creekside Holiday Houses, Restronguet, FALMOUTH, Cornwall
Tel: 01326 372722
• website: www.creeksideholidayhouses.co.uk

Self-Catering
Mrs Terry, "Shasta", Carwinion Road, Mawnan Smith, FALMOUTH, Cornwall TR11 5JD
Tel: 01326 250775
• e-mail: katerry@btopenworld.com

www.holidayguides.com

Self-Catering / Caravan

Mrs A. E. Moore, Hollyvagg Farm,
Lewannick, LAUNCESTON,
Cornwall PL15 7QH
Tel: 01566 782309
• website: www.hollyvaggfarm.co.uk

Self-Catering

Celia Hutchinson,
Caradon Country Cottages, East Taphouse,
LISKEARD, Cornwall PL14 4NH
Tel: 01579 320355
• e-mail: celia@caradoncottages.co.uk
• website: www.caradoncottages.co.uk

Self- Catering

Mr Lowman, Cutkive Wood Holiday Lodges,
St Ive, LISKEARD, Cornwall PL14 3ND
Tel: 01579 362216
• e-mail: holidays@cutkivewood.co.uk
• website: www.cutkivewood.co.uk

Self-Catering

Valleybrook Holidays, Peakswater, Lansallos,
LOOE, Cornwall PL13 2QE
Tel: 01503 220493
• website: www.valleybrookholidays.com

B & B

Heidi Swire, Penrose B & B, 1 The Terrace,
LOSTWITHIEL, Cornwall PL22 0DT
Tel: 01208 871417
• e-mail: enquiries@penrosebb.co.uk
• website: www.penrosebb.co.uk

Self-catering Lodges

Blue Bay Lodge, Trenance, MAWGAN
PORTH, Cornwall TR8 4DA
Tel: 01637 860324
• e-mail: hotel@bluebaycornwall.co.uk
• website: www.bluebaycornwall.co.uk

Self-Catering

Ged & Lora Millward, Churchtown &
Churchgate Cottages, 6 Halwyn Road,
Crantock, NEWQUAY, Cornwall TR8 5RT
Tel: 01637 830046
• e-mail: info@crantockcottages.co.uk
• website: www.crantockcottages.co.uk

Guest House

Mrs Dewolfreys, Dewolf Guest House, 100
Henver Road, NEWQUAY, Cornwall TR7 3BL
Tel: 01637 874746
• e-mail: holidays@dewolfguesthouse.com
• website: www.dewolfguesthouse.com

Caravan / Camping

Quarryfield Caravan & Camping Park,
Crantock, NEWQUAY, Cornwall
Contact: Mrs A Winn, Tretherras, Newquay,
Cornwall TR7 2RE
Tel: 01637 872792
• e-mail:
quarryfield@crantockcaravans.orangehome.co.uk
• website: www.quarryfield.co.uk

Self-Catering

Classy Cottages, POLPERRO, Cornwall
Contact: Fiona and Martin Nicolle
Tel: 01720 423000
• e-mail: nicolle@classycottages.co.uk
• website: www.classycottages.co.uk

Caravan / Camping

Globe Vale Holiday Park, Radnor, REDRUTH,
Cornwall TR16 4BH
Tel: 01209 891183
• e-mail: info@globevale.co.uk
• website: www.globevale.co.uk

Guest House

Mr S Hope, Dalswinton House,
ST MAWGAN-IN-PYDAR, Cornwall TR8 4EZ
Tel: 01637 860385
• e-mail: dalswintonhouse@tiscali.co.uk
• website: www.dalswinton.com

Self-Catering

Mrs R. Reeves, Polstraul, Trewalder,
Delabole, ST TUDY, Cornwall PL33 9ET
Tel: 01840 213120
• e-mail: ruth.reeves@hotmail.co.uk
• website: www.maymear.co.uk

Self-Catering

Whitsand Bay Self Catering, Portwrinkle,
TORPOINT, Cornwall, PL11 3BU
Tel: 01579 345688
• e-mail: ehwbsc@hotmail.com
• website: www.whitsandbayselfcatering.co.uk

Self-Catering

The Garden House, Port Isaac, Near
WADEBRIDGE, Cornwall
Contact: Mr D Oldham, Travella, Treveighan,
St Teath, Cornwall PL30 3JN
Tel: 01208 850529
• e-mail: david.trevella@btconnect.com
• website: www.trevellacornwall.co.uk

Self-Catering

Great Bodieve Farm Barns, Molesworth
House, WADEBRIDGE, Cornwall PL27 7JE
Tel: 01208 814916
• e-mail: enquiries@great-bodieve.co.uk
• website: www.great-bodieve.co.uk

FHG Guides

•CUMBRIA

Self- Catering
Kirkstone Foot Apartments Ltd, Kirkstone Pass Road, AMBLESIDE, Cumbria LA22 9EH
Tel: 015394 32232
• e-mail: enquiries@kirkstonefoot.co.uk
• website: www.kirkstonefoot.co.uk

Guest House / Self- Catering
Cuckoo's Nest & Smallwood House, Compston Road, AMBLESIDE, Cumbria LA22 9DJ
Tel: 015394 32330
• e-mail: enq@cottagesambleside.co.uk
  enq@smallwoodhotel.co.uk
• website: www.cottagesambleside.co.uk
  www.smallwoodhotel.co.uk

Caravan Park
Greenhowe Caravan Park, Great Langdale, AMBLESIDE, Cumbria LA22 9JU
Tel: 015394 37231
• e-mail: enquiries@greenhowe.com
• website: www.greenhowe.com

Hotel / Guest House
Mrs Liana Moore, The Old Vicarage, Vicarage Road, AMBLESIDE, Cumbria LA22 9DH
Tel: 015394 33364
• e-mail: info@oldvicarageambleside.co.uk
• website: www.oldvicarageambleside.co.uk

Self-Catering
43A Quarry Rigg, BOWNESS-ON-WINDERMERE, Cumbria.
Contact: Mrs E. Jones, 45 West Oakhill Park, Liverpool L13 4BN. Tel: 0151 228 5799
• e-mail: eajay@btinternet.com

Self-Catering
Mrs Almond, Irton House Farm, Isel, Near Keswick, COCKERMOUTH, Cumbria CA13 9ST
Tel: 017687 76380
• e-mail: joan@irtonhousefarm.co.uk
• website: www.irtonhousefarm.com

Self-Catering
Fisherground Farm Holidays, ESKDALE
Contact: Ian & Jennifer Hall, Orchard House, Applethwaite, Keswick, Cumbria CA12 4PN
Tel: 017687 73175
• e-mail: holidays@fisherground.co.uk
• website: www.fisherground.co.uk

Self-Catering
2 Moot Hall, Ireby, Near KESWICK, Cumbria CA7 1DU
Contact: Ruth Boyes, Anglers Lodge, Main Street, Helperby, North Yorkshire YO61 2NT
Tel: 01840 213 120
• e-mail: ruthboyes@virgin.net
• website: irebymoothall.co.uk

Self-Catering
Mr D Burton, Lakeland Cottage Holidays, Bassenthwaite, KESWICK CA12 4QX
Tel: 017687 76065
• e-mail: info@lakelandcottages.co.uk
• website: www.lakelandcottages.co.uk

Self-Catering
Mr D Williamson, Derwent Water Marina, Portinscale, KESWICK, Cumbria CA12 5RF
Tel: 017687 72912
• e-mail: info@derwentwatermarina.co.uk
• website: www.derwentwatermarina.co.uk

Inn
Mr I Court, Horse and Farrier Inn, Threlkeld, KESWICK, Cumbria CA12 4SQ
Tel: 017687 79688
• e-mail: info@horseandfarrier.com
• website: www.horseandfarrier.com

Self-Catering
Mrs J Fallon, South Lakes Cottages, Sunset Cottage, 1 Friars Ground, KIRKBY-IN-FURNESS, Cumbria LA17 7YB
Tel: 01229 889601
• e-mail: enquiries@southlakes-cottages.com
• website: www.southlakes-cottages.com

Self-Catering
Mrs S.J. Bottom, Crossfield Cottages, KIRKOSWALD, Penrith, Cumbria CA10 1EU
Tel: 01768 898711
• e-mail: info@crossfieldcottages.co.uk
• website: www.crossfieldcottages.co.uk

Self-Catering
Mr & Mrs Iredale, Carrock Cottages, Carrock House, Hutton Roof, PENRITH, Cumbria CA11 0XY
Tel: 01768 484111
• e-mail: info@carrockcottages.co.uk
• website: www.carrockcottages.co.uk

Guest House / Inn
The Troutbeck Inn, Troutbeck, PENRITH, Cumbria CA11 0SJ. Tel: 01768 483635
• e-mail: info@troutbeckinn.co.uk
• website: www.thetroutbeckinn.co.uk

Caravan & Camping
Cove Caravan & Camping Park, Watermillock, ULLSWATER, Penrith, Cumbria CA11 0LS
Tel: 017684 86549
• e-mail: info@cove-park.co.uk
• website: www.cove-park.co.uk

B & B / Self-Catering
Barbara Murphy, Land Ends Country Lodge, Watermillock, Near ULLSWATER, Cumbria CA11 0NB
Tel: 01768 486438
• e-mail: infolandends@btinternet.com
• website: www.landends.co.uk

Guest House
Mr Shaw, Meadfoot Guest House, New
Road, WINDERMERE, Cumbria LA23 2LA
Tel: 01539 442610
• e-mail: enquiries@meadfoot-guesthouse.co.uk
• website: www.meadfoot-guesthouse.co.uk

Hotel
The Famous Wild Boar, Crook, Near
WINDERMERE, Cumbria LA23 3NF
Tel: Reservations 08458 504604
• website: www.elh.co.uk

•DERBYSHIRE

Self-Catering Holiday Cottages
Mark Redfern, Paddock House Farm Holiday
Cottages, Peak District National Park,
Alstonefield, ASHBOURNE, Derbyshire
DE6 2FT
Tel: 01335 310282 / 07977 569618
• e-mail: info@paddockhousefarm.co.uk
• website: www.paddockhousefarm.co.uk

Self-Catering
Keith & Joan Lennard, Windlehill Farm,
Sutton-on-the-Hill, ASHBOURNE,
Derbyshire DE6 5JH
Tel: 01283 732377
• e-mail: windlehill@btinternet.com
• website: www.windlehill.btinternet.co.uk

Self-Catering
Burton Manor Farm Cottages, BAKEWELL,
Derbyshire DE45 1JX
Contact: Mrs R Shirt, Holmelacy Farm,
Tideswell, Buxton SK17 8LW
Tel: 01298 871429
• e-mail: cshirt@burtonmanor.freeserve.co.uk
• website: www.burtonmanor.freeserve.co.uk

Hotel
Biggin Hall, Biggin-by-Hartington, BUXTON,
Derbyshire SK17 0DH
Tel: 01298 84451
• e-mail: enquiries@bigginhall.co.uk
• website: www.bigginhall.co.uk

Caravan
Golden Valley Caravan Park, Coach Road,
RIPLEY, Derbyshire DE55 4ES
Tel: 01773 513881
• e-mail:
enquiries@goldenvalleycaravanpark.co.uk
• website: www.goldenvalleycaravanpark.co.uk

•DEVON

Self-Catering
Helpful Holidays, Mill Street, Chagford,
DEVON TQ13 8AW
Tel: 01647 433593
• e-mail: help@helpfulholidays.com
• website: www.helpfulholidays.com

Self-Catering
Farm & Cottage Holidays, DEVON
Tel: 01237 459897
• website: www.holidaycottages.co.uk

Self-Catering
Wooder Manor, Widecombe-in-the-Moor,
ASHBURTON, Devon TQ13 7TR
Tel: 01364 621391
• e-mail: angela@woodermanor.com
• website: www.woodermanor.com

Farm B & B
Mrs J Ley, West Barton, Alverdiscott, Near
BARNSTABLE, Devon EX31 3PT
Tel: 01271 858230
• e-mail: ela@andrews78.freeserve.co.uk

Self-Catering / Organic Farm
Little Comfort Farm Cottages, Little Comfort
Farm, BRAUNTON, North Devon EX33 2NJ
Tel: 01271 812414
• e-mail: info@littlecomfortfarm.co.uk
• website: www.littlecomfortfarm.co.uk

Guest House
Woodlands Guest House, Parkham Road,
BRIXHAM, South Devon TQ5 9BU
Tel: 01803 852040
• e-mail: woodlandsbrixham@btinternet.com
• website: www.woodlandsbrixham.co.uk

Farm / Self-Catering / B&B
Mrs Lee, Church Approach Cottages,
Church Green, Farway, COLYTON, Devon
EX24 6EQ
Tel: 01404 871383/871202
• e-mail: lizlee@eclipse.co.uk
• website: www.churchapproach.co.uk

Holiday Park
Manleigh Holiday Park, Rectory Road, COMBE
MARTIN, North Devon EX34 0NS
Tel: 01271 883353
• e-mail: info@manleighpark.co.uk
• website: www.manleighpark.co.uk

Self-Catering / Holiday Park
Mrs Helen Scott, Cofton Country Holidays,
Starcross, Near DAWLISH, Devon EX6 8RP
Tel: 01626 890111
• e-mail: info@coftonholidays.co.uk
• website: www.coftonholidays.co.uk

Inn

The Blue Ball Inn, Countisbury, LYNMOUTH,
Near Lynton, Devon EX35 6NE
Tel: 01598 741263
* website: www.BlueBallinn.com
    www.exmoorsandpiper.com

Self-Catering

G Davidson Richmond, Clooneavin,
Clooneavin Path, LYNMOUTH, Devon
EX35 6EE • Tel: 01598 753334
* e-mail: relax@clooneavinholidays.co.uk
* website: www.clooneavinholidays.co.uk

Self-Catering

C & M Hartnoll, Little Bray House, Brayford,
Barnstable, LYNTON, Devon EX32 7QG
Tel: 01598 710295
* e-mail: holidays@littlebray.co.uk
* website: www.littlebray.co.uk

B & B / Guest House / Farm

Mrs E A Forth, Fluxton Farm, OTTERY ST
MARY, Devon EX11 1RJ
Tel: 01404 812818
* website: www.fluxtonfarm.co.uk

Hotel

Christine Clark, Amber House Hotel, 6
Roundham Road, PAIGNTON, Devon
TQ4 6EZ
Tel: 01803 558372
* e-mail: enquiries@amberhousehotel.co.uk
* website: www.amberhousehotel.co.uk

Guest House

The Commodore, 14 Esplanade Road,
PAIGNTON, Devon TQ4 6EB
Tel: 01803 553107
* e-mail: info@commodorepaignton.com
* website: www.commodorepaignton.com

Hotel / Inn / Self Catering

Port Light Hotel & Bolberry Farm Cottages,
Bolberry Down, Near SALCOMBE, Devon
TQ7 3DY • Tel: 01548 561384
* e-mail: info@portlight.co.uk
* website: www.portlight.co.uk
    www.bolberryfarmcottages.co.uk

Guest House

A J Hill, Beaumont, Castle Hill, SEATON
Devon EX12 2QW
Tel: 01297 20832
* e-mail: jane@lymebay.demon.co.uk
* website:
www.smoothhound.co.uk/hotels/beaumon1.html

FHG Guides

Self-Catering

M Courtney, West Millbrook, Twitchen,
SOUTH MOLTON, Devon EX36 3LP
Tel: 01598 740382
* e-mail: wmbselfcatering@aol.com
* website: www.westmillbrook.co.uk

Self-Catering / Camping

Dartmoor Country Holidays, Magpie Leisure
Park, Bedford Bridge, Horrabridge,
Yelverton, TAVISTOCK, Devon PL20 7RY
Tel: 01822 852651
* website: www.dartmoorcountryholidays.co.uk

Guest House

John O'Flaherty, Overcombe House, Old
Station Road, Horrabridge, Yelverton,
TAVISTOCK, Devon, PL20 7RA
Tel: 01822 853501
* e-mail: enquiries@overcombehotel.co.uk
* website: www.overcombehotel.co.uk

Hotel

Riviera Lodge Hotel, 26 Croft Road.
TORQUAY, Devon TQ2 5UE
Tel: 01803 209309
* e-mail: stay@rivieralodgehotel.co.uk
* website: www.rivieralodgehotel.co.uk

Self-Catering

Marsdens Cottage Holidays, 2 The Square,
Braunton, WOOLACOMBE, Devon
EX33 2JB
Tel: 01271 813777
* e-mail: holidays@marsdens.co.uk
* website: www.marsdens.co.uk

Holiday Park

Woolacombe Bay Holiday Parks,
WOOLACOMBE, North Devon EX34 7HW
Tel: 0844 770 0379
* e-mail: goodtimes@woolacombe.com
* website: www.woolacombe.com

Caravan & Camping

North Morte Farm Caravan & Camping Park,
Mortehoe, WOOLACOMBE, Devon EX34 7EG
Tel: 01271 870381
* e-mail: info@northmortefarm.co.uk
* website: www.northmortefarm.co.uk

•DORSET

Self-Catering

Luccombe Farm Cottages, Luccombe Farm,
Milton Abbas, BLANDFORD FORUM, Dorset
DT11 0BE
Tel: 01258 880558
* e-mail: mkayll@aol.com
* website: www.luccombeholidays.co.uk

Hotel
Southbourne Grove Hotel, 96 Southbourne Road, BOURNEMOUTH, Dorset BH6 3QQ
Tel: 01202 420503
• e-mail: neil@pack1462.freeserve.co.uk
• website: www.bournemouth.co.uk/southbournegrovehotel

Self-Catering
C. Hammond, Stourcliffe Court, 56 Stourcliffe Avenue, Southbourne, BOURNEMOUTH, Dorset BH6 3PX
Tel: 01202 420698
• e-mail: rjhammond1@hotmail.co.uk
• website: www.stourcliffecourt.co.uk

Self-Catering Cottage / Farmhouse B & B
Mrs S. E. Norman, Frogmore Farm, Chideock, BRIDPORT, Dorset DT6 6HT
Tel: 01308 456159
• e-mail: bookings@frogmorefarm.com
• website: www.frogmorefarm.com

Golf Club
Came Down Golf Club, Higher Came, DORCHESTER, Dorset DT2 8NR
Tel: 01305 813494
• e-mail: manager@camedowngolfclub.co.uk
• website: www.camedowngolfclub.co.uk

Self-Catering
Josephine Pearse, Tamarisk Farm Cottages, Beach Road, West Bexington, DORCHESTER DT2 2DF
Tel: 01308 897784
• e-mail: holidays@tamariskfarm.com
• website: www.tamariskfarm.com/holidays

Hotel / Self Catering
Cromwell House Hotel, LULWORTH COVE, Dorset BH20 5RJ
Tel: 01929 400253
• e-mail: catriona@lulworthcove.co.uk
• website: www.lulworthcove.co.uk

Hotel
Fairwater Head Hotel, Hawkchurch, Near Axminster, LYME REGIS, Dorset EX13 5TX
Tel: 01297 678349
• e-mail: info@fairwaterheadhotel.co.uk
• website: www.fairwaterheadhotel.co.uk

Self-Catering
Westover Farm Cottages, Wootton Fitzpaine, Near LYME REGIS, Dorset DT6 6NE
Tel: 01297 560451/561395
• e-mail: wfcottages@aol.com
• website: www.westoverfarmcottages.co.uk

Self-Catering
Mrs E Melville, Wood Dairy, Wood Lane, NORTH PERROTT, Somerset/Dorset TA18 7TA
Tel: 01935 891532
• e-mail: liz@acountryretreat.co.uk
• website: www.acountryretreat.co.uk

Farm / Self-Catering
White Horse Farm, Middlemarsh, SHERBORNE, Dorset DT9 5QN
Tel: 01963 210222
• e-mail: enquiries@whitehorsefarm.co.uk
• website: www.whitehorsefarm.co.uk

Hotel
The Knoll House, STUDLAND BAY, Dorset BH19 3AW
Tel: 01929 450450
• e-mail: info@knollhouse.co.uk
• website: www.knollhouse.co.uk

Self-Catering
Dorset Coastal Cottages, 3 Station Road, Wood, WAREHAM, Dorset BH20 6BL
Tel: 0800 980 4070
• e-mail: hols@dorsetcoastalcottages.com
• website: www.dorsetcoastalcottages.com

Guest House
Kemps Country House, East Stoke, WAREHAM, Dorset BH20 6AL
Tel: 0845 862 0315
• e-mail: info@kempscountryhouse.co.uk
• website: www.kempshotel.com

Inn / Self-Catering
The Lugger Inn, 30 West Street, Chickerell, WEYMOUTH, Dorset DT3 4DY
Tel: 01305 766611
• e-mail: info@theluggerinn.co.uk
• website: www.theluggerinn.co.uk

Guest House / Self-Catering
Olivia Nurrish, Glenthorne, 15 Old Castle Road, WEYMOUTH, Dorset DT4 8QB
Tel: 01305 777281
• e-mail: info@glenthorne-holidays.co.uk
• website: www.glenthorne-holidays.co.uk

•ESSEX

Farm House B&B / Self-Catering
Mrs Brenda Lord, Pond House B & B and Self-Catering, Earls Hall Farm, St Osyth, CLACTON ON SEA, Essex CO16 8BP Tel: 01255 820458
• e-mail: brenda_lord@farming.co.uk
• website: www.earlshallfarm.info

•GLOUCESTERSHIRE

Hotel

Tudor Farmhouse Hotel, CLEARWELL,
Forest of Dean, Gloucs GL16 8JS
Tel: 01594 833046
* **e-mail: info@tudorfarmhousehotel.co.uk**
* **website: www.tudorfarmhousehotel.co.uk**

Guest House

Mr John Sparrey, Parkview Guest House, 4
Pittville Crescent, CHELTENHAM, Gloucs
GL52 2QZ
Tel: 01242 575567
* **e-mail: stay@parkviewguesthouse.me.uk**
* **website: www.parkviewguesthouse.me.uk**

Hotel

Tudor Farmhouse Hotel, CLEARWELL Near
Coleford, Gloucs GL16 8JS
Tel: 01929 450450
* **e-mail: info@tudeorfarmhousehotel.co.uk**
* **website: www.tudorfarmhousehotel.co.uk**

Self-Catering

Two Springbank, 37 Hopton Road, Cam,
DURSLEY, Gloucs GL11 5PD
Contact: Mrs F A Jones, 32 Everlands, Cam,
Dursley, Gloucs G11 5NL
Tel: 01453 543047
* **e-mail: info@twospringbank.co.uk**
* **website: www.twospringbank.co.uk**

Caravan & Camping

Tudor Caravan Park, Shepherds Patch,
SLIMBRIDGE, Gloucestershire GL2 7BP
Tel: 01453 890483
* **e-mail: fhg@tudorcaravanpark.co.uk**
* **website: www.tudorcaravanpark.com**

Guest House

Elizabeth Warland, Hambutts Mynd, Edge
Road, PAINSWICK, Gloucs GL6 6UP
Tel: 01452 812352
* **e-mail: ewarland@supanet.com.**
* **website:**
www.accommodation.uk.net/painswick.htm

Self-Catering

Nicky Cross, Wharton Lodge Cottages,
Weston-Under-Penyard, ROSS-ON-WYE,
Gloucs HR9 7JX
Tel: 01989 750140
* **e-mail: ncross@whartonlodge.co.uk**
* **website: www.whartonlodge.co.uk**

B & B

Mrs A Rhoton, Hyde Crest, Cirencester Road,
Minchinhampton, STROUD, Gloucs GL6 8PE
Tel: 01453 731631
* **e-mail: stay@hydecrest.co.uk**
* **website: www.hydecrest.co.uk**

•HAMPSHIRE

Holiday Park

Downton Holiday Park, Shorefield Road,
MILFORD-ON-SEA, New Forest, Hampshire
SO41 0LH
Tel: 01425 476131 / 01590 642515
* **e-mail: info@downtonholidaypark.co.uk**
* **website: www.downtonholidaypark.co.uk**

•ISLE OF WIGHT

Farmhouse B & B / Self-Catering Cottages

Mrs F.J. Corry, Little Span Farm, Rew Lane,
Wroxall, VENTNOR, Isle of Wight PO38 3AU
Tel: 01983 852419
* **e-mail: info@spanfarm.co.uk**
* **website: www.spanfarm.co.uk**

•KENT

Hotel

The Hanson, 41 Belvedere Road,
BROADSTAIRS, Kent CT10 1PF
Tel: 01843 868936
* **e-mail: hotel.hanson@yahoo.co.uk**
* **website: www.hansonhotel.co.uk**

Hotel

Mr M Collins, The Bell Hotel, The Quay,
SANDWICH, Kent CT13 9EF
Tel: 01304 613388
* **e-mail: reservations@bellhotelsandwich.co.uk**
* **website: www.bellhotelsandwich.co.uk**

Self-Catering

Mr A Vincent, Golding Hop Farm, Bewley
Lane, Plaxtol, SEVENOAKS, Kent TN15 0PS
Tel: 01732 885432
* **e-mail: info@goldinghopfarm.com**
* **website: www.goldinghopfarm.com**

•LINCOLNSHIRE

Lodges / Touring Caravan Park

Mr & Mrs A Potts, Walnut Lake Lodges &
Camping Park, Main Road, Algarkirk,
BOSTON, Lincs PE20 2LQ
Tel: 01205 460482
* **e-mail: mariawalnutlakes@yahoo.co.uk**
* **website: www.walnutlakes.co.uk**

www.holidayguides.com

Lodges / Touring Caravan Park
Mrs D Corradine, Woodland Waters,
Willoughby Road, Ancastet, GRANTHAM,
Lincs NG2 3RT
Tel: 01400 230888
• e-mail: info@woodlandwaters.co.uk
• website: www.woodlandwaters.co.uk

Farm B & B / Self-catering cottage
Mrs C.E. Harrison, Baumber Park, Baumber,
HORNCASTLE, Lincolnshire LN9 5NE
Tel: 01507 578235/07977 722776
• e-mail: mail@baumberpark.com
        mail@gathmanscottage.co.uk
• website: www.baumberpark.com
        www.gathmanscottage.co.uk

Self Catering / B & B
Mr A Tuxworth, Poachers Hideaway Holiday
Cottages, Flintwood Farm, Belchford,
HORNCASTLE, Lincolnshire LN9 5QN
Tel: 01507 533555
• e-mail: info@poachershideaway.com
• website: www.poachershideaway.com

Farmhouse B & B
S Evans, Willow Farm, Thorpe Fendykes,
SKEGNESS, Lincolnshire PE24 4QH
Tel: 01754 830316
• e-mail: willowfarmhols@aol.com
• website: www.willowfarmholidays.co.uk

B & B
Mrs Hodgkinson, Kirkstead Oldmill Cottage,
Tattershall Road, WOODHALL SPA,
Lincolnshire LN10 6UQ
Tel: 01526 353637
• e-mail: barbara@woodhallspa.com
• website: www.woodhallspa.com

Hotel
Petwood Hotel, Stixwould Road,
WOODHALL SPA, Lincolnshire LN10 6QG
Tel: 01526 352411
• e-mail: reception@petwood.co.uk
• website: www.petwood.co.uk

• MERSEYSIDE

Guest House
Holme Leigh Guest House, 93 Woodcroft Road,
Wavertree, LIVERPOOL, Merseyside L15 2HG
Tel: 0151 734 2216
• e-mail: info@holmeleigh.com
• website: www.holmeleigh.com

• NORFOLK

Hotel
The Hoste Arms, The Green, BURNHAM
MARKET, Norfolk PE31 8HD
Tel: 01328 738777
• e-mail: reception@hostearms.co.uk
• website: www.hostearms.co.uk

Self-Catering
Blue Riband Holidays, HEMSBY,
Great Yarmouth, Norfolk NR29 4HA
Tel: 01493 730445
• website: www.BlueRibandHolidays.co.uk

Board /Farm
Mrs L Mack, Hempstead Hall, HOLT, Norfolk
NR25 6TN
Tel: 01263 712224
• website: www.hempsteadhall.co.uk

Hotel
The Stuart House Hotel, 35 Goodwins Road,
KING'S LYNN, Norfolk PE30 5QX
Tel: 01553 772169
• e-mail: reception@stuarthousehotel.co.uk
• website: www.stuarthousehotel.co.uk

Self-catering
Scarning Dale, Dale Road, SCARNING,
Dereham, Norfolk NR19 2QN
Tel: 01362 687269
• e-mail: jean@scarningdale.co.uk
• website: www.scarningdale.co.uk

Self-Catering
Winterton Valley Holidays, Edward Road,
WINTERTON-ON-SEA, Norfolk NR29 4BX
Contact:15 Kingston Avenue, Caister-on-
Sea, Norfolk NR30 5ET
Tel: 01493 377175
• e-mail: info@wintertonvalleyholidays.co.uk
• website: www.wintertonvalleyholidays.co.uk

• NORTHUMBERLAND

Inn
The Bay Horse Inn, West Woodburn,
HEXHAM, Northumberland NE48 2RX
Tel: 01434 2710218
• e-mail: enquiry@bayhorseinn.org
• website: www.bayhorseinn.org

Self Catering
Mr A. P. Coatsworth, Gallowhill Farm,
Whalton, MORPETH, Northumberland
NE61 3TX
Tel: 01661 881241
• website: www.gallowhillfarm.co.uk

FHG Guides

Self Catering
Mrs J Younger, Burradon Farm Houses &
Cottages, Burradon Farm, Cramlington,
NEWCASTLE-ON-TYNE, Northumberland
NE23 7ND
Tel: 0191 2683203
• e-mail: judy@burradonfarm.co.uk
• website: www.burradonfarm.co.uk

•NOTTINGHAMSHIRE

Caravan & Camping Park
Orchard Park, Marnham Road, Tuxford,
NEWARK, Nottinghamshire NG22 0PY
Tel: 01777 870228
• e-mail: info@orchardcaravanpark.co.uk
• website: www.orchardcaravanpark.co.uk

B & B
Willow House, Burton Joyce,
NOTTINGHAM, NG14 5FD Nottinghamshire
Tel: 01159 312070 / 07816 347706
• website: www.willowhousebedand
breakfast.co.uk

•OXFORDSHIRE

Leisure Park
Cotswold Wildlife Park, BURFORD,
Oxfordshire OX18 4JN
Tel: 01993 825728
• website: www.cotswoldwildlifepark.co.uk

B & B / Guest House
June Collier, Colliers, 55 Nethercote Road,
Tackley, KIDLINGTON, Oxfordshire, OX5 3AT
Tel: 01869 331255 / 07790 338225
• e-mail: colliers.bnb@virgin.net
• website: www.colliersbnb.com

B & B / Self Catering
Julia Tanner, Little Acre, 4 High Street,
Tetsworth, THAME, Oxfordshire OX9 7AT
Tel: 01844 281423
• e-mail: julia@little-acre.co.uk
  info@theholliesthame.co.uk
• website: www.little-acre.co.uk
  www.theholliesthame.co.uk

•SHROPSHIRE

Hotel
Longmynd Hotel, Cunnery Rd, CHURCH
STRETTON, Shropshire SY6 6AG
Tel: 01694 722244
• e-mail: info@longmynd.co.uk
• website: www.longmynd.co.uk

Self Catering
Mrs N Adams, The Anchorage, Anchor,
Newcastle-on-Clun, CRAVEN ARMS,
Shropshire S77 8PR
Tel: 01686 670737
• e-mail: nancynewcwm@btinternet.com
• website: www.adamsanchor.co.uk

Self-Catering
Clive & Cynthia Prior, Mocktree Barns
Holiday Cottages, Leintwardine, LUDLOW,
Shropshire SY7 0LY
Tel: 01547 540441
• e-mail: mocktreebarns@care4free.net
• website: www.mocktreeholidays.co.uk

Self-Catering
Jane Cronin, Sutton Court Farm Cottages,
Sutton Court Farm, Little Sutton, LUDLOW,
Shropshire SY8 2AJ
Tel: 01584 861305
• e-mail: enquiries@suttoncourtfarm.co.uk
• website: www.suttoncourtfarm.co.uk

•SOMERSET

Farm / Guest House / Self-Catering
Jackie Bishop, Toghill House Farm, Freezing
Hill, Wick, Near BATH, Somerset BS30 5RT
Tel: 01225 891261
• e-mail:
accommodation@toghillhousefarm.co.uk
• website: www.toghillhousefarm.co.uk

Guest House
Mrs C Bryson, Walton Villa, 3 Newbridge
Hill, BATH, Somerset BA1 3PW
Tel: 01225 482792
• e-mail: walton.villa@virgin.net
• website: www.walton.izest.com

Self-Catering
Westward Rise Holiday Park, South Road,
BREAN, Burnham-on-Sea, Somerset TA8 2RD
Tel: 01278 751310
• e-mail: info@westwardrise.com
• website: www.westwardrise.com

Self-Catering
Leone & Brian Martin, Riscombe Farm
Holiday Cottages, Riscombe Farm, EXFORD,
Minehead, Somerset TA24 7NH
Tel: 01643 831480
• e-mail: brian@riscombe.co.uk
• website: www.riscombe.co.uk

Self-Catering / Holiday Park / Touring Pitches
Mary Randle, St Audries Bay Holiday Club,
MINEHEAD, Somerset TA4 4DA
Tel: 01984 632515
• e-mail: info@staudriesbay.co.uk
• website: www.staudriesbay.co.uk

Farm / B & B
North Down Farm, Pyncombe Lane,
Wiveliscombe, TAUNTON, Somerset TA4 2BL
Tel: 01984 623730
• e-mail: jennycope@btinternet.com
• website: www.north-down-farm.co.uk

B & B
The Old Mill, Netherclay, Bishop's Hull,
TAUNTON, Somerset TA1 5AB
Tel: 01823 289732
• website: www.theoldmillbandb.co.uk /
www.bandbtaunton.co.uk

Farm / Guest House
G. Clark, Yew Tree Farm, THEALE,
Near Wedmore, Somerset BS28 4SN
Tel: 01934 712475
• e-mail: enquiries@yewtreefarmbandb.co.uk
• website: www.yewtreefarmbandb.co.uk

B & B
Mrs S Crane, Birdwood, Bath Road, WELLS,
Somerset BA5 3EW
Tel: 01749 679250
• e-mail: susancrane@mbzonline.net
• website: www.birdwood-bandb.co.uk

Caravan
C G Thomas, Ardnave Holiday Park,
Kewstoke, WESTON-SUPER-MARE,
Somerset BS22 9XJ
Tel: 01934 622319
• e-mail: enquiries@ardnaveholidaypark.co.uk
• website: www.ardnaveholidaypark.co.uk

•STAFFORDSHIRE

Caravan & Camping
Star Caravan & Camping Park, Woodside
Lodge, Ramshorn, Near ALTON TOWERS,
Staffordshire ST10 3DW
Tel: 01538 702219
• website: www.starcaravanpark.co.uk

Farm B & B / Self-Catering
Mrs M. Hiscoe-James, Offley Grove Farm,
Adbaston, ECCLESHALL, Staffs ST20 0QB
Tel: 01785 280205
• e-mail: enquiries@offleygrovefarm.co.uk
• website: www.offleygrovefarm.co.uk

Self-Catering
T.A. Mycock, Rosewood Cottage, Lower
Berkhamsytch, Bottom House, Near LEEK,
Staffordshire ST13 7QP
Tel: 01538 308213
• website: www.rosewoodcottage.co.uk

FHG Guides

•SUFFOLK

Self-Catering
Annie's Cottage, BUNGAY, Suffolk
Contact: Mrs L Morton, Hill Farm, Beccles,
Suffolk NR34 8JE
Tel: 01956 781240
• website: www.hillfarmholidays.com

B & B / Guest House
Dunstin Guest House, 8 Springfield Road,
BURY ST EDMUNDS, Suffolk IP33 3AN
Tel: 01284 767981
• e-mail: anndakin@btconnect.com
• website: www.dunstonguesthouse.co.uk

B & B
Mrs Sarah Kindred, High House Farm,
Cransford, Woodbridge, FRAMLINGHAM,
Suffolk IP13 9PD
Tel: 01728 663461
• e-mail: b&b@highhousefarm.co.uk
• website: www.highhousefarm.co.uk

Self-Catering
Kessingland Cottages, Rider Haggard Lane,
KESSINGLAND, Suffolk.
Contact: S. Mahmood, 156 Bromley Road,
Beckenham, Kent BR3 6PG
Tel: 020 8650 0539
• e-mail: jeeptrek@kjti.co.uk
• website: www.k-cottage.co.uk

Self-Catering / Caravan
Mr D. Westgate, Beach Farm Holiday Park,
Arbor Lane, Pakefield, LOWESTOFT, Suffolk
NR33 7BD
Tel: 01502 572794
• e-mail: beachfarmpark@aol.com
• website: www.beachfarmpark.co.uk

•SURREY

Self-Catering / B & B
Mrs J Howell, Little Orchard B & B, 152
London Road North, Merstham, REDHILL,
Surrey RH1 3AA
Tel: 01737 558707
• e-mail:jackie@littleorchardbandb.co.uk
• website: www.littleorchardbandb.co.uk

•EAST SUSSEX

Self-Catering
Best of Brighton & Sussex Cottages,
Laureens Walk, Nevill Road,Rottingdean,
BRIGHTON, East Sussex BN2 7HG
Tel: 01273 308779
• e-mail: enquiries@bestofbrighton.co.uk
• website: www.bestofbrighton.co.uk

B & B

Maon Hotel, 26 Upper Rock Gardens, BRIGHTON, East Sussex BN2 1QE
Tel: 01273 694400
- **e-mail: maonhotel@aol.com**
- **website: www.maonhotel.co.uk**

Self-Catering

"Pekes", CHIDDINGLY, East Sussex
Contact: Eva Morris, 124 Elm Park Mansions, Park Walk, London SW10 0AR
Tel: 020 7352 8088
- **e-mail: pekes.afa@virgin.net**
- **website: www.pekesmanor.com**

Guest House / Self-Catering

Longleys Farm Cottage, Harebeating Lane, HAILSHAM, East Sussex BN27 1ER
Tel: 01323 841227
- **website: www.longleysfarmcottage.co.uk**

Hotel

Grand Hotel, Grand Parade, St Leonards, HASTINGS, East Sussex TN38 0DD
Tel: 01424 428510
- **e-mail: info@grandhotelhastings.co.uk**
- **website: www.grandhotelhastings.co.uk**

• WEST SUSSEX

Self-Catering

Mrs M. W. Carreck, New Hall Holiday Flat and Cottage, New Hall Lane, Small Dole, HENFIELD, West Sussex BN5 9YJ
Tel: 01273 492546
- **e-mail: norman.carreck@btinternet.com**
- **website: www.newhallcottage.co.uk**

•WARWICKSHIRE

Caravan Touring Park

Dodwell Park, Evesham Road, STRATFORD-UPON-AVON, Warwickshire CV37 9SR
Tel: 01784 204957
- **e-mail: enquiries@dodwellpark.co.uk**
- **website: www.dodwellpark.co.uk**

•EAST YORKSHIRE

Hotel

The Old Mill Hotel, Mill Lane, Longtoft, DRIFFIELD, East Yorkshire YO25 3BQ
Tel: 01377 267284
- **e-mail: enquiries@old-mill-hotel.co.uk**
- **website: www.old-mill-hotel.co.uk**

•NORTH YORKSHIRE

Farmhouse B & B

Mrs Julie Clarke, Middle Farm, Woodale, COVERDALE, Leyburn, North Yorkshire DL8 4TY • Tel: 01969 640271
- **e-mail: j-a-clarke@hotmail.co.uk**
- **www.yorkshirenet.co.uk/stayat/middlefarm/index.htm**

Farm

Mrs Linda Tindall, Rowantree Farm, Fryup Road, Ainthorpe, DANBY, Whitby, North Yorkshire YO21 2LE • Tel: 01287 660396
- **e-mail: krbsatindall@aol.com**
- **website: www.rowantreefarm.co.uk**

Farmhouse B&B

Mr & Mrs Richardson, Egton Banks Farmhouse, GLAISDALE, Whitby, North Yorkshire YO21 2QP
Tel: 01947 897289
- **e-mail: egtonbanksfarm@btconnect.com**
- **website: www.egtonbanksfarm.agriplus.net**

Self-Catering / Lodges & Caravans

Reynard Crag Holiday Park, Reynard Crag Lane, High Birstwith, Near HARROGATE, North Yorkshire HG3 2JQ
Tel: 01423 772828 / 07793 049567
- **e-mail: reynardcrag@btconnect.com**
- **website: www.reynardcragpark.co.uk**

Guest House

The New Inn Motel, Main Street, HUBY, York, North Yorkshire YO61 1HQ
Tel: 01347 810219
- **enquiries@newinnmotel.freeserve.co.uk**
- **website: www.newinnmotel.co.uk**

Self-Catering

Allaker in Coverdale, West Scrafton, LEYBURN, North Yorkshire DL8 4RM
Contact: Mr Adrian Cave, 21 Kenilworth Road, London W5 5PA Tel: 020 856 74862
- **e-mail: ac@adriancave.com**
- **www.adriancave.com/allaker**

Self-Catering

Abbey Holiday Cottages, MIDDLESMOOR. 12 Panorama Close, Pateley Bridge, Harrogate, North Yorkshire HG3 5NY
Tel: 01423 712062
- **e-mail: info@abbeyhallcottages.com**
- **website: www.abbeyholidaycottages.co.uk**

Self-Catering

Waterfront House, RIPON
Contact: Mrs C. Braddon, Chantry Bells, Chantry Court, Ripley, Harrogate HG3 3AD
Tel: 01423 770704
- **e-mail: chris1.braddon@virgin.net**
- **website: www.dalesholidayripon.co.uk**

www.holidayguides.com

Guest House / Self-Catering
Sue & Tony Hewitt, Harmony Country Lodge,
80 Limestone Road, Burniston,
SCARBOROUGH, North Yorkshire YO13 0DG
Tel: 0800 2985840
• e-mail: mail@harmonylodge.net
• website: www.harmonycountrylodge.co.uk

Self-Catering
Mrs Jones, New Close Farm, Kirkby Malham,
SKIPTON, North Yorkshire BD23 4DP
Tel: 01729 830240
• e-mail:
brendajones@newclosefarmyorkshire.co.uk
• website: www.newclosefarmyorkshire.co.uk

Self-Catering
Greenhouses Farm Cottages, Near WHITBY.
Contact: Mr J.N. Eddleston, Greenhouses
Farm, Lealholm, Near Whitby, North
Yorkshire YO21 2AD. Tel: 01947 897486
• e-mail: n_eddleston@yahoo.com
• www.greenhouses-farm-cottages.co.uk

Guest House
Mr & Mrs R Brew, The Arches, 8 Havelock
Place, WHITBY, North Yorkshire YO21 3ER
Tel: 0800 915 4256 / 01947 601880
• e-mail: archeswhitby@freeola.com
• website: www.whitbyguesthouses.co.uk

B & B
Mr & Mrs Leedham, York House, 62 Heworth
Green, YORK, North Yorkshire YO31 7TQ
Tel: 01904 427070
• e-mail: yorkhouse.bandb@tiscali.co.uk
• website: www.yorkhouseyork.co.uk

Self-Catering
York Lakeside Lodges Ltd, Moor Lane,
YORK, North Yorkshire YO24 2QU
Tel: 01904 702346
• e-mail: neil@yorklakesidelodges.co.uk
• website: www.yorklakesidelodges.co.uk

•SCOTLAND

•ABERDEEN, BANFF & MORAY

Hotel
Glen Lui Hotel, 14 Invercauld Road,
BALLATER, Aberdeenshire AB35 5PP
Tel: 01339 755402
• e-mail: info@glen-lui-hotel.co.uk
• website: www.glen-lui-hotel.co.uk

•ANGUS & DUNDEE

Golf Club
Edzell Golf Club, High Street, EDZELL,
Brechin, Angus DD9 7TF
Tel: 01356 648462
• e-mail: secretary@edzellgolfclub.net
• website: www.edzellgolfclub.net

•ARGYLL & BUTE

Self-Catering
Ardtur Cottages, APPIN, Argyll PA38 4DD
Tel: 01631 730223
• e-mail: pery@btinternet.com
• website: www.ardturcottages.com

Self-Catering
Blarghour Farm Cottages, Blarghour Farm,
By Dalmally, INVERARAY, Argyll PA33 1BW
Tel: 01866 833246
• e-mail: blarghour@btconnect.com
• website: www.self-catering-argyll.co.uk

Self-Catering
Inchmurrin Island Self-Catering Holidays,
Inchmurrin Island, LOCH LOMOND G63 0JY
Tel: 01389 850245
• e-mail: scotts@inchmurrin-lochlomond.com
• website: www.inchmurrin-lochlomond.com

Self-Catering
Colin Mossman, Lagnakeil Lodges,
Lerags, OBAN, Argyll PA34 4SE
Tel: 01631 562746
• e-mail: info@lagnakeil.co.uk
• website: www.lagnakeil.co.uk

Hotel
Falls of Lora Hotel, Connel Ferry, By OBAN,
Argyll PA37 1PB
Tel: 01631 710483
• e-mail: enquiries@fallsoflora.com
• website: www.fallsoflora.com

Self-Catering
Airdeny Chalets, Glen Lonan, TAYNUILT,
Oban, Argyll PA35 1HY Tel: 01866 822648
- e-mail: **jenifer@airdenychalets.co.uk**
- website: **www.airdenychalets.co.uk**

•AYRSHIRE & ARRAN

Farmhouse / B & B

Mrs Nancy Cuthbertson, West Tannacrieff,
Fenwick, KILMARNOCK, Ayrshire KA3 6AZ
Tel: 01560 600258
- e-mail: **westtannacrieff@btopenworld.com**
- website: **www.smoothhound.co.uk/hotels/
westtannacrieff.html**

•BORDERS

Guest House

Mr A & Mrs C Swanston, Ferniehirst Mill
Lodge, JEDBURGH, Roxburghshire
TD8 6PQ
Tel: 01835 863279
- e-mail: **ferniehirstmill@aol.com**
- website: **www.ferniehirstmill.co.uk**

Self-Catering

Mrs C. M. Kilpatrick, Slipperfield House,
WEST LINTON, Peeblesshire EH46 7AA
Tel: 01968 660401
- e-mail: **cottages@slipperfield.com**
- website: **www.slipperfield.com**

•DUMFRIES & GALLOWAY

Self-Catering

Barend Holiday Village, Barend Farmhouse,
SANDYHILLS, Dalbeattie, Dumfries &
Galloway DG5 4NU
Tel: 01387 780663
- e-mail: **info@barendholidayvillage.co.uk**
- website: **www.barendholidayvillage.co.uk**

Self-Catering

Ae Farm Cottages, Gubhill Farm, Ae,
DUMFRIES, Dumfriesshire DG1 1RL
Tel: 01387 860648
- e-mail: **gill@gubhill.co.uk**
- website: **www.aefarmcottages.co.uk**

Farm / Camping & Caravans / Self-Catering

Barnsoul Farm Holidays, Barnsoul Farm,
Shawhead, DUMFRIES, Dumfriesshire DG2
9SQ. Tel: 01387 730249
- e-mail: **barnsouldg@aol.com**
- website: **www.barnsoulfarm.co.uk**

Self-Catering
Rusko, GATEHOUSE OF FLEET, Castle
Douglas, Dumfriesshire DG7 2BS
Tel: 01557 814215
- e-mail: **info@ruskoholidays.co.uk**
- website: **www.ruskoholidays.co.uk**

Self-Catering

Hope Cottage, THORNHILL, Dumfriesshire
G3 5BJ
Contact: Mrs S. Stannett Tel: 01848 331510
- e-mail: **a.stann@btinternet.com**
- website: **www.hopecottage.co.uk**

•EDINBURGH & LOTHIANS

Guest House

International Guest House, 37 Mayfield
Gardens, EDINBURGH EH9 2BX
Tel: 0131 667 2511
- e-mail: **intergh1@yahoo.co.uk**
- website: **www.accommodation-edinburgh.com**

•FIFE

Self-Catering

Pitcairlie House, AUCHTERMUCHTY, Fife
KY14 6EU
Tel:01337 827418
- e-mail: **reservations@pitcairlie-leisure.co.uk**
- website: **www.pitcairlie-leisure.co.uk**

•HIGHLANDS

Self-Catering

Cairngorm Highland Bungalows, AVIEMORE.
Contact: Linda Murray, 29 Grampian View,
Aviemore, Inverness-shire PH22 1TF
Tel: 01479 810653
- e-mail: **linda.murray@virgin.net**
- website: **www.cairngorm-bungalows.co.uk**

Self-Catering

Frank & Juliet Spencer-Nairn, Culligran
Cottages, Struy, Near BEAULY, Inverness-
shire IV4 7JX . Tel: 01463 761285
- e-mail: **info@culligrancottages.co.uk**
- website: **www.culligrancottages.co.uk**

Self-Catering

Tyndrum, BOAT OF GARTEN, Inverness-shire
Contact: Mrs Naomi C. Clark, Dochlaggie,
Boat of Garten PH24 3BU
Tel: 01479 831242
- e-mail: **dochlaggie99@aol.com**

Self-Catering
Carol Hughes, Glenurquhart Lodges, Balnain,
DRUMNADROCHIT, Inverness-shire IV63 6TJ
Tel: 01456 476234
• e-mail: carol@glenurquhartlodges.co.uk
• website: www.glenurquhart-lodges.co.uk

Hotel
The Clan MacDuff Hotel, Achintore Road,
FORT WILLIAM, Inverness-shire PH33 6RW
Tel: 01397 702341
• e-mail: reception@clanmacduff.co.uk
• website: www.clanmacduff.co.uk

Caravan & Camping
Auchnahillin Caravan & Camping Park,
Daviot East, INVERNESS, Inverness-shire
IV2 5XQ • Tel: 01463 772286
• e-mail: info@auchnahillin.co.uk
• website: www.auchnahillin.co.uk

Hotel
Dunain Park Hotel, Loch Ness Road,
INVERNESS, Inverness-shire IV3 8JN
Tel: 01463 230512
• e-mail: info@dunainparkhotel.co.uk
• website: www.dunainparkhotel.co.uk

Hotel
Kintail Lodge Hotel, Glenshiel, SHIEL
BRIDGE, Ross-shire IV40 8HL
Tel: 01599 511275
• e-mail: kintaillodgehotel@btinternet.com
• website: www.kintaillodgehotel.co.uk

Hotel
Whitebridge Hotel, Whitebridge, LOCH
NESS, Inverness-shire IV2 6UN
Tel: 01456 486226
• e-mail: info@whitebridgehotel.co.uk
• website: www.whitebridgehotel.co.uk

Self-Catering
Innes Maree Bungalows, POOLEWE,
Ross-shire IV22 2JU • Tel: 01445 781454
• e-mail: info@poolewebungalows.com
• website: www.poolewebungalows.com

Self-Catering
Mr & Mrs S Dennis, Riverside House,
Invergloy, SPEAN BRIDGE, Inverness-shire
PH34 4DY • Tel: 01397 712684
• e-mail: enquiries@riversidelodge.org.uk
• website: www.riversidelodge.org.uk

• LANARKSHIRE

Caravan & Holiday Home Park
Mount View Caravan Park, Station Road,
ABINGTON, South Lanarkshire ML12 6RW
Tel: 01864 502808
• e-mail: info@mountviewcaravanpark.co.uk
• website: www.mountviewcaravanpark.co.uk

• PERTH & KINROSS

Self-Catering
Loch Tay Lodges, Remony, Acharn,
ABERFELDY, Perthshire PH15 2HR
Tel: 01887 830209
• e-mail: remony@btinternet.com
• website: www.lochtaylodges.co.uk

Self-Catering
Laighwood Holidays, Laighwood,
DUNKELD, Perthshire PH8 0HB
Tel: 01350 724241
• e-mail: holidays@laighwood.co.uk
• website: www.laighwood.co.uk

Self- Catering
Atholl Cottage, Killiecrankie, PITLOCHRY,
Perthshire
Contact: Mrs Joan Troup, Dalnasgadh,
Killiecrankie, Pitlochry, Perthshire PH16 5LN
Tel: 01796 470017
• e-mail: info@athollcottage.co.uk
• website: www.athollcottage.co.uk

Self-Catering Cottages
Dalmunzie Highland Cottages, SPITTAL OF
GLENSHEE, Blairgowrie, Perthshire
PH10 7QE Tel: 01250 885226
• e-mail: enquiries@dalmunziecottages.com
• website: www.dalmunziecottages.com

• STIRLING & TROSSACHS

Hotel
Culcreuch Castle Hotel & Estate, Kippen
Road, FINTRY, Stirlingshire G63 0LW
Tel: 01360 860555
• e-mail: info@culcreuch.com
• website: www.culcreuch.com

• ORKNEY ISLANDS

Caravan & Camping
Point of Ness, STROMNESS, Orkney
Tel: 01856 850262
• e-mail: recreation@orkney.gov.uk
• website: www.orkney.gov.uk

Caravan & Camping
Pickaquoy Centre, KIRKWALL, Orkney
Tel: 01856 879900
• e-mail: enquiries@pickaquoy.com
• website: www.pickaquoy.co.uk

www.holidayguides.com

•WALES

Self-Catering
Quality Cottages, Cerbid, Solva,
HAVERFORDWEST, Pembrokeshire SA62 6YE
Tel: 01348 837871
* **e-mail: reserve@qualitycottages.co.uk**
* **website: www.qualitycottages.co.uk**

•ANGLESEY & GWYNEDD

Self-Catering / Caravan Site
Bryn Gloch Caravan and Camping Park,
Betws Garmon, CAERNARFON, Gwynedd
LL54 7YY Tel: 01286 650216
* **e-mail: eurig@bryngloch.co.uk**
* **website: www.bryngloch.co.uk**

Self-Catering Chalet
Chalet at Glan Gwna Holiday Park, Caethro,
CAERNARFON, Gwynedd
Contact: Mr H A Jones, Menai Bridge,
Caernarfon, Gwynedd LL59 5LN
Tel: 01248 712045
* **e-mail: hajones@northwales-chalet.co.uk**
* **website: www.northwales-chalet.co.uk**

Self-Catering
Parc Wernol, Chwilog Fawr, Chwilog,
Pwllheli, CRICCIETH, Gwynedd LL53 6SW
Tel: 01766 810506
* **website: www.wernol.co.uk**

Self-Catering
Mrs E A Williams, Tyddyn Heilyn, Chwilog,
PWLLHELI, Gwynedd LL53 6SW
Tel: 01766 810441
* **e-mail: tyddyn.heilyn@tiscali.co.uk**

Caravan & Camping Site
Marian Rees, Dôl Einion, Tal-y-Llyn, TYWYN,
Gwynedd LL36 9AJ
Tel: 01654 761312
* **e-mail: marianrees@tiscali.co.uk**

•NORTH WALES

Guest House
Park Hill/Gwesty Bryn Parc, Llanrwst Road,
BETWS-Y-COED, Conwy LL24 0HD
Tel: 01690 710510
* **e-mail: welcome@park-hill.co.uk**
* **website: www.park-hill.co.uk**

Guest House
Mr D E Morgan, The Northwood, Rhos
Road, Rhos-on-Sea, COLWYN BAY, Conwy
LL28 4RS
Tel: 01492 549931
* **e-mail: welcome@thenorthwood.co.uk**
* **website: www.thenorthwood.co.uk**

• PEMBROKESHIRE

Self-Catering
Timberhill Farm, BROAD HAVEN,
Pembrokeshire SA62 3LZ
Contact: Mrs L Ashton, 10 St Leonards
Road, Thames Ditton, Surrey KT7 0RJ
Tel: 02083 986349
* **e-mail: lejash@aol.com**
* **website: www.33timberhill.com**

Hotel
Michael & Suzy Beales, Castell Malgwyn
Hote, LLechryd, CARDIGAN, Pembrokeshire
SA43 2QA
Tel: 01239 682382
* **e-mail: reception@malgwyn.co.uk**
* **website: www.castellmalgwyn.co.uk**

Country House
Angelica Rees, Heathfield Mansion, Letterston,
Near FISHGUARD, Pembrokeshire SA62 5EG
Tel: 01348 840263
* **e-mail: angelica.rees@virgin.net**
* **website: www.heathfieldaccommodation.co.uk**

Guest House
Ivybridge, Drim Mill, Dyffryn, Goodwick,
FISHGUARD, Pembrokeshire SA64 0JT
Tel: 01348 875366
* **website: www.ivybridgeleisure.co.uk**

Caravan & Camping
Nolton Cross Caravan Park, NOLTON
HAVEN, Haverfordwest, Pembrokeshire
SA62 3NP
Tel:01437 710701
* **e-mail: info@noltoncross-holidays.co.uk**
* **website: www.noltoncross-holidays.co.uk**

Self-Catering
Capri Cottage, The Ridgeway,
SAUNDERSFOOT, Pembrokeshire
SA69 9LD.
Contact: R Reed, Trevayne Farm,
Saundersfoot, Pembrokeshire SA69 9LD
Tel: 01834 813402
* **e-mail: info@camping-pembrokeshire.co.uk**
* **www.saundersfoot-holidaycottage.co.uk**

Self-catering
Ffynnon Ddofn, Llanon, Llanrhian, Near ST DAVIDS, Pembrokeshire. Contact: Mrs B. Rees White, Brick House Farm, Burnham Road, Woodham Mortimer, Maldon, Essex CM9 6SR. Tel: 01245 224611
• e-mail: daisypops@madasafish.com
• website: www.ffynnonddofn.co.uk

Guest House
Mrs M. Jones, Lochmeyler Farm, Pen-Y-Cwm, Near Solva, ST DAVIDS, Pembrokeshire SA62 6LL
Tel: 01348 837724
• e-mail: stay@lochmeyler.co.uk
• website: www.lochmeyler.co.uk

Self-Catering
Mrs M. Pike, Porthidaly Farm Holiday Cottages, Abereiddy, ST DAVIDS, Pembrokeshire SA62 6DR
Tel: 01348 831004
• e-mail: m.pike@porthiddy.com
• website: www.porthiddy.com

•POWYS

Self-Catering
Old Stables Cottage & Old Dairy, Lane Farm, Paincastle, Builth Wells, HAY-ON-WYE, Powys LD2 3JS
Tel: 01497 851 605
• e-mail: lanefarm@onetel.com
• website: www.lane-farm.co.uk

Self-Catering / Guest House
Park House Motel, LLLANDRINDOD WELLS, Powys LO1 6RF
Tel: 01597 851201 / 07918 660647
• website: www.parkhousemotel.net

•SOUTH WALES

Caravan Park
Mr G. Watkins, Wernddu Caravan Park, Old Ross Road, ABERGAVENNY, Monmouthshire NP7 8NG
Tel:01873 856223
• e-mail: info@wernddu-golf-club.co.uk
• website: www.wernddu-golf-club.co.uk

Self-Catering Cottages
Mrs Norma James, Wyrloed Lodge Holiday Cottages, 3 Wyrloed Lodge Cottage, Manmoel, BLACKWOOD, Caerphilly, South Wales NP12 0RN
Tel: 01495 371198
• e-mail: norma.james@btinternet.com
• website: www.wyrloedlodge.com

Country House Hotel
Egerton Grey Country House Hotel, Porthkerry, Rhoose, CARDIFF, Vale of Glamorgan, South Wales CF62 3BZ
Tel: 01446 711666
• e-mail: info@egertongrey.co.uk
• website: www.egertongrey.co.uk

Self-Catering
Cwrt-y-Gaer, Wolvesnewton, CHEPSTOW, Monmouthshire, South Wales NP16 6PR
Tel: 01291 650700
• e-mail: john.llewellyn11@btinternet.com
• website: www.cwrt-y-gaer.co.uk

FHG Guides

Index of Towns and Counties

Abbotsbury, Dorset	SOUTH WEST
Aberfeldy, Perthshire	SCOTLAND
Aberporth, Ceredigion	WALES
Abersoch, Anglesey & Gwynedd	WALES
Aberystwyth, Ceredigion	WALES
Achiltibuie, Highlands	SCOTLAND
Alford, Lincolnshire	MIDLANDS
Alnmouth, Northumberland	NORTH EAST
Alnwick, Northumberland	NORTH EAST
Alva, Stirling & The Trossachs	SCOTLAND
Ambleside, Cumbria	NORTH WEST
Anglesey, Anglesey & Gwynedd	WALES
Appin, Argyll & Bute	SCOTLAND
Ardgay, Highlands	SCOTLAND
Ardnamurchan, Argyll & Bute	SCOTLAND
Ashbourne, Derbyshire	MIDLANDS
Ashburton, Devon	SOUTH WEST
Ashford, Kent	SOUTH EAST
Ashwater, Devon	SOUTH WEST
Askrigg, North Yorkshire	YORKSHIRE
Auchtermuchty, Fife	SCOTLAND
Aviemore, Highlands	SCOTLAND
Avington, Hampshire	SOUTH EAST
Avoch, Highlands	SCOTLAND
Axminster, Devon	SOUTH WEST
Bacton-on-Sea, Norfolk	EAST
Bala, Anglesey & Gwynedd	WALES
Ballantrae, Ayrshire & Arran	SCOTLAND
Ballyvaughan, Co Clare	IRELAND
Bamburgh, Northumberland	NORTH EAST
Bangor, Anglesey & Gwynedd	WALES
Barnoldby-Le-Beck, Lincolnshire	MIDLANDS
Barnoldswick, Lancashire	NORTH WEST
Barnstaple, Devon	SOUTH WEST
Bath, Somerset	SOUTH WEST
Battle, East Sussex	SOUTH EAST
Beadnell, Northumberland	NORTH EAST
Beaminster, Dorset	SOUTH WEST
Beauly, Highlands	SCOTLAND
Beaumaris, Anglesey & Gwynedd	WALES
Belford, Northumberland	NORTH EAST
Belper, Derbyshire	MIDLANDS
Berwick-upon-Tweed, Northumberland	NORTH EAST
Bicester, Oxfordshire	SOUTH EAST
Biggar, (Clyde Valley), Lanarkshire	SCOTLAND
Bishop Auckland, Durham	NORTH EAST
Bishop Wilton, North Yorkshire	YORKSHIRE
Blairgowrie, Perth & Kinross	SCOTLAND
Blandford Forum, Dorset	SOUTH WEST
Boat of Garten, Highlands	SCOTLAND
Bodmin, Cornwall	SOUTH WEST
Bodorgan, Anglesey & Gwynedd	WALES
Boncath, Pembrokeshire	WALES
Bonchester Bridge, Borders	SCOTLAND
Bonnybridge, Stirling & The Trossachs	SCOTLAND
Bosherton, Pembrokeshire	WALES
Bournemouth, Dorset	SOUTH WEST
Bowness-on-Windermere, Cumbria	NORTH WEST
Brayford, Devon	SOUTH WEST
Brechin, Angus & Dundee	SCOTLAND
Bridlington, East Yorkshire	YORKSHIRE
Bridport, Dorset	SOUTH WEST
Bristol, Gloucestershire	SOUTH WEST
Bristol, Somerset	SOUTH WEST
Brixham, Devoon	SOUTH WEST
Broadwoodwwidger, Devon	SOUTH WEST
Brockenhurst, Hampshire	SOUTH EAST
Bronwydd Arms, Carmarthenshire	WALES
Broughton in Furness, Cumbria	NORTH WEST
Bude, Cornwall	SOUTH WEST
Bungay, Suffoolk	EAST
Burnaston, Derbyshire	MIDLANDS
Burton Bradstock, Dorset	SOUTH WEST
Bury St Edmunds	EAST
Caernarfon, Anglesey & Gwynedd	WALES
Cairndow, Argyll & Bute	SCOTLAND
Caister-on-Sea, Norfolk	EAST
Callander, Stirling & The Trossachs	SCOTLAND
Campbeltown, Argyll & Bute	SCOTLAND
Cannington, Somerset	SOUTH WEST
Canterbury, Kent	SOUTH EAST
Cardigan Bay, Ceredigion	WALES
Carloway, Scottish Islands/Isle of Lewis	SCOTLAND
Castle Douglas, Dumfries & Galloway	SCOTLAND
Cawdor, Highlands	SCOTLAND
Chalford, Gloucestershire	SOUTH WEST
Chard, Somerset	SOUTH WEST
Charmouth, Dorset	SOUTH WEST
Cheddar, Somerset	SOUTH WEST
Chulmleigh, Devon	SOUTH WEST

Cirencester, Gloucestershire	SOUTH WEST	Garthmyl, Powys	WALES
Clitheroe, Lancashire	NORTH WEST	Gendaruel, Argyll & Bute	SCOTLAND
Clun Valley, Shropshire	MIDLANDS	Glencoe, Highlands	SCOTLAND
Cockburnspath. Borders	SCOTLAND	Glenfarg, Perth & Kinross	SCOTLAND
Cockermouth, Cumbria	NORTH WEST	Goodwick, Pemebrokeshire	WALES
Colinsburgh, Fife	SCOTLAND	Grange-over-Sands, Cumbria	NORTH WEST
Combe Martin, Devon	SOUTH WEST	Grantham, Lincolnshire	MIDLANDS
Comrie, Perth & Kinross	SCOTLAND	Great Malvern, Worcestershire	MIDLANDS
Coniston, Cumbria	NORTH WEST	Great Yarmouth, Norfolk	EAST
Conwy Valley, North Wales	WALES	Grosmond, North Yorkshire	YORKSHIRE
Conwy, North Wales	WALES	Guernsey, L'Ancresse	CHANNEL ISLANDS
Corbridge. Northumberland	NORTH EAST	Gunnerton, Northumberland	NORTH EAST
Coverdale, North Yorkshire	YORKSHIRE	Haltwhistle, Northumberland	NORTH EAST
Crackington Haven, Cornwall	SOUTH WEST	Happisburgh, Norfolk	EAST
Cramlington, Northumberland	NORTH EAST	Hardraw, North Yorkshire	YORKSHIRE
Craven Arms, Shropshire	MIDLANDS	Harlech, Anglesey & Gwynedd	WALES
Crediton, Devon	SOUTH WEST	Harrogate, North Yorkshire	YORKSHIRE
Crianlarich, Perth & Kinross	SCOTLAND	Hartington, Derbyshire	MIDLANDS
Criccieth, Anglesey & Gwynedd	WALES	Haverfordwest, Pembrokeshire	WALES
Croft, Pembrokeshire	WALES	Hawick, Borders	SCOTLAND
Crymych, Pembrokeshire	WALES	Hawkshead, Cumbria	NORTH WEST
Cullompton, Devon	SOUTH WEST	Hayle, Cornwall	SOUTH WEST
Dalbeattie, Dumfries & Galloway	SCOTLAND	Hay-on-Wye, Powys	WALES
Dalmally, Argyll & Bute	SCOTLAND	Heathfield, East Sussex	SOUTH EAST
Dartmouth, Devon	SOUTH WEST	Helensburgh, Argyll & Bute	SCOTLAND
Dawlish Warren, Devon	SOUTH WEST	Helston, Cornwall	SOUTH WEST
Delabole, Cornwall	SOUTH WEST	Henfield, East Sussex	SOUTH EAST
Dent, Cumbria	NORTH WEST	Hexham, Northumberland	NORTH EAST
Devizes, Wiltshire	SOUTH WEST	Holmrook, Cumbria	NORTH WEST
Diss, Norfolk	EAST	Honiton, Devon	SOUTH WEST
Dorney, Berkshire	SOUTH EAST	Horncastle, Lincolnshire	MIDLANDS
Drummore, Dumfries & Galloway	SCOTLAND	Hornsea, East Yorkshire	YORKSHIRE
Drumnadrochit, Highlands	SCOTLAND	Hunstanton, Norfolk	EAST
Dulverton, Somerset	SOUTH WEST	Inveraray, Argyll & bute	SCOTLAND
Dumfries, Dumfries & Galloway	SCOTLAND	Ipswich, Suffolk	EAST
Dunkeld, Perth & Kinross	SCOTLAND	Isle of Anglesey, Anglesey & Gwynedd	WALES
Durham, Durham	NORTH EAST	Isle of Seil, Argyll & Bute	SCOTLAND
Dursley, Gloucestershire	SOUTH WEST	Jedburgh, Borders	SCOTLAND
Ely, Cambridgeshire	SOUTH EAST	Kelso, Borders	SCOTLAND
Evie, Scottish Islands/Orkney	SCOTLAND	Kessingland, Suffolk	EAST
Exmoor, Devon	SOUTH WEST	Keswick, Cumbria	NORTH WEST
Exmoor, Somerset	SOUTH WEST	Kildonan, Ayrshire & Arran	SCOTLAND
Eye, Suffolk	EAST	Kilham, East Yorkshire	YORKSHIRE
Falmouth, Cornwall	SOUTH WEST	Killiecrankie, Perth & Kinross	SCOTLAND
Felton, Northumberland	NORTH EAST	Kilmory, Ayrshire & Arran	SCOTLAND
Flamborough, East Yorkshire	YORKSHIRE	Kincraig, Highlands	SCOTLAND
Fochabers, Aberdeen, Banff & Moray	SCOTLAND	King's Nympton, Devon	SOUTH WEST
Fort William, Highlands	SCOTLAND	Kingsbridge, Devon	SOUTH WEST
Fowey, Cornwall	SOUTH WEST	Kingston-upon-Thames	SOUTH EAST
Fraserburgh, Aberdeen, Banff & Moray		Kington, Powys	WALES
	SCOTLAND	Kinlochleven, Argyll & Bute	SCOTLAND

Kirkby Lonsdale,Cumbria	NORTH WEST	Millport, Ayrshire & Arran	SCOTLAND
Kirkby Stephen, Cumbria	NORTH WEST	Minehead, Somerset	SOUTH WEST
Kirkby-in-Furness, Cumbria	NORTH WEST	Morecambe, Lancashire	NORTH WEST
Kirkoswald,Cumbria	NORTH WEST	Morfa Nefyn, North Wales	WALES
Kirkwall, Scottish Islands/Orkney	SCOTLAND	Morpeth, Northumberland	NORTH EAST
Laide, Highlands	SCOTLAND	Mundesley-on-Sea, Norfolk	EAST
Lairg, Highlands	SCOTLAND	Mungrisdale, Cumbria	NORTH WEST
Lake District, Cumbria	NORTH WEST	Muthill, Perth & Kinross	SCOTLAND
Lamplugh, Cumbria	NORTH WEST	Nayland, Suffolk	EAST
Langport, Somerset	SOUTH WEST	Nether Kellet, Lancashire	NORTH WEST
Largs, Ayrshire & Arran	SCOTLAND	Nethy Bridge, Highlands	SCOTLAND
Launceston, Cornwall	SOUTH WEST	New Forest, Hampshire	SOUTH EAST
Lauragh, Co Kerry	IRELAND	Newby Bridge, Cumbria	NORTH WEST
Laxfield, Suffolk	EAST	Newgale, Pembrokeshire	WALES
Leek, Staffordshire	MIDLANDS	Newport, Pembrokeshire	WALES
Leominster, Herefordshire	MIDLANDS	Newport-on-Tay, Fife	SCOTLAND
Lerwick, Shetlands	SCOTLAND	Newquay, Cornwall	SOUTH WEST
Liskeard, Cornwall	SOUTH WEST	Newton Abbot, Devon	SOUTH WEST
Llanddona, North Wales	WALES	Newton Stewart, Dumfries & Galloway	
Llandrindod Wells, Powys	WALES		SCOTLAND
Llanfair Caereinion, Powys	WALES	Newtown, Powys	WALES
Llangrannog, Ceredigion	WALES	North Berwick, Edinburgh & Lothians	
Loch Broom/Ullapool, Highlands	SCOTLAND		SCOTLAND
Loch Crinan, Argyll & Bute	SCOTLAND	North Perrott, Dorset	SOUTH WEST
Loch Goil, Argyll & Bute	SCOTLAND	Northallerton, North Yorkshire	YORKSHIRE
Loch Lomond, Argyll & Bute	SCOTLAND	Norwich, Norfolk	EAST
Loch Lomond, Dunbartonshire	SCOTLAND	Noss Mayo, d'evon	SOUTH WEST
Loch Ness, Highlands	SCOTLAND	Nottingham, Nottinghamshire	MIDLANDS
Loch Rannoch, Perth & Kinross	SCOTLAND	Oban, Argyll & Bute	SCOTLAND
Lochgilphead, Argyll & Bute	SCOTLAND	Old Hunstanton, Norfolk	EAST
Loddon, Norfolk	EAST	Olney, Buckinghamshire	SOUTH EAST
Longhorsley, Northumberland	NORTH EAST	Padstow, Cornwall	SOUTH WEST
Looe Valley, Cornwall	SOUTH WEST	Paignton, Devon	SOUTH WEST
Looe, Cornwall	SOUTH WEST	Pately Bridge, North Yorkshire	YORKSHIRE
Louth, Lincolnshire	MIDLANDS	Penrith, Cumbria	NORTH WEST
Low Bentham, North Yorkshire	YORKSHIRE	Penzance, Cornwall	SOUTH WEST
Ludlow,Shropshire	MIDLANDS	Perranporth, Cornwall	SOUTH WEST
Lyme Regis, Dorset	SOUTH WEST	Perth, Perth & Kinross	SCOTLAND
Lyng, Norfolk	EAST	Pickering,North Yorkshire	YORKSHIRE
Lynton, Devon	SOUTH WEST	Pirnmill, Ayrshire & Arran	SCOTLAND
Lynton/Lynmouth, Devon	SOUTH WEST	Pitlochry, Perth & Kinross	SCOTLAND
Malvern, Worcestershire	MIDLANDS	Port Isaac, Cornwall	SOUTH WEST
Marazion, Cornwall	SOUTH WEST	Porthmadog, Anglesey & Gwynedd	WALES
Market Rasen, Lincolnshire	MIDLANDS	Portnahaven, Scottish Islands/Islay	SCOTLAND
Melrose, Borders	SCOTLAND	Portpatrick, Dumfries & Galloway	SCOTLAND
Methven, Perth & Kinross	SCOTLAND	Portwrinkle, Cornwall	SOUTH WEST
Mevagissey, Cornwall	SOUTH WEST	Powerstock/Bridport, Dorset	SOUTH WEST
Middlemarsh/Sherborne, Dorset	SOUTH WEST	Preston, Lancashire	NORTH WEST
Middleton-in-Teesdale, Durham	NORTH EAST	Pwllheli, Anglsesy & Gwynedd	WALES
Milford-on-Sea, Hampshire	SOUTH EAST	Quantocks,Somerset	SOUTH WEST

Rhayader, Powys	WALES
Ripon, North Yorkshire	YORKSHIRE
Rosewell, Edinburgh & Lothians	SCOTLAND
Rugby, Warwickshire	MIDLANDS
Scarborough, North Yorkshire	YORKSHIRE
Seaton, Devon	SOUTH WEST
Sidmouth Devon	SOUTH WEST
Skipton, North Yorkshire	YORKSHIRE
Sliddery, Ayrshire & Bute	SCOTLAND
Solva, Peembrokeshire	WALES
South Molton, Devon	SOUTH WEST
Spean Bridge, Highlands	SCOTLAND
St Agnes, Cornwall	SOUTH WEST
St Andrews, Fife	SCOTLAND
St Davids, Pemebrokeshire	WALES
St Ives, Cornwall	SOUTH WEST
St Margaret's Bay	SOUTH EAST
St Mawes, Cornwall	SOUTH WEST
St Tudy, Cornwall	SOUTH WEST
Staithes, North Yorkshire	YORKSHIRE
Stanton by Bridge, Derbyshire	MIDLANDS
Stockton-on-Forest, North Yorkshire	YORKSHIRE
Stratford-upon-Avon, Warwickshire	MIDLANDS
Swaffham Prior, Cambridgeshire	EAST
Sway, Hampshire	SOUTH EAST
Tarbert, Argyll & Bute	SCOTLAND
Taunton, Somerset	SOUTH WEST
Tavistock, Devon	SOUTH WEST
Taynuilt, Argyll & Bute	SCOTLAND
Tenby, Pembrokeshire	WALES
Tenbury Wells, Worcestershire	MIDLANDS
Thame, Oxfordshire	SOUTH EAST
Thirsk, North Yorkshire	YORKSHIRE
Thurlestone, Devon	SOUTH WEST
Thurne, Norfolk	EAST
Tiverton, Devon	SOUTH WEST
Torquay, Devon	SOUTH WEST
Torrington, Devon	SOUTH WEST
Totland, Isle of Wight	SOUTH EAST
Trearddur Bay, Anglesey & Gwynedd	WALES
Trowbridge, Wiltshire	SOUTH WEST
Ullswater, Cumbria	NORTH WEST
Ventnor, Isle of Wight	SOUTH EAST
Wadebridge, Cornwall	SOUTH WEST
West Bexington, Dorset	SOUTH WEST
Weston-super-Mare, Somerset	SOUTH WEST
Westward Ho, Devon	SOUTH WEST
Wetherby, North Yorkshire	YORKSHIRE
Weybourne, Norfolk	EAST
Weymouth, Dorset	SOUTH WEST
Whitby, North Yorkshire	YORKSHIRE
Whitland, Pembrokeshire	WALES
Whitney-on-Wye, Herefordshire	MIDLANDS
Wigton, Cumbria	NORTH WEST
Windermere, Cumbria	NORTH WEST
Wolsingham, Durham	NORTH EAST
Woolacombe, Devon	SOUTH WEST
Wye/Elan Valley, Powys	WALES
York, North Yorkshire	YORKSHIRE

Please note

All the information in this book is given in good faith in the belief that it is correct. However, the publishers cannot guarantee the facts given in these pages, neither are they responsible for changes in policy, ownership or terms that may take place after the date of going to press. Readers should always satisfy themselves that the facilities they require are available and that the terms, if quoted, still apply.

Other FHG titles for 2010

FHG Guides Ltd have a large range of attractive
holiday accommodation guides for all kinds of holiday opportunities throughout Britain.
They also make useful gifts at any time of year.
guides are available in most bookshops and larger newsagents but we will be happy
post you a copy direct if you have any difficulty. POST FREE for addresses in the UK.
We will also post abroad but have to charge separately for post or freight.

£7.99

£8.99

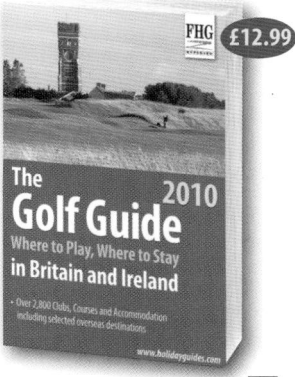
£12.99

Family Breaks ☐
in Britain
• Accommodation, attractions and resorts
• Suitable for those with children and babies

Bed & Breakfast Stops ☐
in Britain
• For holidaymakers and business travellers
• Overnight stops and Short Breaks

The Golf Guide ☐
Where to play, Where to stay.
• Over 2800 golf courses in Britain with convenient accommodation.
• Holiday Golf in France, Portugal, Spain, USA and Thailand.

£9.99

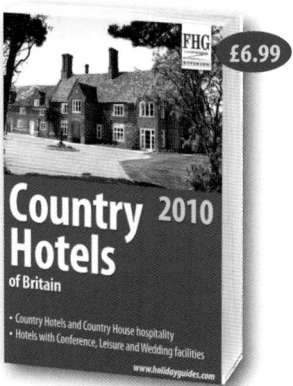
£6.99

£7.99

The Original Pets Welcome! ☐
• The bestselling guide to holidays for pets and their owners

Country Hotels ☐
of Britain
• Hotels with Conference, Leisure and Wedding Facilities

Caravan & Camping Holidays ☐
in Britain
• Campsites and Caravan parks
• Facilities fully listed

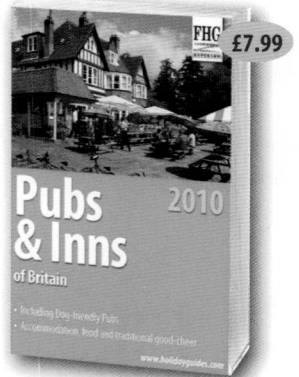 **£7.99**
 **£7.99**

**Pubs
& Inns**
of Britain
• Including Dog-friendly Pubs
• Accommodation, food and
traditional good cheer

**500
Great Places to Stay**
in Britain
• Coast & Country Holidays
• Full range of family
accommodation

**Weekend
& Short Breaks**
in Britain
• Accommodation for holidays
and weekends away

Tick your choice above and send your order and payment to

**FHG Guides Ltd. Abbey Mill Business Centre
Seedhill, Paisley, Scotland PA1 1TJ
TEL: 0141- 887 0428 • FAX: 0141- 889 7204
e-mail: admin@fhguides.co.uk**

Deduct 10% for 2/3 titles or copies; 20% for 4 or more.

Send to: NAME ....

ADDRESS ....

....

....

POST CODE ....

I enclose Cheque/Postal Order for £ ....

SIGNATURE ....DATE ....

**Please complete the following to help us improve the service we provide.
How did you find out about our guides?:**

☐Press   ☐Magazines   ☐TV/Radio   ☐Family/Friend   ☐Other